The Corrigible and the Incorrigible

Social History, Popular Culture, and Politics in Germany
Kathleen Canning, Series Editor

Recent Titles

Stop Reading! Look! Modern Vision and the Weimar Photographic Book
Pepper Stetler

The Corrigible and the Incorrigible: Science, Medicine, and the Convict in Twentieth-Century Germany
Greg Eghigian

An Emotional State: The Politics of Emotion in Postwar West German Culture
Anna M. Parkinson

Beyond Berlin: Twelve German Cities Confront the Nazi Past
Gavriel D. Rosenfeld and Paul B. Jaskot, Editors

Consumption and Violence: Radical Protest in Cold-War West Germany
Alexander Sedlmaier

Communism Day-to-Day: State Enterprises in East German Society
Sandrine Kott

Envisioning Socialism: Television and the Cold War in the German Democratic Republic
Heather L. Gumbert

The People's Own Landscape: Nature, Tourism, and Dictatorship in East Germany
Scott Moranda

German Colonialism Revisited: African, Asian, and Oceanic Experiences
Nina Berman, Klaus Mühlhahn, and Patrice Nganang, Editors

Becoming a Nazi Town: Culture and Politics in Göttingen between the World Wars
David Imhoof

Germany's Wild East: Constructing Poland as Colonial Space
Kristin Kopp

Colonialism, Antisemitism, and Germans of Jewish Descent in Imperial Germany
Christian S. Davis

Africa in Translation: A History of Colonial Linguistics in Germany and Beyond, 1814–1945, Sara Pugach

Between National Socialism and Soviet Communism: Displaced Persons in Postwar Germany, Anna Holian

Dueling Students: Conflict, Masculinity, and Politics in German Universities, 1890–1914
Lisa Fetheringill Zwicker

The Golem Returns: From German Romantic Literature to Global Jewish Culture, 1808–2008, Cathy S. Gelbin

German Literature on the Middle East: Discourses and Practices, 1000–1989
Nina Berman

Franz Radziwill and the Contradictions of German Art History, 1919–45
James A. van Dyke

For a complete list of titles, please see www.press.umich.edu

The Corrigible and the Incorrigible

Science, Medicine, and the Convict in Twentieth-Century Germany

Greg Eghigian

University of Michigan Press
Ann Arbor

Published in the United States of America by the
University of Michigan Press
Manufactured in the United States of America
♾ Printed on acid-free paper

2018 2017 2016 2015 4 3 2 1

A CIP catalog record for this book is available from the British Library.

Library of Congress Cataloging-in-Publication Data

Eghigian, Greg, 1961– author.
The corrigible and the incorrigible : science, medicine, and the convict in twentieth-century Germany / Greg Eghigian.
pages cm. — (Social history, popular culture, and politics in Germany)
Includes bibliographical references and index.
ISBN 978-0-472-11965-3 (hardcover : alk. paper) — ISBN 978-0-472-12137-3 (ebook)
1. Criminals—Rehabilitation—Germany—History—20th century. 2. Sex offenders—Rehabilitation—Germany—History—20th century. 3. Corrections—Germany—History—20th century. 4. Criminal behavior—Germany—History—20th century. 5. Criminal psychology—Germany—History—20th century. 6. Criminal justice, Administration of—Germany—History—20th century. I. Title.

HV9358.E44 2016
365'.6409430904—dc23

2015021565

For Natascha

Acknowledgments

As I worked on this project, a host of people and institutions provided vital and generous assistance. First and foremost, I thank the staffs of the numerous archives and libraries I visited: the Brandenburgisches Landeshauptarchiv, the Bundesarchiv in Berlin and Koblenz, the Bundesbeauftragte für Stasiunterlagen, the Institut für Geschichte der Medizin in Berlin, the Landesarchiv Baden-Württemberg, the Landesarchiv Berlin, the Niedersächsisches Hauptstaatsarchiv Hannover, the Staatsarchiv Hamburg, the Stadtarchiv Frankfurt am Main, and the Staatsbibliothek in Berlin. Their skillful help and guidance consistently reaffirmed my view that Germany's archivists and librarians are among the most professional and accomplished in the world.

Funding for research was made possible by grants and fellowships from the Deutscher Akademischer Austauschdienst, the National Science Foundation, the Wood Institute of the College of Physicians in Philadelphia, and Penn State University's College of the Liberal Arts, Department of History, and Institute for the Arts and Humanities.

Along the way, I have also received crucial comments, criticisms, and advice from a host of insightful colleagues and friends, including Paul Betts, Karl-Heinz Bomberg, John Burnham, John Christman, Winson Chu, David Crew, Matthew DeMichele, Sace Elder, Eric Engstrom, Jennifer Evans, Moritz Foellmer, Rüdiger Graf, Volker Hess, Andreas Killen, Ulli Klöppel, Jan Logemann, Alf Lüdtke, Julia Moses, Eve Rosenhaft, Sajay Samuel, Russell Spinney, Marcel Streng, Klaus Weinhauer, Richard Wetzell, Benjamin Ziemann, the members of the Philadelphia Area Workshop in Modern German History and of the History of Medicine Working Group at the Philadelphia Area Center for the History of Science, and two anonymous readers. I apologize if I have inadvertently left anyone out.

Last but not least, I thank my chanteuse in life, Natascha, who always ensured that the process involved in this project was accompanied by adventure and joy.

Contents

Chapter 1

An Introduction to the Correctional Imagination in Modern Germany

The Punitive Turn and Correctional Rehabilitation

In 1974, Robert Martinson published his now-famous essay "What Works? Questions and Answers about Prison Reform." Examining study after study assessing the success or failure of various treatments to rehabilitate convicts, he concluded, "With few and isolated exceptions, the rehabilitative efforts that have been reported so far have had no appreciable effect on recidivism."[1] Martinson qualified this statement and made it clear that the evidence raised questions less about the inherent corrigibility of offenders than about the disease model of criminality and the effectiveness of prisons. Nevertheless, victims' rights groups and conservative politicians and parties picked up on the article and boiled down Martinson's conclusion into a two-word mantra: "Nothing works."

The "nothing works" movement has been widely seen as a reaction to the buoyantly optimistic efforts in the sixties and early seventies to handle crime and delinquency as pathologies—in other words, to understand antisocial behavior as the result of dysfunctional environments and to apply psychotherapy to treat the offender as the sufferer of a malady. Proponents of the "nothing works" approach, by contrast, have largely dismissed the notion of treating crime as a disease, as naive, amoral, and overly sentimental. Instead of considering criminals as needy patients, a new generation of observers and policies has placed its emphasis on retributive justice, public and private partnerships aimed at crime prevention, surveillance, and the punitive segregation and long-term incapacitation of convicts.[2]

The United States has generally been taken as the paradigmatic example of this historical sea change in punishment. Over the past three and a half decades, in place of clinical, remedial measures based on scientific research, the United States has come to rely increasingly on mass incarceration and the preventive surveillance of its citizens.[3] At the same time, fears over terrorism and sex offenders have emboldened states there to find ways to place dangerous convicts in preventive custody and under perpetual monitoring.[4]

These developments have helped reinforce the international perception that the American legal system is out of step with western European standards.[5] Admittedly, contemporary western European countries have not resorted to punitive, mass imprisonment on the scale seen in the United States. Upon closer inspection, however, a nation like contemporary Germany—associated with a progressive, rehabilitative system of criminal justice—presents a more ambiguous picture.

Despite an astounding decrease in violent and serious crime in Germany since 1992—declines by 75 percent in auto theft, 50 percent in bank robbery, 45 percent in breaking and entering, and 45 percent in sexual murders between 1993 and 2004—the number of prisoners rose more than 40 percent by the mid-2000s. This was primarily due to judges increasingly giving out more and lengthier prison sentences.[6] A similar trend can be observed in the country's application of so-called preventive detention and involuntary commitment since passage of the 1998 Law to Combat Sexual Offenses and Other Dangerous Crimes. The number of people being held in preventive detention increased from 299 in 2002 to 503 by the end of November 2010. Meanwhile, forensic commitments to psychiatric facilities rose from 3,764 in 1987 to 9,361 in 2007.[7] Even during the years 1983–89, when the number of prisoners held declined from 62,294 to 50,910, West Germany saw the number of its long-term prisoners double between 1975 and 1988.[8]

Attention to the United States has been mirrored by similar interest in Scandinavia's turn, since the late 1970s, to more-punitive policies toward drugs and violent crime.[9] Both cases have raised questions about the fate of what Francis Allen called "the rehabilitative ideal," which characterized American and Scandinavian penal systems before the rise of the new emphasis on punitiveness.[10] While criminologists have often pointed to the lackluster, empirically measured impact of rehabilitative projects on recidivism, those studying the history of punishment have chalked up the shift to a number of interrelated social developments: economic recession and austerity, the rise of right-wing political parties, changes in cultural values, the impact of new social movements, and a growing reliance on actuarial models in criminal policy.[11]

Despite their differences, many on both the political right and left seem to share a tacit understanding of the modern history of punishment. From the vantage point of the late twentieth and early twenty-first centuries, the suspicion toward correctional rehabilitation represented a conservative/neoliberal backlash—fueled by populist, anti-intellectual sentiments—against the perceived failures of earlier socially progressive, humanistic, and social scientifically based ideas and professionals. By extension, then, correctional rehabilitation supposedly reached its peak during roughly the middle two quarters of the twentieth century.

Legal scholar David Garland largely agrees with this periodization, seeing the years circa 1930–80 as a kind of heyday for a correctional configuration he refers to as "penal welfarism."[12] Garland describes penal welfarism at this time as a form of intervention characterized by having experts help reform criminals using individualizing, indeterminate, and discretionary custodial arrangements rhetorically couched in pathos.[13] Given these features, it is perhaps easy to understand how American and British observers have been prone to seeing the rise of correctional rehabilitation as intimately bound up with expansion of social and progressive democracy and the growth of humanitarianism. This explanation rings hollow, however, once we begin considering developments outside the Anglo-American context.

German history, of course, presents a starkly different picture. One would be hard pressed to speak of an unbroken line of socially progressive liberal humanism informing the treatment of crime and punishment in the years 1930–80. Instead, conservative, National Socialist, communist, Christian and Social Democratic, and liberal parties, governments, and values all played a formative role in criminal justice.

This very fact, however, makes twentieth-century Germany an ideal place to examine the history and fate of the correctional configuration described by Garland. Just as Germany has not been immune to punitive currents in contemporary criminal justice, it experienced the flourishing of rehabilitative idealism and reform that was occurring elsewhere in the north Atlantic world at the same time. To what extent did regime change affect the understanding and treatment of deviance, criminality, and convicts? What kinds of experts and knowledge played a role in how regimes administered correctional rehabilitation? What kinds of continuities and breaks were there in the history of punishment in Germany, and how do these map onto political and social changes? In what ways has the twentieth-century German experience with correctional rehabilitation been comparatively exceptional or representative? These are some of the questions this book is intended to address.

The History of Penal Correction and Modern Germany

Historians have identified a number of different types of detention that societies have employed over time. Forced confinement—removing someone from the general community and interning that person in some kind of confined space—dates back to ancient times. Ancient, medieval, and early modern societies all built and used a variety of detention spaces (*gaols*) for lawbreakers: among them were underground chambers, dungeons, isolation cells in monasteries and towers, rooms or holes in the foundations of fortifications, and cellars of town halls. By and large, however, these forms of confinement were treated as places of temporary custody for those being investigated or tortured, those believed to be flight risks, debtors, refractory slaves, and those awaiting execution. Into the eighteenth century, exile, public shaming, fines, penal servitude, corporal punishment, and death were far more commonly accepted and practiced as forms of punishment.[14]

Over the course of the sixteenth, seventeenth, and eighteenth centuries, the custodial confinement of those exhibiting socially unacceptable behavior underwent a series of changes. As Pieter Spierenburg has shown, by the mid-seventeenth century, some northern European cities had carceral workhouses mixing charity and discipline, where primarily beggars and vagrants were housed. Over time, municipalities began establishing criminal prisons that catered mostly or exclusively to delinquents. Prison regimens, in turn, centered around forced labor. The obligation to work was, in part, justified as a means to instill diligence. In general, however, attempts to reform inmates were couched in terms of saving souls and were operationalized in the form of religious instruction and discipline, the latter enforced using corporal punishment and the revocation of privileges.[15] Well into the nineteenth century, places like workhouses were marked by a fixed, daily routine of rising early, cleaning and tidying, religious instruction, and working either intramurally for a prison enterprise or extramurally for a local employer.[16]

The period from the second half of the eighteenth century to the end of the 1920s witnessed a set of profound, though nonlinear, changes directly affecting how delinquents were dealt with in central Europe. Among other things, these involved the reform and codification of criminal law; the establishment of a clearer division of labor between institutions of confinement; the emergence of new supervisory, advisory, and research professionals; and a growing interest in the differentiated treatment of those convicted and confined.[17] Taking shape in the process were four interconnected principles of carceral punishment, which came to serve as the foundation for a secular vision of correctional rehabilitation: guiding prisoners to reform themselves, the importance of knowing the character of inmates, a demand that punishment involve an atoning for one's crimes, and an insistence on protecting society from dangerous elements.

By the mid-nineteenth century, German states largely had reduced the number of types of punishments to four (capital punishment, imprisonment, fines, reprimand), while recognizing three different kinds of incarceration: the standard prison, the penitentiary (for those sentenced to hard labor), and the workhouse.[18] This new economy of punishment reflected the fact that nineteenth-century criminal justice experts and authorities came to attribute a variety of purposes to punishment. Retributive and theological justifications for criminal punishment increasingly had to make room for other considerations, such as deterrence, convict reform, restitution, discipline, social control, and conflict resolution.[19]

These new considerations, in turn, helped promote a growing interest in differentiating and individualizing the treatment of convicts and prisoners. Throughout the nineteenth century, an international network of penal reformers pressed central European lawmakers to consider making what they deemed "humanitarian" changes in the accommodation of inmates.[20] To reformers, this meant redesigning carceral facilities to better express the general and special prevention[21] purposes of punishment by offering alternatives to conventional communal housing, through such methods as classification and segregation by offense and behavior and the use of individual confinement.

While continuity stamped the principal means used in midcentury practices for reforming prisoners—a reliance on work, religious instruction, and schooling[22]—enthusiasm grew during the second half of the nineteenth century for what was referred to as "progressive stage incarceration" (*Stufenstrafvollzug*). Originating in Ireland,[23] progressive stage incarceration was first proposed to the Prussian National Assembly by Johann Louis Tellkampf in 1874 as an expedient way to prepare "the convict for his return back to human society."[24] The basic idea was to set up three stages of incarceration through which every inmate would pass before being released. These stages were to be associated with successively greater freedom and privileges, starting with an initial phase of individual isolation, followed by a period of communal work and holding in an individual cell, and ending with preparation for release. Progressive stage incarceration proved to be among the most discussed proposals among prison planners and legislators in imperial Germany, but parliaments continually rejected the scheme, delaying its introduction until the 1920s.[25]

The liberalization of criminal law and the growing interest in differentiating between convicts served as both cause and effect of a related change in how scholars, administrators, and jurists made sense of criminal behavior. Michel Foucault famously claimed that the rise of the prison was part of a larger shift in how society not only treated but also understood human subjectivity in the wake of the Enlightenment.[26] While Foucault's portrait of the nineteenth-century prison as a rationalized and totalizing form of discipline has been rightly criticized,[27] historians of Germany have since confirmed that experts there did look to the human sciences for answers. Reformers, in particular, drew inspiration from psychiatry, pedagogy, and engineering, in seeing convicted criminals as ill-bred (*unerzogen*) or sick (*krank*) and thus requiring commensurate remedial assistance.[28] As Falk Bretschneider has pointed out, attempts were made during the second half of the century to ascertain and institutionalize the scientific principles behind the reform and recovery (*Besserung*) of convicts, but they invariably failed to live up to the claims of both their advocates and Foucault.[29]

Nevertheless, nineteenth-century German scholars and administrators of criminal justice demonstrated a growing curiosity in the psychological makeup of criminals and delinquents. An assortment of jurists, philosophers, psychologists, and physicians, attentive to the emergence of new diagnoses such as monomania, argued for the necessity of attending to those mental factors potentially inhibiting the exercise of free will. This knowledge, it was claimed, was especially relevant in determining a defendant's competency to stand trial, as well as for determining an appropriate sentence.[30] By the last two decades of the nineteenth century, these lines of questioning crystallized in the form of the new academic subfields and clinical specializations of forensic psychiatry, forensic psychology, and criminology, the latter being a field dominated in Germany by psychiatrists.[31]

The emergence of new research agendas and professions dedicated to studying and handling criminal conduct heralded the growing jurisdiction of the human sciences in public affairs. Lutz Raphael has dubbed this general process "the scientification of the social," and some historians of crime and punishment have understood the rise of the criminal sciences and medicine as part of this development.[32] Raphael's terminology is especially apt for describing the ambitions of a number of prominent criminal and legal scholars in the decades leading up to World War I.

Among the most influential voices were those of jurist Franz von Liszt (1851–1919) and his followers, who comprised the so-called modern school of law. Liszt gave expression to the growing sense of some that German criminal law's traditional focus on retribution and atonement was out of step with the modern state's legal framework (*Rechtsstaat*) and its social policy ambitions. As an alternative, he proposed that the criminal justice system heed the knowledge and methods of the human sciences, in order to pursue the goal of deterring criminality. The key, according to Liszt, rests in making the criminal, not the crime, the focal point of criminal justice. In practice, this meant relying on empirical research to identify the causes of criminal behavior and on experts from the human sciences to counsel judges about the individual personality of each offender.[33]

Liszt's ideas were carried forward after his death in 1919 by a number of prominent criminologists and legal scholars, including Gustav Aschaffenburg (1866–1944), Franz Exner (1881–1947), Hans-Walter Gruhle (1880–1958), Moritz Liepmann (1869–1928), Gustav Radbruch (1878–1949), Eberhard Schmidt (1891–1977), and Rudolf Sieverts (1903–80). Together, they and others articulated a vision of criminal justice that stressed the importance of criminological research, the need for psychological and psychiatric assessment, and the realization of crime prevention through remedial correction. As we will see, these notions assumed, over time, an ever more prominent place in German thought and practice about the treatment of convicts.

These principles were first operationalized on a large scale by the prison physician Theodor Viernstein (1878–1949) in post–World War I Bavaria. In June 1923, the Reich states of Bavaria, Hamburg, and Prussia set down prison guidelines citing the correction of convicts as a principal goal of imprisonment. The wording of their agreement demonstrated that authorities remained wedded to traditional notions of moral correction through discipline and work. "Through incarceration," it stated, "prisoners should, insofar as it is necessary, become accustomed to order and work and become so morally fortified, that they never again commit an offense. . . . Prisoners are to be treated earnestly, fairly, and humanely. Their sense of honor is to be preserved and reinforced."[34] By 1926, these principles were accepted by other states and served as guidelines for establishing progressive stage incarceration throughout the country.

The institutionalization of progressive stage incarceration took place in Bavaria already in 1921. Its introduction there served as the inspiration for Theodor Viernstein, the prison physician at Straubing Penitentiary, to devise a method for determining how to classify convicts for assignment to one of the three stages of imprisonment. The key, to Viernstein's thinking, lie in a prognostic assessment of how likely it was for an individual convict to reoffend upon release. With the backing of the Bavarian minister of justice at the time, Franz Gürtner, Viernstein established the so-called Criminal Biological Data Collection Center (Kriminalbiologische Sammelstelle) in Munich in 1924, designed to study convict recidivism. Over the course of the 1920s, other German states and cities—Saxony, Hamburg, Prussia—followed suit and created their own centers, modeled more or less on Viernstein's.[35]

Viernstein and his staff studied criminal records, conducted medical examinations, and administered a standardized survey to identify factors common among recidivist criminals, such as work history patterns, level of intelligence, and family status.[36] The results were used not only for epidemiological purposes but also to determine whether individual convicts would be among a corrigible "select few" (*Auslese*) prepared for transfer to one of the more advanced stages of incarceration.[37] By 1933, the Munich center had examined some 17,500 prisoners and analyzed the relevant data. As Thomas Kailer has observed, Viernstein's project was predicated on the assumption that convicts could be credited with either a capacity or an incapacity for reform (*Besserungsfähigkeit, Unverbesserlichkeit*). This attribute was equated with the individual's ability and willingness to conform to social norms, inclinations presumed to be the results of both genetic and acquired factors affecting character and free will.[38] Hereditary constitution, milieu, moral capacity, and willpower—these four facets, Viernstein believed, played decisive roles in forming and reforming delinquents.

Over time, Viernstein's team grew increasingly pessimistic about the ability of most convicts to be resocialized. Whereas his center found 68 percent of subjects in 1928/29 to be corrigible, the figures were virtually inverted by 1931/32, with 38 percent deemed corrigible and 62 percent deemed incorrigible.[39] This growing cynicism about the capacity of adult convicts to reform themselves would become a hallmark of National Socialist penology.

The Year 1933 as a Starting Point

Historians of criminal justice have conventionally pointed to 1923 as a convenient starting point for the introduction of correctional rehabilitation in Germany. Admittedly, since the mid-nineteenth century, several German states and a number of individual prisons had already been embarking on projects aimed at the "moral reform" of inmates through their "inner transformation." As mentioned earlier, however, not until 1923 did the Reich government formally recognize rehabilitation as a principal goal of incarceration for both juveniles and adults, intended to be realized through the introduction of progressive stage incarceration.[40] As Nikolaus Wachsmann and Herbert Schattke have shown, however, despite the avowed claims of federal states to embrace the goal of prisoner rehabilitation, progressive stage incarceration during the Weimar Republic remained little more than a system for allocating more or less privileges to inmates.[41] In the face of budget cuts and the resistance of prison personnel, the Weimar penal system offered no special rehabilitative services by trained experts and nothing substantive by way of transitional assistance.[42]

Instead of 1923, a better candidate for marking the start of the contemporary rehabilitative era in German penology is 1933. In November of that year, the Reich government passed the Law against Dangerous Habitual Criminals and on Rehabilitative and Preventive Measures. That law and its immediate impact are discussed in detail in chapter 2. For now, it is enough to acknowledge that the law had a profound impact on the future of German criminal law, by systematically formalizing a new, second track of criminal sanctions alongside criminal punishment: so-called executive measures (*Maßregel*). From this point forward,[43] courts were granted the authority to order that any individual deemed a dangerous repeat offender be indefinitely detained within one of several institutions of confinement—namely, a psychiatric facility, a center for substance abuse treatment, a workhouse, or a preventive detention facility. In the first three instances, an inmate's release was contingent on a clinical evaluation of his or her successful rehabilitation, in the form of a prognostic risk assessment. Preventive detention, in turn, was reserved for those individuals determined to be, for the most part, hopelessly incorrigible.

The establishment of the two-track system of criminal sanctions (see table 8, in this book's conclusion) represented the realization of the reform ambitions of Franz von Liszt and the modern school of law. While German law had previously recognized the state's prerogative to carry out a number of individual executive measures (e.g., police supervision, confiscation of property, the deportation of foreigners), these had never been systematically linked to rehabilitation.[44] It took the rise to power of the National Socialists to turn the dream of a legal order based on preventive incapacitation into a reality.

Therein lies the rub. To historians of Nazi Germany, the 1933 law has been seen as an expression of National Socialist race policy.[45] This perspective, no doubt accurate, has helped reinforce the sense that when it comes to criminal justice, the Third Reich represents either the end or the interruption of an era. As a glance at this book's notes demonstrates, historians of crime and punishment in modern Germany have generally either used 1933 as the end point of their studies or focused solely on the years 1933–45. In both cases, the repressive brutality, lawlessness, and racism of the Third Reich is frequently contrasted with earlier efforts aimed at reform. Even in cases such as Immanuel Baumann's 2006 study,[46] where scholars take their narrative beyond World War II, the primary focus has been on the retention of Nazi-era justice officials and the persistence of racist categories.

By contrast, I follow some legal scholars in recognizing National Socialism and the Third Reich as the beginning of an era,[47] the era of a form of clinical correction in Germany. By "clinical correction," I mean what I referred to earlier as ostensibly caring forms of intercession characterized by professional experts attempting to reform criminals using individualizing, indeterminate, and discretionary custodial arrangements. In ushering in a second track of criminal sanctions, National Socialism broadened the horizons of punishment. It opened up new vistas for imagining and realizing remedial interventions, recognizing the authority of specialists in the human sciences and endorsing their forms of knowledge. Of course, the irony of all this rests in the fact that correctional rehabilitation was sparked in Germany by the very regime that dedicated itself to the relentless annihilation of social outsiders.

Another paradox lies at the heart of the Dangerous Habitual Offender Law. Namely, it institutionalized correctional rehabilitation and preventive detention in the same moment. In doing so, the law conceded that some criminals would prove irredeemably dangerous and need to be permanently incapacitated. By linking treatment and security, it signaled that correctional rehabilitation was predicated on the assumption that human beings could and should be divided into two categories: the corrigible and the incorrigible. That distinction, which predated and outlived National Socialism, has proven to be the central defining question in German penology.

A History of the Correctional Imagination

This book is not a history of the prison. Nor is it a history of penology, criminology, or forensic psychiatry. The history of twentieth-century correctional rehabilitation—informed by multiple actors, institutions, and ways of knowing—cannot be accurately represented by a conventional institutional or disciplinary history. The planned rehabilitation of convicts has been historically framed as a project for both society and individuals. Jean-Paul Sartre emphasized this idea of understanding personhood as a project, highlighting its two facets: (1) seeing humans as beings directing themselves toward a projected, nonexistent future and (2) treating personhood as an undertaking or plan that must be completed.[48] Twentieth-century political ideologies, states, institutions, and human sciences generally shared the outlook that society should steer its members toward an ideal projected future, while they encouraged individuals to treat their own lives as projects to be fulfilled.[49] Correctional rehabilitation was one such project.

To better capture these dimensions, I herein offer a history of the correctional imagination in Germany since 1933. By the term *correctional imagination*, I refer to the ensemble of ideas, values, policies, practices, subjects, and objects associated with public attempts to reform and rehabilitate criminals.

This framing allows us to understand incarceration as more than simply an instrumental, reflexive reaction to crime. In the process, it allows us to thematize something that has been a consistent feature in the history of prisons: the chronic disparity between plans and realities. Correctional rehabilitation has been an aspirational project of collective imagining, an enterprise onto which states, experts, and the general public have projected ideals of good and bad, normal and pathological, corrigible and incorrigible. If most plans ultimately foundered when put into practice, they nonetheless played a lasting role in propagating influential visions of crime, the criminal, and human nature. The history of crime and punishment in the twentieth century is therefore also part of the history of the modern knowledge society (*Wissensgesellschaft*).[50] The reform of criminal law, the reform of the human sciences, and the reform of prisoners were all intimately bound up with one another.

The term *correctional imagination* might lead one to believe that I am gesturing in the theoretical direction of Cornelius Castoriadis and others who have invoked the notion of the social imaginary.[51] In part, I am sympathetic to Charles Taylor's use of the term *imaginary* as a means to incorporate expectations and hopes, alongside mundane realities, into the history of correctional rehabilitation.[52] After all, so much of the latter's history has been about perpetual plans and reforms and about the resulting disappointment in their failure to live up to expectations. Similar to Taylor, I wish to underscore the imaginative in order not to lose sight of the fact that hopes and ambitions can be communicated not only in theories and designs but also in images, stories, and emotions. However, I have no interest in Castoriadis's or Taylor's projects aimed at finding a general term to describe the overarching habitus driving society: I have no wish to contribute to building up a reified and ultimately reductive concept of the social imaginary. Rather, along the lines of Claudia Strauss, I wish to call attention to the imaginary aspects of scientific, medical, legal, and administrative life.[53]

Criminals, Biopolitics, and Sexuality

My chief interest is in understanding how, in the modern and contemporary context, science, medicine, and criminal justice came together to shape a historically new set of ways to interrogate and manage criminal behavior and the fate of offenders. In this, I draw on the works of such scholars as Erving Goffman, Joseph Gusfield, and Edwin Sutherland, all of whom stressed the need to study the process of problematization, that is, how "an issue or problem emerges as one with a public status, as something about which 'someone ought to do something.'"[54] Along with Foucault, however, I am especially concerned with how a public problem like criminality emerges as a remedial problem, viewed and managed through scientific, medical, legal, and administrative eyes and techniques.[55]

Considered in this manner, the history of the correctional imagination in Germany reveals itself to be intimately bound up with questions over the limits of state sovereignty, the enforcement of boundaries of social normality and deviance, and the ways in which institutions such as psychiatry and law sanction forms of personhood. These themes have been of central importance to those interested in the study of biopolitics. Here again, Foucault has played the pivotal theoretical role, first systematically discussing the concept in the first volume of his history of sexuality.

The thrust of Foucault's contention is that, in contrast to earlier forms of institutional power in which sovereignty was exercised through depriving subjects of things and services, modern institutions have come to exercise power over life and death through efforts aimed at regulating the population and disciplining the individual's body.[56] This development has not been limited to the prerogatives of state, according to Foucault, but has been accomplished with the complicity of the human sciences and civil society. Thus, following Thomas Lemke, the term *biopolitics* can be taken to refer to the emergence of scientific, medical, and administrative techniques that "make it possible to analyze processes of life on the level of populations and to 'govern' individuals and collectives by practices of correction, exclusion, normalization, disciplining, therapeutics, and optimization."[57]

It is no coincidence that Foucault raised the idea of biopolitics in the context of the history of sexuality. After all, human sexuality lies at the heart of efforts aimed at disciplining bodies and regulating populations. Whether one is discussing the political economics of the eighteenth century, the psychopathologization of homosexuality in the nineteenth, or eugenics and genetic engineering in the twentieth, sexual conduct has consistently been a prominent target for modern scientific analysis and social steering.

This is especially evident in the case of sexual crimes and their perpetrators and victims. Georges Vigarello has argued that, at least in the case of France, the figure of the rapist as a mentally defective type of man only emerged over the course of the nineteenth century. This occurred just as criminal law was increasingly placing the spotlight on the intent and willpower of offenders and as psychiatry was pathologizing sexual violence and deviations as forms of perversion.[58]

Nevertheless, the history of rape, it would seem, has been marked by continuities, chief among them being a tendency to treat it as a primitive, animalistic act. In Germany in the late nineteenth and early twentieth centuries, sexual assaults were widely presumed to occur outside of civilized, bourgeois society and to be committed by "indecent" (*unsittliche*) social outsiders and among the proletariat and peasant populations. Even then, male sexual violence—including individuals targeting children—was largely naturalized, in that it was assumed that males possessed a normally aggressive sexual drive that was inherently directed at a naturally receptive female. Forensic experts from psychology and psychiatry reinforced this thinking by positing the inherent fickleness of children and the biological imperatives of male sexual desire and female passivity.[59] Similar sentiments supported the criminalization of homosexuality as an unnatural act of sodomy, as well as its psychopathologization as a form of abnormal sexual perversion.[60]

Admittedly, writing about the history of sexual crime is fraught with methodological challenges. Historical differences in age of consent, changing standards and norms of tolerance, and questions about the veracity of records all have to be kept in mind.[61] Moreover, it is important to remember that the legal category of "sex offenses" has covered a range of actions at any given time (from sexually motivated murder to adult consensual homosexuality) and that certain forms of sexual crime (e.g., sexual assaults on males) have been chronically underreported.

All this has implications for the historical study of crime in general and sexual crime in particular. For one thing, it means we must exercise critical restraint in all-too-easily accepting crime and prison statistics at face value. For instance, reports from the western occupied zones of Germany after World War II that cite a precipitous rise in sex offenses (see chapter 6) remain equivocal. Can the figures be taken to reflect a social reality within the population? Or might the numbers be a function of a shift in state priorities, only then allowing for the accurate collection of statistics? Or might they represent a change in how such crimes were being defined? It is often impossible to definitively adjudicate such matters. Nevertheless, historical statistics can provide us with a glimpse into the perspectives and changing cultural sensitivities of those who gathered them and debated their meaning.

The relative capaciousness of the legal concept of sexual crimes also means that it would be inaccurate to consider all sex offenders either as unfairly stigmatized outsiders or as ruthless predators.[62] Awareness of this should serve as a warning against too facilely adapting the history of criminal sanctions against sex offenders to a Whiggish story about those who furthered or hindered sexual liberation.[63] Instead, we should be led to consider how the punishment of sex offenders has served didactic and controlling functions not altogether dissimilar from other aspects of social life.[64]

The disciplining of sex offenders is therefore a particular focus of this study, but not simply out of theoretical considerations. Rather, the empirical evidence indicates that the modern criminal justice system and its ancillary sciences and professions afforded sex offenders a special place within the carceral regime. As we will see, these criminals were widely understood to share a number of different features. First, by posing a threat primarily to women and children, they were perceived as presenting a particular danger to patriarchal and parental authority and to especially prized values, such as childhood innocence, personal honor, discretion, and family safety. Second, the fact that their crimes revolved around a biological function appeared to make them receptive to therapeutic interventions. No group of convicts was seen by the criminal sciences as more suited to treatment than sex offenders, and they have remained one of the few groups of criminals who have had rehabilitative programs designed specifically for them. Yet—and this is the third point—sex offenders were consistently associated with a high rate of psychopathology and recidivism and were widely considered by both the lay public and experts to be incorrigible. This paradox and tension between the imagined treatability and the perceived chronic recidivism of sex offenders offers a chance to track how the possibilities and limits of correctional rehabilitation were discussed and institutionalized.

Any historical study must necessarily limit its focus, and mine is no exception. I herein focus almost solely on adult convicts processed through the criminal justice system, considering juvenile correction and the use of concentration camps under the Nazis only when those topics prove especially relevant to this adult population. In addition, my intent is to analyze how and with what effects science, medicine, and their practitioners came to play a role in correctional rehabilitation. My interest along these lines extends to their relationships with the objects of their attention, the convicts. Despite the starkly hierarchical nature of this relationship, the latter were able to exercise varying degrees of agency, which I have tried to acknowledge with the sources available to me. It must be conceded, however, that the convicted and incarcerated encountered problems with society that antedated the intervention of criminal justice institutions.[65] A history of criminal deviance and its correction could well be written about the vernacular terms of everyday social stigmatization. This is beyond the scope of my project, but I hope to make it clear that I see professional and lay forms of stigma management to be inseparably linked with one another.

Chapter 2 examines the correctional imagination of Nazi Germany. Despite its avowed rejection of rehabilitation, Nazism helped institutionalize the correctional framework that would come to dominate punishment in twentieth-century Germany. Criminal justice was reimagined under the Nazis as a kind of moralizing social hygiene, lending incarceration the character of both moral corrective and quarantine. Under National Socialism, penologists focused on developing prognoses for, categorizing, and sorting inmates, ultimately creating three carceral pathways for convicts. The ideal was to create a total "pedagogical atmosphere" within prison walls. Staff then attempted to identify those convicts who still had proven moral sensibilities and to spur their willpower in order to help build "character." Character, in this context, was associated with the virtues of strength, stability, personal responsibility, self-discipline, stamina, and self-sacrifice. Receptive prisoners who served their sentences were then released, while those flagged as incorrigible were either placed in indefinite preventive detention or transferred to a concentration camp. A third alternative, castration and supervised release, was reserved for dangerous sex offenders and was justified on medical, therapeutic grounds. While punishment assumed increasingly more draconian features after 1939, researchers and clinicians during the war continued to see brutality as a tool for both correction and risk assessment.

Chapter 3 explores how East Germany approached the general problem of correctional rehabilitation. In looking at penology in East Germany, observers have been struck by the dissonance between its progressive pretensions and its abusive realities. Both political and fiscal realities account for this contradiction. East German officials in the 1950s were skeptical about the impact rehabilitative methods could have on convicts. This skepticism was grounded in three things: the carryover of personnel and essentializing ideas from the Third Reich, Marxism-Leninism's consideration of all crime as a political act, and infrastructural shortcomings. By the late fifties, the situation began to change. From 1959 to 1971, officials turned to the human sciences to help shape new ways of understanding and treating the prison population. From this point on, penal correction in East Germany focused on steering "socialist personalities," that is, righting the attitudes and habits of those delinquent individuals whose personal development was believed to be no longer converging with that of socialist society. During the 1970s and 1980s, the influence of détente meant that international innovations, such as victimology, social psychiatry, and standards for humane treatment, began playing a stronger role in East German penology. Eventually, a public health approach to crime emerged, one that placed its emphasis on enlisting the knowledge and skills of researchers and clinicians, tracing the etiology of crime to environmental factors, and adopting a preventive strategy based on epidemiological research. Yet, for all these changes, East German criminal justice retained its earlier emphasis on prognosis and the sorting of prisoners according to their relative corrigibility. Within prisons, overworked and poorly trained staff members were able to offer little by way of resocializing assistance, instead concentrating mostly on putting prisoners to work and keeping order.

In chapter 4, I examine how the German Democratic Republic dealt with sex offenders. Up until around 1960, experts in East Germany treated sexual crimes as the acts of depraved individuals whose personalities lacked the fortitude necessary to resist their deviant urges. This began to change in the early 1960s, when forensic psychiatrist and psychologist Hans Szewczyk, in East Berlin, began to map out a new approach toward sexual criminals, contending that environmental factors played the definitive role in shaping sex offenders. In his daily work, he moved beyond clinical examinations and started to include interviews with families and friends and to use psychometric testing for diagnostic and prognostic purposes. His ideas ultimately led him to press for the creation of special facilities for psychopaths in East Germany, in order to provide the most refractory offenders with treatment until they could be released into the general public. Such psychopath units were never created in the GDR, so he and his colleagues adopted a strategy of using psychiatric facilities there as de facto preventive detention facilities in order to indefinitely institutionalize many sex offenders. The emergence of chemical castration in the 1970s only reinforced the notion that antisocial sexual deviance should and could be treated as a medical problem. Changes in sexology throughout the seventies and into the eighties, however, led to the growing acceptance of approaches to sexual deviance that were more multidimensional and less drawn to utilizing psychiatric typologies.

Chapter 5 considers how the Federal Republic established an ambitious correctional rehabilitation program. Penology in the early Federal Republic was marked by two countervailing trends. On the one hand, the criminal justice system retained many of its Nazi-era personnel, while the fields of criminology and penology continued to be dominated by psychiatrists and legal scholars. On the other hand, the occupying powers sought to inflect the German penal system with a resocializing purpose. In both scholarship and administration, a new perspective emerged during the 1950s, drawing less from German medicine and the life sciences than from American social psychology, diagnostic testing, and sociology. The result was a new, decidedly psychological outlook on the convict's personality. Selfhood presumably took shape and was revealed interpersonally and interactively, with the individual using personal resources to respond situationally to changing circumstances. As a result, the convict was increasingly viewed as a neurotic individual. The criminal psychologist's job now involved not only evaluation but also offering supportive and informed guidance. This change in perspective informed a government reform of the criminal justice system, beginning in 1953 and eventually ending with the establishment of the resocializing prison system in 1977. Yet, despite paying lip service to universalism, policy makers and experts remained wedded to models that led them to treat convicts differently based on the latter's relative corrigibility. Standard imprisonment was thought to be suitable for most prisoners, while psychiatric facilities continued to be available for the criminally mentally ill. Finally, there remained preventive detention for those deemed incorrigible, dangerous criminals.

Chapter 6 chronicles how West Germany attempted to transform sex offenders into patients by establishing a new institution. There was a good deal of continuity between National Socialist and early West German efforts aimed at combating sex crime. Policy makers and the human sciences in the fifties and sixties primarily sought ways to therapeutically incapacitate repeat sex offenders using clinical methods. Two solutions, inspired by precedents in Nazi Germany and Scandinavia, became the chief objects of research and debate: the practice of castration and the creation of special therapeutic units. Though some concern was expressed about the ethics and efficacy of castration on sex offenders, a voluntary system was established in 1969, allowing both surgical and chemical castration under certain conditions. Meanwhile, the attention being paid to the most recalcitrant and dangerous criminals led specialists to deem many repeat sex offenders "psychopaths," a group of mentally abnormal delinquents considered immune to the effects of conventional punishment and treatment. Inspired by special psychopathic units in Denmark and the Netherlands, federal justice officials advocated the creation of similar institutions in the FRG. Heavily influenced by trends in social psychiatry, the "social therapeutic facility," as it was called, was imagined as an integrated "therapeutic community," staffed by doctors, psychologists, social workers, teachers, and occupational rehabilitation specialists. As archival records reveal, however, the facilities retained a highly selective process for intakes, accepting only those individuals judged receptive to their methods. In so doing, the social therapeutic facilities helped not only in providing treatment to hundreds of inmates but also in the transfer of a growing number of "incorrigible" sex offenders to preventive detention.

In this book's conclusion, I discuss the significance of Germany's two-track system of criminal law, criminal prognosis, and resocialization efforts. Throughout the last century, the correctional imagination in Germany, while distinctive, has hardly followed some kind of "special path" (*Sonderweg*). Rather, developments there should be thought of as representing variations on a theme being considered and debated throughout much of the world at the same time—an ideal of crime management stressing risk aversion, constant surveillance, and preventive intervention. Prognosis, not therapy, proved to be the centerpiece of twentieth-century correction.

The rise and spread of this paradigm has been explored perhaps most notably by Michel Foucault and others interested in the theory of biopolitics. Their view that this way of knowing and acting in the world centered on historically peculiar concepts of life and improvement is borne out by the history of criminal correction in Germany. Yet there is little cause to be as confidently sanguine as Nikolas Rose, who sees postwar biomedical technologies as pluralizing and democratizing, or as reductively grim as Giorgio Agamben, who sees contemporary politics as a reduction of life to "bare life" through the spread of states of exception and the integration of medicine and politics. Consistently, the aspirations of reformers were tempered, the impact of new methods were limited, and, subsequently, expectations for change were lowered. The history of the correctional imagination has been as much about resignation and expected failure as about promise and innovation. Drawing on Erving Goffman's notion of "people-work," we might better understand the correctional rehabilitation as a modern psychagogic enterprise extending well beyond the prison gates, demanding that the convict treat his or her own life as a moral project, in order to become a particular kind of proper person.

CHAPTER 2

The Correctional Imagination of Nazi Germany

The Third Reich is widely understood to have represented a radical break with the rehabilitative thinking that came to prominence in reform penology during the first third of the twentieth century. Nazi prisons, Nikolaus Wachsmann has shown, grew increasingly arbitrary and punitive toward criminals, delinquents, and convicts.[1] In addition, the vast literature on the institutional treatment of psychiatric patients during the Third Reich has chronicled the regime's reliance on an essentializing, racist worldview organized around practices of classifying, segregating, and exterminating.[2] Informed by a reductive race hygiene and relatively more confident of its citizens' loyalty than postwar communism in East Germany, National Socialism appears, at first glance, to have been unconcerned with micromanaging people's motivations and life course. The regime's eugenic agenda seems to have had physiognomies and spaces as its object and to have acted as a political parasitology played out on bodies, populations, and territories.[3] The few studies looking at the question of correctional rehabilitation in the Third Reich have argued that what little interest Nazi officials showed toward reforming so-called asocials and repeat offenders was limited to the local level and confined to the prewar years.[4] Histories of psychiatry at the time, having focused almost exclusively on the sterilization and "euthanasia" programs, have helped encourage the judgment that National Socialism offered a simple, fatalistic worldview of human nature.

Yet archival and published sources from the thirties and forties tell a more complicated and, in some ways, discomforting story. They reveal that policy makers, researchers, and the criminal justice system were far more curious about knowing and changing the hearts and minds of deviants than one might first be led to believe. Even if crime experts in the years 1933–45 often understood "asocial" and antisocial behavior primarily as expressions of hereditary traits, this did not mean that they considered criminals to be automatons who could not be reached. As historian of science Heiko Stoff has demonstrated, essentializing models from the life sciences at the turn of the century hardly precluded therapeutic interventions.[5] Moreover, the concepts of character, personality, self-control, conscience, and virtue all figured prominently in the ways in which German science, medicine, and administration at the time treated convicts. All were considered possible contact points for transforming the inclinations of lawbreakers.

Rethinking Punishment

Curiosity

The National Socialists came to power in 1933 on a law-and-order party platform, siding with other conservative groups in insisting on a return to retributive justice and strict prison discipline.[6] Yet for all the party's emphasis on retribution and atonement in punishment, administrators and criminologists in the years before World War II spent far more time discussing crime prevention. Under the new legal order, as Otto Thierack explained soon after becoming

TABLE 1. Inmates in German Penal Institutions (Altreich) and Prison Rate, 1933–44

Month and Year	Number of Inmates	Estimated Prison Rate (Inmates per 100,000 Population)
1933	95,000 (estimate)	144
July 1934	102,832	155
December 1935	113,641	170
December 1936	117,756	175
December 1937	112,388	166
December 1938	101,901	149
June 1939	101,152	(152)
November 1940	105,814	(159)
December 1941	118,254	(178)
December 1942	143,495	(216)
December 1943	143,245	(216)
December 1944	153,137	(230)

Source: Data on the number of inmates is from Nikolaus Wachsmann, *Hitler's Prisons* (New Haven: Yale University Press, 2004), 394–95. Rounded estimates here are based on population figures from B. R. Mitchell, *International Historical Statistics: Europe, 1750–2005* (Basingstoke: Palgrave, 2007), 86–87.

Note: The Altreich here refers to penal institutions controlled by the Ministry of Justice within the German borders up to 1937, along with the addition of a few Polish districts added during the war. There is no reliable population data available for the years 1939–45; the prison rates here for those years have been calculated on the basis of the average between the estimated population in 1938 and 1946.

president of the People's Court (*Volksgerichtshof*) in 1936, justice was meted out in the name of the "national racial community" (*Volksgemeinschaft*). In such a society, the purpose of punishment was not only to make criminals pay for their actions but also to protect respectable society. To do this, in turn, required a carefully calibrated system of punishment. "It's not the damage that the perpetrator has effected, the injury to a legal interest," Thierack declared, "[but, rather,] the very person of the perpetrator, his more or less strong criminal volition, the extent of his irreverence or indifference, that justifies the sense and purpose of the punishment. They alone are the benchmarks for sentencing."[7]

National Socialism's penchant for racist, categorical judgment and brutal, collective treatment of those deemed deviant has been well documented.[8] The regime's use and promotion of the eugenically inspired fields of race hygiene and criminal biology have reinforced the notion that the Third Reich represented the culmination of a process by which criminal policy and justice were medicalized.[9] Yet, as Richard Wetzell has pointed out, National Socialist leaders in the twenties and early thirties disagreed about the viability of criminology as a discipline. It took the work of prominent crime researchers and criminal biologists, such as Gustav Aschaffenburg, Franz Exner, Adolf Lenz, and Theodor Viernstein, to convince officials in the new government to recognize the usefulness of the field.[10] Even then, the success of criminology—particularly criminal biology—was limited during the Third Reich both by disputes between experts over research methods and results and by the growing interference of the Schutzstaffel (SS) in police, crime policy, and prison affairs after 1937.

Two things are worth noting, however, about Thierack's declaration. First, he associated National Socialism with reform. Thierack made it clear that while the new legal order would adopt some past features of criminal justice, it intended to usher in fundamental change.[11] Second, this change involved a recentering of criminal justice, away from assessing the damages caused by the perpetrator and toward evaluating the criminal proclivities of the offender. Thierack's vision of National Socialist punishment served, then, as both description of and prescription for the handling of criminals.

In so doing, it effectively highlights a somewhat surprising aspect of criminal justice during the Third Reich: the regime's drive to identify and isolate "alien" elements in society not only contributed to its retributive and destructive tendencies but also helped feed disaggregating and correctional impulses in policy. As historians of science have shown, fascism did not preclude knowledge.[12] On the contrary, sound knowledge was considered vital to fulfilling party and state tasks.[13] The science, medicine, and administration of crime and punishment under the Nazis demonstrated a remarkable curiosity about the psychological makeup of convicts. To many, effective prevention of crime could only be achieved by weeding out habitual offenders from the general criminal population, something that required the ability to differentiate between corrigible and incorrigible criminals. The problem of finding reliable ways to do this provided the space for researchers and clinicians to play a role in Nazi penology.

Within the human sciences, two scholarly projects helped to set the terms and agenda for research and intervention in the punishment of convicts. The first was criminology, particularly criminal biology.[14] As outlined in this book's introduction, German criminology of the late nineteenth and early twentieth centuries was dominated by psychiatrists. This helps explain why criminology in the twenties and thirties was so easily drawn to hereditary, pathological, and characterological explanations of criminal behavior. Richard Wetzell is certainly correct in noting that this situation did not preclude criminologists from acknowledging the importance of environmental and situational factors in promoting crime.[15] But most criminologists during the Third Reich with an interest in criminal recidivism adopted a clinical, casework approach borrowed from medicine and oriented around a diagnostic and prognostic assessment of individuals in custody. Already by 1933, forensic specialists had developed an extensive questionnaire for profiling the psychology of criminals, covering such things as family history, interpersonal relations, recreational outlets, temperament, intelligence, and moral values. Within a few years after the Nazi seizure of power, Franz Exner (1881–1947), a powerful advocate of criminal biology, could claim that criminology offered the criminal justice system a range of professional services: informed diagnostic and prognostic judgments about offenders, expert opinion about criminal motivations and life histories, and empirically grounded information about penal correction.[16]

Criminal biology garnered early government acceptance through the Reich Ministry of Justice. Playing a key role in this was the national-conservative politician Franz Gürtner (1881–1941), who served as the Reich minister of justice from 1932 until his death in 1941. Gürtner had earlier served as justice minister in Bavaria from 1922 to 1932 and there acted as the enthusiastic patron of the work of Theodor Viernstein, approving the creation of the first German criminal biological data collection center in 1924, to conduct research into the family, criminal, and medical histories of thousands of convicts.[17] Under Gürtner, the Reich Ministry of Justice promoted the widespread use of criminal biological examinations throughout Prussia and Germany, eventually authorizing the creation of the national Criminal Biological Research Office in November 1937, with examination centers in seventy-three prisons.[18]

A second line of influence on Nazi-era penology emerged from discussions about legal doctrine and new legislation. Since the late nineteenth century, proponents of the modern school of law had argued for the need to treat law as a tool for protecting society.[19] Already in 1883, Franz von Liszt laid out a carceral scheme, which drew a growing number of supporters over time. According to Liszt, three types of criminals warranted three types of punishment: "(1) reform for the corrigible and those criminals needing reform, (2) deterrence for those criminals not needing reform, (3) incapacitation [*Unschädlichmachung*] for incorrigible criminals."[20] This plan, especially the proposal to create some form of special detention for incorrigibles, continued to be debated and elaborated on in the 1920s and 1930s by jurists and welfare administrators. Some, such as the legal scholar Edmund Mezger (1883–1962), looked to criminal biology in arguing for the need to reorient criminal justice toward the identification and permanent isolation of dangerous, incorrigible offenders.[21] Others, like Agnes Neuhaus, Hans Maier, and Helene Simon, lobbied for a special detention law that would allow welfare providers to preventively detain "weak-willed" juvenile delinquents, alcoholics, prostitutes, and vagrants. Their emphasis was placed on the moral failings of targeted groups and the missionary need to save such social outsiders from themselves. While eugenic justifications eventually made their way into these conversations about the need for special detention, welfare advocates largely remained wedded to seeing the problem posed by dangerous, chronic offenders as a matter of virtue combating vice.[22]

The concern with dangerousness, morality, and character also underpinned the National Socialist legal theory of *Willensstrafrecht* (volitional criminal law). As Benedikt Hartl has described it, "the point of departure for this theory was the fundamental conviction that the state via criminal law should not respond to a legal infraction as a form of objective damage or injury to the public peace or a public interest but, rather, must apprehend the criminal will of the perpetrator as soon as it manifests itself as impeachable."[23] Advocated by eventual president of the People's Court Roland Freisler (1893–1945), the Academy for German Law, the National Law Office of the National Socialist German Workers' Party (NSDAP), and the justice ministry's Criminal Law Commission, *Willensstrafrecht* was built on the central premise of free will. Proponents argued that to protect the public, it was necessary for the state to identify dangerous criminals and decisively punish them early on in their delinquent careers. To do this, criminal justice needed to uncover and neutralize the "hostile" (*volksfeindlichen*) will of dangerous offenders, by either sparking their consciences to reform or removing them from society altogether.[24]

Correction, Custody, and Prevention

By the time of the Nazi seizure of power then, a number of prominent organizations, politicians, scholars, and administrators had outlined a bold new agenda for criminal justice. Naming the preservation of public safety the chief purpose of law and order, they emphasized crime prevention, which, in turn, was operationalized as the thwarting of criminal recidivism. From this perspective, criminal justice was reimagined as a kind of moralizing social hygiene, lending incarceration the character of both moral corrective and secure quarantine. Correction (*Erziehung*) and custody (*Verwahrung*) quickly became the focal points of Nazi-era penology.

Already within months of National Socialism's consolidation of its power in 1933, the Reich interior and justice ministries began drafting a new law that would address the issue of preventing criminal recidivism. The result of their deliberations was the Law against Dangerous Habitual Criminals and on Rehabilitative and Preventive Measures, passed on 24 November 1933 and made effective beginning 1 January 1934.[25] Several features of the new law came to play a pivotal role in the correctional imagination and penology of the Third Reich. First, it gave judges the authority to deem as a "dangerous habitual offender" anyone who was convicted of a felony, who had at least two previous felony convictions (the last occurring within the past five years), and whose past actions warranted that label. In cases where "public safety demand it," a dangerous habitual offender was not only to be given a prison term but also to be placed in "preventive detention" (*Sicherungsverwahrung*) after having served his or her sentence.[26] For those criminals found to be chronic vagrants or of diminished mental capacity, the court was to order, alongside a prison sentence, a commitment to a psychiatric hospital, substance abuse facility, or workhouse. In all of these cases, including preventive detention, "the commitment lasts," according to section 42f of the law, "as long as required." Finally, courts were given the authority to order the castration of chronic or dangerous sex offenders over the age of twenty-one, as a means to prevent their committing such acts again. Table 2 shows how many individuals were subject to the new measures from 1934 up to the last quarter of 1942. As Christian Müller has observed, the relatively small numbers involved testify to how seriously authorities accepted the law as targeting a very specific population.[27]

The impact of the new law, however, was felt far beyond the relatively small circle of targeted convicts. By establishing an array of institutions and treatments for those deemed most incorrigible, authorities had made it necessary for judges, prison administrators, and forensic experts to evaluate all convicts on the basis of their relative capacity to reform. In 1935, for instance, several specialists suggested that the inmate population needed to be differentiated and segregated in order to keep corrigible prisoners from the influence of "bad apples." Punishments, incentives, instruction, and hard work were all recommended, to inspire a deepening sense of responsibility in convicts.[28] Even preventive detention was presumed to have its rehabilitative purposes, but as two prominent jurists explained, the effect "depends on the personality of the detainee. If a reasonable amount of effort at correction accomplishes the reform of the detainee, then this will only be welcomed."[29]

From clinical assessment of new prisoners to the supervision of released convicts, the tasks and challenges presented by the Dangerous Habitual Offender Law altered the landscape of confinement. Prison surveillance wards, first established in the nineteenth century for the clinical evaluation of mentally ill inmates, found themselves increasingly called on to serve as treatment centers for unruly, refractory criminals.[30] Many of the inmates formerly interned by welfare providers in closed asylums were redirected into the network of treatment and preventive detention centers.[31] Throughout the country, mental hospitals, alcoholic treatment units, workhouses, and prison administrations were forced to either build new facilities or renovate old ones in order to accommodate the new intakes.[32] By the spring of 1935, some preventive detention facilities reported working well over their capacity, although a small number of detainees were being successfully released.[33]

The Dangerous Habitual Offender Law was especially taxing for psychiatric facilities. Hospitals and homes for the mentally ill and disabled became

TABLE 2. Number of Cases Committed by Courts to Rehabilitative and Preventive Measure, 1934–42

Type of Measure	1934	1935	1936	1937	1938	1939	1940	1941	1942[a]
Psychiatric Facility	553	728	880	902	992	1,087	—	—	—
Alcohol and Substance Abuse Facility	97	126	138	150	148	226	—	—	—
Workhouse	1,832	1,409	1,413	1,094	1,026	729	—	—	—
Preventive Detention	3,723	1,464	946	765	964	1,827	1,916	1,651	1,095
Castration	613	343	230	189	195	238	—	—	—
Banned from Performing Occupation	131	158	215	252	269	294	—	—	—

Source: Data from Christian Müller, *Das Gewohnheitsverbrechergesetz vom 24. November 1933: Kriminalpolitik als Rassenpolitik* (Baden-Baden: Nomos), 53–54.

[a]Data for 1942 is for the first three quarters.

convenient dumping grounds for dangerous and difficult criminals committed on the basis of sections 42 and 51 of the criminal code.[34] Follow-up studies of the law's impact yielded surprising results. Government statistics consistently showed that 80–90 percent of those placed in prevention detention were primarily there for committing crimes against property, while 35–55 percent of those committed to psychiatric institutions were sex offenders, the vast majority of whom had been convicted on multiple counts of child molestation.[35] With a reputation for disruption and recalcitrance, psychopaths in particular—individuals considered legally sane but possessing clinically abnormal antisocial personalities—were often passed on to mental hospitals by prisons and welfare providers.[36] Psychiatric facilities responded in kind, attempting to transfer the most difficult criminal patients to workhouses, preventive detention units, and concentration camps.[37] As the director of an asylum in Thuringia complained in 1941, he and his colleagues had had to deal with "personalities with severe congenital psychopathologies of their impulses, volition, affects, and comprehension," individuals "with only a very slight possibility of being influenced in the long term."[38]

During the early years of the Nazi regime, however, problems such as these did little to dampen the enthusiasm of reform advocates, who often showed great interest in tracking developments and innovations in prison systems and methods abroad. From 1933 to 1937, criminological journals and conferences were venues for countless reports that bureaucrats, judges, prosecutors, wardens, and criminologists gave on their experiences with their foreign counterparts. England's borstal system, chain gangs and prisoner segregation in the United States, open-air forced labor in the USSR, Denmark's prison for psychopaths, and Italy's special detention centers and reliance on "biocorrectional research" to reshape criminal personalities all drew the attention of experts, who often personally visited the institutions in question.[39]

In fact, one of the most talked about penological works of the thirties was Franz Exner's *A Criminalistic Report on a Trip to America*, published in 1935. During his visit to the United States in the summer of 1934, the Munich-based criminologist was surprised to find that the American prison system had largely abandoned individualized treatment of prisoners yet had succeeded in matching prisoners with specifically tasked prisons, by using casework units and clinics, classification commissions, and clearinghouses to typologize inmate personalities.[40] He was also deeply impressed by the work done by American criminologists in collecting statistical data on risk factors and, in turn, translating that data into social prognostic tables for use by parole boards.[41] Still,

Exner and others believed that importing any American ideas and methods would necessarily be hampered by the "mechanical" and "materialist" nature of the latter's criminal justice system.[42]

More than anything else, then, the Dangerous Habitual Offender Law succeeded in orienting German criminal justice and penology around prognostication. Forecasting the probability of an inmate committing a new offense became the focal point for correctional science and interventions. In a legal context where the aim was no longer to calculate culpability but, rather, to determine relative dangerousness, the criminal act was now seen as emerging from a chronic disposition of the perpetrator, a symptom of the individual's flawed character.[43] What now needed to be established was the peculiar nature of a criminal's personality. In the 1936 edition of the *Handbook of Criminology*, jurists Josef Schafheutle and Fritz Hauptvogel expressed this nature in terms that would be echoed well into postwar West Germany. "The significant indicator of the habitual criminal in this sense," they argued, "is the tendency [*Hang*] to commit crimes, an inner criminal attitude rooted within the personality of the perpetrator, out of which constantly arises a new willingness to engage in criminal activity."[44]

Forensic Forecasting: Social Prognosis

As already mentioned, Bavarian Theodor Viernstein first developed the examination and prognostic assessment of large numbers of convicts, as a response to the establishment of progressive incarceration. During the twenties and early thirties, Viernstein and his Criminal Biological Data Collection Center had not been alone in generating information about convicts for criminal justice purposes, but only in Bavaria—and, beginning in 1930, in Prussia—did researchers and authorities in the Weimar Republic justify this work on the basis of its correctional applications.[45] Viernstein's "criminal biological examination" of inmates was a product of knowledge gained from a variety of human sciences at the time: criminology, pedagogy, psychiatry, characterology, race hygiene, moral theology, and criminal anthropology.[46] The examination consisted of a survey interview, a clinical examination, and an analysis of prisoner records, with the data then entered into a standardized form. His survey served as the template for other centers, covering family background, education, work history, physiognomy, physical and cognitive abilities, physical and mental development and health, personality traits, and general mien.[47]

Once collected for an individual, the new information was compared with general recidivism patterns, allowing judgments to be made about the relative receptiveness of different types of criminals to correction.

Viernstein's influence grew markedly following the Nazi seizure of power, owing to the fact that his patron in Bavaria, Franz Gürtner, became Reich minister of justice. Gürtner used his position to promote Viernstein's ideas and methods throughout Germany. Already in August 1933, Gürtner put his support behind a twenty-point report drafted by Viernstein in which the Straubing physician sought to place criminal biology firmly at the center of the new legal order. In particular, he insisted that courts, prisons, and postrelease transitional care providers all rely on and provide data for criminal biological examinations of convicts. "The primary goal of this examination of the individual criminal personality for court assistance," he emphasized, "is to gauge the relative degree of its social fitness or unfitness and, afterward, to suggest the necessary conclusions to be drawn for either a reforming and rehabilitative treatment and care program or preventive detention and sterilization."[48]

Until 1936, Viernstein's criminal biological examination methods and results were the orientation point for scholarly discussions about social prognosis. By 1933, he and his staff had examined over seventeen thousand cases, and his work enjoyed the support of criminal justice officials, confessional groups, and colleagues. During the early years of the Third Reich, numerous criminologists and forensic psychiatrists attempted to expand on Viernstein's findings, agreeing that the limitations of both prisons and the labor market made the scientific identification of incorrigibility essential to criminal justice.[49] "Are there incorrigible criminals?" asked the director of the Altscherbitz psychiatric facility in Saxony, in a lecture published in 1933.[50] His emphatically affirmative response was echoed by other criminal biologists, particularly those relying on the Bavarian data. A 1935 study of five hundred repeat offenders from Viernstein's center, for instance, concluded that some 80 percent of repeat offenders were "constitutionally predisposed criminals" requiring permanent "segregation and isolation" from society, "since their criminogenic character structure is irreparable and can neither be cured through correction nor inhibited by disincentives in realizing its true nature."[51]

Viernstein's methods and conclusions were not immune from criticism, however. Prison medical staff in Bavaria, for instance, expressed frustration at having to take on the new task of administering the criminal biological questionnaire to inmates. In addition, some scholars openly questioned the scientific validity of Viernstein's results, most prominently Werner Petrzilka and Rudolf Sieverts, who criticized both the survey and the interviewers for their biases and for not taking into account the shortcomings of the penal system itself.[52]

The biggest challenge to Viernstein's seeming monopoly over the science of social prognosis came in the form of a dissertation by a law student at the University of Munich, working under the supervision of Franz Exner. In 1936, Robert Schiedt published *A Contribution to the Problem of Recidivism Prognosis*, proposing a new way to determine the likelihood of inmates to reoffend. Instead of trying to identify the often obscure etiological factors behind a criminal career, Schiedt argued, one could focus on something far more accessible: symptomatology. Borrowing the actuarial methods of life insurers, he proposed using criminal records to flag characteristics of individual perpetrators and their crimes that reliably correlated with repeat offending following release. Once enough data was collected and once those factors positively correlating with recidivism were singled out, it would then be possible to create a prognostic table of risk factors, which could then be used in assessing individual offenders.[53]

The inspiration for Schiedt's model based on risk factors came from researchers in the United States. In particular, Ernest Burgess and his colleagues had used a similar method, awarding convicts a demerit point for each negative risk factor, in helping to advise the Illinois parole board about cases involving indeterminate sentences.[54] Around the same time, the criminologists Sheldon and Eleanor Glueck studied five hundred parolees in Massachusetts, similarly finding that the more demerit points a convict received, the more likely he or she was to be rearrested.[55]

Schiedt adopted the methods of the Americans and applied them to the cases of five hundred randomly selected released convicts examined by Viernstein's Munich data collection center.[56] Based on his findings, Schiedt was able to develop a fifteen-point system, which, he claimed, could be used for determining the statistical probability of a prisoner becoming a repeat offender (see tables 3 and 4): convicts scoring three or fewer points enjoyed a favorable prognosis, while those with ten points or more were seen as almost certain to reoffend. Intermediate point totals indicated an indeterminate prognosis, although, depending on the score, a comparatively poor or good prognosis could be indicated.[57]

Schiedt's calculation of probability rates based on manifest, sometimes mundane attributes of offenders represented a challenge to the German criminological establishment, since it radically diminished the role of the clinical evaluator. Schiedt, however, went still further, comparing his findings about recidivism rates among prisoners examined by the Munich data collection center with those of examining physicians there. He found a marked disparity between reality and the assessments of the Munich clinicians. Not only did some of the latter's prognostic factors—for instance, body type (based on Ernst Kretschmer's typology), marriage status, and focus of criminal activity—not correlate with outcomes, but physicians at Viernstein's center were coming up with false positives and false negatives in around one in every four cases.[58]

Schiedt was no doubt emboldened by the endorsement of his academic adviser, the prestigious Franz Exner. In the immediate aftermath of the publication of Schiedt's study, Exner took the lead in promoting it and defending its findings against critics.[59] Criticism came, expectedly enough, from Viernstein's Bavarian supporters. In 1937, one of the leading criminology journals published a posthumous article by Hans Trunk, a longtime medical officer at the prison in Straubing where Viernstein had developed his methods. Trunk took one hundred cases from the Bavarian Criminal Biological Data Collection Center and compared the veracity of his own clinical prognoses with predictions indicated by Schiedt's table of risk factors. Trunk's results showed that the two methods differed little in their accuracy when it came to making specific prognoses (with accuracy rates of 88 percent for Schiedt and 85.6 percent for clinical assessors), but he found that the tabular method was for more likely than clinicians to reach an inconclusive judgment. If one treated these cases as failures, clinical assessment failed 29 percent of the time, while Schiedt's method had a failure rate of 49 percent.[60] In response, Exner insisted that Trunk's success in predicting recidivism did not undo the fact that, on average, criminal biological prognoses focusing on etiology remained woefully unde-

TABLE 3. Schiedt's Fifteen Factors Associated with Recidivism

1. Hereditary Corruption
2. Increasingly Serious Criminality
3. Poor Rearing Circumstances
4. Poor Schooling Record
5. Discontinuation of Career Training
6. Irregular Work Record
7. First Crime before the Age of 18
8. More Than Four Previous Convictions
9. Especially Short Time between Offenses
10. Interlocal Criminality
11. Psychopathy
12. Alcoholism
13. Poor General Behavior in Prison
14. Release from Prison before the Age of 36
15. Poor Social and Family Circumstances after Release

pendable. Attempting to assuage Trunk's obvious fear that statistics and algorithms were replacing clinical experience and judgment, however, Exner insisted that the prognostic table was nothing more than "condensed experience," meant to supplement, not supersede, the clinician's authority.[61]

The following year, Wilhelm Meywerk (1897–1947), director of the Hamburg Criminal Biological Data Collection Center, published the results of his own follow-up analysis of two hundred cases from the years 1929–33, showing that Schiedt's point system was generally more accurate in predicting recidivism than clinical evaluation. Noting, however, that each of Schiedt's fifteen factors were only present an average of 22.8 percent of the time in successful cases of rehabilitation, he insisted that prognosis tables should never replace the tacit knowledge of experts. "Limiting oneself to objective facts alone is far too simplistic," Meywerk contended, adding, "Moreover, it could lead to an inflation of environmental factors: we run into the danger of remaining stuck in the crassest of materialisms, and then we will have again reached the very nurture theory of individual psychology that we had happily overcome."[62]

In ensuing years, researchers attempted to refine the prognostic table, conducting more careful longitudinal studies, testing for new risk factors, and weighting individual factors according to their relative importance.[63] This went some way toward addressing the concerns of critics, and throughout the rest of the Third Reich, etiologically oriented clinical prognosis and symptom-based risk assessment were, by and large, treated as compatible. The predominance of psychiatrists in both German criminology and forensic assessment, however, meant that clinical evaluation of case histories remained the norm. Still, by the 1940s, a consensus had emerged that a handful of factors were reliable indicators of a poor prognosis in convicts: the presence of endogenous abnormalities, a family history of deviance, early onset of criminal behavior, dimin-

TABLE 4. Schiedt's Prognostic Table

Group	Number of Poor Indicators	Number in Each Group	Percentage of Repeat Offenders/ Nonrepeat Offenders
I	0	30	3.3 / 96.7
II	1–3	101	14.8 / 85.2
III	4–6	170	40.6 / 59.4
IV	7–9	118	68.6 / 31.4
V	10–11	50	94.0 / 6.0
VI	12–15	31	100.0 / 0.0

Source: Data from Robert Schiedt, *Ein Beitrag zum Problem der Rückfallsprognose* (Munich: Münchener Zeitungs-Verlag), 65.

ishing length of time between crimes, frequent relocation, and the lack of a marriage partner.

The intense interest in social prognosis within the human sciences was symptomatic of an even broader trend within German criminal justice during the 1930s. If, as Franz Exner neatly put it in 1935, criminology was "increasingly becoming more like meteorology than physics,"[64] this was because party and government officials, jurists, and prison administrators were actively looking for ways to undercut criminality by singling out repeat offenders early on in their careers, before they could wreak much havoc. Forestalling crime required forensic forecasting.

Interest in preempting crime only grew in importance as the SS took over more police functions during the second half of the thirties. Especially in the wake of the Ministry of Interior's decree of 14 December 1937 announcing a "preventive police campaign against crime," German criminal policy experienced an escalation in crime prevention. German police, in particular, were given a broad mandate to monitor, arrest, and incarcerate those habitual deviants deemed to be a threat to the racial health of the national community.[65] Informed by criminal biology, the new policy assumed hygienic overtones, targeting not only repeat property and violent offenders but also beggars, vagrants, prostitutes, and alcoholics, for police raids and preventive custody.[66] Knowledge gained through social prognosis research about the dangers associated with the early onset of criminal activity helped justify the aggressive approach: since juvenile delinquency could now be seen as representing a prodromal phase in a criminal's career, it made sense to rely more consistently on preventive, indeterminate detention in such cases.[67] Though some dismissed this way of thinking as unsupported by the data,[68] powerful figures, such as Roland Freisler, insisted that preventive detention and social prognosis were essential tools in "isolating the crystallization points of the career criminal class" and thereby ensuring that "the breeding and training grounds for the next generation of criminals dries up."[69]

Character and Willpower

Both etiology-based and symptom-based forms of social prognosis were primarily interested in indicators, that is, signs that reliably pointed to a likelihood of reform or recidivism in convicts. As an applied forensic science, social prognosis was far less concerned with explaining the mechanism by which a criminal mind came to commit its acts. Nevertheless, many researchers, clinicians, and administrators were interested in understanding what drove individuals to a life of crime. What, then, was actually wrong with repeat offenders? The answer was of more than academic interest, since it went to the matter of identifying the very target of correctional rehabilitation.

For some groups, most notably Jews, authorities tended to attribute their purported delinquencies to moral flaws inherent within a supposed racial stock.[70] When it came to gentiles, however, most forensic experts in Germany during the 1930s and 1940s explained recidivism by focusing on the shortcomings of individual perpetrators. In particular, as described in 1938 by the prominent chief physician at the Bodelschwing Hospital in Bethel, Werner Villinger (1887–1961), the problem was anchored in the personality's lack of ability to adapt to the moral norms of society. This deficiency turned on critical faculties that could be summed up by the term *conscience* (*Gewissen*), that is, "the attitude of the perpetrator toward the act, the capacity for self-criticism and genuine remorse, the depth and endurance of moods, and the power to understand moral resolutions and remain loyal to them."[71]

The notion that criminals lacked a proper moral character was hardly new, of course. Now, however, the psychological sciences and medicine were making character a scientific and clinical object at the same time that criminal law was treating it as the object of correctional and preemptive intervention. The two impulses were institutionally linked in the Dangerous Habitual Offender Law of 1933, whereby "dangerousness" was attributed to a delinquent's chronic "inclination" (*Hang*) or "habit" (*Gewohnheit*) toward crime. As commentators noted, this inclination or habit referred not simply to a given quantity of past criminal acts but also to a "constant inner readiness to act."[72] Thus, to speak of an inclination meant that there was evidence of a pattern of behavior derived from an imagined psychological state.

For a criminal to have shown a pattern of committing antisocial acts was therefore not enough for the criminal justice system to consider him or her a dangerous habitual offender. It also needed to be apparent that this pattern was so rooted in the convict's personality that he or she would almost assuredly reoffend after release. German courts largely adhered to this standard as well. As one court explained it in a 1942 case involving an abortion doctor, treatment as a dangerous habitual offender was reserved for an individual "whose impulses, due to the moral disposition that rules over the perpetrator and has found its expression in the number and severity of his crimes, are so dangerous that he must be permanently cast out from the national racial community."[73]

Mastering one's drives and impulses was therefore seen as the key factor separating respectable citizens from repeat offenders. This capacity had a name: willpower.[74] Again, this was not merely an academic term. Prison records show that staff were on the lookout for insights into the relative strength and weakness of inmates' willpower as a way of assessing the chances that an individual prisoner would reoffend after release.[75] This was especially true in cases involving sex offenders.[76] A 1944 report of prisoner conduct from authorities at Plötzensee in Berlin, for example, noted the following about inmate E.W., a man with a history of convictions for theft and homosexuality:

> Character: Humble, self-restrained, correct behavior
> Work Performance: Very industrious, dependable worker. Since a [word missing], he was able to be granted regular supplemental pay, up until his stay in the prison hospital
> Conduct: Unobjectionable
> Since he apparently has the determined will to conduct himself from now on in a law-abiding manner, there is hope that he will never again commit a new offense.[77]

In numerous instances like this, the strength or weakness of the inmate's will was measured against the convict's compliance with disciplinary, work, and even domestic routines.[78]

These routines were believed not only to reveal the willpower of inmates but also to instill—in some of them, at least—a strength of will not yet seen. In 1935, for instance, the warden of a preventive detention facility at Sonnenburg in Brandenburg made the case to his superiors that preventive detainees, too, needed to be provided with meaningful opportunities to work. He justified this on the grounds that such labor helped build character.

> With sufficient and paying work, you have the possibility to offer the preventive detainee the incentive to earn money through diligent work, in order to buy additional food. This kind of incentive is necessary especially for primitive character types. Even if it does not manage to induce him to enjoy working, it might be possible to develop in him the will to work, and it is not altogether out of the question that he becomes accustomed—even if only unconsciously—to consistently working.[79]

Preoccupation with will and willpower was not original to Nazi Germany. During the nineteenth century, psychiatry had come to associate a weak or malformed will with monomania and, later, psychopathy.[80] By the first third of the twentieth century, there was widespread enthusiasm in Germany for projects aimed at therapeutically cultivating the will, in order to address a perceived rise in personal nervous weakness and passivity. This was especially the case in the fields of medicine and pedagogy, where it was proposed that both body and spirit be trained toward achieving the goals of personal strength, self-control, liberation, decisiveness, and leadership.[81] National Socialism called on this intellectual tradition to frame its own ideals of individualism and action, portraying Hitler and its pantheon of heroes as the embodiment of masculinity—courageous, intrepid, and tireless leaders capable of forcing their will on their opponents.[82]

Within criminology circles, however, it was widely acknowledged that appraising an individual's will and motivations presented a challenge. Despite offering an array of models, academic psychology and psychiatry in Nazi Germany tended to see personality as the reflection of a hierarchical architecture, itself tied to a spiritual or material core (e.g., in a hereditary genotype or an inherent constitution).[83] The problem for most any clinician was finding a way to reach this depth within a person.[84] For forensic specialists, the task was made more difficult by the fact that their subjects—criminals—were infamous for their propensity to dissimulate. Particularly after 1937—when police were instructed to preemptively detain individuals suspected of being "asocial"—and, in a second wave, after failures on the Eastern Front during World War II, forensic psychologists and psychiatrists warned against the deceptiveness of appearances in character assessment.[85] Only a thorough, comprehensive exploration of an individual's motivations, actions, thoughts, feelings, and lifestyle, it was argued, could successfully unmask the true nature of a criminal's personality.[86]

Correction as Project

The "Pedagogical Atmosphere"

The Nazi Party had come into power criticizing Weimar penal reform, particularly the institutionalization of the "correctional idea" (*Erziehungsgedanke*) in the form of progressive stage incarceration. The attacks continued after the party took power in 1933. During the first four years of the Third Reich, criminal justice officials were joined by criminologists in dismissing rehabilitation as the embodiment of a misguided and naive humanitarianism that placed the needs of the criminal over those of society.[87] Kiel law professor Friedrich Schaffstein blamed the adoption of American models for "the overemphasis on correctional thinking in the theory and practice of German penology," a perspective mistakenly extolled under the "irrational ideological motto 'humaneness as end in itself and at any price.'"[88] Criticism like this was extended to transitional services for ex-convicts as well.[89]

The picture of Nazi Germany as a merciless law-and-order regime, with little or no interest in rehabilitation, is certainly shared by historians. Nikolaus Wachsmann has justifiably portrayed prison life during the Third Reich as one marked by military drills, beatings, hunger, and forced labor.[90] In addition, the vast literature on concentration camps—including more recent studies on their public functions—leaves little doubt that the camps aimed at demoralizing and degrading inmates, while provoking terror in the general population.[91] Any traces of genuine rehabilitative efforts have mostly been seen as confined to the treatment of juvenile delinquents.[92]

Some recent research on early concentration camps, however, reveals that they were not originally designed for slave labor or mass extermination but, rather, drew their inspiration from workhouses, labor services, and preventive detention, using discipline and intimidation to deter opponents and social deviants.[93] Moreover, during the first three to four years of the Nazi regime, it was not uncommon for prison staff to express optimism about the ability of correction to reform inmates, citing the presence of strong "character values" even among some communist political prisoners.[94] Prison administrators tended to be more restrained but did not altogether abandon the rehabilitative ideal. In a meeting between representatives from the Reich Ministry of Justice and penal facilities in the fall of 1933, most prison officials voiced their support for retaining some kind of progressive stage incarceration but insisted that more needed to be done to direct rehabilitation at only those convicts receptive to it.[95] A draft of new guidelines for progressive incarceration that circulated in 1934 conveyed a new determination to infuse the system with the values of male ruggedness and soldierly fidelity.

> Progressive stage incarceration is supposed to aid in reaching the goals of prison. Its task is to spur, to yoke, and to toughen the will of the prisoner in the service of strict self-discipline [*Selbstzucht*], so that goals can be placed before the inmate that are important for him to reach. By being constantly faced with the demand to mobilize all his strength, the proper sense of responsibility and duty to conform and submit is stirred and promoted, while his attitude toward the state and the national racial community after his release is being constantly directed the way forward.[96]

Experts imagined the penal facility as an extension of Nazi society, with prison staff and transitional care workers acting as reforming intermediaries on behalf of the community. First and foremost, incarceration was considered punishment, a necessary form of atonement for those who had injured the community. Security was prison's second principal function, a task it fulfilled by segregating the dangerous and the delinquent from the rest of society. The "weeding out" (*Aussonderung*) of undesirables was not to stop at the prison gates, however. As mentioned earlier, the existence of preventive detention itself meant that staff were to continue differentiating prisoners according to their relative unruliness and corrigibility.[97] Moreover, as Franz Gürtner, Reich minister of justice, emphasized in a secret memo in January 1939, the commingling of "various types of prisoners [*wesensverschiedener Gefangener*]," such as antisocials and asocials, ran the danger of spreading the latter's discontent and laziness among inmates who were otherwise educable.[98] It therefore remained of signal importance for the penal system to offer incentives and pedagogical support only to those capable of being reintegrated into society.[99]

Most penologists agreed that the goal of correction was ultimately more than just a matter of helping inmates stay out of future trouble. It was to spark "an inner transformation" through recognition of one's personal guilt for the crimes committed. This process, as one expert put it in 1935, began with incarceration itself, an act prompting self-reflection and a deepening sense of responsibility.[100]

During the Third Reich, experts rarely provided specifics or followed any single method for administering correctional measures. Despite the emphasis placed on psychological change, penologist showed little interest in psychotherapy.[101] Instead, they generally advocated the creation and maintenance of a total "pedagogical atmosphere" that could strike "one of the good 'strings' that are hidden in every person" and awaken and strengthen the inmate's sense of honor.[102]

Two elements were deemed critical to correction: strict order and hard work. The Cologne-based jurist H. Gummersbach spoke for many of his contemporaries in his 1934 description of the reforming benefits of discipline and labor. "By getting used to order and work in the facility," he contended, "not only are good inmates corrected; work and order are also the foundations for living together with others in freedom. . . . Joy in work and the genuine will to claim a place for oneself in human society through labor represent a moral fortification that is well suited to avoiding recidivism."[103]

Values

Correctional incarceration under the banner of National Socialism was intended to be nothing short of a schooling in character building. The new penal regimen, declared a prison instructor in Breslau, stressed action, vitality, authenticity, education, competition, combat, and discipline. Together, these values promised to instill in corrigible inmates those character features most needed outside prison walls: "loyalty, a willingness to sacrifice, selflessness, a readiness to help."[104] In this way, prison life could be seen as offering the path for convicts to be "reattached" to the "national racial community."[105]

It is all too easy to dismiss these calls for the creation of a pedagogical atmosphere in prisons as little more than a cynical attempt to give pseudoscientific cover to Nazi brutality. The fact, however, that the pedagogical features and values invoked here mirror those found in other settings at the time speaks, at the very least, to their imagined normative merits. Order, martial discipline, labor, "learning through action" (*Erziehung durch die Tat*), subordination to the racial community, a bifurcation of the population into winners and losers, friends and foes—as Martin Stahlmann and Jürgen Schiedeck have argued, these were all key components in National Socialist education and training generally.[106] If taken seriously, then, efforts to foster a pedagogical national community in prisons can be seen as the Nazi precursor and counterpart to attempts to create a democratic "therapeutic community" in psychiatric and penal facilities following World War II.[107]

As in other variations of therapeutic communities, gender expectations and ideals of domesticity played a key role in correctional thinking during the thirties and forties. As we have seen, broken and dysfunctional families were frequently cited as signs of corruption and causes of criminality. To combat such influences, it was argued, required a responsive and steely prison staff. Book learning would not suffice, as one prison officer from Greifswald explained; rather, the correctional officer needed to possess a commanding personality and the ability to use it to sway the willpower of others.[108] At the very top in men's prisons stood the prison warden, a man whose relationship toward his inmates was imagined to be necessarily both paternalistic and patriarchal.

> He [the warden] is for him [the inmate] the support, the counselor, the mediator, as well as confidant and confessor, yet also exhorter and cautioner, judge and punisher. Still today, the relationship remains that of a father to his disobedient son, only that he does not come to him with open arms, forgiving and excusing everything. Rather, he is the father with the

sturdy stick, who first punishes and then waits to see what the future holds. Then it is time to help.[109]

Female inmates appeared to require a different set of talents from staff. At the time, women's criminality was widely attributed to essential, yet misguided, attributes of "the feminine character," such as vengefulness, jealousy, and oversensitivity.[110] Likewise, it was believed that confinement and correction needed to be specifically tailored to feminine needs and abilities: only forms of physical exercise that were considered suited to women's bodies (e.g., gymnastics) were offered, first-time offenders needed to be separated from the bad influence of seasoned convicts such as prostitutes, and the fulfillment of domestic tasks was the focus of work details and schooling.[111]

Because the penal system was dominated by an overwhelmingly male population, correctional thinking largely assumed a male subject, something that one warden considered problematic. Else Voigtländer, head of the women's section of the penal facility at Waldheim, contended in 1937 that the handling of female convicts was hindered by outdated stereotypes and conventions. The widespread opinion that women prisoners were more unruly than their male counterparts, she argued, was patently false and rooted in a number of misinformed attitudes: lazy criminological arguments attributing all female behavior to the "nature of the female," the reluctance of male staff to lay hands on female inmates, and the male staff's impatience with women's sensitivities and indirect ways of communicating. The military forms of order and discipline common to male prisons, Voigtländer concluded, had no place in facilities for women. Instead, she recommended retaining progressive incarceration, allowing mothers to have regular visits from their children, and providing them with exercise outlets and suitable domestic work, such as sewing.[112]

The Reformed

For both male and female repeat offenders deemed to be especially dangerous, Nazi criminal justice held out the possibility of indefinite imprisonment in a preventive detention unit. Despite being the last outpost within the criminal justice system for an inmate (a repository for those considered most irredeemable), preventive detention was also understood to have rehabilitative functions. Disciplinary measures were applied, and some minor privileges were extended for good behavior. But as two observers noted in separate reports for the *Blätter für Gefängniskunde* in 1937 and 1938, progressive stage incarceration made little sense in this setting. Since their detention had no fixed limit, these inmates lived in a constant state of limbo—preventive detainees in Brandenburg Görden, for instance, reportedly referred to their facility as "Waitburg" (*Wartburg*) and could not be placated by anything other than their release from detention.[113] Thus, faced with a population described as unstable, easily tempted, flippant, soft, wanton, lazy, egotistical, and amoral, staff relied primarily on work and discipline, concentrating their efforts on aiding social prognosis by observing behavior.[114]

Still, while it was conceded that reform was out of reach for most preventive detainees due to their lack of inhibitions, some could reform themselves, as one judge in Hamburg put it in 1935, "if they learn to see that only an inner change (be it through correction or deterrence), and not the passage of time, will open the door to freedom."[115] Records from the city of Cologne, for instance, confirm that through 1938, officials there were releasing some preventive detainees after three or four years in custody.[116] In fact, by the end of April 1938, 701 out of a total of 3,886 preventive detainees throughout the country had been released.[117]

For young and first-time offenders, however, release was at least likely, if not a certainty. During the war, when courts lengthened criminal sentences for even juvenile offenders, early release was extended to inmates considered to have turned over a new leaf. Wartime records regarding sex offenders from the infamous Plötzensee Prison in Berlin provide some insight into what factors led staff to consider an inmate corrigible. A lack of previous convictions, an admission of guilt, and an expression of genuine remorse about the crime or crimes committed all figured prominently in the justifications that prison officials gave.[118] Staff often referred to inmates making a "good impression"; in the case of one prisoner, this meant that he didn't "give the impression of a weak-willed person."[119] A strong work record and a lack of disciplinary problems were also regularly flagged as an indication of a man with an encouraging prognosis.[120] Having a wife or even the prospect of marriage was generally seen as propitious, particularly for sex offenders.[121] One conduct report assessed thirty-nine-year-old artisan E.W., convicted multiple times for homosexuality, as follows:

> Still reformable: According to his statements, W. is not purely homosexual, only bisexually inclined. He has wanted to have regular relations with females. In order to have an external support for this, he foresees marrying after his release.[122]

Once out of prison, convicts faced a dismissive and distrustful public. Many found that "the real sentence first begins with release."[123] Like social prognosis and prison correction, transitional support for released convicts was framed in decidedly austere terms under the National Socialists. The head of the German Association for Court Assistance and Prisoner and Ex-Convict Welfare, Heinz Vogelsang, made this clear to those involved in aiding ex-convicts. The centralization and "coordination" of assistance, he emphasized, carried with it a necessary change in mentality. "Prisoner transitional care also follows the guiding principles of National Socialist social policy, the priority of community, and the strict principle of selection," he insisted in 1935. This meant excluding not just "the stubbornly resistant" but also the "inept and hereditarily craven. A humane and understanding sympathy for these asocials must be set aside in favor of the inexorable claims of the national community."[124] Vogelsang believed that physicians especially were going to have to play a pivotal role in this selection process, by informing state officials about those ex-convicts who should be considered for preventive detention.

Admittedly, Vogelsang's attitudes were not solely an expression of National Socialist ideology. Insistence that career criminals were unsuited to transitional care and that special detention needed to be arranged for "mental inferiors" were both well-established tenets among transitional care workers during the Weimar Republic.[125] National Socialism provided a legitimating framework within which assistance for ex-convicts could be imagined in both stern and ameliorative terms at once. House visits and investigations into domestic circumstances were now colored by criminal biological interest in confirming signs of a hereditary corruption.[126] Party organizations were considered resources for released men and women.[127] Stress was placed on providing ex-convicts assistance based less on the nature of their crimes than on their personalities and willpower.[128]

Most noteworthy from the standpoint of the human sciences is the fact that postrelease assistance for ex-convicts increasingly functioned as an extension of social prognosis, by providing data on the progress of convicts and ex-convicts. Criminal biological data collection centers checked police, prison, and welfare records and interviewed criminals and their families and employers for tracking purposes.[129] Details about how a released man or woman adapted to life inside and outside prison were then used as both a measure of the individual's progress and a source of information for researchers about which factors could serve as reliable indicators of incorrigibility.

A closer look at this research reveals how investigators and administrators operationalized notions like character and willpower in practice. During the fall of 1942, for instance, the Criminal Biological Research Center of the Reich Health Office looked into the backgrounds and habits of prisoners at the penitentiary in Rheinbach near Bonn. The nature and frequency of a repeat offender's crimes figured some into the center's prognostic assessments, but only to a limited extent. Investigators emphasized instead the indicative value of work and family relations in determining a convict's readiness to assume social responsibilities (*Verantwortungsbereitschaft*).[130] Evidence of spotty work habits and alcohol abuse were considered obvious red flags.[131] But gendered ideals of duty and domesticity played an especially prominent role in how the capacity for responsibility was framed. Messy, unsanitary, and ill-reputed households, abusive and neglectful fathering, and philandering were all regarded as signs of hopeless depravity.[132]

The corrigible man, by contrast, was one who took his family obligations seriously, as evidenced, for instance, in one police officer's report to the Hamburg Criminal Biological Data Collection Center about the progress of a released sex offender in 1943. "From every perspective, he treats his family correctly and thoroughly supports them with his income," the officer explained, adding, "He is easily influenced and easily swayed by his household. As long as he is under the influence of his wife, he has been well behaved and very domestic."[133] Besides highlighting the importance of family provision, the officer's evaluation reveals the expectation that wives held the key to keeping a man on the correct path. Wives, therefore, not only were an important source of information about released husbands but also were seen as extensions of correctional discipline. As one physician who studied the fate of parolees found, married men were more likely than single men to avoid getting into trouble again. "Marriage," he concluded, "became for them its own 'preventive detention,' in the best sense of the term."[134]

"The Sharpest Weapon in the Fight against the Sex Offender"

Castration as Correctional Therapy

As we have seen, Nazi Germany offered a number of institutional responses to convicted criminals: capital punishment, a fixed prison sentence, conditional preventive detention (including concentration camps), provisory psychiatric commitment, and supervised release. Each was seen as serving both special and general prevention goals, and each was justified on both punitive and rehabilitative grounds. There was, however, one other form of intervention, described by a Ministry of Interior official as "the sharpest weapon in the fight against the sex offender."[135] Directed specifically at repeat sex offenders and justified solely in therapeutic terms, section 42k of the Dangerous Habitual

Offender Law of 1933 allowed judges to mandate the compulsory castration of a man who was at least twenty-one years old and whose history of sex offenses revealed him to be "a dangerous sex criminal."

As noted earlier, turn-of-the-century criminologists tended to see sex offenders as categorically different from other types of criminals, in that their depravity was believed to be clearly rooted in a psychopathology. This did not change during the Third Reich, and there was broad consensus among forensic specialists during the 1930s and 1940s about the nature of the sex offender's personality. While a sexual drive (*Sexualtrieb*)—understood in thermodynamic terms as a kind of instinctual energy—was attributed to all human beings, the perversions of sex offenders were thought to be a function of three possible deficiencies in the form and/or expression of this drive: the relative strength of the drive, the direction or object of the drive, and the relative strength of one's willpower to resist deviant drives.[136] Little wonder that sex offenders at the time were routinely referred to as *Triebtäter* (drive, or impulse, perpetrators). Although criminal biologists tended to focus on the hereditary aspects of this psychopathology, researchers and clinicians pointed to multiple factors as playing a role in the etiology of sexual criminality, including senility, intoxication, poor rearing, boredom, corruption, and the lack of an available sex partner.[137]

During the thirties and early forties, government and academic researchers collected and analyzed epidemiological data about sex crimes, with an eye toward enhancing both criminal policy and the criminological sciences. By the mid-1930s, it was apparent that sex crime convictions were rising, from 13,178 in 1932 to 15,059 in 1933 and 19,092 in 1936, with about two-thirds of convictions being for sexual assault, rape, sexual abuse of children, and exhibitionism.[138] Studies also revealed some patterns in the behavior and backgrounds of offenders and their victims. Overall, perpetrators were overwhelmingly male (less than 1 percent were female), and the majority of them were married. Psychiatric evaluations also indicated that sex offenders disproportionately manifested symptoms of mental abnormality, most prominently psychopathy, congenital feeblemindedness, epilepsy, and nervous disorders.[139]

When it came to child molesters, there proved to be some surprising findings. In most instances, the criminal act never went beyond the mutual touching of genitalia. Gerhard Wessel revealed that the age distribution of perpetrators clustered at both ends of the life cycle: the largest share were around the ages of eighteen to twenty, while roughly 28 percent were over the age of sixty. He also found that of those convicted of child molestation, very few (2.6 percent) were deemed "dangerous sex offenders."[140] The victims of child molesters were overwhelmingly girls (over 90 percent), with about half being between the ages of twelve and fourteen and with around three-quarters being acquainted with their molester before the crime.[141]

It was in this context that criminal justice experts in Germany explored the application of castration as a response to sexual crime. First performed as a form of psychiatric treatment in Switzerland in 1892, castration began to be taken seriously as a medical remedy during the early twentieth century, as hormones began to be seen as the foundation of human sexuality and personality.[142] Voluntary castration of criminals was first sanctioned in Denmark in 1929, with the first mandatory laws emerging during the 1930s in Denmark, Iceland, Norway, Finland, Sweden, and Japan. Following Swiss and Danish precedents, jurists, scientists, clinicians, and government officials in Germany all agreed that the use of castration on sex offenders was a preventive, safety measure, not an extension of punishment. As such, even in Nazi Germany, it was strictly applied as a therapeutic treatment and, thus, ordered only on the basis of medical indications. As a treatment, however, castration was understood to be limited in its efficacy: the removal of male gonads was assumed to diminish or outright extinguish a criminal's libido and potency, but it was recognized to do nothing to change the object of his sexual desires or his willpower. Changing the latter two, it was believed, was best left to psychotherapy.[143] In fact, prominent criminologists and physicians, such as Albrecht Böhme, Emil Lange, and Wilhelm Meywerk, were strong advocates of combining castration with a range of psychotherapeutic techniques, including hypnosis and suggestion, psychoanalysis, self-discovery and will therapy (*Erkenntnis- und Willenstherapie*), and association therapy (a nascent form of cognitive behavioral therapy).[144]

Physicians were well aware that the operation did not always have the desired effect and that it could be accompanied, more often than not, by troubling side effects. After being castrated, some men continued to have an active libido and occasionally even achieved erection. There was general agreement that the procedure had limited impact on those with homosexual orientations. Many castrated men were beset with headaches, dizziness, sweats, weight gain, loss of muscle and hair, and bouts of depression, moodiness, and rage.[145] Still, archival records show that particularly in the case of child molesters, both clinicians and their castrated patients often characterized the effects of the operation as a "liberation" (*Befreiung*) from unnatural drives.

Ordering, Performing, and Evaluating the Operation

The Dangerous Habitual Offender Law of 1933 made it clear that the operation could only be prescribed compulsorily for those repeat offenders deemed "dangerous sex offenders." It was left to courts and physicians to operationalize the concept for everyday use. Both judge and physician were to direct their attention to the future, meaning that the offender need not manifest any signs of possessing a constitutional inclination (*Hang*). Rather, there needed to be evidence pointing to the probability that he would reoffend if he were not castrated. A judge could reject the idea of castration, for instance, in a case where there was evidence that the man was undergoing psychotherapy to extinguish his deviant impulses or that he had married or changed professions and thus would no longer pose a threat to a particular category of victims.[146] To be sure, some dangerous sex offenders could be considered dangerous habitual offenders and could thus be eligible for preventive detention even after castration. But for the most part, castration served as a kind of screening procedure, through which convicts who might otherwise have been placed in preventive detention could be diverted to supervised release.[147]

Forensic researchers and clinicians were eager to use section 42k of the Dangerous Habitual Offender Law as an opportunity to investigate the physical and mental effects of castration on men in general and on criminals in particular. Already in May 1934, Prussia required that prison doctors conduct follow-up examinations on castrated offenders in order to collect data for investigators. Under Franz Gürtner, the Reich Ministry of Justice played an active role in promoting the scientific study of castration, and on 10 October 1936, it mandated standardized procedures for the examination of men earmarked for castration, as well as follow-up examinations of postoperative convicts. Criminal biological data collection centers were ordered to fill out and gather three forms: a medical report on the patient's medical, sexual, and personal history, filled out by the attending physician; information on how the operation was performed and on the patient's reaction to it; and, finally, a medical report on the effects of the castration on the patient (including naked "before" and "after" pictures), focusing not only on the man's libido and sexual potency but also on his family, work, and interpersonal relations. Follow-up examinations were to be performed after one month, one year, three years, and five years.[148]

With the Reich Ministry of Justice's announcement in November 1937 of the creation of the centralized Criminal Biological Service, a mechanism was set up for the creation of a national catalog for the data collected.[149] In practice, however, things worked far from smoothly. Criminal biologists reported that they routinely met resistance from prison and police officials, who associated research with being soft on criminals. Prisoners were sometimes being released before they could be examined. Local civil servants often either were not sharing their information or provided too little detail about the domestic lives of released prisoners. Photographs were frequently of poor quality.[150]

A closer look at records from one criminal biological data collection center provides some insight into how researchers operationalized their evaluations of prisoners and the effects of castration. A criminal biological research department was first established in the Hamburg region by the psychiatrist Otto Matthey at the Fuhlsbüttel prison hospital in 1927. In 1930, Matthey, along with another physician, by the name of Clemenz, began conducting criminal biological examinations modeled on Viernstein's methods in Bavaria. Wilhelm Meywerk then replaced Matthey as director of the Hamburg Criminal Biological Data Collection Center in January 1935, a position he held until 1944. Under Meywerk, the Hamburg center moved quickly to become one of the premier data collection centers in the country, examining around 450 convicts, setting up a criminal biological catalog with information on some 4,700 forensically examined criminals, and beginning work on the creation of a comprehensive registry of all mental patients and their relatives (ca. 40,000–50,000 cases) in the Hamburg region.[151]

As at other data collection facilities, staff members at the Hamburg center were deeply involved in the administration and evaluation of the castration of convicts: they provided diagnostic reports for the courts, oversaw the operation, and conducted the required follow-up examinations on castrated men. In the Hamburg region, the castrations were performed at either the central interrogation jail in the city or the municipal hospital in Bremen. In the city, at least, the operation was done by a surgeon on staff, along with a municipal physician, neither of whom were compensated for their labor.[152] The procedure itself was described as "simple" by one of the physicians: a small cross section of skin on the scrotum, just underneath the root of the penis, was opened up, allowing the removal of the testicles. Most of the operations were done with only a local anesthetic, and it was reported that some men needed to be physically restrained for the procedure.[153]

In an article published in 1943, Meywerk reported that between 1 January 1934 and 30 June 1942, 402 convicts were castrated in Hamburg. By far, the largest share of those castrated were convicted child molesters, followed by exhibitionists and those guilty of aggravated sexual assault. The youngest man to be castrated was twenty-one years old, and the oldest was sixty. Over 55 percent of the men were between the ages of thirty-one and fifty.[154]

Meywerk came to strongly believe in the efficacy of castration on sex offenders. He announced that in almost all cases, both libido and sexual potency were either completely or almost completely extinguished following the surgery. Results of 609 periodic follow-up examinations by the Hamburg center were even more encouraging. They revealed that of the 402 men castrated, 91 were still incarcerated, 36 had died, 25 were in preventive detention, 12 were committed to psychiatric facilities, and 3 had been committed to some other kind of facility by the summer of 1942. The remaining 235 men were released, and only six of those had committed another sexual offense—a recidivism rate of only 2.6 percent. These results, Meywerk noted, could be still further improved on, "if the means and ways are found to underscore the success of the operations through psychotherapy and thereby firmly anchor it mentally."[155]

This was not enough evidence of efficacy to convince the Marburg medical scholar Albrecht Langelüddeke (1889–1977), an expert who would come to play a prominent role in the related debate in West Germany. Langelüddeke went over Meywerk's data and found shortcomings. In particular, he criticized Meywerk for using inexact and unstandardized criteria for determining whether a castrated man had improved or not, criteria contributing to a marked inflation in the reported success rate.[156]

How, then, did forensic specialists go about evaluating sex offenders both before and after castration? Helmut Wolf's 1941 study of sex offenders committed to the psychiatric facility in Göttingen, for instance, revealed some common features in the background of those earmarked for castration: multiple sex offenses, no prospect of improvement through correctional measures, and chronic difficulties at home and work.[157] Records from the Hamburg Criminal Biological Data Collection Center paint a similar picture, showing that clinicians and courts paid most attention to the chronic nature of sex offenders' criminal behavior—the number, rapidity, and increasing severity of offenses. Because castration was seen as a form of therapy, not a punishment, indications that a convict still had redeeming qualities often led assessors to recommend castration. Thus, in the case of a child molester who had nine convictions dating back to 1914, observers took note of his honesty and receptiveness to correction.[158] In another instance, the courts resisted sentencing a twenty-nine-year-old man to death for repeated homosexual relations with boys (some under the age of fourteen), due in large measure to his admission and expressions of regret about the crimes.[159]

Such candor was not necessary, however, in order for authorities to favor castration. For instance, in the case of a fifty-year-old man accused and convicted multiple times of the sexual molestation of girls, including his stepdaughters, both the medical examiner and the court found the unrepentant man prey to an unusually strong, deviant sex drive. Castration, the physician in the case argued, offered a viable solution. "Such men with elevated and inverted sexual drives," he noted, "can be cured of their malady, if one takes on the cause of their actions, namely, freeing them of [these drives], so that through the distribution of hormones their sexual drives will be perpetually kept in check."[160] Clinical assessments like these proved pivotal in decision making about castrating offenders: in virtually every case I have encountered, courts deferred to the judgment of medical examiners when deciding the question.

Criminal biologists and psychiatrists were also given the task of conducting the periodic evaluations of postoperative sex offenders. As was the case with the justifications given for sanctioning castration, a pattern can be seen in the criteria used for judging the relative success of the operation. Criteria considered key evidence of improvement included a quiet, serene home life; a consistent work record; a lack of disciplinary and legal problems; and being on good terms with family, neighbors, and workmates[161]—in general, being "hard-working, amenable, correct in behavior."[162] Investigators went still further, delving into the men's attitudes and moods, looking for indications of happiness (*lebensfroh*, *lebenslustig*), affability, and a diminished libido. For their part, castrated men themselves demonstrated an ability, at the very least, to mimic what was expected of them. "Just a sexual thought would have required an extraordinary act of willpower, and that doesn't happen to me," explained one man, who added, "I have my will, I think, under control, since I no longer am ruled by pathological drives."[163]

In Hamburg, where Meywerk held an optimistic view of castration's inhibiting effects on recidivism, even the most hardened criminals appeared to show remarkable signs of reform. K.F., for instance, was forty-two years old when he was castrated in October 1934. Though he had four previous convictions dating back to 1920, they had all been for theft. What had precipitated the castration order was evidence showing that F. had spent the previous five years sexually molesting a girl whose parents shared his house, repeatedly threatening to kill her if she told anyone. He was eventually released in June 1937. From May 1938 to July 1943, the staff of the Hamburg Criminal Biological Data Collection Center periodically followed up on F. to see how he was getting on. Time and again, they found him to be withdrawn, quiet, and even-tempered. He eventually married in June 1938 and went into business breeding domestic animals. The last information from local police reported, "F. is leading a withdrawn, quiet family life."[164]

All told, a conservative estimate is that around twenty-four hundred convicts were castrated in Germany under section 42k of the Dangerous Habitual Offender Law during the years 1934–43.[165] On average, this represented between 1.7 and 2.7 percent annually of all convictions for sex offenses, a figure testifying to the commitment of authorities to use castration for strictly limited, therapeutic purposes.[166] By and large, the program was deemed a success by criminal biologists and government officials, but not without caveats. Studies at the time found that some men continued to have erections or sexual desires well after the operation, while many others reported bouts of depression and listlessness. In 1944, the physician Nikolaus Jensch summarized a decade's worth of data on the effects of castration on German sex offenders, adding analysis of his own investigation into the fate of 693 castrated offenders. He found that the majority of those ordered to be castrated were child molesters (many of whom had engaged in homosexual and incestuous relations). Only 11.3 percent had reoffended, and most of those men were previously involved in other kinds of criminal activities. Still, Jensch found, the operation had its shortcomings: it had no discernible impact on the sexual orientation of offenders, and many complained of strong, physical side effects. Most importantly, only about half of the men were able to be effectively resocialized; the rest moved from job to job and ultimately proved incapable of fully reintegrating into society. "The prognosis for castration," Jensch concluded, "is worst for homosexuals, better for all other sexual drive anomalies, also for late-developing criminals and postencephalitics—all told, however, judged to be more modest than previously [thought]."[167]

The Correctional Imagination during the War

Rehabilitation and Brutality

Without question, the war—particularly events following the outbreak of war against the Soviet Union in June 1941—had a profound impact on German criminal justice. The war years witnessed what has been referred to as an "escalation of legal terror," in the form of more frequent application of the death penalty (from 1,292 cases in 1941 to 4,457 in 1942 to around 9,600 over the years 1943–44), stricter sentencing by judges, increasing reliance on police and the concentration camp system, and the criminalization of more mundane acts of social deviance.[168] In addition, the SS and the police were given increasingly broad powers to detain, confine, and kill criminals and nonconformists, all at the expense of traditional criminal justice procedures.[169] The unequivocal viciousness and lethality of the Third Reich during the years 1939–45 appears to have signaled the end of any semblance of rehabilitation and nuance in Germany at the time. It is therefore surprising, when examining criminal justice records and penological literature, to see persistent traces of correctional thinking during these bleak years. Their presence testifies neither to the regime's interest in keeping up appearances nor to a need for us to reconsider our assessment of National Socialism's ruthlessness. Rather, these records highlight the extent to which it was possible to see rehabilitation and brutality as compatible.

It is not a coincidence that expressions of faith in resocialization were most prominent within the criminal justice establishment. Under Franz Gürtner and his immediate successor, Franz Schlegelberger, the Ministry of Justice had fought—by and large unsuccessfully—the insinuation of SS, police, and interior ministry officials in criminal justice affairs, insisting on the professional competence of scholarly jurists and legalistic methods.[170] By late April 1942, when Hitler, in his final speech before the Reichstag, railed at the judiciary and claimed to be the sole authority in legal affairs, the justice system had increasingly become an object of scorn in many important party circles. After Otto Georg Thierack (1889–1946) took over as Reich minister of justice on 20 August 1942, he embarked on a reform of the judiciary aimed at bringing it more closely in line with the party and establishing a new division of labor alongside the police and the SS.[171] In February 1943, Thierack spelled out his plan for criminal justice, envisioning a legal system that would leave the internment of incorrigibles and racial enemies to the police and that would leave the fate of the remaining offenders to the judiciary.[172]

As totalizing and autocratic as Hitler's wartime criminal policy was imagined, then, there remained areas and instances where continuities in correctional thinking and practice were able to be maintained. The picture of the habitual offender, for instance, remained fairly constant, as a figure whose actions arose out of a criminal predilection, rather than out of a momentary passion or dire circumstance.[173] Criteria for social prognosis continued to emphasize family history, the relative stability of work and marriage relations, and evidence of character virtues, such as willpower, selflessness, and self-restraint.[174] While personnel shortages and a shift in labor priorities presented challenges for reintegration programs, their focus primarily remained matching ex-convicts to jobs and employers and reporting on the progress of released men.[175]

The continuation of business as usual in the handling of convicts during the war led, in at least one instance, to ruffling the feathers of prominent party officials. Records show that at least through the end of 1944, individual judges and clinicians continued to draw distinctions between perpetrators based on their social prognoses, sometimes leading to the imposition of a lighter sentence or release.[176] Such practices eventually came to the attention of the Reich Chancellery and its head Martin Bormann. Writing from Hitler's headquarters in September 1942, Bormann castigated Minister Thierack, judges, and prosecutors for their misguided leniency, particularly in cases involving child molestation. Too often, he claimed, mitigating circumstances were being used to justify a lighter sentence for individual suspects. "The reasons for the present sentencing practice might be found in the fact that courts are granting too much weight to the personal circumstances of the perpetrator, his frequently advanced age, and his psychopathic constitution," Bormann suggested.[177] He added that judges should instead consider the damage done to the victims and the deterrent impact of a harsh sentence.

Bormann's insistence on the deterrent function of punishment offers some insight into how, despite some continuities, the war altered the correctional imagination of Nazi Germany. In many ways, the changes brought about by World War II were a matter of degree more than kind. By 1941, correctional thought in Germany had already largely adopted the soldierly language and ideals of National Socialism, stressing self-control, duty, discipline, obedience, and self-sacrifice. In the context of total war, these values were revalorized with a new urgency.[178]

Peter Longerich and others have observed that from early 1942 onward, a sense of desperation manifested itself in the form of a growing intolerance toward ever more mundane behavior that was perceived to undermine the war effort.[179] One of the surprising results of this was the increasing reliance on psychopathological explanations for antisocial actions. For example, Ernst Kühn, the director of the university psychiatric clinic at Jena, argued that the disorder and instability incited by domestic political opponents mirrored the latter's disturbed and unstable personalities. Many of their crimes, he maintained, were little more than the "expression of a situational conflict at work, in the family, in marriage, etc." of "primitively structured people."[180] While it was acknowledged that some criminals did suffer from mental disabilities such as "feeblemindedness," the mental shortcomings of most criminals, experts argued, did not rise to the level of being deemed a disease. By the last years of the war, however, it had become more commonplace to see and treat all sorts of asocial and antisocial behavior as indicative of mental "weakness" or disturbance.[181]

One might see in this development evidence of the medicalization or racialization of criminality. But there is good reason to understand it in a broader context, as a function of German criminal law's emphasis on the subjectivity of perpetrators, social prognosis, and prophylactic intervention. Take, for instance, the extension of the death penalty to dangerous repeat offenders in the fall of 1941.[182] Legal experts at the time did not justify the change in the law on the basis of its retributive function; instead, they focused almost solely on it serving the purpose of removing incorrigibles from society. Within the criminal justice system, the death penalty was intended to be reserved, then, for those dangerous repeat offenders whose personalities were judged to be incapable of reform and who would likely cost more than they would produce if placed in preventive detention.[183] As one prominent legal scholar put it, "Guilt goes from referring to a guilty deed to [referring to] a guilty way of life."[184] The German high court (*Reichsgericht*) affirmed this interpretation of the law in the spring of 1942, stating that the key to passing a death sentence in these instances was the presence of "a personality, which, as a result of a hereditary constitution or an acquired tendency, repeatedly breaks the law," as well as evidence that this "inner tendency . . . is so ingrained that neither reform attempts nor fear of a harsh sentence can keep it under control."[185] Thus, the legal extension of the death penalty to include repeat offenders arose out of the logic of correctional thinking, an elaboration on the ideas of incapacitation and preventive detention.[186]

From Correcting Convicts to Eliminating Prodromes

The war accentuated the preventive features and purposes of the correctional imagination in Germany. Patrick Wagner's characterization of policing during the final years of the Third Reich is equally valid for criminal justice in general at this time. The regime began shifting its attention from criminal phenotypes to delinquent genotypes.[187]

The psychiatrist and criminal biologist Robert Ritter (1901–51) played a key role in realizing the vision of a truly totalitarian rehabilitative ideal. Ritter began his career as a youth psychiatrist, studying medicine and psychology in Tübingen and Munich. In the early 1930s, he became active in criminal biology, researching "asocial" youth. Moving to Berlin in 1936, he started working on the concept of "preventive crime fighting," under the auspices of the Reich and Prussian ministries of interior and the Reich Health Office. Here, he focused his attention on "gypsies," a group he believed hereditarily tied to asociality, feeblemindedness, and criminality. Ritter quickly came to the attention of powerful figures in the Nazi establishment, and by 1942, he had been chosen to head both the Criminal Biological Institute of the research branch of the Reich Health Office as well as the Criminal Biological Institute of the Reich Criminal Police. He was eventually named head of the entire Reich Health Office in November 1943.[188]

One of Ritter's wartime initiatives involved the application of criminal biological diagnosis and social prognosis in welfare assistance for delinquent youth. "For it goes without saying," as he explained in a 1942 article, "that the next criminal generation springs from their [youth's] ranks and that our work can only succeed if we can predict already at the moment of the first commission of a crime whether we are also dealing with the first in a criminal life."[189] In Ritter's view, the future of criminal investigation and criminal justice resided in the use of psychology to assess young delinquents' heredity, personality traits, and psychological development in order to determine their relative receptiveness to correction and punishment. In an effort to operationalize these ideas, Ritter helped in the design and maintenance of so-called youth detention camps (*Jugendschutzlager*), intended as a form of indefinite detention for wayward "Aryan" youths ages sixteen to twenty-one. Two camps were established in Germany: a camp for four hundred boys in Moringen (Lower Saxony), starting operations in August 1940, and a camp for six hundred girls in Uckermark (Brandenburg), beginning its work in June 1942.[190] Both were maintained by the police and the SS and fell under the jurisdiction of the Reich Criminal Police Office.

In their mission and methods, the youth detention camps were a direct expression of the correctional and prophylactic impulses within criminal justice. Administrators saw the facilities as the last chance for especially refractory young people to prove themselves capable of being reformed.[191] "Through ongoing examination by youth caseworkers, the key here is determining whether all correctional options have been exhausted that could be suitable to reforming someone into a productive member of the national racial community," explained Brandenburg's provincial youth office in January 1943.[192]

What made these new camps unusual was the emphasis placed on achieving crime prevention through early detection and correction within the life course of delinquents. In a meeting held for youth welfare officials in January 1941, one of the architects of the program, Paul Werner (SS-Standartenführer and Police Colonel in the Reich Security Headquarters), laid out the raison d'être of this form of detention. An official in attendance summarized Werner's gist as follows:

> Whether the case involves a youth with environmental damage or hereditary damage is insignificant. The youths are to remain in the youth detention camp until the conclusion can be reached that, in the future, they will no longer disturb the community. The length of the confinement is therefore indeterminate. If no success is evident by age 21, then the youngsters are to be transferred to a concentration camp for preventive custody.[193]

Robert Ritter and his staff took on both analytical and directive duties at Moringen and Uckermark. He and his team conducted biological examinations on all new intakes, noting body type, racial features, genealogy, psychological development, life history, and character traits. Data from these assessments were used not simply for research purposes but also for administering treatment plans. The evaluations were relied on both to establish a baseline for individual inmates against which future behavior could be measured and to serve as the basis for assigning inmates to different "blocks" in the camps.[194] At Moringen, eight blocks were created to house different groups of inmates based on their personalities and form of deviance.[195]

Once in camp, inmates were subjected to discipline and work. Correction, as Paul Werner openly admitted, was regimented and tough: "When it comes to correction itself, it is organized strictly, soldierly, and, when necessary, also severely. To begin with, the inmates are placed face-to-face with correctional officers and other staff who demand the most stringent manliness, discipline, soldierly demeanor, diligence, and punctuality."[196] A ten-hour workday filled the daily routine, with a range of disciplinary measures, from lost privileges to corporal punishment, meted out for violations of the rules.

Supervising and evaluating the inmates were correctional officers, or *Erzieher*, from the SS. By the summer of 1943, fifteen such officers—six of whom were trained in pedagogy—were distributed among the different blocks at Moringen. One of the principal duties of correctional officers was tracking inmate conduct and recording anything noteworthy about the habits and attitudes of individual boys and girls. Every six months, the correctional officer was required to submit a conduct report on each of his charges. The evidence from these reports was then combined with data from inmate records and a psychological interview conducted by Ritter and his assistants. In the end, Ritter used the results to determine the relative corrigibility of each inmate.[197] While few records from these camps have been recovered, one source indicates that up to July 1944, a total 351 inmates at Moringen were either released or transferred, including 45 sent back home, 138 released to the Wehrmacht, and 52 moved to a psychiatric facility, 53 to a concentration camp, and 27 to a penal facility.[198]

The youth detention camps at Moringen and Uckermark point in the direction of the Third Reich's growing interest in spotting those exhibiting early signs of delinquency or criminal prodromes. With most of its political and "racial" opponents subdued by 1944, late National Socialism showed signs of turning its attention to the identification, isolation, and indefinite detention of those considered likely to become enemies of the racial community.[199] An expression of this came in the form of the final draft of the Gemeinschaftsfremdengesetz (Law on Those Alien to the Community) in 1944.

The idea of creating a "community alien" law dated backed to discussions between the Ministry of Interior and the Reichsführer SS in 1935. Although a rough first draft was being circulated in government circles in 1939, the justice ministry only became involved in deliberations in August 1942. The proposed law aimed at empowering authorities to identify, monitor, arrest, intern, castrate, sterilize, and/or otherwise remove from society anyone "who, on the basis of personality and lifestyle—in particular, those with an extraordinary lack of understanding or character—show themselves to be incapable of satisfying the most minimal demands of the national racial community."[200] A 1942 version of the law pointed not to specific deeds but to personality types—"failures, ne'er-do-wells, freeloaders, do-nothings, or disruptives"—as the targets of the law.[201] Within the context of the war, the law was framed in terms of public hygiene and deemed a preventive measure justified on the basis of hereditary theory and criminal biology.[202]

Conclusions

Despite the Nazi Party's avowed rejection of Weimar penal reform and the regime's increasing reliance on extralegal terror and violence, the Third Reich provided space for discussing and carrying out the correctional rehabilitation of prisoners. By and large, these deliberations took place within the jurisdiction of the Reich Ministry of Justice and were often driven by medically trained criminal biologists. Not surprisingly, the reform of convicts was often couched in race hygienic terms, adopting categorical distinctions and emphasizing the importance of physical stigmata as signs of hereditary corruption. Applying clinical prognosis to single out incorrigibles for incapacitation, correctional efforts increasingly focused on finding ways to identify criminal prodromes.

As a biopolitical project, rehabilitation under National Socialism was not strictly confined to the somatic, however. Instead, the correctional imagination of Nazi Germany proved remarkably interested in the minds of convicts, and researchers, clinicians, and administrators sought to uncover the inner workings of the "criminal personality" in a fashion that could be best described as a forensic characterology of suspicion. An offender's past life, dealings with staff, physical and mental health, and work performance were all monitored and assessed for indications believed to reveal essential truths about the person's willpower, moral fortitude, and, ultimately, relative corrigibility.

Thus, while historians are quite right in stressing how incarceration was used as a tool of exclusion in Nazi Germany,[203] we need to recognize that confinement could also serve the ideals of inclusion, integration, and reintegration. The use of and debate about castration, for instance, show how a twentieth-century tool of criminal justice can be difficult to map neatly onto a normative distinction drawn between rehabilitative inclusion and punitive exclusion. In fact, historians of Stalin's gulag have pointed to some similar trends in the Soviet Union at this time.[204] Evidence indicates that around 20 percent of all prisoners there were released annually. Within the Soviet camps, forced labor had both explicitly productive and correctional purposes, educational workers were hired to reform inmates, and prisoner conduct was used to differentiate between the reformable and the irredeemable. The examples of Stalinist Russia and Nazi Germany demonstrate that it has been perfectly possible for brutality and rehabilitation to coexist and, indeed, to underpin one another.

Yet it would be an overstatement to suggest, as natural law proponents in postwar West Germany and others have, that National Socialism's harsh treatment of deviants was the culmination of social engineering and rehabilitative impulses.[205] Traditional notions of atonement and retribution, as Thomas Roth has observed, remained leitmotifs in punishment during the Third Reich.[206] To these could be added other prominent concepts and ideals with much longer histories than the human sciences: moral turpitude, free will, authenticity, social expulsion as punishment.

What, if anything, did National Socialism introduce, then, that was new to the German correctional imagination? The movement and the regime borrowed heavily from earlier precedents, so that any conclusions drawn in this regard must be qualified. The idea of special forms of detention was not original to the Nazis, but enacting the Dangerous Habitual Offender Law of 1933 was. Social prognosis was hardly an innovation of the regime, but the creation of a nationwide system for identifying criminal prodromes was. Likewise, the castration of sex offenders was not a new project, but its compulsory realization was. The transinstitutionalization of deviants, delinquents, and criminals was not unique in German history, but the existence of concentration and death camps was. The distinction between the corrigible and the incorrigible was not a Nazi invention, but the grim fate awaiting those who failed to change was.

The changes under National Socialism were sweeping, but they were not without parallel. Especially before World War II, German penology experts could well claim that their research and efforts were well within the mainstream of international science and medicine, if not downright pioneering. So it should come as no surprise that 1945 represented far from a sudden and definitive end to most of the changes that had occurred under the Nazi regime. The legal scholar Joachim Vogel has pointed to five lines of development in twentieth-century criminal law to which National Socialism contributed: expansion of the social reach of law, the formal operationalization of law, the introduction of ethics into legal thought, emphasis on the importance of the criminal's subjectivity, and the instrumental use of law in the service of policy.[207] The extent to which these and other trends were reinforced and thwarted in the two postwar German states will be considered in the following chapters.

Chapter 3

Correcting the Disoriented Socialist Personality

None of the twentieth-century German states managed to live up to the ideals they set for themselves when it came to rehabilitating prisoners. That reality—as well as that fiction—is an integral part of the story of correctional rehabilitation. One can argue, however, that the disparity between ideal and practice was greatest in the German Democratic Republic. Here, the ruling Socialist Unity Party (SED) laid claim to having one of the most advanced rehabilitative penal systems in the world. In reality, conditions in East German prisons were more often than not dismal, rife with human rights violations, and populated by tens of thousands of political prisoners.

Reports from former inmates and historical studies conducted since 1989 have lent credence to the claim that the GDR all but abandoned any semblance of correctional rehabilitation.[1] There is a great deal of truth in this assessment, but it needs to be acknowledged that much of the criticism heaped on East German prisons has been motivated by an understandable desire to provide a counterpoint to the inflated claims of the former regime. The picture painted of a hypocritical and callous Communist Party, however true, has made it that much easier to treat the East German experience with prisons as an anomaly in German history, best considered part of a fraternity of totalitarian criminal justice systems alongside the Third Reich.

While it may be comforting to adopt a normative definition of correctional rehabilitation that conveniently excludes Nazi Germany and the GDR from consideration, it hardly reflects historical realities. The correctional imagination in East Germany was beset by many of the same kinds of challenges and pitfalls encountered elsewhere. If rehabilitation fell victim there to ideological imperatives, chronic shortages, short-term expediency, and secrecy, these were obstacles also encountered elsewhere. East German prisons failed to live up to the aspirations proclaimed by their administrators and reformers. That this happened was hardly unique. What were unique, however, were the ways in which this discrepancy was articulated and managed. Considered in this manner, correctional rehabilitation—either in principle or in practice—did not disappear from East Germany but, rather, took shape as "real existing socialism's" inadequate response to crime in a postfascist world.

Early Reform Initiatives

At first, the Soviet occupation of eastern Germany brought with it a swift and noteworthy change in penology. On 27 July 1945, the Soviet Military Administration in Germany created a department of prisons within the German Central Administration for Justice. The selection of the department's head signaled a marked shift in thinking about how prisons were to be run. Dr. Werner Gentz had been a reform-minded jurist during the Weimar Republic, serving as an official in the penal system department of the Prussian Ministry of Justice and as a faculty member at the University of Berlin, until his dismissal from both posts by the Nazis in 1933. Already by the midtwenties, Gentz had made a name for himself as a vocal advocate of rehabilitative prisons based on the methods of the human sciences.[2]

For Gentz, prisoner rehabilitation was about reaching the willpower and moral core of a convict, to instill in him or her a sense of responsibility through respect for order and work. In October 1945, Gentz called on his earlier ideas and experiences to frame a set of guidelines for the East German penal system, announcing, "The inmate must go from being an object of to a subject in prison; he must internally participate in what prison presents to him. . . . No military drills but, rather, group pedagogy and the formation of a sense of community."[3]

Over the next three years, Gentz put forward a vision of penology that harkened back to Weimar reform ideas, one committed to the abandonment of retributive justice. Setting his ideas against the backdrop of, on the one hand, Nazi brutality and, on the other, postwar shortages in resources and labor, he contended that the legal and juridical logic of criminal justice was largely incapable of addressing the social dislocation and economic devastation faced by most prisoners. That most inmates were between the ages of sixteen and twenty-eight made it urgent that criminal justice be recast as a form of welfare (*Fürsorge*), to prevent "the rise of a generation of genuine criminals."[4] This meant, according to Gentz, seeing most of those behind bars as victims of their times and ensuring that they received the kind of material and social assistance needed to mitigate the brutalizing effects of incarceration.

To this end, Gentz proposed developing a prison system around five prin-

TABLE 5. Number of Prisoners and Arrested in Custody in the GDR, 1953–87 (Annual Average, Rounded Estimate)

Year	Total	Prisoners	Arrested in Custody	Compulsory Work	Prison Rate (Inmates per 100,000 Population)
1953	51,829	39,214	12,615		216
1954	43,092	36,439	6,653		202
1955	48,457	41,804	6,653		233
1956	34,331	30,615	3,716		173
1957	24,304	20,573	3,731		117
1958	36,158	28,884	7,472		166
1959	35,151	29,687	5,464		172
1960	32,639	27,010	5,629		157
1961	28,445	22,828	5,166	451	133
1962	32,625	27,028	4,537	1,060	158
1963	23,916	20,028	3,242	646	117
1964	25,680	21,610	3,065	1,005	127
1965	21,694	16,651	3,717	1,326	98
1966	27,058	20,504	4,393	2,161	120
1967	31,082	23,274	5,077	2,731	136
1968	30,466	23,713	3,586	3,070	136
1969	28,324	21,120	3,979	3,225	124
1970	29,766	21,439	4,998	3,329	126
1971	34,416	24,325	6,045	4,045	143
1972	34,318	24,208	5,717	4,393	142
1973	28,904	15,728	7,827	5,349	93
1974	47,693	30,093	5,665	11,935	178
1975	46,974	30,644	4,966	11,364	182
1976	41,598	27,548	4,167	9,883	164
1977	35,632	30,895	4,737		184
1978	35,375	29,448	5,927		176
1979	37,175	31,830	5,345		190
1980	36,153	30,827	5,326		184
1981	40,958	36,179	4,779		216
1982	40,589	35,410	5,179		212
1983	39,756	34,658	5,098		208
1984	38,917	33,846	5,071		203
1985	35,015	30,248	4,857		182
1986	33,259	28,151	5,108		169
1987	28,872	24,546	4,326		148

Source: Most of the table from Johannes Raschka, *Justizpolitik im SED-Staat: Anpassung und Wandel des Strafrechts während der Amtszeit Honeckers* (Cologne: Böhlau, 2000), 336–37; "prison rate" data included by the author.

ciples: classification, individualization, vitalization, collectivization, and humanization. Prisoners and facilities needed to be distinguished and segregated according to attributes such as sex, age, health, severity of offense, and risk of reoffending. This would allow prison staff to take full advantage of training in character analysis, psychology, and pedagogy, to arrive at a scientifically rigorous diagnosis of an inmate's personality as well as a correctional plan tailored to his or her circumstances. Work was the centerpiece in Gentz's scheme, with self-run worker collectives serving as the means by which inmates would come to learn the value of community and responsibility. Prison labor would then be supplemented by leisure activities, such as schooling, lectures, music, and sports, all designed to break the monotony of conventional prison life and to nurture more stable ties to the outside world.[5]

Gentz was not alone at this time in his advocacy for correctional rehabilitation. Like Gentz, Walther Hoeniger was a left-leaning jurist whose career dated back to the Weimar Republic. Joining the SED in May 1946, he quickly rose to become head of the Brandenburg Justice Administration, where he supported initiatives aimed at turning convicts "as quickly as possible into useful members of human society."[6]

In early 1946, Brandenburg's prisons, faced with shortages of cell space, clothing, food, equipment, and trained personnel, began to grant some first-time offenders the opportunity to work extramurally on public works projects in exchange for a reduced sentence. In contrast to earlier prison labor, participation in the program was voluntary. Participating inmates were organized into work collectives and set to work at limestone quarries or railway construction sites, alongside nonoffender workers and for the same wages. The performance of inmates was tracked, recorded, and used to determine whether they should be eligible for early release.[7] All told, Hoeniger reported, around three thousand prisoners took part in the conditional release program by the end of February 1948. Of those prisoners, only seventy were dismissed for poor performance, and only forty-eight committed another offense during their work details.[8]

As Hoeniger readily admitted, however, the reform initiative in Brandenburg faced ongoing resistance from a number of sources. Conventional laborers resented working next to convicts receiving equivalent wages, perceiving the practice to be a denigration of their social status. Cynical prison officials refused to invite inmates to apply to the program, while many officials dismissed the project as an indulgent watering down of criminal justice.

Equally strong were the countervailing currents within the administration of Soviet-occupied Germany. Soviet authorities, under the direction of then head of civil affairs Major General Ivan Kolesnitchenko, took a decidedly hands-on approach in their oversight of the German justice system. Waves of decrees, instructions, and guidelines from the Soviet Military Administration directed German officials on policy.[9] While Gentz and Hoeniger were given relatively free reign early on to pursue their reforms, Soviet officials increasingly encouraged a hard-line approach to criminal justice.

Signs of this were already evident by late in the spring of 1945, when Soviet officials sanctioned the use of former Nazi concentration camps as "special camps" to incarcerate former Nazi Party members and officials, war criminals, and perceived opponents. During the ten years of the camps' existence, around 154,000 prisoners were held in them, and Soviet indifference to the fate of the prisoners led to roughly 44,000 of them dying, primarily due to neglect.[10] Already by the summer of 1946, then, Soviet officials were criticizing Gentz's reform notions as going "too far" in trying "to turn prisons into correctional homes and asylums."[11]

By the summer of 1950, Gentz lost the patronal support of justice minister Max Fechner, and on 22 August, the Politburo formally announced the transfer of all authority of the East German prison system to the Ministry of Interior and the police.[12] It took six years for control of the entire penal system to be handed over to the interior ministry. From the start, however, officials made it clear—as did a police decree in April 1951—that security would trump "the false humanitarianism, which increasingly insinuated itself into penal facilities in the postwar period and which served to dilute the idea of prison."[13] From this point on, the Ministry of Interior played the role of hard-liner in prison affairs. Under the leadership of former Communist Party functionary and "Moscow cadre" August Mayer during the years 1951–59, the department of prisons within the ministry insisted on subjecting convicts to a retributive and harsh regime of isolation, discipline, military drills, and harassment, all with the ostensible purpose of protecting society by breaking the will of offenders.[14]

Thus, when the constitution of the newly founded German Democratic Republic declared, in October 1949, that "prison is based on the idea of the correction of corrigible individuals through common, productive work," it signaled the end, not the start, of postwar reform. Correction (*Erziehung*) was now carefully qualified. Tied to work that contributed to the planned economy, correction was now limited to those convicts deemed corrigible.

In practice, by the early 1950s, little remained of the rehabilitative plans of Gentz and Hoeniger except for their ideals. Yet these values were not without significance. The historical consensus that East German penal reform vanished once the Ministry of Interior took over prisons overlooks the fact that terms and concepts had been introduced for imagining incarceration in new terms—for bringing scientific and clinical know-how to prison management, blurring the boundaries separating prisons and the outside world, thinking of prison labor as a form of therapy, and making individual self-reliance the goal of correction. East German prisons may never have lived up to these principles, but they nevertheless provided advocates of rehabilitation in the 1950s and 1960s with a means to moor their ideas to what were officially considered legitimate ideals.[15]

Medical and Legal Understandings of the Criminal in the Fifties

In stark contrast to their counterparts in West Germany, party and state officials in East Germany throughout most of the 1950s not only distanced themselves from psychiatric and psychopathological explanation in understanding crime but abandoned criminology and forensic psychology altogether. Dismissing both sciences as "bourgeois" endeavors that were inadequate for understanding antisocial conduct in a socialist society, legal scholars and party leaders in the GDR defined crime as a political expression of class struggle. This meant, as one police textbook put it in 1955, that "personal" motivations were invariably declining as the immediate causes of crime, whereas "terrorist groups, saboteurs, agents, and spies," as well as other "enemies of worker and peasant power," were exerting a growing influence.[16]

That this view of crime as class struggle was elevated to official doctrine did not, however, entirely wipe away the vestiges of forensic psychiatry and psychology in postwar East Germany. For one thing, the disciplines of psychiatry and psychology did not disappear: practitioners continued to pursue the same research programs and professional goals they had pursued for decades, albeit with more limited resources. Over the course of the 1950s, psychiatric research and services were slowly reestablished and firmly oriented toward a biological view of mental illness, while psychological institutes remained fixed on pedagogical applications of their studies.[17] Researchers in forensic psychiatry, too, found receptive audiences for their findings, among fellow clinicians at conferences and through scholarly journals.[18]

Coupled with this persistence was the fact that criminal law in the fifties remained more or less the same as that under the Nazis. It was particularly relevant for psychiatrists that the criminal code's sections 42b (involuntary commitment to a psychiatric institution) and 51 (diminished capacity of the offender) remained in force, thus requiring courts to solicit psychiatric assessments of individual defendants in appropriate cases. These clinical evaluations took on an increased importance in the GDR in comparison to Nazi and West Germany, because East German law did not allow for court-ordered treatment as part of sentencing. In addition, a Supreme Court decision of 23 December 1952 struck down the practice of preventive detention, declaring it to be based on the "fascist theory of criminal types."[19] Psychiatric commitment, therefore, served as the only legal means to order a treatment course or preventive incarceration for convicted offenders.

Published and archival sources from this period reveal the striking continuities in criminological practice during the Third Reich and the early GDR. Until the last third of the decade, forensic psychiatrists in the fifties relied almost exclusively on prewar literature and data, with little distinguishing their methods and notions from earlier criminal biology.[20] Records from the Charité hospital's Department of Forensic Psychiatry in Berlin confirm this. Over the course of the decade, clinicians there were asked to evaluate over four thousand cases. Until 1956, feeblemindedness, debility, and psychopathy predominated among the diagnoses assigned to prisoners. Psychiatrists paid particularly close attention to signs of a "character predisposition" (*charakterliche Veranlagung*), examining court records and interviewing inmates and their families for information about early childhood quirks, habits, and achievements.[21]

The data collected was then interpreted in relation to the medical history of the criminal's parents and siblings. It was considered critical, as one examiner put it, to investigate the "hereditary circumstances" in a given case, in order "to get a longitudinal perspective on the personality structure."[22] A deficient upbringing was routinely understood to be the probable indicator of a hereditary defect, as in the case of one man with an alcoholic father, a suicidal mother, and seven sisters who dabbled in prostitution. "His little-inhibited, unstable character structure," noted Dr. Ziese, the senior examining physician in the case, "becomes psychologically intelligible when one becomes familiar with the unfavorable family circumstances in which K. grew up. In all probability, he got his poor hereditary disposition from his father."[23] Ziese's perspective on the hereditary risks posed by alcohol abuse was shared by his colleague Dr. Geisler, who considered one offender's "character shortcomings" the likely result of "germ damage brought on by chronic alcoholism."[24]

The invocation of blastophthoric degeneration—a eugenic idea that dated back to Auguste Forel's work at the turn of the century and that informed the Nazi sterilization program—shows the extent to which criminal biology remained a force in East German forensic science and medicine of the 1950s.[25]

It is little wonder, then, that related concepts from the Nazi era were also carried over into a regime outwardly sworn to the destruction of fascism. One of the most prominent of these was the term and figure of the "asocial." As Sven Korzilius has shown, authorities in the GDR labeled as asocial the same group of "deadbeats," "feebleminded" people, alcoholics, drug addicts, prostitutes, and vagrants as had the Third Reich.[26] While administrators and researchers bemoaned the insufficient work ethic (*Arbeitsmoral*) of such "parasites," it remained common to attribute the flaw to hereditary causes.[27] Forensic records at the Charité are, once again, instructive. When clinicians there were asked in 1950 to determine whether a twenty-eight-year-old woman with syphilis and multiple convictions involving theft and forgery was asocial, the examiners concluded, "It is the prominent character trait of such personalities that they simply can learn nothing from life and are always reverting back to making the same old mistakes. . . . This kind of behavior should be understood as an expression of a *congenital character structure*, similar to what occurs in weak-willed psychopaths."[28]

Thus, at least until the second half of the 1950s, East German psychiatrists and psychologists—including those with an interest in criminal behavior—were largely able to continue to work and pursue research interests in the same areas in which they had been involved before 1945.[29] It is clear that their perspectives exercised an influence, albeit a circumscribed one, on criminal justice. In official party and legal discussions about crime, however, their voices were marginalized.

This marginalization was due to the fact that the SED sanctioned an explicitly politicized view of law and crime. East German state and legal theory was organized around the principle of "socialist lawfulness" (*sozialistische Gesetzlichkeit*). The concept understood law as the "objective" expression of the interests and will of the working classes and thereby also as a reflection of existing material and social circumstances. Socialist lawfulness, however, assumed a highly centralized and hierarchical notion of the will of the people, in that the party was accepted as the vanguard leader of workers. As a result, jurists were instructed to ensure that the legal order sufficiently realized the party's will and, in the name of clarity, eliminated all forms of deviation.[30]

At that time, Marxism-Leninism also treated crime itself as an ideological act, awarding most perpetrators a status equivalent to that of counterrevolutionaries. In assessing the actions of any individual offender, legal scholars emphasized that it was critical to look at the person's social class, political views, and work discipline in order to establish whether the antisocial or criminal behavior was consistent with or deviated from the perpetrator's life history. Court records show that judges did just that, collecting information on the habits of defendants from workmates, neighbors, family members, social workers, teachers, victims, and direct interrogation in the courtroom.[31]

Despite the SED's insistence that criminals be understood in Marxist-Leninist terms, its class struggle theory of crime was never really successful in defining judicial or penal practice. Jurists found it to be of little use in deciding cases, especially cases with no apparent political relevance.[32] In the meantime, prison authorities faced pressing administrative challenges demanding pragmatic, improvised solutions. Particularly in the early 1950s, living conditions in facilities were grim, and overcrowding became routine at middecade, as over forty thousand prisoners were eventually serving sentences behind bars. At the same time, recruiting qualified, reliable personnel remained a constant challenge. By 1960, hundreds of open staff positions remained unfilled, while one in every five guards was over the age of fifty.[33] Circumstances like these made security the central priority, above all else, within the East German penal system, its sole purpose being the isolation of "parasites" from society.[34]

Imagining the East German Prison after Stalin

In the wake of Stalin's death in March 1953, the June 1953 uprising, and the Twentieth Party Congress of the Soviet Communist Party in February 1956, the class struggle theory of crime began to meet resistance from within party circles. After meetings in June and July of 1953, the Central Committee of the SED announced that it was now necessary to distinguish between "crimes" (*Verbrechen*), considered to be attacks on the state or party organizations, and "delicts" (*Gesetzesverletzungen*), violations committed out of a lack of discipline, a deficient sense of responsibility, or economic and personal difficulties.[35] Krushchev's later insistence on the "restoration of socialist rule of law" set in motion the official abandonment of the class struggle theory of crime. Lawmakers and legal scholars now placed the Cold War firmly at the center of a criminal policy intended to distinguish between friends and foes. Ideological commitment, as the Fifth Party Congress of the SED announced in June 1958, became the benchmark for assessing civic conduct.[36]

The demise of the class struggle theory of crime signaled the return of correctional rehabilitation as an acceptable topic for discussion and study. Now flagging residual bourgeois attitudes and habits as the sources of antisocial and asocial behavior, the SED opened the way for considering how best to didactically and therapeutically counter them. Contrary to the view of many historians of crime and punishment in the GDR, then, correctional work was not abandoned during the fifties.

Instead, for those tasked with developing rehabilitative plans, it was a matter of finding a niche for correctional interventions. Proponents of correction rehabilitation had to navigate a terrain marked by an unstable ideological climate, institutional resistance, and administrative constraints. Hedwig Scholz's 1953 panegyric to the socialist penal system, based on a lecture she gave before the Soviet House of Culture in Berlin two weeks after Stalin's death, testifies to the limits and opportunities available at that time. *They Should Become Full-Fledged Human Beings Again* dedicates most of its time denouncing criminal justice in capitalist societies, particularly the United States, as inhumane. "Uninhibited extermination through bodily mutilation, sterilization, and castration, complete isolation from society through indeterminate preventive detention, mental and physical mutilation through monotonous and long prison sentences as well as sentences of hard labor or—even worse—given no work at all"—this, according to Scholz, was the legacy of punishment in the capitalist world.[37] By contrast, she emphasized, socialist justice understood criminal law as a form of social law (*Sozialrecht*), oriented around returning the corrigible convict to society, using work to bolster his or her sense of self-confidence and discipline. Heavy on platitudes and vague about specifics, Scholz's talk was a mythic retelling of the history of penology in Marxist-Leninist terms. If its function was more performative than anything else, it nevertheless helped sustain an ideal-cum-mantra that would be repeated over and over in the GDR.

Like Scholz, Herbert Kern, in his 1958 monograph *Correction in Prison*, donated half of his book to chronicling the historical failings of bourgeois incarceration. As a member of the SED's Justice Sector since the early 1950s, Kern had helped centralize the East German judiciary as well as train prosecutors and court personnel in party fidelity. In his book, he dismissed the bourgeois penal system as little more than the capitalist state's tool for class exploitation, profiting from coerced prison labor, while impoverishing those who performed it. Bourgeois correction, in his view, was a cover for the ruling class to teach inmates "slavish obedience," something that was "merely a form of instruction in individualism and egotism, in traits which define bourgeois morality and stand in direct contradiction to moral codes."[38] By contrast, Kern emphasized, prisons in the GDR sought to actively resocialize inmates through productive work and political-cultural education. "In our state," he added, "punishment is supposed to not only produce inhibitions but also nurture responsible conduct toward society."[39]

In practice, however, correction was hardly operationalized in a way consistent with the public pronouncements of pedagogues, lawmakers, and administrators. Yes, productive work did increasingly become the focal point of correctional work. By middecade, almost every East German inmate was given work, and government regulations in 1952 and 1954 mandated an appropriate reduction in sentence for convicts working and fulfilling production targets in heavy industry. But the rationale for this labor was its contribution to economic planning, not its service to rehabilitative goals.[40]

Likewise, the management of inmate behavior was tailored to meet institutional, not personal, needs and demands. According to reports from those incarcerated at Bautzen Prison in Saxony during the 1950s, which are substantiated by the prison's house rules from November 1957, the daily regimen there was oriented around subordination to staff, procedures, and timetables. When inmates spoke with a guard, they were to address him as "Herr," along with the latter's rank, and to remove their caps; cells and work spaces were to be clean and orderly; only thirty minutes a day were set aside for recreation; inmates moving between activities were marched in group formation; correspondence with the outside world was limited to one letter a month; and visitors were limited to one visit every three months.[41]

Conforming to this rigid order played a critical role in how prison staff assessed the degree of success of an inmate's rehabilitation. A glance at prisoner conduct reports—progress reports filled out by staff on inmates they directly supervised—is especially revealing in this regard. For those convicts who had committed high crimes against the state, prison officials and the Stasi monitored them for signs of "ideological" change. Regular "correctional conversations" (*Erziehungsgespräche*) between supervisors and prisoners were used to question the latter about their attitudes toward the GDR and socialism. Conversations with fellow inmates about political issues as well as the enthusiasm with which prisoners involved themselves in political reeducation were noted. Finally, special care was taken to follow the reading habits of prisoners, with subscription to the party newspaper *Neues Deutschland* taken as an especially promising sign of improvement.[42]

These reports also reveal that officials were equally focused on these same concerns when it came to nonpolitical prisoners. Correctional progress was measured by conscientiousness in following house rules, politeness and responsiveness toward staff, cleanliness, and productivity at work. The reports of one leader of a work detail at Luckau Prison in Brandenburg, for instance, make constant reference to institutional benchmarks. Terms like "good work ethic," "orderly and respectable person," "to be prodded into order, discipline, and cleanliness," "disciplined," "very calm and reserved," and "according to the rules" pepper the Luckau supervisor's reports.[43] Thus, East German correctional staff did something quite common among personnel in custodial institutions of confinement in other historical settings: they assumed that rules intended to maintain prison order were inherently rehabilitative and, therefore, that they offered a reliable yardstick by which to measure inmate behavior.

The Return of the Human Sciences and the Rise of the Socialist Personality, 1958–72

It has been argued that Herbert Kern's *Correction in Prison* represented the crowning moment in the "demise of correctional thought in the East Germany prison system."[44] This judgment, however, overlooks some strikingly new terms and concepts employed by Kern. Crime and antisocial behavior in the GDR, he argued, demonstrated that perpetrators were not yet accustomed (*hineingewachsen*) to socialist society. Their shortcoming was the expression of a "defective consciousness" that had nothing to do with biological abnormalities but, rather, was the result of defective social relations. The key to developing a socialist society was therefore a matter of promoting the "development of socialist points of view in the heads of people." This, Kern concluded, had direct implications for prison correction.

> The new relationships between human beings emerging from the process of productive labor, the proper relationship toward the collective, the emotional sense of interdependence, these must become rooted in the head of the prisoner. In other words, the relationships objectively arising out of labor must become subjectively conscious through political-cultural education, transforming his feelings, attitudes, and thinking and finding their expression in qualitatively new relations with society.[45]

For all of Kern's self-congratulatory bluster, his claims for socialist penology presented a novel rationale for prison correction in the GDR. The targets for intervention here were those attitudes, thoughts, and feelings that precipitated delinquent behavior. The process of rehabilitation needed to simply reverse this order. It was to rely on collective inducement as a way of changing the minds of prisoners and making them appreciate collective interdependence. Kern thus pointed correctional thought in a new direction, toward a curiosity about the inner workings of criminals and convicts.

Kern can be only partly credited with this innovation. By directing its attention to the motivations of criminals and delinquents, it was the "friend-foe" doctrine—debated and refined during the second half of the 1950s, then formally endorsed by the State Council in January 1961—that opened up legal thought to this line of questioning. In so doing, it paved the way for not only a new judicial philosophy but also a new research agenda. In the years that followed, party leader Walter Ulbricht led the call for police and social services to scientifically pinpoint the causes behind the fact that socialist norms were apparently not being effectively internalized.[46]

Science and technology occupied a prominent place in the SED's plans for building a socialist society. In part, this had to do with a long-standing German tradition of state sponsorship of research and development.[47] The party's faith in science and technology, however, was also informed by its conviction, rooted in the intellectual history of Marxism-Leninism, that society followed natural laws of development and that the party's own ideology was inherently scientific.[48] By the time of the development of the First Five-Year Plan (1951–55), party and state leaders already understood the building of a socialist state not only as a political project but also as a social scientific project, requiring the skills of scholars, scientists, and engineers.[49]

Yet officials remained deeply suspicious about the East German intelligentsia throughout the late 1940s and the 1950s. During the thirties and forties, professionals such as doctors, psychiatrists, neurologists, and engineers had joined the Nazi Party in significant numbers—as many as 50 percent of all physicians were card-carrying members of the party by 1945—and over the course of the 1950s, they represented a disproportionately large group among those fleeing the GDR into the Federal Republic.[50] As was the case in West Germany, Soviet and East German administrators found it necessary, after an initial phase of denazification, to retain in key postwar positions and institutions many highly skilled personnel who had been active during the Third Reich. Adopting a "policy of alliance" (*Bündnispolitik*) with the bourgeois intelligentsia, the regime sought to stem the emigration tide westward by giving academics a stake in the new order.[51]

Party officials, however, continued to harbor grave doubts about the political reliability of the country's experts. In response, the planning of scientific research was centralized, Soviet and natural scientific models were privileged, and the influence of the Communist Party at all levels was secured. The result was not so much a routine of political interference in scientific work but, rather, the emergence of a peculiarly politicized style of scientific practice, engaged in by functionaries and researchers alike: party dogma and scientific knowledge were to be defended and protected from fractious and corrupting influences; ideologically acceptable "lines" of questioning and thinking were prescribed; knowledge was treated as cumulative, not dialectical, its growth reciprocally linked to the "development" of socialism; "deviations" from sanctioned lines of inquiry were to be rooted out, and their proponents were to be "educated" (*parteierzogen*) to abandon their positions.[52]

Just as de-Stalinization prompted sweeping changes in policy, however, it had an impact on science throughout communist Europe. Debates within party and scholarly circles in the USSR beginning in 1954 resulted in a reorganization of the Soviet Academy of Sciences by 1961. The effect of this change was a reversal of the conventional Stalinist relationship between science and ideology. The principle of "partymindedness" (*partiynost*) in science was formally dropped, and it now became the task of ideologues "to adapt their interpretations, at least superficially, by incorporating the lessons of the newest scientific achievements," rather than vice versa.[53]

The form of official scientific discourse and that of the prevailing political discourse thus mirrored one another, both emphasizing the defense of the party line's projection for the development of socialist knowledge and a socialist society. Just as the intelligentsia did not always behave in the ways the SED hoped, however, the general population in East Germany did not always behave as "planned."[54] Jurists, police, and party officials increasingly chalked up crime and everyday resistance to reactionary elements inside and outside the GDR as well as to an insufficient "political consciousness" within the citizenry.[55] By the second half of the 1950s, party leaders began attacking the problem by embarking on a concerted plan to rear a new generation of "respectable human beings" (*wohlanständige Menschen*). The educational system was reformed and oriented toward raising party activists and so-called comprehensively developed personalities (*allseitig entwickelte Persönlichkeiten*).[56] Conventional stereotypes about the public role of women were called into question, as the state and party glorified and encouraged women's equal access to jobs and careers.[57] Eventually, new rules of everyday decency and discipline were publicized, culminating in July 1958 with Walter Ulbricht's announcement of the "Ten Commandments for the New Socialist Person."[58]

When the party announced the so-called New Economic System (1963–69) in June 1963, hailing "scientificness" (*Wissenschaftlichkeit*), technical innovation, creativity, and expert know-how, it signaled that the way was open for a new generation of engineers, social scientists, psychologists, psychiatrists, physicians, jurists, and social workers to actively contribute to public policy in the 1960s.[59] Fields once categorically dismissed as "bourgeois" were resuscitated, such as empirical sociology.[60] Programs and research centers were quickly built up, recruiting academics and staff from existing institutes and departments of philosophy, political economy, modern history, pedagogy, psychology, Marxism-Leninism, and hygiene. Using standard methods and tools, such as surveys, questionnaires, experiments, and observation, studies focused especially on social group formation, political and consumer attitudes, and patterns of social behavior.[61]

Psychology was yet another field reinvigorated during the 1960s. While the "pavlovization" of Soviet psychology in the fifties had a limited impact in East Germany,[62] the new intellectual climate and the presence of the Berlin Wall made it possible for psychologists there to organize themselves nationally for the first time, founding the Society for Psychology in the GDR in 1962. Subsequent meetings of the society in 1964 and 1968 extolled "psychology as a socially productive force," whose subfields offered a way to augment worker proficiency and contribute to the development of "the socialist human community" (*sozialistische Menschengemeinschaft*).[63]

Psychology also appeared well suited to grapple with a growing public concern. The participation of young people in the unrest of 1953, the large numbers of them fleeing to the West, and their receptiveness to American popular culture led East German officials to see the young as one of the principal risks to national security.[64] A marked rise in the crime rate around 1960, widely attributed to juvenile delinquents, reinforced anxieties.[65] For the SED, which represented itself as a parental figure in the lives of East German youth, the key to addressing these issues lay in more effective rearing and education.[66] The historical association of German psychological institutes with pedagogical applications of their research made psychology appear to be a logical ally in reforming young people. As a result, there was a wave of research on child development and pedagogy during the 1960s, much of it centered at universities in Jena and Berlin and combining cybernetics and evolutionary theory with behavioral, cognitive, and Gestalt psychologies.[67]

The renaissance in the human sciences of learning and childhood was part of a sweeping change in the broad conceptualization of subjectivity in the GDR. Similar to their West German counterparts at the time, East German psychologists, educators, and policy makers began abandoning the language and emphasis on character that had informed their work in previous decades. From the mid-1960s to the mid-1970s, inspired by the international attention being awarded to "personality," they revamped the Marxist-Leninist notion of "the socialist personality," a concept that had previously been employed primarily by philosophers and party ideologues.[68] Fostering "comprehensively developed socialist personalities" became a ubiquitous mantra across party and state planning circles. As the vice president of the Academy of Pedagogical Sciences in the GDR expressed it at a major conference in 1972, the task was to promote "personality features such as mental flexibility, adherence to principle and courage, decisiveness, inexhaustible thirst for knowledge, discipline, industriousness, conscientiousness, consideration, thoroughness, and dependability."[69]

This revised concept of the socialist personality retained many of its utopian features, invoking the promise of a bold, collectivist, egalitarian, and politically energized consciousness that was expected to accompany advanced socialism. At the same time, however, it invested the individual with a more complicated psychology than earlier philosophical formulations. Renouncing a psychodynamic view of the self, East German theorists of the socialist personality understood it as the product of interaction between an individual's constitutional dispositions and the social conditions under which he or she was raised. In actively engaging the outside world, the human being learned how to be a social being, as external influences were internalized. Biological and psychological development were portrayed as unfolding progressively in stages that were more or less universal. The trope of "development" is what presumably linked the ontogenetic development of the individual with the phylogenetic development of socialist society.[70]

The Criminal Sciences and the State

The SED's newfound enthusiasm for the human sciences considerably altered the ways in which criminals and their potential rehabilitation were understood in East Germany. Beginning early on in the 1960s, scientific researchers and clinicians were called on to analyze delinquent behavior, forecast crime trends, and assess the efficacy of state actions. While party and state leaders sanctioned this recruitment of data and scholars in the service of criminal justice, the GDR was by no means unique in this. The Fourth International Criminological Congress, held in The Hague in September 1960, passed a series of resolutions calling for the promotion of empirical research about the effectiveness of treatments, as well as the incorporation of the criminological sciences into legal and medical training.[71] This was taken to heart in the USSR, where a central criminological institute was founded in Moscow in May 1963, and law schools began introducing criminology into the curriculum during the 1964/65 school year. Both individual republics and states subject to the Warsaw Pact soon followed suit.[72]

In the GDR, the return of empirical criminology and penology in the 1960s took place against the backdrop of ongoing discussions about the reform of the criminal code and calls for a scientific-technological revolution.[73] In 1964, the Central Committee of the SED and the East German State Council instructed both the Chief Prosecutor's Office and the Ministry of Interior to establish their own scientific advisory boards. The boards were expected to do two things: enhance the knowledge that policy makers had about crime in the country and improve the rehabilitative services offered to prisoners.[74]

The fifteen-member board of the Ministry of Interior was to include a pedagogue, legal scholars, a psychologist, a psychiatrist, and a labor economist, in addition to prison and government officials. Recruiting members and ironing out the body's governing statutes, however, proved to be complicated. Questions invariably arose about bureaucratic jurisdictions, the relationship of research to political ideology, and the extent to which scholarly conclusions could inform practice.[75] It was April 1970 before the Ministry of Interior's advisory board first convened.

Things moved more quickly at the Chief Prosecutor's Office, where leading criminologists Erich Buchholz, Hans Hinderer, Walter Orschekowski, and Joachim Renneberg began meeting with officials in Department IX (Scientific Research on Criminality) in December 1964, to map out the interdisciplinary work of its board.[76] Already in mid-January 1965, the group was able to identify several areas for focused research at a number of East German universities, including the causes of different kinds of criminal activity, the sources of recidivism, the effectiveness of correctional measures, and the use of pedagogical, psychological, and psychotherapeutic techniques in prisons.[77] A few months later, Department IX was ready to outline a preliminary five-year research plan for evaluating the "objective and subjective, social and personal, material and mental, political, ideological, and psychological causes and conditions of criminal activity and behavior in individuals and groups."[78]

By the eve of the promulgation of the new criminal code on 12 January 1968, members of the scientific advisory boards, criminal justice officials, academicians, and clinicians were not altogether agreed on the most effective ways to prevent crime. They did, however, reach a consensus on an overarching strategy. Following international precedents, they adopted a public health approach to criminality, which focused on identifying, tracking, and institutionalizing "endangered" youth (*Gefährdete*), coupled with coordinated action against alcohol abuse and all forms of antisocial behavior.[79] The emphasis on crime prevention and the management of risk factors led experts throughout the 1960s back to a perennial problem: recidivism and its causes and solutions.

Recidivism, Criminal Prognosis, and the Limits of Forensic Science and Medicine

By the early 1960s, when the SED and the state began welcoming the human sciences back for consultation, two groups of experts were poised for recruitment in the campaign to combat recidivism. As noted previously, legal scholars early on had played a dominant role in shaping the official party line on crime and penology. The jurists' and party's adoption of the "friend-foe" doctrine over the course of the late fifties ensured that they would continue to have an influential voice in scholarly and government circles about the reform of criminal justice. The second group of specialists braced for enlistment were psychiatrists, who, as we have seen, remained active throughout the fifties in the study and assessment of prisoners. Both groups occupied seats on the scientific advisory boards of the sixties, and their historical involvement in criminology gave them established and respected professional tools for taking up the work of reform.

When it came to the correctional rehabilitation and social prognosis of individual prisoners, however, psychiatrists had the advantage of clinical experience evaluating and treating patients and inmates. Like their counterparts in jurisprudence, forensic psychiatrists began showing signs already in the late 1950s of abandoning their earlier notions about criminal behavior. A pivotal moment came with the World Congress of Doctors for the Study of Present-Day Living Conditions, held in Vienna in 1953, which inspired the international study of public health over subsequent years. Researchers and officials in the GDR joined the effort, when the Ministry of Health called on the newly founded East German Medical Science Society to investigate the public health impact of living conditions there. In short order, forensic psychiatry's focus on heredity defects to explain criminal behavior was supplanted by a new emphasis on environmental factors, under the rubric "milieu."[80]

All of this sparked a wave of empirical studies on the interpersonal and psychological dimensions of antisocial and criminal behavior, which began appearing in print in the early 1960s. For the most part, a new generation of scholars and clinicians, trained primarily in medicine, psychiatry, and psychology, led the way. They included such psychologists as Harry Dettenborn, who worked out of the Department of Legal Science at the Humboldt University of Berlin and whose textbooks in forensic psychology became canonical reading in the 1970s and 1980s, and Hans Hiebsch, under whose direction in the 1960s the Psychological Institute in Jena became the center of Marxist social psychology. Prominent physicians in the field of criminological research included

Ehrig Lange, a trained psychiatrist and director of the Clinic for Psychiatry and Psychotherapy at the Technical University in Dresden (1968–87), and child psychiatrist Hanns Schwarz, cofounder of the journal *Psychiatrie, Neurologie, und medizinische Psychologie* in 1949 and one of the few figures with a career dating back before the war.

Arguably the most influential figure throughout the 1960s and 1970s was Hans Szewczyk (1923–94). A clinician trained in psychology and medicine, Szewczyk first worked as an assistant in Kurt Gottschaldt's Institute for Psychology at the Humboldt University of Berlin but then transferred to the psychiatric clinic of the Charité hospital. There, he habilitated in the field of psychiatry under the direction of Karl Leonhard (1904–88). Appointed director of the Department of Forensic Psychiatry and Psychology at the Charité in 1961, Szewczyk used his position to institutionalize forensic psychiatry and psychology as an empirical science and clinical tool in the GDR. His success had as much to do with his willingness to work interdisciplinarily with physicians, psychologists, sociologists, jurists, criminologists, and government officials as it did with his prolific record of over 250 publications, including twenty-one monographs and six textbooks.[81]

Szewczyk convened and chaired the first major forensic psychiatry symposium in postwar East Germany, on 8 and 9 March 1963. Opening the meeting, he noted that, until recently, the psychiatrist's role in the criminal justice system had been largely limited to reporting on the defendant's capacity to stand trial. The reform of the criminal code, however, brought with it a new set of priorities and needs.

> In the future, the correction of the criminal according to the most modern methods of science, with research into causes, conditions, and reasons behind criminal activities as well as their elimination, should occupy center stage. The perspective of our field requires knowledge about the personality of perpetrators and their general and unique development. Psychiatry and its foundational sciences of psychology and psychopathology have at their disposal results, models, and practical experience that should be condensed at this conference and presented as proposals for legal reform and the new criminal code.[82]

The key to undercutting recidivism, Szewczyk argued, was concentrating on the peculiar motivations of criminals. This involved finding ways to gauge the impact of various factors on personality, including hereditary predispositions, psychological development, organic injuries, and social circumstances.

This work, he maintained, fell directly under the purview of the medical and psychological sciences.[83]

Lucie von Ehrenwall (justice of the East German Supreme Court), Gerhard Göllnitz (director of the Department of Child Neurology and Psychiatry at the University Psychiatric Clinic in Rostock), Hans Hinderer (director of the Institute for Criminal Law at Martin Luther University in Halle), Helmut Schmidt (head of the Department of Law within the Ministry of Justice), and Hans-Ehrenfried Stelzer (director of the Institute for Criminology at the Humboldt University of Berlin) joined Szewczyk in insisting that experts in psychiatry and psychology needed to be involved at each stage of criminal prosecution and punishment. This meant enlisting their expertise not only in assessing a defendant's capacity to stand trial but also for aiding judges in determining guilt and sentence, assessing the likelihood of a relapse, and determining the convict's suitability for specific kinds of correctional therapies and treatments.[84] By 1966, Szewczyk was confident enough to brag publicly that government officials were taking these suggestions seriously.[85]

But while Szewczyk and his colleagues were eager to proclaim their expertise in criminal prognosis and rehabilitation, the reality was that the speed of political reform in East Germany far outpaced that of scientific research on these subjects. After the gutting of the human sciences during the 1950s, there was little empirical data to which one could appeal. Moreover, convincing prison officials to share the SED's newfound enthusiasm for scholars and research remained difficult, as Karl Leonhard and Hans Szewczyk discovered early in 1963. At the time, the two were conducting a study on recidivism, and they requested the opportunity to conduct psychiatric examinations on one hundred incarcerated repeat offenders. The head of the East German prison system denied the request, informing his colleagues, "According to secret information, Prof. Dr. Leonhard has not been given a positive assessment, and scientific value of his work is questionable."[86] Nervous as well about the two researchers delving into the circumstances of prisoners charged with state crimes, officials restricted Leonhard and Szewczyk to conducting their examinations on released inmates convicted of crimes against property or persons.[87]

These impediments help explain a pattern evident in public and private discussions about criminal correction throughout much of the 1960s. With little data to which to point, experts were left to invoke their tacit knowledge, at the same time that they called for sponsorship of an aggressive research agenda. While terms such as *personality*, *motivation*, *milieu* and *development* were bandied about, operationalizing them was going to take time. All this added up to a peculiar and short-lived dialogue about criminals and their rehabilitation, marked by an uncommon open-endedness, as ideological abstractions were countered by an insistence on empirical rigor.

Political leaders and scientific and clinical experts agreed on the need for an accurate way to forecast recidivism and for an effective system for reforming convicts. In both cases, however, disagreement surrounded the question of scale. Government officials, for instance, were enamored with the idea of criminal prognosis, while researchers were far more tempered in their enthusiasm. At a meeting of the Scientific Advisory Board to the Chief Prosecutor's Office in the fall of 1967, Hans Szewczyk and legal scholars Michael Benjamin and John Lekschas stressed the need for much more interdisciplinary research, on both the macro and micro levels, before any social patterns could be reliably identified. Even then, they insisted, the data would only be useful at an epidemiological level, correlating state interventions with the incidence and prevalence of specific crimes.[88] This hardly dissuaded criminal justice officials, who placed their faith in establishing an infrastructure for maintaining documents and sharing information, in order "to reach a flow of information with the least amount of lost time and information."[89] Researchers shared the interest in data collection and exchange but admitted that East German scholarship was still not up to speed. "It is necessary to conduct concrete research about the effects of different kinds of punitive and correctional interventions," Gerhard Stiller (director of the Institute for Criminal Justice and Crime Control in Potsdam) pointed out in 1968. He continued,

> In addition legal scholarship needs to develop a sustained body of sociological research. The present system of document analysis no longer suffices. What is far more needed are interviews with criminals and their relatives as well as with the collectives in which they live and work. Methods like sociometry—which can be applied at different points in time in the development of a collective and to the status of the perpetrator within that collective—and scaling and statistical methods are all crucial. If properly applied, psychological testing will also provide deeper insights than has been the case up until now.[90]

Understanding criminal motivations was seen as another important aspect in developing accurate prognostic techniques. Richard Hartmann, a member of Hans Szewczyk's research team, made the point that the causes and motives behind criminal acts in individual cases were multiple, complex, and reciprocal. "We cannot confine ourselves to a linear notion of causality," he pointed out at the 1963 forensic psychiatry symposium, "nor should we start from the presumption of a mechanistic stimulus-response model, nor can we conceive of the 'internal conditions' of the perpetrator as something static and unchanging. Rather, we have to see these as the result of a social process of maturation."[91]

Other prominent criminologists echoed Hartmann's demand that scholars and policy makers recognize the effects of multiple factors on human behavior. Nevertheless, it was necessary, especially in more public forums, to calibrate this message to fit the party's "friend-foe" legal doctrine. Social structure, policies, and public institutions remained above reproach, of course, so observers relied on the categories of dialectical materialism to draw a distinction between the "objective conditions" (the natural and social environment) and the "subjective conditions" (consciousness and its relationship to this environment) that surrounded crime. Using this framework, investigators centered their attention on malignant mind-sets and habits within the population, locating the problem both interpersonally and intrapersonally—on the one hand, in maladaptive attitudes picked up at work, in the home, and among acquaintances; on the other hand, in "psychopathies, neuroses, or anomalous drives and compulsions."[92]

Thus, over the course of the sixties, a new generation of forensic specialists fashioned a less overtly politicized, public health perspective on crime in the GDR. Criminality could now be understood to be the result of virulent values or morbid conditions, while its etiology could be couched in more complex psychological terms. As a result, it not only triggered studies into the motivations of offenders but more generally reinforced the authority of clinicians and their casework approach to correctional rehabilitation.[93]

Assessing the Inmate's Personality

Forays into correctional rehabilitation during the sixties were dominated by talk about the need to "differentiate" the prison population and "individualize" correction according to personality features. Before the Fifth Party Congress of the SED in July 1958, Walter Ulbricht declared that effective correctional rehabilitation was only possible through a more careful segregation of the prison population, which soon resulted in the categorization of inmates according to the severity of their offenses: those found guilty of state offenses or especially heinous crimes were to be incarcerated together with repeat offenders but separate from the rest of the inmates. The sudden rise in the prison population following the construction of the Berlin Wall in August 1961,[94] however, made it difficult for prisons to adhere to this policy. So it was not until the spring of 1962 that the justice and interior ministries began working with the German

Academy for State Science and Law in Potsdam-Babelsberg to determine how best to match inmates with particular kinds of incarceration, work details, and correctional regimes.[95]

A decree on 4 April 1963 spurred more discussions by requiring that the penal system be reorganized, with each facility assigned a specific subgroup of convicts. The plan called for assigning prisoners to one of three different categories of confinement—ranging from restrictive (category 1) to general (category 2) to minimum security (category 3)—based on the relative severity of their most recent offenses as well as their general criminal record.[96] Redistribution of the entire prison population was scheduled to be completed by the end of 1963.[97]

In practice, however, the new classification system proved difficult to realize. In the spring of 1964, prison officials reported that judges were not adhering to the new division of labor, leaving facilities in places like Waldheim, Karl-Marx-Stadt, Leipzig, Gera, and Magdeburg to complain that up to a third of their new inmates were wrongly classified.[98] In the following year, the Prison Administration within the Ministry of Interior attempted to clarify exactly who was allowed to commit a convict to a specific facility and on what basis. While the Prison Administration recognized the autonomous authority of courts in sentencing, it made it clear that it considered wardens the final authority on whom their facilities would accept. This, officials added, was a decision based on both security and rehabilitative concerns.[99]

Like their counterparts in the human sciences, East German prison administrators regularly invoked the personality of convicts as a critical factor in deciding how to handle them. Archival sources, however, reveal that prison staff largely regarded "personality" as a kind of conceptual placeholder, a relatively generic notion, into which they could place any seemingly relevant considerations beyond the convict's particular sentence.[100] The relative vagueness of the concept as it was translated into practice accounts, in part, for a pattern of miscategorized prisoners in the late 1960s and early 1970s.

Records, for instance, detail the persistent efforts of the head of the Prison Administration in 1968, Col. Hans Tunnat, to set straight local prison officials wishing to transfer inmates to stricter categories of confinement. For example, a major at the Untermaßfeld facility in Thuringia sought to transfer the prisoner K.B.—a prisoner married three times, with five children born out of wedlock, and serving a thirteen-month sentence for state slander and refusing to pay child support—from category 3 to category 2 detention. The major at Untermaßfeld justified the reassignment on the basis of B.'s behavior and attitudes, citing B.'s "extremely immoral" past, his pattern of frequently changing jobs, his inability to accept criticism, his rejection of state policies, and his undisciplined and insulting behavior toward staff.[101] Tunnat dismissed the major's decision as unjustified, pointing to indications in B.'s dossier that the man had a strong prison work record and no disciplinary demerits.[102]

The same major's name crops up again in the case of F.S., a man serving a ten-month sentence for state slander, whom the major, "based on the inmate's personality," sought to transfer. S., he contended, had a history of alcohol abuse, took no instruction from his work collective, and bad-mouthed his boss. Once again, Tunnat rejected the request, saying that the files showed S. to be orderly, disciplined, and clean in his habits and work ethic.[103]

In examining the transfer reports from prison wardens and staff that came before Tunnat that year, a clear pattern emerges. Time and again, personnel cited lack of motivation and breaches of orderliness, cleanliness, and discipline as evidence of shortcomings in the "character" of inmates. Adjectives like *undisciplined*, *negative*, *indifferent*, *combative*, and *insolent* feature prominently.[104] Thus, prisoners' responses to institutional structures and demands served as the criteria by which their corrigibility was assessed. Those responses, in turn, were attributed not to the situation at hand but to the personality of the individual convict.

A similar logic was at work in cases of suspected mental illness. In the early 1960s, physician Manfred Ochernal established and served as medical director of the penal hospital for psychiatry at Waldheim. There he also ran an observation unit, which conducted diagnostic examinations on inmates in Stasi custody who were believed to be suffering from a psychiatric disorder but, for security reasons, could not be sent to a conventional psychiatric hospital for evaluation. Prison officials wishing to have someone in custody examined at Waldheim were directed to outline the reasons for the transfer.[105] These transfer records and evaluations provide some insight into the kinds of behavior prison authorities considered aberrant.

E.R., for example, was a twenty-year-old woman sentenced to over twenty months in prison for defamation of the state in May 1966 and incarcerated at the prison in Görlitz. An official there reported that R. had been behaving aggressively ever since her arrest. After being placed in custody, she broke lightbulbs, lamps, and windows, cutting her wrists with the shards, and told police that they "were going to be stunned at how she was going to behave." It turned out that this was not just bluster on her part. At Görlitz, her horseplay on work details prevented others from doing their jobs; she attempted suicide, howled like a dog, and painted her arms with sayings such as "My head belongs to the executioner."[106] Over and over again, prison officials cited things like suicide attempts, unpredictable behavior, and disruptions to work routines as key reasons for sending inmates to Waldheim for observation.[107]

In the relatively small number of cases I encountered from the years 1965–67, I found no evidence to support the claim that the Stasi, criminal justice officials, or Ochernal were, at the time, systematically attempting to use psychiatric confinement as a way of punishing or isolating political prisoners. Rather, in case after case, officials were faced with individuals whose behavior struck them as patently bizarre and uncontrollable. For instance, staff at the Bützow-Dreibergen facility were clearly at their wit's end in the winter of 1965/66 over thirty-year-old G.H. A repeat offender with a long history of institutionalization in mental hospitals, homes for asocials, and prisons, H. proved impossible for Bützow to manage. He refused to work, destroyed property, sang fascist songs, insulted guards, and smeared feces on his cell wall.[108] After observing him for three months, Ochernal determined, "We are dealing here with a feebleminded, unstable, emotionally incontinent, asocial psychopath with disruptive tendencies, who is only fit for incarceration under the conditions of psychiatric observation, something prohibitive for the prison. A change in behavior is hardly to be expected."[109]

Faced with instances of hallucination, delusion, severe depression, mood swings, and suicidality, Ochernal remained focused on determining two things: whether the inmate presented symptoms of a psychiatric disorder and whether he or she was best treated in a psychiatric facility. He was especially interested in differentiating between presenting symptoms triggered by incarceration and those predating confinement.[110] There was even an instance when Ochernal and a colleague of his berated guards at Brandenburg Prison for poking fun at one inmate who had been ruled mentally incapable, stating that if the allegation was true, "we are of the opinion that this is not the most appropriate form of fulfilling the correctional function of prison."[111]

Thus, rather than pointing to the cynical abuse of psychiatry in the service of Stasi expediency, the Waldheim commitment records in this particular instance reveal how East German criminal justice in the sixties continued to struggle with handling refractory inmates. More than anything else, the evidence points to a common problem facing both West German and East German officials in the 1960s: namely, how to accommodate their most unsettling and unmanageable convicts. As we will see in chapters 4 and 6, the Federal Republic addressed this problem by creating new therapeutic penal facilities, while administrators in the GDR were left to improvise a solution.

From Correction to Reintegration

In the midsixties, the Scientific Advisory Board to the Chief Prosecutor's Office established a research project whose purpose was to study the mechanisms by which correctional interventions had their impacts on individual behavior. In the fall of 1966, criminologist Erich Buchholz presented the advisory board with an outline "for research on the social and individual effects of punishment." Compared to earlier East German discussions about correctional rehabilitation, Buchholz's paper is noteworthy for its reliance on models and results from psychological research to justify its proposals.

Appealing to behaviorism, cybernetics, and the teachings of the Soviet pedagogue Anton Makarenko, Buchholz argued that correctional rehabilitation was a matter of learning and, like all learning, necessarily involved the proper "internalization" of social norms through positive and negative reinforcement. As a form of negative feedback, punishment was most effective, Buchholz explained, when it was administered promptly, forcefully, and as a reflection of collective judgment. Changing behavior meant providing the right incentives and disincentives to prompt the delinquent to become more responsive to the interests of society.[112]

Buchholz's sketch of correctional punishment captures the tenor of penal reform thinking in East Germany during the sixties. The ambition was to effect radical change in the personality of the offender through a combination of positive and negative reinforcements, instilling in the convict a moral disposition adapted to socialist society. Society's influence within the individual could only be effective, it was insisted, if the individual were successfully placed back inside society. Reintegration (*Wiedereingliederung*) of ex-convicts into society was therefore considered not merely a goal but itself part of the correctional process.

As noted earlier, reintroducing ex-convicts back into society had been a concern for the German criminal justice system since the nineteenth century. But within the GDR, reintegration was a new emphasis for authorities. In this context, it emerged as an extension of correctional rehabilitation, removing it from the confines of the prison and setting it firmly within society at large.

Reintegration presented authorities with challenges. Chief among them were finding the ex-convict a home and job, getting local communities involved, and coordinating efforts. Toward the end of 1966, representatives from the Chief Prosecutor's Office and the German Academy for State Science and Law conducted on-site inspections of reintegration efforts in the district of Quedlinburg, around the city of Halle. In speaking with local officials along with factory personnel at the Leuna Factory, the task force discovered that things worked far from smoothly once ex-convicts were released back into the community.

As a rule, within two weeks before a prisoner's release, officials were supposed to inform the factory's personnel department of the convict's arrival, his or her future residence, and the nature of his or her crimes. A minder (*Betreuer*) was then to be assigned to the released individual, and meetings with local officials and conflict commissions were to be held in cases where the ex-convict's performance was lacking. In reality, however, inspectors found that factory personnel were often not informed about the identity and number of prisoners assigned to the plant until their arrival and that the former were not receiving any instructions on how to go about reforming the ex-convict. In addition, some minders neglected their jobs, and little was being done to work with the families of released men and women.[113]

On 12 January 1968, the Penal and Reintegration Law (Strafvollzugs- und Wiedereingliederungsgesetz) was announced, the same day a new criminal code was issued. Intended to codify prison administration and rehabilitation efforts, the law formally made individualized correctional rehabilitation the centerpiece of East German criminal justice. Penologists portrayed it as the culmination of modern scientific research and clinical know-how and as reaffirmation of socialism's commitment to social inclusion.[114] The law's language of differentiation and individualization, however, was an admission that distinctions were still being drawn between the corrigible and the incorrigible.

The Correctional Imagination under Honecker

By the time Erich Honecker became first secretary of the Central Committee of the SED and head of state in 1971, reformers had succeeded in outlining the structure and agenda for a science- and medicine-based penology. Along with legal scholars, psychologists and psychiatrists had come to play pivotal roles in shaping a public health approach to correctional rehabilitation. Their vision stressed the impact of interpersonal "milieu" on character development, the need to flag risk factors for recidivism, and an insistence on synchronizing the attitudes, motivations, and moral orientations of offenders with the expectations of socialist society.[115] The variety of research methods recognized as suitable for criminology and penology—clinical personality and witness assessment, observation, interviews, controlled experimentation, surveys, statistics, work production analysis, and the study of documents—had still yielded few empirical studies by 1971.[116]

When it came to correctional work, the East German Ministry of Interior followed the lead of its counterpart in the USSR in turning its back on medical interventions and instead embracing learning models drawn from pedagogy and psychology. By 1970, Soviet penology relied heavily on the ideas of three sets of thinkers. First and foremost was the pedagogue Anton Makarenko, whose notions about the use of collective discipline, mutual surveillance, and coerced habit formation had become canonical by the 1950s.[117] Over the course of the 1960s, Makarenko's ideas were supplemented by the "activity theories" of Aleksei Leontiev and Sergei Rubinstein: these theories emphasized the need to understand consciousness relationally, as constructed through its interaction with the material world, an interaction mediated by the subject's use of tools to achieve goals. A third thread drew from the "interiorization theory" of the pedagogue Pyotr Galperin, which stressed the internalization of external instruction as a system of mental self-regulation.[118] All told, as one of the canonical textbooks in educational psychology explained it, the aim of all instruction was "falling into line within society" (*Einordnung in die Gesellschaft*), and for this task, three areas were seen as essential: "the shaping of a political worldview, development of a socialist attitude toward work, and training in socialist relationships with others (including with those of the opposite sex)."[119]

As a result, penology was imagined as a system of "reform and reeducation" that attempted to spark a "self-correction" through the internalization of external coercions from staff and fellow inmates.[120] This correctional process, it was argued, worked by using institutional activities to recondition attitudes and behaviors toward two ends:[121] "the simultaneous removal of old points of view, habits, and personality traits and the formation of new ones in the consciousness of individuals."[122] The criteria for deciding on the relative success of a prisoner's rehabilitation ultimately rested in evidence of improvements in relationships, particularly with party doctrine, law and order, public property, work, and collectives.[123]

Yet, as noted earlier, the underdevelopment of the human sciences in the GDR, a lack of qualified personnel, and the resistance of prison staff hindered implementing the ideas of reformers. The case of a thirty-two-year-old prisoner, M.S., in the summer of 1970 testifies to the dissonance between science and administration that carried over into the seventies and eighties. At some point (most likely in the early 1960s), S. moved from West Germany to the GDR, after having spent a year in prison in the west. From 1963 to 1967, he committed a string of offenses, most under the influence of alcohol, including insulting a party member, drunk and disorderly public conduct, and several attempts to cross the border back to West Germany. For these crimes, he served several stints in East German prisons up until the spring of 1970. During his incarceration, S. proved to be a recalcitrant inmate, and a summary of his progress reports declared that "in the case of S., we are dealing with an extremely inaccessible person, who is unwilling to voluntarily reeducate himself."[124] In July 1970, police in Potsdam interrogated S., who was now being held in custody as a suspect in a new crime. During the interrogation, S. was asked for his assessment of the correctional rehabilitation process.[125] His frank response reveals just how far implementation often deviated from planning.

Based on his experience, S. said, no inmate ever left prison reformed (*umerzogen*): most simply reoffended. Correctional rehabilitation within prison walls existed in name only. Repeat offenders, for instance, were the very ones who tended to be given positions of authority, such as brigade leaders, owing to their experience of having served in them before. When an inmate broke a rule, such as speaking in the stairwell, everyone in the group was indiscriminately punished. Moreover, S. added, staff were hardly effective reformers of men. "Our station leader often gave us prisoners uninformed speeches," he told interrogators, "making it clear that he didn't have the faintest pedagogical capabilities." As for the reintegration program, it was "just as much of a calamity." S. was promised a room in Potsdam upon his release, but it never materialized, and a second accommodation was refused him by its landlord. He ended up having to sleep at bus stops, until returning, unwelcome, to the house of his stepmother and brother.

S.'s case was hardly an isolated one. Criminal justice and security officials in the seventies were well aware that the reintegration of prisoners was failing to meet expectations. A student at the Edwin Hoernle School for State Science in Weimar conducted a study of reintegration efforts in the city of Magdeburg during the years 1971–77. His findings, forwarded on to Stasi headquarters in Berlin, showed that one in every five ex-convicts in the area had reoffended and that a contributing factor was the lack of communication between prisons and municipal authorities. Examining final prison reports on released inmates, he found that only 37 percent of the reports he examined were submitted on time and that 24 percent of these reports never reached local authorities in time to be of any use.[126]

The care and concern that reformers voiced for prisoners was not only mitigated by challenges in the field. The rehabilitative impulse that had emerged by the seventies also carried with it a mind-set of suspicion and an obsession with defending the party line. By making risk factors in the psychological development of the individual the key to understanding criminal behavior, the human sciences and public policy had placed a premium on observing, registering, screening, and redirecting individuals. Simply put, as prevention assumed a greater importance, ever more mundane forms of deviance could be seen as socially or politically threatening. One of the more pointed examples of this came in the summer of 1973, as preparations were being made for the Tenth World Festival of Youth and Students in East Berlin. In an effort to remove from the streets "all negatively appearing persons who might damage our image," the Ministry of Interior, the Chief Prosecutor's Office, the police, and workers in youth welfare apprehended hundreds of drug addicts, alcoholics, prostitutes, and homeless persons and committed them to psychiatric facilities throughout the GDR.[127] Few of these individuals, if any, met the criteria for involuntary commitment.

As Leonore Ansorg and Johannes Raschka have documented, criminal justice under Honecker was largely marked by a clampdown on criminal and deviant behavior, though it was punctuated by moments of liberal reform. By and large, there were four periods in the development of crime policy during Honecker's tenure as head of the GDR. From 1971 to 1974, the state took a hard-line approach to crime, especially to repeat offenders, in response to both détente and a precipitous rise in criminal and antisocial activity. More convictions led to prison sentences and more prisoners were assigned to work details than ever before, and in 1974, the government created a fourth, even stricter form of incarceration (*verschärfter Vollzug*). Economic difficulties, the rise of an indigenous emigration movement, and standards laid down in international treaties prompted a change in course, culminating in the Penal Law of 1977: general prison conditions were improved, the four types of incarceration were reduced to two, and a more moderate rhetoric about punishment emerged. The years 1978–86, however, saw the return of a more punitive attitude toward criminal justice and a growing reliance on the services of the Stasi, both being a reaction to an escalation in Cold War and domestic tensions as well as an increase in the number of GDR citizens leaving the country. Finally, the last years of the SED regime witnessed a pronounced relaxation in traveling restrictions, the elimination of the death penalty, and the institution of a general amnesty.[128]

The human sciences could not help but be caught up in the SED's Janus-faced approach to public problems like crime. State security in the seventies and eighties showed a growing interest in the work of the human sciences. As talk of reform came and went and as relations between West Germany and East

Germany thawed in the 1970s, the Stasi experienced a phase of unprecedented growth during the years 1961–82.[129] Under Erich Honecker and Stasi head Erich Mielke, state security sought to expand the network of reliable "unofficial collaborators" (*inoffizielle Mitarbeiter*) within the population by using the most modern technologies of surveillance and subversion. Here, as they did in education, criminal justice, and social work, officials placed a premium on identifying and steering specific personality types.[130] To this end, academic fields like psychology, pedagogy, sociology, and psychiatry, along with their practitioners, were used in Stasi training centers to establish a new human science, "operative psychology," whose ultimate goal was to exploit and subvert human weaknesses in the service of overtly political goals.[131]

At the same time that security concerns were occupying a more prominent place in policy-making circles, images of nurturing, kindness, and protection also assumed a higher profile in public life, as social policy and consumption occupied a central place in Honecker's vision for the GDR.[132] In what was dubbed the new "mommy politics" (*Muttipolitik*) of the 1970s, the SED reasserted the value of domesticity, family, and motherhood, as a response to falling birthrates and a stagnant economy.[133] In the process, the language and policies of maternalism helped revivify ideals of humanism and social activism, all of which had been linked with one another in East German social welfare discourse since the 1950s.[134] Human scientists' explanations for crime and their proposals for reforming convicts often struck these chords of social concern, a fact that regularly prompted some hard-liners to respond with skepticism, if not outright hostility.

Yet authorities increasingly came to see the impulses of security and care as two sides of the same coin. This is particularly evident in the East German state's approach to recidivism during the eighties. By 1980, criminal justice and security officials were convinced that, while crime rates were generally going down, the incidence and prevalence of reoffending were on the rise. Their attention focused increasingly on "asocials," who were seen as impromptu recruiters for career criminals.[135]

In June 1980, the Supreme Court, minister of interior, minister of justice, and chief prosecutor issued a directive outlining their "shared standpoint on effectively combating criminally asocial behavior."[136] The directive heralded the beginning of a concerted effort by criminal justice officials and the Stasi to more effectively accent their public health approach to delinquency.[137] This meant studying the causes of and proposing solutions to recidivism. In a report prepared for Erich Mielke's deputy in the Ministry for State Security in April 1982, the case was made that the problem of reoffenders was inseparable from that of asocials. Around two-thirds of those convicted for asocial conduct, the report noted, had previous convictions. Meanwhile, during the period 1971–81, reintegration back into society ended with a new conviction for 41 percent (around eighty-one thousand) of all released convicts, and that figure was only rising over time (to 47 percent in 1981).[138]

In response, criminal justice and health care authorities put forward a plan designed to institutionalize three types of repeat offenders. For those deemed especially refractory (estimated at around 420 individuals), whose "parasitic life" was marked by "instability, indifference, callousness, and brutality," the plan was to expand section 48a of the criminal code and allow for their preventive detention for up to ten years. New, therapy-centered "homes for resocialization" were to be built to house a second group of recidivists, whose "personality is stamped by instability, shortcomings, and, in part, primitiveness" and who demonstrated little ability to manage their own lives (around four thousand individuals). Finally, an estimated twenty-seven hundred individuals, whose problems were rooted in "feeblemindedness," psychopathy, or substance abuse and for whom correction and reintegration were deemed "essentially hopeless," were to be committed to appropriate health care facilities.[139]

The new, three-pronged offensive against recidivists—emulating West Germany's tripartite network of preventive detention units, social therapeutic facilities, and mental health institutions—represented a subtle shift in how party and state officials were thinking about the incorrigibles in their midst. If the Ministry of Health now insisted that "homes for resocialization" be built as new, independent structures with their own uniquely trained staff, it was because authorities there understood that what the targeted population had in common was a stubborn criminal predilection, not a diagnosis.[140] A government resolution on 9 January 1985, dictating that "mentally conspicuous" (*psychisch auffällige*) asocials be earmarked for special surveillance and social therapeutic intervention, signaled that pedagogical and clinical tools were to play an increasingly prominent role in the treatment of incorrigibles.[141] Yet, while at least one East German apologist has attempted to portray this approach as a scientifically and medically sound attempt to aid the many asocials who "were not malicious, but simply inept,"[142] Stasi records show that the groups singled out for special treatment extended well beyond substance abusers and the mentally disabled. By June 1985, criminal police were monitoring over thirty-five hundred individuals, around 48 percent of whom either were convicted of actually attempting or were simply threatening to leave the GDR.[143] Thus, the attempt to combat recidivism through therapeutic means served only to help feed the criminalization of deviant behavior in East Germany.

Nevertheless, by the 1980s, it had become acceptable to discuss and even experiment with the use of psychotherapeutic techniques on the convict population. Already in the seventies, pilot programs in Magdeburg and Berlin were held up as models. There, psychologists and pedagogues prepared inmates before their release, while physicians offered advice to family members and psychotherapy to those ex-convicts requiring treatment.[144] At the same time, the ideas and approaches associated with group therapy and social therapy were discussed and applied to a small number of prisoners and juvenile delinquents.[145]

By the early eighties, then, East German penology had settled into a relatively stable self-image of correctional rehabilitation. Prisons were designed to serve three functions: security, correction, and economic productivity. The reform of inmates was to be achieved by effecting a moral change in the development of a convict's personality, itself achieved through the management of privileges and sanctions, the assignment of supervised work, and reeducation and training. Personal conduct was evaluated on the basis of consistency of performance, the enthusiasm and dedication shown in fulfilling duties, and subordination to authority.[146]

The basic unit in a prison consisted of a station comprised of somewhere between sixty and one hundred inmates, all under the supervision of a "correctional educator" (*Erzieher*). Training for these educators differed according to their rank, with basic training consisting of four to five months of education at a Ministry of Interior penal school—with courses in Marxism-Leninism, penology, criminal law, psychology, pedagogy, and sports—followed by a six-month practicum. As one moved up the ladder, training became increasingly more academic, focusing on the human sciences of Marxism-Leninism, psychology, pedagogy, and penology. At all levels, however, emphasis was placed on demonstrating a resolute "socialist state consciousness."[147]

The correctional educator enforced order and discipline, supervised all forms of correction, doled out punishments and privileges, and wrote up reports on the conduct of prisoners. He or she also delegated responsibilities, a key function, since a degree of collective self-governance was granted to inmates. The lives of prisoners, in turn, were dominated by collectives of various kinds: work brigades, educational circles, cultural groups (centered around music, sports, hobbies). Everyday life in the collectives was run by fellow inmates selected by the correctional educator—so-called elders (*Älteste*), stewards (*Ordner*), brigadiers, and actives (*Aktivs*)—whose jobs ranged from ensuring punctuality, to reporting on inmate misbehavior, to enforcing discipline during work and leisure activities.[148]

Records and reports from former inmates, however, reveal that penal facilities rarely, if ever, worked as imagined. All prisons experienced overcrowding. That inmates in leadership positions tended to exploit the others, while the Stasi actively recruited informants, undermined any collective esprit de corps. Drills and work assignments tended to be petty and tedious. Former East German inmates have often complained that correction existed in name only: correctional educators are talked about as being distant and unfriendly, relying mostly on punishment, especially the threat of isolation, to keep prisoners in line. As a result, those incarcerated tended to game the system, often feigning illness to avoid work.[149]

Former staff members have confirmed that East German prisons hardly lived up to the rehabilitative ideals set for them. In conversations that former guards, correctional educators, and administrators had with Torsten Heyme in 1990, personnel contended that the expectations for correction were routinely unfulfilled due to institutional realities. Educators were largely ill equipped to deliver the kinds of correctional services being touted by pedagogues and psychologists. One deputy director explained, "[Our correctional educators] didn't arrive with the necessary pedagogical, psychological, or basic human prerequisites and abilities. . . . They had gotten some physical exercise and political ideological training, but they were given few tools."[150]

On the job, correctional educators were granted a good deal of latitude in how they performed their duties. Thus, the content of conduct reports differed in how detailed they were. Grounds for ordering an inmate to isolation were left to the staff's personal judgment. Although work performance, rule compliance, and character development were the stated criteria for evaluating an inmate's rehabilitation, they were never effectively operationalized in practice. In the overcrowded and understaffed environment of East German prisons, recounted staff members, correctional educators relied primarily on conversation and the threat of punishment to manage prisoners' contact with others and the outside world.[151]

Upon release, ex-convicts also found the reintegration process deeply flawed. During the years 1979–84, government investigations confirmed that reintegration was plagued by numerous shortcomings: released inmates often found that either no or inadequate housing and work arrangements had been made for them; insufficient information was being given to work and residential supervisors; local supervisors were sometimes reluctant to assist ex-convicts; and distinctions were not being made between types of prisoners.[152] Ex-convicts and Stasi and criminal justice officials agreed that the shortcomings of the reintegration process, especially during the first six months after release, were a main reason why so many released prisoners fell back on their former bad habits and reoffended.[153]

Stasi leaders considered the failures of reintegration a public relations problem that created its own set of security problems. The security ministry in Berlin was well aware of the general public's aversion to ex-convicts. So, when the largest general amnesty of prisoners in the history of the GDR—involving the release of over twenty-five thousand inmates—was announced on 17 July 1987, officials tracked public opinion. One report made it clear that a large segment of the population was none-too-happy with the release of the prisoners. "Numerous times, it's been sarcastically said that 'bananas should be thrown over at them,'" the report noted, continuing, "Many have said that 'GDR citizens who never get into trouble, who don't peer over at the West, and who work honestly are, in the end, the dumb ones.'"[154] A study conducted by criminal police revealed that, with the exception of a higher recidivism rate in Halle, fewer than 10 percent of the released convicts had committed a new offense by year's end. Yet this appears to have done little to assuage the anxieties and resentments of the public.[155]

Conclusions

Critics are quite right in pointing to the disparity between the GDR's inflated rhetoric about correctional rehabilitation and the reality of its prison system. Given, however, that this represents a chronic problem in the history of institutions of confinement and public policy, it is worthwhile to ask what was different about the way this played out in East Germany. The tendency, of course, has been to see this divergence between ideal and fact as a grand lie, a fraud perpetrated on the public by a corrupt and malicious party and state.

There is, in my estimation, little reason to argue with the portrayal of the SED and Stasi state as an unscrupulous and repressive institution. That East Germans were compelled to live with such an open secret for so long, however, raises questions about how this system functioned. How did administrators, researchers, clinicians, staff, and convicts operate within this open secret?

A common approach was one taken by inmates since the birth of prisons themselves: gaming the system. Prisoners and personnel found ways to simply "get by" on a daily basis, using official rhetoric instrumentally. For instance, once it was clear that emphasis was being placed on the "personality" of offenders, staff routinely used that term's vagueness and plasticity as a means to justify their administrative tactics. Higher-ups and experts from the human sciences bristled at what they considered to be the sloppy nontechnical ways in which personnel in the field used the concept. But it proved difficult, if not impossible, for decision makers at the center to enforce their abstractions at the local level.

This is not to say, however, that the East German rhetoric of correctional rehabilitation can be dismissed as merely bombast. Sandra Pingel-Schliemann and Hubertus Knabe have spoken of there being "soft" or more "subtle" forms of persecution at work in the GDR.[156] Whether or not one wishes to accept this kind of description, it is clear that in policy-making circles, East German authorities themselves recognized the existence of "soft" and "hard" approaches to public problems. By the late 1970s and 1980s, the methods and approaches of the human sciences were widely associated with social caring. They represented the "soft" line in contrast to the "hard" line of ideologues and police.

Thus, in the context of the criminal justice system, the language and techniques of psychology, psychiatry, psychotherapy, social work, sociology, and pedagogy offered some leverage for those interested in realizing correctional rehabilitation. As their emphasis on hierarchical models of learning demonstrates, these fields were not somehow inherently more pluralistic and democratic than others. Rather, they proved to be relatively permeable, embracing empirical methods and increasingly open to international influences.

Nevertheless, the correctional imagination in East Germany, similar to both Nazi Germany and West Germany, was stamped by its ideological commitments. By the late 1960s, the criminal archetype in the GDR was widely understood as a disoriented personality, an individual whose personal development failed to properly converge with that of socialist society. The job of correctional rehabilitation was therefore couched in didactic terms, as a collective project aimed at transforming a mind out of step with its social surroundings.

CHAPTER 4

Civilizing Deviant Sexuality under Socialism

In June 1961, just weeks before the construction of the Berlin Wall, the East German Ministry of Justice received word that a recent court decision in the jurisdiction of Neuruppin involving a long-standing member of the Communist Party had provoked the ire of the local population there. On 8 June 1961, the district court in Neuruppin had convicted sixty-five-year-old P.G. of sexually molesting children and had sentenced him to three years in prison and to the loss of his civil rights for five years. Though G. denied the charges, testimony from numerous witnesses convinced the court that he had been exposing himself to children since at least 1952. In the case for which he was convicted, G. apparently had become bolder: he had invited a number of schoolchildren to his home, where he proceeded to lecture them about what "fucking means," attempted to have sex with several of them, demonstrated different sexual positions, and explained, "in an ugly and cynical manner," how girls sexually matured and how one girl he knew let herself be penetrated by a dog.[1] Around two hundred people showed up at his sentencing, and though most appeared to have been satisfied with the verdict, an article in the press some days later indicated that many in the community found the sentence too lenient.[2]

Setting this case apart from other cases of sexual molestation at this time was the political setting and circumstances surrounding it. G. was a decorated veteran in the communist movement. Becoming a member of the Spartacus League after World War I, he joined the KPD (Kommunistische Partei Deutschlands) in 1920, spent the better part of the Nazi years in concentration camps, aided the Soviet command in Vienna in 1947, and was an active member of the SED since 1950. G.'s misconduct and subsequent sentencing had the dangerous potential to cast the party in a corrupt light. Moreover, there remained the unenviable task of trying to explain such outrageous and licentious behavior—a decadence the regime had always publicly associated with the West—in a man whose biography appeared to mesh so seamlessly with twentieth-century communist ideals of personhood.[3]

In laying out the legal justifications for its decision, the district court attempted to respond to these thorny questions by simultaneously situating the convicted man's conduct in relation to both the ontogenetic development of children and the evolutionary development of socialism. What made G.'s vulgar "lessons" in sex so heinous, according to the court, was that experience showed that the normal sexual and psychological development of children was easily disturbed and inhibited by early traumas. "In just a few hours," the court announced, "the accused has undone the arduous rearing efforts of parents, school, and youth organization. He has endangered the health of these children as well as their development into joyfully creative human beings." G. was thus understood to have undermined one of the fundamental pillars of socialism: raising the next generation of socialist subjects. In this, the court explained, G. showed "that he no longer possesses the right to consider himself to be a progressive part of the worker class." The term *fortschrittlich* (progressive) here held the key to making sense of the man's crimes.

> In our republic, having removed the economic roots of capitalism, we have created the preconditions for fundamentally reshaping relations between people. They are no longer inhuman and impersonal. Rather, only in our order is the kind of true love which characterizes human beings really possible between the sexes. That means that in our society, the preconditions have been created for relations between people—in particular, between the sexes—to be truly humane, genuine, and moral. The accused has not overcome the old, inhuman morality of the bourgeois state.

In justifying its sentence, however, the court made clear that the justice system in the GDR was dedicated to the principle that "in everyone, including those who stumble, there is good core." Thus, the court concluded that the appropriate response should be not a harsh sentence but "to help him find his way back to society."[4]

P.G.'s case provides a telling example of the kinds of problems sex offenses could pose for the political, legal, and social order in East Germany. His case is particularly instructive in that the trial took place in the summer of 1961, at a time when the SED was embarking on a new, post-Stalinist phase in the development of its socialist experiment. The Berlin Wall was to be only one element in a more comprehensive reform of the country's economic, legal, health care, educational, and cultural systems, eventually culminating in the so-called New Economic System (1963–69). In this context, child molestation and G.'s state of mind shared something in common: they were both seen as sad relics from the past, holdovers from a self-centered moral order that threatened to subvert and divert the development of a truly socialist consciousness among East Germany's young people.

As Dagmar Herzog has noted, sexual desire was a highly politicized subject in Europe in the decades following World War II.[5] This was the case, too, in East Germany, where unbridled sexuality was something associated particularly with youth, a group the party and the state quickly came to perceive as a principal threat to national security.[6] Seen in this context, G.'s case and, indeed, sex crimes in general raise interesting questions about the relationship between communist ideology and institutional forms of knowledge in making sense of social deviance.

As the East German Communist Party attempted to reconceptualize virtually all knowledge through the idiom of Marxism-Leninism, sex crime, too, was reexamined and recast in socialist terms. Assessing and defining criminally deviant sexual behavior, however, posed a number of peculiar problems for the criminal justice system. Most glaringly, postwar socialist criminology adhered to the principles that crime was historically and socially conditioned and thus eradicable. However, the continued presence of sex offenders—a group of criminals historically conventionally associated with a high rate of psychopathology and recidivism and considered by most experts at the time to be largely incurable—fundamentally challenged the historicism, social determinism, and pedagogical optimism of official doctrine.

Together, criminology, forensic psychology, and the criminal justice system in East Germany provided a venue for talking about and defining the boundaries of desire in a society where self-gratification was widely perceived as politically significant and potentially seditious. In the end, authorities and researchers came to see sex offenders much as the courts did in the case of P.G., that is, as primitive relics of both a biological evolutionary and a more recent historical past. As such, it was believed, sex offenders were men requiring civilization in the form of modern, scientifically based treatment and therapy.[7]

Psychopaths, Dirty Old Men, and Sexual Harassers during the Fifties

Notwithstanding its claims of representing a revolutionary new political and social order, East German law throughout most of the fifties and sixties retained and recognized most of the German criminal code developed under the Weimar Republic and the Nazi state. Nowhere was this continuity more evident than in the area of sex offenses, where the litany of criminal sexual acts was mostly the same as would have been found in the years 1918–45. Those forms of abnormal sexual conduct deemed criminal included rape, sexual harassment and intimidation, sexual abuse of minors, sexual intercourse in public, prostitution, distribution of pornographic literature, incest, indecent exposure, bestiality, and homosexuality. The latter two were eventually decriminalized in 1968.

There was one important way, however, in which East German criminal justice differed from both previous decades and the Federal Republic. As mentioned before, in 1952 the practice of preventive detention was deemed incompatible with the GDR constitution and from that point on, courts were no longer able to indeterminately incarcerate repeat sex offenders under sections 20a and 42e of the imperial criminal code. With no recognized precedent in German jurisprudence for court-ordered therapy,[8] commitment to a mental hospital, drug abuse facility, or workhouse represented the only legal means to place someone in indefinite custody. For this reason, questions about the relative risk, prognosis, and treatment of individual sex offenders were addressed for the most part during legal proceedings exploring soundness of mind (*Zurechnungsfähigkeit*) and suitability for psychiatric hospitalization.

These limiting factors served to reinforce the influential role played by psychiatrists in the study and handling of sex offenders. Similar to conversations in West Germany, East German discussions in the fifties about sex crime were consistently couched in psychopathological terms, with investigators seeking to determine the origins, development, and symptoms of sexual deviance as manifestations of mental disorder. Well into the last years of the decade, clinicians saw little reason to depart from the terminology and conclusions relied on during the Third Reich. Hugo von Keyserlingk, a leading psychiatrist based at the university psychiatric clinic in Jena, conducted a study of 801 of the clinic's patients (678 men, 123 women) who had undergone a court-mandated examination over the years 1920–50 and found that 42.2 percent of males and 53.7 percent of females were classified as "psychopathic personalities." He conceded that the proportion of psychopaths among sex offenders in general was not as high as that found among other groups of criminals. He did discover, however, that up until age fifty-four, the overwhelming majority of those committing sex crimes against children were deemed psychopaths, while sex offenders aged fifty-five and over were most often described in other terms, such as "hysterical, degenerative, asocial, impulsive, submissive, primitive-infantile." At the same time, both psychopaths and sex offenders had been disproportionately granted the protection of section 51 (presence of a mitigating mental state) during the previous three decades.[9]

Records from the Charité hospital's Department of Forensic Psychiatry in Berlin reveal that criminal biology's influence was felt there well into the 1950s. Especially in sexual crime cases, clinicians focused their attention on signs of congenital and acquired forms of nervous degeneration in the defendants they examined. In two separate cases involving incest in 1950, for instance, psychiatrists pointed to a weak personality structure as the main culprit. The "feebleminded behavior" (*schwachsinniges Verhalten*) of twenty-four-year-old E.P.—she had spent her youth sleeping with numerous men, had contracted both gonorrhea and syphilis, and was now having frequent sex with her abusive, alcoholic father—was tied to her low intelligence, itself traced back to her truancy and a congenital retardation (*angeborene Minderbegabung*).[10] G.W., a twenty-three-year-old male who had spent the years 1942–46 in youth homes for sex offenses and was now suspected of numerous sexual assaults on children under the age of ten (including his sister), was thought to be the victim of a "hereditary corruption" (*familiäre Belastung*). Citing the facts that W.'s father was divorced, his mother had an "unstable personality" and frequent run-ins with the law, and his brother was plagued with learning problems, Charité clinicians concurred with an earlier report that he was a "docile object of his own impulses and milieu influences" and incapable of "leading an independent life."[11]

As noted in the previous chapter, *milieu* became an increasingly prominent term in the East German criminology of the fifties, and forensic psychiatric reports from the time confirm its ubiquitous presence in clinical settings. In the GDR, the expression referred to the material and interpersonal circumstances presumed to shape different facets of an individual's life, such as family, neighborhood, and workplace. In the context of criminal justice, however, the talk most often was of "milieu impairments" (*Milieuschäden*), developmental maladies considered to have arisen from poor rearing and education. The concept was capacious enough to encompass both biological and sociopsychological explanations, as in the case of thirty-year-old lesbian M.B., convicted numerous times for vagrancy, lack of identity papers, and falsifying documents. Examining psychiatrists ultimately deemed her to be a psychopath with transvestite perversions (she and other self-identified lesbians enjoyed going to the Sascha Club in Berlin, where she dressed in men's clothing and referred to herself as "Jonny"). The examiners considered B.'s maladies to be the result of a latent schizophrenia, combined with sexual abuse at the hands of her father and a female teacher as well as her confinement in a youth concentration camp during the war. Examiners noted in their report, "It goes without saying that, in a concentration camp, there is no possibility for an already damaged young person to mature and develop into a feeling human being."[12]

In looking over psychiatric reports during the early years of the GDR, it is striking how many of them capture the peculiar uncertainties, flux, and violence characteristic of the war and immediate postwar years.[13] Particularly during the years 1941–49, Germany was dominated by a culture of destruction, where "collapse" (*Zusammenbruch*) was one of the central defining images in public discourse.[14] It was a world that many described living through with a sense of unreality, a feeling of passively being acted on by events, along with a desire for new sources of safety and security.[15] Psychiatrists and their patients did not fail to see a connection between the broken lives and mental states of the latter and the destruction surrounding them.

An especially disturbing example of this involved the 1952 case of F.S., a fifty-year-old itinerant, blinded by an injury in 1937, who admitted to having sex with his stepdaughter and four of his own children over the years 1944–52. Physicians at the Charité clinic were clearly bemused by S., interviewing him five separate times during the summer of 1952. Inquiring into his motivations, examiners learned that S. claimed to have committed the crimes not merely to satisfy his lust but as a means to exact revenge on his wife, whom he suspected of cheating on him.

Although there were disparities in the chronologies provided by S. and his wife, staff at the Charité were able to reconstruct the following. S. had spent most of his childhood and youth on the move, living first in orphanages and then in correctional houses and finally wandering around a series of European countries as a traveling vendor. He met his wife shortly after he lost his eyesight. They married in 1940 and returned to Germany around 1942, eventually having four children. Sex between the two became ever more infrequent, however, and S. became increasingly jealous of both other men and the children. Over the years 1939 to 1944, he suffered under the growing conviction that he was not the only man in his partner's life, so he turned to his children. "His hope for an improvement in their marriage situation was never fulfilled," clinicians explained, "and so, over several years, he seized on a plan to get even with his wife in such a way that would hurt her as much as he had been injured by her infidelity." While S. expressed the worry that his children might now see him as a criminal, he continued, even in custody, to feel that he had no choice in his actions.

S.'s troubling sense of masculine entitlement to sexual gratification, reassurance, and retribution could well be understood as a—albeit extreme—reflection of the insecurities facing many German men during and after World War II.[16] Psychiatrists at the Charité, however, labeled him a schizoid psychopath who "tends toward autism, toward introversion"—a man stamped by flightiness and volatility. "No woman, no experience has been in the position to lead him back to a regular, settled, ~~bourgeois~~, socially integrated existence," they noted in their report. Here was a form of illegal emigration (*Republikflucht*) of a different kind, an abandonment of the very virtues that the East German state increasingly came to embrace as its own—endurance, conscientiousness, and a sedentary lifestyle. In the end, examiners strongly recommended that S. be committed to a psychiatric facility.[17]

S.'s case demonstrates how neatly psychopathological explanations could sometimes map onto socialist ideals of sexual personhood. Both Dagmar Herzog and Josie McLellan have noted that despite some surprisingly open and tolerant attitudes about sexuality, SED functionaries and East German experts tended to see sexuality in conservative terms, guided by the assumptions that natural sex was between a man and woman and oriented around marriage and that excessive or unusual sexual activities represented dangerous perversions.[18] Perhaps, then, the ubiquitous application of the diagnosis of psychopathy in so many of the sexual assault cases examined by forensic psychiatrists should come as no surprise, since psychopathy's reliance on the notion of a lack of self-control over depraved impulses simultaneously informed and reflected East German conventions about sexual desire at the time.

This was especially evident in cases where elderly men were the perpetrators. Psychiatrists were frequently called on to forensically examine older males involved in exhibitionism or the sexual provocation of children, since officials always considered senility (*Altersabbau*) a possible explanation in such cases. Memory loss, a diminished capacity for critical thinking, and an inability to control emotions and urges were often cited as mitigating circumstances, even in cases involving incest.[19] Lewd behavior toward children by elderly men in their sixties and seventies was common enough to earn its own moniker, "old-timer criminality" (*Greisenkriminalität*), which referred to "becoming a first-time offender during old age along with physical and mental signs of aging."[20] The social prognosis for such older criminals was considered somewhat challenging: while physical frailty might prevent some from being a threat to others, the degenerative nature of their mental conditions seemed to hold out little hope for a remedy. As a result, the men were either committed to a psychiatric facility or released into housing settlements where family members and/or residents could keep a watchful eye out for their interactions with children.[21]

Anxieties about the persistence of sexual assaults on children, particularly by older men, eventually inspired one of the first and most influential attempts to systematically bring a Marxist-Leninist perspective to the problem of sex crime. It came from the legal scholar Gerhard Feix, in a monograph entitled *The Fight against Child Molesters*, based on his 1959 Humboldt University dissertation. By relying on legal and forensic science, jurisprudence, and Marxism-Leninism to shed light on the sexual abuse of children, Feix established himself as one of the leading experts on child molestation in the GDR, and his ideas and findings were cited extensively throughout the sixties and seventies. Feix's investigation, based on scientific studies conducted in the West and on the analysis of East German police statistics, painted a picture of child molestation—comprising 35.6 percent of all sex crimes in the GDR in 1957—that looked similar to that found in other countries at the time. The crime could not be associated with any particular class, but the vast majority of perpetrators were male, married, relatively old, attracted to girls, and tended to work alone.[22]

Feix explained the presence of such sex offenders in the GDR by invoking the "friend-foe" thesis increasingly being endorsed by SED leaders around 1960. For instance, his evidence showed that 61 percent of convicted child molesters in the years 1930–45 were between the ages of twenty-six and fifty-five, while 61.7 percent of perpetrators in the years 1946–58 were over forty (33.8 percent were over fifty). In Feix's view, the reality of the stereotypical "dirty old man" served not only to indicate the presence of a physiological component associated with aging but also to confirm that child molestation was a relic from the past that would "increasingly disappear from the life of our society in the process of an ever growing socialist consciousness and the realization of the socialist lifestyle."[23] Thus, while he believed that a host of biological factors—for instance, senility, mental retardation, alcohol intoxication, early onset of puberty—helped account for the incidence of child molestation in the GDR, he thought that "the causes of this kind of crime in our state lies in the residue of the old, bourgeois attitude toward the child and toward sexual relations as well as the influence of the decadent western lifestyle from the imperialist camp."[24]

Within medical circles, however, the ages and genders of sex offenders and their victims played an integral part in how experts perceived the gravity of crimes. Males far outnumbered females among offenders of all kinds: throughout the 1950s, the percentage of women in East German prisons ranged from a high of 17.7 percent in 1956 to a low of 13.9 percent in 1959.[25] The figure for females convicted of violent sex offenses was undoubtedly lower still. When it came to crimes with a sexual component, women were most often tried for prostitution, asocial conduct, and incest. Clinicians frequently explained the motivations for their crimes in much the same way as they did for women committing other kinds of crime—as the product of an infantile personality, itself the result of a damaged, retarded psychological development.[26] This line of thinking was particularly prominent in the understanding of filicidal mothers.[27] In a three-year study of fifteen women who had murdered their own children, physician Joachim Gerchow found that the women largely shared a set of related traits, including, among others, developmental inhibitions, assimilation difficulties, introversion, and sexual insecurity. In sum, he concluded, they tended to exhibit a juvenile personality, which predisposed these women to respond to external pressures in an impulsive manner.[28]

Clinicians were equally inclined to understand the motivations behind sex crimes by young males—particularly pedophiles—as a consequence of the latter's lack of psychosexual maturity. Twenty-one-year-old H.K. from West Berlin, for instance, was found to have groped numerous eight- and nine-year-old girls in separate incidents. K. believed his attraction to young girls arose out of his insecurities about having grown up with a pronounced lisp and a significantly shorter right leg that made him appear like a "cripple." Examiners deemed him an "insecure psychopath, unstable, having an infantile sexual structure," although they did not believe he was legally incompetent. His criminal prognosis, they concluded, was not altogether poor, since he was sufficiently intelligent enough to learn from his punishment.[29]

Experts typically saw young sex offenders of both genders as psychologically and sexually immature psychopaths, handicapped in their ability to control their impulses and desires. The focus on arrested psychological development led East German psychiatrists to look back at the milieu in which perpetrators were raised for the origins of their deviance. This was paralleled by a commensurate concern over the impact that sexual assaults could have on the emotional and social development of victims. Though it was not assumed that molestations (even on children) necessarily had a traumatizing effect on victims,[30] the potential for lasting psychological harm was recognized. The gender and age disparity that often existed between offenders and victims reinforced the sense that most sex crimes represented an exploitation of dependents and subordinates, which challenged the rearing and correctional efforts of the SED state.[31]

In this way, courts were able to integrate psychiatric knowledge with the legal demand for "socialist lawfulness," seeing the sex offender as an individual unable or unwilling to resist capitalist hedonism, which resulted from a regressive attitude toward self-gratification and constituted a threat to socialist progress. This point was made explicitly in sexual harassment cases, such as the case of fifty-six-year-old B.F., a box manufacturer who employed a number of women under the age of twenty-one and was convicted of violating section 174 of the criminal code (sexually indecent abuse of a dependent relationship) in 1959. F. had apparently used his position to fondle and assault his female employees on a regular basis. He defended himself by arguing that since the women in question were neither interns nor apprentices and since he was a private entrepreneur, section 174 was irrelevant. The district court of Suhl rejected this argument, stating that private owners of capital also had the responsibility to look after the moral upbringing of the country's youth.[32]

During the 1950s, courts and clinicians generally agreed that rehabilitating sex offenders posed enormous difficulties for the East German criminal justice system. Deeming so many perpetrators as "psychopaths" meant that they were associated with recalcitrance and incorrigibility by definition. The old age of some of the perpetrators only served to reinforce the image of sexual criminals as refractory personalities largely immune to penal and therapeutic interventions. In addition, criminal justice in the GDR lacked two tools on which National Socialism and the Federal Republic were able to rely in their treatment of sex offenders: preventive detention and castration. Prescription of castration for repeat offenders was rejected on both medical and legal grounds, both as ineffective in altering sexual inclinations such as homosexuality and as a breach of Order Number 6 of the Soviet Military Administration, which revoked the Nazi sterilization law of 1933.[33]

Despite the institutional differences between the Nazi state and the GDR, many East German specialists in the fifties continued to see correctional rehabilitation as an extension of medicine and the biological sciences. "For the study of criminals is a kind of sociological pathobiology, which makes therapy and prophylaxis necessary, as is the case in the rest of medicine," argued one criminologist at a meeting of the Medical Society in February 1960. That expert continued, "Resocialization, on the one hand, and isolation on the other, are measures that have their long-standing analogue in the fight against contagious disease. The fight against and prevention of crime must increasingly pay more attention to the experiences of medicine and natural science."[34] Especially in the case of psychopathic sex offenders, it was thought that a careful assessment of each convict's personality was necessary, to determine whether to sentence offenders to prison or to commit them to a psychiatric clinic. Examiners looked for signs providing insight into the "character" of the criminal, such as a strong work record, a sense of shame, a desire to atone, a stable marriage, and moral discipline.[35] Hugo von Keyserlingk noted in 1951 that while it was invariably difficult to treat such psychopaths, the influences of work therapy and collective life could achieve much "to integrate the individually mentally abnormal lawbreaker into society."[36]

The Charité System: The New Psychopathology of Sex Offenders

Up until around 1960, experts in East Germany treated sex crimes largely as the acts of depraved individuals whose personalities tended to lack the fortitude necessary to resist their deviant urges. Vestiges of criminal biology continued to exercise an influence on forensic clinicians, as they remained wedded to the idea of the sex offender as an "impulse criminal" (*Triebtäter*), a product of a hereditary predisposition and poor milieu. Admittedly, Marxism-Leninism's insistence on the priority of environmental over endogenous factors in the formation of human subjectivity meant that explanations for sex criminals accentuated upbringing and development more than had been the case under the Third Reich. Yet, in forensic clinical practice of the 1950s, sex offenders were consistently diagnosed as weak-willed, unstable, and immature psychopaths, incapable of governing their feelings and drives.

At the Charité clinic, these notions simultaneously informed and resulted from a relatively routinized method for evaluating criminal suspects and convicts. During the fifties, forensic assessors at the Charité typically relied on two sources of information about the defendant: court records and an outpatient psychiatric exploration covering both physical and mental health, lasting one session. The physical exam involved a clinical observation of the skin, extremities, sensory organs, and general physiognomy, with the subject's body assigned a type according to Ernst Krestschmer's nosology, similar to what Viernstein had done in Bavaria in the twenties and thirties. This examination was accompanied by a neurological one, testing reactions, reflexes, coordination, motors skills, and memory. Some suspects were also tested for venereal diseases.

The psychological part of the examination consisted of a partly structured clinical interview of the prisoner. Psychiatrists were first interested in determining whether the individual was firmly oriented in time and space. Responses to examiner questions were noted for signs of a "flight of ideas" (still associated today with those suffering from bipolar disorder). The intelligence of examinees was also tested, as they were asked to respond to a number of exercises, such as reciting the alphabet backward, explaining the meaning of such concepts as "courage" and "loyalty," naming different kinds of fruits, and describing what they would do if they won the lottery.[37] Clinicians then asked direct questions about family, childhood, and educational background, with particular attention paid to any noteworthy mental illnesses, criminal charges, interruptions in schooling or work, or sexual abnormalities among family members or in the suspect's own past. Finally, the assessors asked the examinee to talk about the crime in question, that is, the circumstances surrounding it, his or her motivations, and his or her attitudes toward the crime after the fact.

Karl Leonhard

Beginning in the late1950s, examination techniques and the language and conclusions of forensic reports at the Charité psychiatric clinic began to change. One reason for this change was the arrival of Karl Leonhard (1904–88) as director of the clinic in 1957, a position he held until 1970. Leonhard traced his intellectual heritage back to Carl Wernicke (1848–1905), studying with Wernicke's student Karl Kleist (1879–1960) at the University of Frankfurt am Main. Hoping to one day assume his mentor's position, Leonhard moved to Erfurt in the GDR in 1955, before being offered the position of director of the university psychiatric clinic at the Charité. When he finally was given the opportunity to take the post he desired in Frankfurt in 1964, East German authorities declined his request to leave the country. An accomplished researcher—he wrote twenty-one monographs and 263 other publications between 1928 and 1988—Leonhard did little, if anything, to accommodate prevailing Marxist-Leninist doctrine in his writings. He therefore earned an oddly independent status in the GDR, simultaneously respected and mistrusted.[38]

By the time he arrived in Berlin, Leonhard had outlined his approach to psychiatric work. To his thinking, observation was the foundation of all psychiatry. To examine someone psychiatrically required more than running tests with quantified results: it demanded that the clinician skillfully note the external manifestations of the patient's inner states through the latter's facial expressions, mannerisms, and gestures. In addition, it required an ability to describe these observations and to differentiate between disturbances in perception, thinking, feeling, ethical character, psychomotor skills, and desire. For Leonhard, the differentiation of symptoms was critical, since he shared the view of those in the so-called Wernicke school that matching discrete symptoms to specific neurological evidence discovered in labs would provide the key to a more refined diagnosis, prognosis, and, ultimately, treatment program for patients.[39] In this regard, Leonhard wished to place psychiatry on a firm biological footing.

During his years as director of the Berlin clinic, Leonhard also focused his attention on prognosis and treatment. Neither, he believed, could be deemed reliable without clinical evidence, so he insisted on the need for catamnestic studies, as he and his team followed up on the progress of hundreds of released patients.[40] Leonhard contended that virtually all forms of neurosis, at least, were curable, and his treatment methods for such maladies had much in common with behavioral therapy. The psychiatrist's task was to teach patients how to avoid succumbing to their idée fixe, by incrementally acclimating them to the object of their obsessions and then showing them how they could divert their minds away from their pathological habits.[41]

According to Leonhard, sex offenders posed a thorny set of problems for the clinician. Leonhard's views on sexuality, particularly abnormal sexuality, were rooted in a biological evolutionary perspective. By the 1960s, he had come to the view that various aspects of sexuality were driven by discrete instincts that evolved over time and were largely immune to correction: while men were moved by more assertive and domineering sets of instincts, women were naturally more passive, subordinate, and nurturing in sexual and erotic relations.[42] Leonhard was hardly unique in accepting these notions, as evolution-based explanations of human attachment emphasizing the role of instincts enjoyed international currency among researchers in the human sciences at the time.[43]

Examining and interviewing 194 forensic patients (130 men, 64 women) from his clinical practice, Leonhard claimed to have found some interesting trends among sex criminals. Obsessive and compulsive features were prominent among many of them, and it was not uncommon for male and female perpetrators to have physical characteristics conventionally associated with the opposite sex. His main conclusion, however, was that sex offenders followed instincts that were either primitive (from the standpoint of evolutionary development) or more natural to the opposite sex. Exhibitionists, Leonhard argued, expressed a subordinate instinct innate to females in that they sought to attract sexual partners by presenting their genitals, a sexual behavior evident among lower forms of animals, whereas violent rapists commonly grabbed their victims by the throat, a manifestation of a domineering Ur-instinct in male animals now wholly sublimated in the modern form of romantic courting.[44]

Though anchored in evolutionary biology, Leonhard's research agenda deviated significantly from earlier criminal biology in renouncing any interest in drawing racial distinctions. His ideas about and methods in psychopathology helped structure the Charité clinic's work around identifying the biological origins of disorders, the importance of differentiating patients and symptoms, treating psychiatry as a clinical art built around trained observation, and being attentive to catamnestic evidence in prognosis. He himself also played a role in the forensic work of the clinic, called in at times to examine patients and advise on cases in which his subordinates felt he would likely take an interest.

Hans Szewczyk

When it came to the evaluation of forensic patients, Hans Szewczyk played a more direct and formative role than his mentor Karl Leonhard. As mentioned in the previous chapter, Szewczyk had trained in both psychology and medicine. In 1961, he was appointed director of the Department of Forensic Psychiatry and Psychology at the Charité, where his forensic reports start appearing in clinic records beginning in 1960. His tireless dedication to institutionalizing forensic psychiatry and psychology in the GDR is confirmed by the fact that he authored or coauthored the overwhelming majority of my sampling of the over eighteen hundred forensic reports found in the clinic's archives for the years 1960–67. Szewczyk's positions as both the director of the leading forensic psychiatric unit in the country and an agenda-setting pioneer in forensic psychiatric research make his clinical reports especially instructive.

Szewczyk's reports are substantially different from those drafted at the Charité clinic during the 1950s. Most striking is his reliance on multiple sources of information about the suspects and perpetrators he examined. Szewczyk was not content with simply material culled from court records and the statements of examinees. Instead, in face-to-face interviews and correspondence, he also routinely queried family members, friends, neighbors, employers, fellow workers, treating doctors and professional caretakers, and crime victims.

Szewczyk believed that information gathered from extramural sources offered insights into criminals' long-term tendencies. In addition, he was concerned that particularly when trying to determine the mental capacity of perpetrators, statements and assessments made during and after the trial were ill suited to shedding light on a potentially unstable offender's mental state at the time of the crime. He explained, in a case in 1964, that by widening the scope of the examination process, examiners "can thereby rely on a larger number of extensive examinations and interviews."[45]

Szewczyk did not stop at questioning a suspect's acquaintances to gain relevant data. Unlike some of his older colleagues, he proved to be more comfortable with newer techniques in medicine and psychology. Following Leonhard's lead, Szewczyk routinely administered an electroencephalogram (EEG) to record the electrical activity of the brains of examinees. International forensic medicine had been using EEG analysis since the early 1950s, primarily to confirm clinical symptoms of brain damage, epilepsy, and trauma in civil and criminal cases. During the 1960s, however, researchers found that a high percentage (around 50 percent) of diagnosed psychopaths showed abnormal EEG results, which reinforced the notion of its effectiveness in confirming diagnoses in forensic patients.[46] While Szewczyk advocated the use of electroencephalography as a means to more precisely and objectively corroborate a diagnosis of psychopathy in individual cases, he nonetheless believed that EEG results were only useful for psychiatric diagnosis if other supporting evidence about the examinee's social conduct could be presented.[47]

Szewczyk was also guardedly supportive about using psychometric testing in forensic practice. During the sixties and early seventies, there were deep divisions among psychiatrists and psychologists—both internationally and in the GDR—over the relative validity and efficacy of, on the one hand, loosely structured clinical exploration and, on the other, standardized, objective personality tests. The debate mirrored disagreements during the Third Reich over the use of clinical prognosis versus prognostic tables. Skeptics of clinical observation dismissed its loosely structured interview method as garnering little more than inconsistent results, no more reliable than chance when it came to diagnosis and prognosis. At the same time, critics of testing argued that by focusing on individual personality traits and structures, objective tests were largely inattentive to situational factors and incapable of identifying precipitating causes.[48]

For his part, Szewczyk steered a middle course. In an article he published in 1970, he conceded that classical exploration was often plagued by vague definitions, wide disparities between observers, and the cognitive bias of the halo effect. He contended, however, that these shortcomings could be offset by gathering accurate data on life history, directing an interview on the basis of previously administered test results, limiting oneself to broad conclusions, relying on the opinions of multiple observers, and employing only well-trained interviewers. Psychometrics, in his estimation, was best restricted to addressing narrowly defined questions, situations where the setting of the examination was largely irrelevant, cases related to assessing functions and not dynamic developments, and patients capable of following extensive instructions.[49] Enamored with the work of German-born psychologist Hans Eysenck, Szewczyk was especially fond of using the former's Maudsley Personality Inventory,[50] a questionnaire designed to measure the relative extraversion/introversion and neuroticism of subjects, with a scale that replaced static characteristics with facets and capacities capable of changing over time.[51]

Alert to the limitations of the results of personality tests, Szewczyk tended to place greater confidence in the traditional clinical examination when it came to etiological and prognostic questions. His forensic reports show a pattern of probing extensively into the family and interpersonal histories of those he examined, looking for signs of childhood disease, family dysfunction, inadequate rearing and education, and psychological trauma. Szewczyk emphasized the "development" and "milieu" of the perpetrator's personality, themes noted in the previous chapter as enjoying wide currency in East German official discourse during the 1960s. Particularly in the case of sex offenders, Szewczyk shared his mentor Leonhard's evolutionary view that family and social circumstances worked dialectically with biological instincts and drives to shape and direct sexual impulses.

Take, for instance, the case of a thirty-four-year-old married man, J.K., who admitted, in separate incidents during the summer of 1962, to instructing two boys (aged twelve and eleven) to play a game in which they were to try to strangle him. As one of the boys put it later, "he said to me that he is a concentration camp inmate and that I should murder him." Interviews with K. and his wife revealed, according to Szewczyk, a "soft" and "passive" temperament, a man remarkably shy, weak, and weepy as a child. When asked to discuss his sexual habits, K. revealed that he had barely had sex with his wife of six years, finding it difficult to keep an erection except when his throat was grabbed at the same time. His sexual deviance, Szewczyk concluded, represented a classic case of what Leonhard referred to as a form of archaic, primitive sexual instinct.[52]

Even in instances like K.'s, however, where innate instincts or drives were seen as the chief culprit, Szewczyk believed that upbringing played a crucial role in shaping sex offenders. For instance, in dealing with a number of cases involving homosexual men, Szewczyk made the point that two groups needed to be distinguished. In some homosexuals, the origin of their deviance rested in a hereditary disposition, apparent already at an early age. But most homosexuals coming before the courts, he claimed, were those "who come to homosexual activities out of impulsive waywardness, a lack of opportunity to meet women, or being biologically incapable of having sexual relations."[53]

Social circumstances were critical, in Szewczyk's eyes, to the development of antisocial personalities. By the early 1970s, modeling his thinking along the lines of the educational and social psychologists Aleksei Leontiev,

Walter Friedrich, Adolf Kossakowski, and Hans Hiebsch, Szewczyk had come to see delinquency as something rooted in a failed process of socialization. The inability of family, school, and the immediate milieu to effect the internalization of proper norms, roles, traits, and values in an individual, he contended, could set in motion a vicious circle of social isolation, substance abuse, sexual depravity, and crime.[54]

The Social Prognosis of Sex Offenders

For Szewczyk, like so many forensic specialists in the human sciences, the etiology of sexual misconduct was the key to knowing about the personality structure of offenders, and that structure served, in turn, as the chief indicator for social prognosis. In contrast to most of his German counterparts of the thirties, forties, and fifties, however, Szewczyk did not simply take signs of an endogenous psychopathology as indicating incorrigibility. Instead, he consistently calibrated his prognoses to specific options for surveillance and confinement: prison, psychiatric commitment, treatment in a substance abuse facility, long-term custodial care, and outpatient treatment. In this way, social prognosis was an appraisal as much of institutional conditions of possibility as of a prisoner's state of mind.

Among the things that led Szewczyk to award sex offenders a poor or a good social prognosis, he often took intelligence and education as a reliable measure of corrigibility. In 1962, he examined twenty-nine-year-old H.K., a chronic inebriant who had molested a thirteen-year-old girl during a drinking binge. Asked to determine whether K. should be committed to an alcoholism treatment center, Szewczyk rejected the idea. Citing K.'s hypomanic personality traits, evidence of marked "feeblemindedness" (*Schwachsinn*), and a history of behavioral problems, Szewczyk found that K. was not so much sexually deviant as he was a victim of neglect in his sexual education. Though his judgment was clearly clouded by alcohol, Szewczyk concluded, an alcoholism treatment program was futile: "His alcohol withdrawal will take place in the course of serving his sentence. . . . [But] influencing him in this or any other way is hardly possible. There is not the slightest inkling that he will be able to avoid alcohol in the future. We therefore fear that, in the future, the accused will be a good worker but, at the same time, will again get in trouble with the law."[55]

Szewczyk tended to privilege relatively more articulate and educated examinees in his social prognoses, a trend that has been found to be common among psychotherapists in general.[56] This is apparent, for example, in the 1964 case of J.K. (discussed above),[57] who had encouraged two boys to strangle him. Szewczyk's exploration revealed K. to be a well-spoken and well-mannered musician, licensed in piano instruction, who primarily socialized with educated professionals. Combined with other circumstances in the case, Szewczyk concluded that K. was perfectly capable of living constructively within society and that psychotherapy at the Charité offered the best means to achieve that end.

Two factors, then, seem to have been most critical to Szewczyk's determination of corrigibility in individual cases: the subject's personal resources (e.g., sense of self-worth, social integration, access to support, robust values) and a suitable institutional regimen for his or her correction. In fact, he considered these two variables so important that they could even outweigh age in importance. R.P., for instance, was a fifty-eight-year-old man who admitted to having fondled his thirteen-year-old stepdaughter's genitals. P. presented signs of arteriosclerosis and senile dementia, leading Szewczyk to conclude that organic processes affected the man's ability to control his emotions and sexual desires. Despite this, however, Szewczyk believed that there was reason for optimism: "Given the otherwise correct life the accused has led, which indicates positive characteristics in his premorbid personality, his incarceration may well have an adequate correctional impact."[58]

By contrast, Szewczyk was relatively pessimistic about the chances for twenty-six-year-old P.M., an exhibitionist who had masturbated multiple times in front of groups of girls at Hackescher Markt and Monbijou Park in Berlin. Szewczyk found M. to be only slightly diminished in his intellectual and emotional capacities and willpower and did not consider his actions anything other than compensation for a lack of normal sexual activity. "Experience shows that prison punishments have no effect on exhibitionists like this," Szewczyk noted, "since many, including M., try to work against their forms of behavior and [since] a prison sentence only reinforces their sense of insecurity." Believing psychotherapy also to be futile, the forensic specialist recommended that the young man be committed to a home for asocials.[59]

Preventive Detention Workarounds

Like many of his colleagues, Szewczyk expressed frustration with the institutional limits of East German confinement. As mentioned earlier, the GDR Supreme Court had deemed the practice of preventive detention incompatible with the GDR constitution in 1952, leaving psychiatric commitment as the only legal means to place someone in indefinite custody. By the 1960s, criminal justice officials and clinicians alike voiced their growing vexation with finding appropriate institutional spaces for those inmates who fit the profile of neither the prison nor the mental hospital.

Szewczyk shared this exasperation and advocated the creation of special detention units for psychopaths, along the lines being considered in West Germany at the time.[60] In the meantime, however, he and others remained faced with the task of accommodating refractory prisoners whose mental states were clearly abnormal yet did not rise to the level of a certifiable pathology.[61] Archival records show that Szewczyk attempted to resolve this problem in individual cases by often using his position as a court-appointed assessor to divert apparently incorrigible sex offenders away from the penal system and place them in the care of psychiatric or welfare facilities.[62] He did this sometimes with and sometimes without the tacit understanding of justice officials, using his extensive knowledge of criminal justice practices to steer judges, prosecutors, and administrators to his way of thinking.

This approach is perhaps best observed in the case of a sickly fifty-one-year-old man examined by Szewczyk in July 1964. P.G. was charged with having homosexual relations with a minor in his apartment. Though G. stated that he sexually preferred women over men, he had a history of homosexual relations dating back to 1941. In fact, he was convicted of an unspecified sex crime that year, sent to prison, and then transferred to several concentration camps, where he contracted tuberculosis. Found guilty of having sex with male minors and adults in 1949 and again in 1960, G. spent time in treatment centers, prisons, and psychiatric facilities over the course of the fifties and early sixties. Even during his incarcerations and furloughs, he persisted in his "illicit activities." During this time, he was examined and evaluated by psychiatrists from both the Charité (1952) and the Hufeland Hospital in Berlin-Buch (1958). The former found him to be feebleminded, while clinicians in Buch offered a grim prognosis. They argued, Szewczyk noted, that "a change in his abnormal disposition is not going to be accomplished" and that in the case of another offense, he should be "left to feel the entire severity of the law."

In his discussions with G., Szewczyk found the man to be intellectually and physically slow, with deficits in concentration, leading Szewczyk to suspect the beginnings of age-associated memory impairment. Despite G.'s history of homosexuality, Szewczyk believed that there was strong evidence to consider his homosexual acts the result of a lack of sexual opportunities with women. Psychologically limited in his self-control and repeatedly punished for his offenses, G. "was torn from the normal social path." Szewczyk therefore concluded that the man could not be held responsible for his actions. At the end of his report, Szewczyk offered officials a solution.

> Commitment to a psychiatric hospital, however, can mean his safekeeping—and with it, his isolation—from society, since any kind of therapeutic influence is still hardly possible and [since] it remains at this point to be determined whether such a therapeutic influence has ever been at all possible, given the attitude of G.
>
> . . . The recommendation of sec. 42b of the criminal code is an indication that therapy for the man is not possible and that commitment appears to be the sensible choice, if the high court approaches this from the perspective that lifelong isolation of the man from society is urgently necessary. His commitment in this case can have nothing other than a warehousing purpose.[63]

Here is a clear instance of how the practice of preventive detention was able to function in the GDR, despite its being formally outlawed. Multiple records testify to the fact that psychiatrists and criminal justice officials in East Germany regularly relied on the mental health system to perform what sociologists have referred to as "workarounds," that is, "ad hoc temporary solutions and strategies to problems arising when the official protocol is perceived as hindering the assigned task."[64] Throughout the sixties and seventies, Szewczyk and others spoke out about the need to build special indefinite detention centers to hold and treat offenders like P.G.[65] No such facilities were ever constructed, so by the mid-1970s, the Chief Prosecutor's Office called on psychiatric hospitals to beef up security in order to provide space to isolate psychopathic deviants—one estimate put the figure at more than fifteen thousand—from the general public.[66] Staff in the Ministry of Health made it clear, however, that health care professionals wanted nothing to do with warehousing potentially dangerous individuals whose psychological problems did not rise to the level of a certifiable illness. In its view, such a development would thwart ongoing reform efforts in establishing an open-door system in facilities and would overburden staff, spread criminal behavior within the general residential population, and undermine public perceptions of psychiatric hospitals as treatment centers.[67] Yet, despite the fact that neither criminal justice nor health care officials believed that psychiatric centers were best suited to the task, subsequent studies have revealed that workarounds and shortcuts were consistently used to preventively detain chronic offenders in mental hospitals throughout the last two decades of the GDR.[68]

Female Victims, Male Perpetrators, and Gender in Forensic Psychiatry

Until at least the mid-1970s, research in forensic psychiatry and criminology centered almost exclusively on the study of perpetrators. In clinical settings, forensic evaluators like Hans Szewczyk spent most of their time assessing suspects and convicts. Victims, by contrast, often received little, if any, attention in scholarship and forensic clinical practice. Practitioners typically only showed interest in victims when questions were being raised about the competency of the victims or the veracity of their claims. This was especially true in cases involving sexual assault, where there was a long history of questioning the character of female accusers.[69] Particularly in cases involving sex offenses against children, as Brigitte Kerchner has shown, scholars in the human sciences expressed doubts, since the turn of the century, about the assumption of "childhood innocence."[70] By the 1930s, pedagogues, psychologists, and psychiatrists, relying on the new field of testimony psychology (*Aussagepsychologie*), were effective in convincing courts of the need for experts to evaluate whether accusing girls were honest victims, pathological liars, or corrupted seductresses.[71]

Clinicians at the Charité clinic were also called on to assess and report on the victims of sexual assaults, including children. Comparing the cases I have examined with those discussed by Kerchner reveals a great deal of continuity in the ways in which examiners in the 1950s and 1960s assessed the probity of child accusers. Precociousness, a history of moral lapses, and inconsistencies in depositions counted heavily against accusers. For instance, H.K., a fifteen-year-old girl who accused her father of sexually molesting her over the years 1955–59, was dismissed by clinicians as an "attention-seeking psychopath," after it was revealed that she had started menstruating a year earlier, was known to steal, and repeatedly embellished her story.[72] By contrast, ten-year-old M.H., who accused a family friend of inappropriately touching her on multiple occasions, was deemed, by her examiner, "a well-raised, gifted, realistic, and dependable child." H.'s naive description of events, her lack of sexual knowledge, and the manifest intelligence and integrity of her mother were cited as grounds for believing the girl.[73] Thus, the ideal female witness was also the idealized German girl, possessing a sexual naïveté, a sense of right and wrong, and a demure mien.

The assessment of a child's truthfulness and rectitude did not always result in a clear-cut decision to side with one of the parties in question. Seven- or eight-year-old S.F. (the record is not clear on her age) was one of several girls who, in 1966, accused sixty-four-year-old K.B. of sexually molesting her.[74] Born out of wedlock, S.F. was referred to by a teacher as "a troubled child," abandoned by her mother when the latter fled to the west in 1961 and left by her father in the care of his eighty-year-old mother. Her school described her as restless and combative, adding, "Her behavior indicates that she is sexually well developed." The accused K.B. claimed that S.F. and the other girls in question had taken the initiative with him, egging him on to kiss and touch them out of an aggressive sexual curiosity.

Hans Szewczyk was asked to interview the girl in order to help determine the veracity of her claims. The transcript of the interview shows how his questions grew increasingly more directed and suggestive.

(Do you know why you are here) . . .
(Do you want to say something) . . .
(Huh, S.?) . . .
(You know it.) . . . "Because I always go after men."
(What do you like more, old or young men?) "Old ones."
(How old do they have to be, as old as me?) "Older."

Szewczyk and the girl briefly discussed her friendliness toward one man in the neighborhood, and then Szewczyk attempted to get around to the topic of K.B.

(To which old man are you still going?) . . .
(To whom are you still going?) "To Herr B."
(And what do you want from him, why are you going to him?) . . .

S. was initially reluctant to speak about this but then explained that she met him in the park several times. There, she claimed, the two kissed each other on the cheek and mouth, and she sat on his lap. Encountering more reticence from the girl as to specifics, Szewczyk decided to ask her more pointed questions about where B. touched her: the back? (yes), the arm? (don't know), the head? (once), breast? (no), leg or thigh? (no), genitals or bottom? (no). At this point, Szewczyk became more confrontational with the girl.

(You told the police that he touched you under your skirt?) She is entirely amazed.
(Isn't that true?) . . .
(Isn't that true?) "Yes."
(Is it also true that he did it, or have you been fibbing a bit?) "That's true."

(It's true that he touched you under your skirt? But I just asked you whether he touched you, and you said no, so what's true?) "I think I had a petticoat on, and I showed it to him, and he touched the petticoat."
(Do you know boys who are real swine?) "Yes."
(What do they do?) . . .
(Do they do something to girls?) "Yes."
(Hit them?) "I was once in the entranceway, and a bike was standing there, and I wanted to ride it, and they said, go ahead, and I didn't really see much, and I turned around. . . ."
(What does that have to do with anything?) "F. und K. were there, [and] they said, I'm not letting you go."
(Did you pull them [underwear] down?) "I had to, yes."
(What did he do, did he touch you?) Long silence.
(S.?) "Yes."
(Where did he touch you?) . . .
(How long did he touch you?) "Not long."
(Was it nice?) "No."
(How many boys have touched you?) "2."
(And how many men have touched you?) . . .
(Huh?) "One."
(Who then?) . . . "Herr B., but I showed him the petticoat, and then he touched it, and then I put the skirt back down, and I showed him how the skirt twirls."

Szewczyk ultimately determined that S.'s lack of a stable upbringing led her to develop an abnormal sexual interest in physical contact with both older boys and older men. "In her active and seeking nature, she is the prototype of the so-called 'victim' who appears in the records to repeatedly be a victim but in reality reveals taking and having taken the initiative." He acknowledged that the girl was unusual in placing responsibility for the sexual encounters on herself rather than on the adults around her. Her sense of guilt made it difficult to get straight answers from her, though Szewczyk suspected that much more went on between the child and K.B. than either was letting on. The contradictions in her stories made it impossible, Szewczyk concluded, to legally rely on her testimony. Despite this, the evidence against B. was overwhelming, and the Charité clinician recommended that the man be placed in a nursing home after his release, to preclude his access to young girls.[75]

Even more so than in the cases of adult perpetrators, Szewczyk's interview of S. reveals the hierarchical nature of the forensic examination. The situation differed little from what had typically been the case decades earlier, weighted in favor of the "respectable," adult male authority who directs the proceedings, demanding a girl explain her intimate thoughts, feelings, and conduct. It is also worth noting how quickly the exchange could turn from inquisitorial to adversarial to accusatory. Szewczyk presents his revelations here as mandates, so S.'s silences and circumspection are treated as evasiveness, a lack of cooperation. This is not simply a generic interview: taking place in the setting of both a criminal and a clinical investigation, it is interrogatory in style. Professional imperatives of law and medicine demanded reliable answers, and laypersons—even neglected and abused girls—were pressed to acquiesce in the work of experts.

The disparity between male expert and female victim is visible in adult cases as well and is especially evident in an unusual case Szewczyk took on in 1964. J.P., a forty-seven-year-old internist at a major East German polyclinic, was accused of violating "the sexual integrity of women by abusing his authority."[76] P., who became chief physician in 1957, admitted to having sexual relations with eleven separate patients, ranging in age from twenty to twenty-seven, during the years 1959–63. The sexual encounters often took place in connection with gynecological exams P. administered, which he used as a pretext to make his sexual advances. Justice officials asked Szewczyk to determine whether P., whom many described as subject to severe mood swings, suffered from manic depression and should be found mentally incompetent and committed to a psychiatric facility.

Since P. was an accomplished physician, the circle of those with information about his past included numerous medical professionals. Szewczyk not only looked over past medical records but also considered statements and comments from P.'s academic colleagues and coworkers, P.'s brother (also a doctor), and several friends of the man, all of whom were physicians. Together with his wife—who said she would stand by her husband because she still loved him and because it was "in her nature" to do so—P.'s family, friends, and colleagues presented a consistent picture of a man prone to, at times, effusive and irritable periods and, at other times, bouts of deep depression. In fact, P. was hospitalized for depression twice, in 1960 and 1962, when he was treated with propaphenin, hexobarbital, tincture of opium, and electroconvulsive therapy.

In his interview with Szewczyk, P. contended that his sexual indiscretions occurred during manic and hypomanic phases of his disorder. While he recognized that his actions were unethical, he did not believe they were criminal.

(Did you have the impression that some of the women had to be coerced?) "No, in my estimation that was never the case."

(Did you have the impression that there was a kind of delayed resistance?) "In part—a kind of stalling resistance was presented, where I had the impression that it wasn't genuine." To some extent, there was no resistance at all. By and large, the ladies came back to him after these encounters.

(Do you see yourself as guilty?) "Now, sure. Now I see the horrible moral guilt I bear, that I went too far with people who were entrusted in my care, that I was wholly wrong in my conduct from a physician's standpoint. I am ashamed about these actions."

(Do you feel legally guilty?) "I personally am convinced that I am ill."

Szewczyk ultimately concluded that P. suffered from a genuine case of manic depression and that his mental capacity was sufficiently diminished to mitigate his criminal culpability. His crimes, Szewczyk explained,

> are the typical forms of criminality associated with the hypomanic, i.e., he tends toward pathological states, elevated moods, disinhibition, and pathologically determined sexual impulsivity leading to actions such as the ones he committed here. Dr. P. still partly had the appropriate determination and willpower to resist his disinhibitions. The fact that he did not do this is, in our view, due to the fact that the girls offered no real resistance or, at the very least, some form of resisting provocation. Given his form of personality and his pathological state, genuine, true resistance in all likelihood would have led to the accused breaking off his attempts. . . . [T]he man's chief guilt lies in the fact that he abused the medical examination situation and thus gravely undermined the trust of at least the patient who goes to a physician for the first time in hope of assistance.

Szewczyk's assessment is remarkable on a number of counts. Chief among them is the fact that he places a good deal of the responsibility for P.'s actions on the women themselves. His train of thinking in this regard is a bit veiled, but his other comments indicate his belief that P.'s moral conscience as a doctor would have been piqued had the women made any serious effort at resisting. In short, Szewczyk expects that P.'s professional ethos would have kicked in. Instead, P.'s hypomanic state betrayed his sense of duty, and it was this betrayal of the responsibility of his position as a doctor that Szewczyk considered the real violation. He ultimately recommended that P. be transferred to a nursing home and banned from having any more female patients, thus treating the man's conduct as little more than a breach of a professional code of conduct.

Thoroughly inattentive to the psychological effects of the discrepancy in power between an older, established physician and a young, female patient and to how this might have had an effect on the women's purported acquiescence, Szewczyk applied his training in social psychology solely toward understanding P.'s behavior. It is hard not to read Szewczyk's appraisal in this case as a reflection of professional sympathy for a colleague of similar stature. At the same time, his appraisal also demonstrates the extent to which a forensic physician's bias toward accepted clinical authority could leave him unaccustomed to thinking more deeply about the effects of crime on its female victims. If it was society's task to civilize and tame the primitive passions of men like P., then, according to Szewczyk, women also needed to play a preemptive role in that collective enterprise.

Sex Offenders and Sexual Deviance in the Seventies and Eighties

The Banning of Castration

Hans Szewczyk proved instrumental in expanding the reach of psychiatry and psychology within East German criminal justice. In particular, he and his colleagues at the Humboldt University successfully advocated granting forensic examiners a broader mandate. No longer was the job of examining psychiatrists limited to the evaluation of a suspect's mental competency.[77] Instead, through social prognosis, the expert was now to be understood as the first instance of correction. The forensic examiner, as two psychologists explained it in 1972, needed, first, to distinguish those social circumstances that reinforced deviant behavior from those that might curb it in a particular individual and, second, to point out positive and negative forms of reinforcement that were likely to succeed in changing the person's character.[78]

As noted in the previous chapter, the human sciences emerged from the 1960s having won the recognition of party and criminal justice officials.[79] But as we have seen, there were factors limiting what science and medicine could do within East German penology. This was especially so in the case of castration.

Early on in postwar eastern Germany, ethical, legal, and scientific reasons were all cited for rejecting the use of castration on sex offenders. Already on 8

January 1946, the Soviet Military Administration in Germany formally revoked the July 1933 sterilization law that had provided a legal underpinning for compulsory reproductive surgeries. In 1950, East German health officials turned down the request of psychiatrists to castrate a "feebleminded" homosexual man in custody, "since homosexuality cannot be significantly reduced or eliminated by castration."[80] Records show that a number of psychiatrists and parents of sex offenders were eager to see the operation performed on those in their charge. But the Ministry of Justice insisted, as in a 1956 case involving a thirty-eight-year-old mentally disabled man convicted of accosting a child, that operations could only be performed in order to save a patient's life or to treat a life-threatening illness.[81]

Interestingly enough, though, the matter was never definitively settled by the courts in the GDR. As a result, during the 1960s and 1970s, a small but steady stream of sex offenders continued to request castrations as a way of treating their criminal impulses.[82] This led the Ministry of Health to solicit the opinions of psychiatrists and clinic directors about the operation, beginning around 1970. Most considered the procedure an effective therapeutic tool for mitigating the relative strength of a man's sex drive. By 1975, the ministry was voicing its support for the voluntary castration of sex offenders, but only in cases where all other forms of rehabilitation promised no signs of success and when the convict gave his explicit consent.[83] Still, the matter continued to be debated among health care officials, with a number of experts expressing concerns about the extent to which a convicted sex offender's consent could ever be seen as "voluntary."[84]

A new solution to the ethical problems posed by surgical castration seemed to be possible, however, after the antiandrogen Androcur (a brand name for cyproterone acetate) made its appearance in the sixties and seventies. Often referred to as a form of reversible chemical castration due to its inhibiting effects on the male libido, Androcur was first developed in 1961 and tested on men in 1966. It was then introduced in East Germany at clinics in Berlin, Dresden, and Leipzig in 1973. Androcur was promoted as a treatment for directly reducing sex drive and, thus, inhibiting the impulse to commit new sexual crimes.[85] During the 1970s, patients were typically given a daily dose of one hundred to two hundred milligrams, and within two to four weeks, both libido and sexual potency were strongly reduced. Over the course of the seventies, the drug was increasingly coupled with psychotherapy.[86] Yet, despite its reversibility, experts in forensic medicine remained adamant that Androcur should only be used on a voluntary basis.[87]

The Emergence of New Perspectives

The enthusiasm over Androcur reflected a growing receptiveness among East German experts toward new, internationally accepted forms of treatment for sex offenders. Admittedly, Karl Leonhard's pessimistic views about psychotherapy's impact on sexual disorders—he held that only frigidity and psychogenic impotence could be effectively treated—continued to enjoy some currency into the early 1970s.[88] By and large, however, Leonhard's atavistic notion of sexual disorders made way for multidimensional perspectives stressing environmental factors, the subjective experience of "deviants," and the need to take into account the counterproductive effects of prison on behavior.[89] By the 1980s, specialists were regularly reporting on the successful use of aversion and behavioral therapies, cognitive therapy, group therapy, and social pedagogy on a range of sexual "deviants."[90]

As Herzog and Evans have observed, the last two decades of the GDR witnessed an unprecedented broadening of both professional and lay discussions about sexuality, the beginnings of which began in the late 1960s.[91] Serving mostly as a science of social hygiene and family planning, the field of sexology underwent a renaissance similar to other human sciences in the wake of new family legislation in 1966. The establishment of treatment-oriented centers for marriage and sexual counseling (160 in 1967) gave East German sexology an institutional anchor for both research and therapeutic application.[92] Psychologists, psychiatrists, physicians, and pedagogues quickly began using these new facilities to conduct surveys about sexual attitudes, behaviors, and problems within the East German population, eventually culminating in Peter Hesse's three-volume handbook *Sexology: Sex, Human, Society*, published over the years 1974–78.[93]

For the general population, the new East German sexology generally reached them through government educational initiatives and was perhaps little distinguishable from other party efforts aimed at promoting the development of a responsible and healthy socialist citizenry.[94] For specialists in forensic science and medicine, however, sexology offered yet another empirical tool, alongside psychological testing and victimology, for reimagining deviance. Beginning around 1970, researchers increasingly adopted a multidimensional approach to sexual deviance and were less drawn to identifying the ostensibly stable features of criminal personalities. Disorders, offenders, and victims of crime all became objects of investigation aimed at disaggregating their dynamics, experiences, and histories.[95] Victimological studies moved the focus toward the interactions between and interpersonal relationships of victims and their offenders, in the hope of identifying those factors predisposing one to becoming a victim or perpetrator of a sex crime.[96] At the same time, the growing emphasis on interpersonal relationships led scholars such as Paul Fehlow, Hans-H. Fröhlich, Eckhard Littmann, and Joachim Morgner to treat behavior like rape, exhibitionism, and pedophilia no longer as the result of abnormal sexualities but, rather, as the consequence of unique constellations of mostly exogenous factors in a perpetrator's life (e.g., a broken home or a history of sexual rejection).[97] In the words of one leading researcher at the time, when considering the exhibitionist, "the exhibition as sexually primitive behavior should be seen less as a transgression or 'deviation' . . . than as a unsuccessful step toward the norm," an absurdly flawed attempt at making contact with a partner.[98]

By the 1980s, East German researchers were well on their way toward establishing a new, less pathologizing concept of sexuality and sex offenders. Earlier forensic psychiatrists and psychologists had been drawn to a delinquency model using a simple casework approach and seeking the truth about the sex criminal "inside" the male sex offender, in his sexual drives and instincts. Now these same kinds of experts relied on testing methods aimed at measuring the offender's cognitive skills, interpersonal styles, and recurrent ways of thinking. The results of batteries of tests exploring multiple variables at once could be graphically depicted and used to compare offenders. In this instance, the truth of sex criminality was to be found in patterns or clusters of responses that could then be compared to standardized results.

In the process, a new, more decentered image of the sex offender emerged. This one was "flatter." Less interested in plumbing the depths of character, it offered a less essentializing view of the human subject. No longer seen as the inner core of a person, personality was treated as the convenient shorthand for the sum and form of the subject's interactions and habits. This approach opened up new possibilities for acknowledging the relative normality and heterogeneity of sex offenders. As Eckhard Littmann, a forensic psychiatrist at the Charité psychiatric clinic, put it bluntly in 1985, "Sexually delinquent behavior in the overwhelming majority of cases should be considered a behavioral deviation lying within the range of normal variation and not equivalent to illness or a pathology."[99] As the behavior of perpetrators began to be treated less as symptoms, the sexuality attributed to them also changed. Sexuality could now take on new meaning as "a social and communicative phenomenon."[100] In this way, the sex offender's problem was relocated, situated not in an abnormal sexual drive but, instead, in a diminished ability to express sexual desires in socially appropriate ways.

Conclusions

Examining the role played by American psychiatry in the treatment of sexual criminals following World War II, Simon Cole has argued that one does not see evidence of an ever-widening medicalization or psychopathologization of sex offenders. Rather, while psychiatric knowledge and practitioners were prominent in the criminal justice system during the 1950s and 1960s, the period since the late 1970s has seen a "retreat of psychiatry from the diagnosis and treatment of sex offenders and the ceding of the field to rival, nonmedical, professional groups."[101] That we can see some similar trends in the GDR at this time testifies not only to the fact that the human sciences in East Germany were relatively open to international trends from both sides of the iron curtain but also to the fact that political ideology alone cannot account for its handling of sex offenders there.

Throughout the first two and a half decades of the GDR, however, experts were wedded to medicine to explain the behavior of sex offenders, much as they were when considering other kinds of criminals. Whether one assumed, like Karl Leonhard, that deviant sexual desires were the manifestation of an underdeveloped character structure or, like Hans Szewczyk, that sex offenders were victims of a deficient personality structure aggravated by an equally inadequate upbringing, researchers and clinicians continued to see the perpetrator as a pathological delinquent. As such, his or her chief failing was an arrested psychological development, a "moral feeblemindedness" expressed in the form of a sexual retardation and primitiveness.

Gerhard Feix helped to show how this psychopathological line of thinking could be integrated with Marxism-Leninism through the idiom of evolutionary development. The male sex offender's purported inhibited development, his deviation "from the normal social path," represented a regressive immaturity and backwardness. Similar to some of the girls accusing them, the lack of maturity on the part of male sex criminals was not taken as cause for assuming their moral innocence. Instead, sexual underdevelopment was framed as sedition, a threat to the very foundations of socialist society.

What occurred over the course of the 1960s and 1970s, then, was the mutual superimposition of psychiatry's psychopathological and developmental view of abnormal sexuality over Marxism-Leninism's linear notion of the development of a socialist society and vice versa. In effect, the contribution that the East German human sciences made to the study of sex crime was to comprehend the danger posed by such offenses as a threat both to the individual development of young people and to the phylogenetic or evolutionary development of socialist sexual society. In this sense, East German criminal justice experts treated their interventions as attempts at civilizing primitive, developmentally regressive men. This civilizing mission not only called on the long intellectual history of Western conceptions of savagery.[102] It was also indebted to prevailing evolutionary explanations of human behavior, which treated expressions of attachment and affection as instinctual. The study and treatment of sex offenders thus represented nothing short of an effort to establish East Germany as the paragon of a healthy, naturally humane, and loving society—as the embodiment of civilization itself.

By the mid-1970s, forensic psychologists had arrived at a very distinctive concept of sexual selfhood: an evolutionary notion of the person as a "biopsychosocial creature,"[103] stressing consistency of personality, stability in lifestyle and interpersonal relations, personal growth, and a maturing into socialist values and attitudes. The ideal sexual man was therefore a man who treated his heterosexuality as a controlled project—a man able to understand the proper limits of his desires, to govern his drives, and to direct his behavior toward socially progressive goals. As victims and potential victims, girls and women were cast in a role analogous to one the party awarded to society as a whole—that of naive, fragile objects all too easily corrupted and thus warranting vigilant protection. Only in the last decade of the regime did a new perspective emerge among forensic specialists to challenge this ideal: the notion of sex as a form of communication and self-expression.

CHAPTER 5

Democratizing Punishment in the Federal Republic

Like its eastern counterpart, West Germany confronted the problem of crime while having to adapt to a radically new set of circumstances following World War II. Not only did the atrocities committed under the National Socialists call into question the legal legacy left behind by the Third Reich, but unconditional surrender meant granting the occupying forces of the United States, Great Britain, and France unprecedented influence over criminal justice affairs. Even after the founding of an independent Federal Republic of Germany (FRG) in May 1949, researchers, clinicians, and administrators involved in crime policy and prison affairs were constantly being drawn toward western European and Anglo-American ideas and methods. The long process of internationalizing law and legal science, which had begun in the nineteenth century, continued, but this time it was necessarily skewed by the omnipresence of the Cold War.

In contrast to the USSR and the GDR, the Western allies and West Germany proved less inclined to distance themselves from the legal precedents and personnel that rose to prominence during the years 1933–45. Numerous Nazi-era judges, scholars, and civil servants retained their posts and came to play important roles in the country's legal and penal reforms. Criminal biology continued to exercise considerable influence on criminology and penology throughout the 1950s, and the FRG retained and even expanded on criminal sanctions inherited from the Third Reich, such as preventive detention and castration.

Nevertheless, despite some marked continuities, correctional rehabilitation in the Federal Republic underwent its own reform. As West German policy makers and social scientists attempted to reestablish the country's international reputation, they were drawn ever more to accommodate the thinking of their new Western allies. Similar to the role played by the Soviet Union within the GDR, exemplars and innovations from the United States served as models for experts in the FRG during the fifties and sixties, according to which correc-

TABLE 6. Number of Prisoners and Detainees in the Federal Republic, 1955–89

Year	Number of Adult Prisoners	Adults Committed to Psychiatric Facility on Basis of Executive Measure	Adults Committed to Alcohol or Drug Abuse Treatment Facility on Basis of Executive Measure	Adults Committed to Workhouse on Basis of Executive Measure	Adults Committed to Preventive Detention
1955		508	191	681	163
1956		493	166	531	176
1957		469	183	602	188
1958		429	223	589	208
1959		448	214	641	230
1960		459	229	565	210
1961	40,607	437	246	530	232
1962	40,809	450	247	519	225
1963	42,581	426	237	459	204
1964	42,876	430	252	485	206
1965	44,836	355	228	329	213
1966	41,841	357	171	397	236
1967	43,439	297	288	270	239
1968	43,767	323	239	227	268
1969	42,279	300	192	93	219
1970	32,038	257	164		110
1971	28,960	295	189		116
1972	29,176	303	183		114
1973	31,269	305	155		84
1974	32,300	310	174		69
1975	30,397	282	209		52
1976	33,253	335	286		60
1977	35,386	311	325		51
1978	36,899	314	377		35
1979	37,692	297	472		44
1980	37,745	304	499		41
1981	38,819	324	446		57
1982	40,911	355	470		38
1983	43,287	361	463		27
1984	44,642	380	465		36
1985	44,390	366	489		39
1986	41,746	354	505		40
1987	44,903				1,190
1988	44,804				1,071
1989	43,900				1,068

Source: Data from Statistisches Bundesamt, *Statistisches Jahrbuch für die Bundesrepublik Deutschland, 1962–1991* (Stuttgart: W. Kohlhammer, 1962–91).

Note: The number of adult prisoners is from either 31 March or 31 December in any given year. The figures for 1987–89 equal the total number of all prisoners. The category "adults committed to workhouse on basis of executive measure" no longer existed after 1 September 1969. The figures for 1987–89 for adults committed to preventive detention equal the total number in preventive and other forms of special detention.

tional rehabilitation was reimagined as a form of participatory counseling in democratic citizenship. By the mid-1970s, many in West Germany were making the case that the pupil had now outpaced the teacher in realizing the dream of creating a truly therapeutic prison system.

Economic woes in the late 1970s and the 1980s raised questions about the feasibility of such an ambitious agenda. Fiscal bottom lines brought with them a growing emphasis on efficacy and efficiency. The enthusiasm of earlier reformers was increasingly muted by scientific and administrative auditors, who raised doubts about the claims made on behalf of correctional rehabilitation.

Reform and Correction in the Late Forties and Early Fifties

Just as eastern Germany was occupied by Soviet troops and fell under the jurisdiction of Soviet military administration, western Germany found itself occupied and under the authority of American, British, and French militaries during the years 1945–49. Authorities across the western occupied zones faced an array of challenges in maintaining law and order. Chief among them was rampant crime. In 1949, Karl Bader, the chief prosecutor in Freiburg, provided a sociological description of postwar criminality that painted a bleak picture. In 1946 and 1947, the general crime rate was around 500–600 percent higher than that of 1938. The number and intensity of sex offenses, murders, and robberies in particular, he reported, rose markedly, the latter often being committed by gangs of home-invading men. Young men and women appeared to be especially drawn to these criminal gangs.[1] Responsibility for the postwar escalation in crime tended be directed at widespread anomie, itself prompted by mass destruction, economic misery, and loss of the rule of law during the Third Reich.[2]

The criminal justice system faced its share of problems as well. Occupying authorities were often unclear as to whether and which German laws remained in force. In the British zone, for instance, prosecutors in late 1945 declared themselves unsure of what to do with preventive detainees left over from Nazi Germany, after hearing rumors that the military government was releasing them all.[3] Officials eventually clarified the issue in the summer of 1946, declaring the institution to be "much older" than National Socialism, "not to have been an expression of National Socialist thought," and therefore still valid.[4] A shortage of space, however, made it difficult for administrators to find facilities with the appropriate balance of security and correctional elements to house the detainees.[5] A lack of housing and staff for the criminally mentally ill in the British zone created similar problems, eventually leading the military government to develop plans for building its own criminal justice asylum for five hundred patients.[6]

Most important to the future of the West German correctional imagination was the occupying powers' insistence on reorienting the German penal system around rehabilitation. The U.S. military government, in particular, gave the rehabilitative impulse a legal form, in the shape of Control Council Directive 19 (12 November 1945), which formally made the "rehabilitation and reeducation" of prisoners the principal purpose of incarceration.[7] Directive 19 was the product of discussions between the four occupying powers and was billed as a return to the reform ideals of the Weimar years. While the American, British, and French prison administrations differed in style and emphasis at times, all three included German officials, who were subordinate to the allies' legal departments. The American and British administrations, in particular, sought to involve German experts in the reconstruction of the country's prison system. To that end, from March 1946 until August 1948, German authorities toured penal facilities in the United States and the United Kingdom, and representatives from all three countries held a series of meetings to agree on basic principles and structures.[8]

The allies' emphasis on penal reform encouraged those who wished to return to the rehabilitative ideas circulating prior to the Nazi seizure of power, such as members of the Working Group for the Reform of the Prison System. First formed in 1923, the working group's postwar members included returned-from-exile psychologist Curt Bondy (1894–1972), penologist and warden Helga Einsele (1910–2005), criminologist Rudolf Sieverts, and criminal law professor Eberhard Schmidt. After holding a series of meetings between September 1948 and August 1951, the group issued and circulated a number of resolutions and guidelines for the reform of the penal system. Throughout, their demands focused on themes that could be traced back to Franz von Liszt and the modern school of law: social-pedagogical training of prison staff, psychotherapeutic training for prison physicians, classification and institutional assignment of all convicts based on personality features, and the free exchange of ideas and experiences with foreign counterparts.[9] The working group and others also called for a thorough reform of the criminal code, something that had not been done since 1871.[10]

By 1950, the West German prison system had hardly succeeded in reorienting itself around the rehabilitation and reintegration of convicts. For example, the response to a call for all Lower Saxony prisons to provide information about the kinds of "intellectual and mental care" being offered to their inmates at the end of 1949 left the chief prosecutor there flabbergasted. Facilities were largely limiting themselves to playing records or hosting lectures via slide shows, with prisoners playing the role of passive listeners. The chief prosecutor berated his subordinates, writing to them the following summer, "With all these efforts I am missing the necessary planning and the attempt to build a sensible infrastructure for general correctional work."[11]

Still, a change in language, expectations, and attitude was being registered, one especially noticeable in the contributions to the newly founded (1950) journal *Zeitschrift für Strafvollzug* (Journal for the penal system). Less scholarly than its criminological and legal counterparts, the journal was intended to serve as a forum where those working in the prison system could keep track of trends and reflect on experiences. In this journal, much of the parlance that had stamped correctional thought during the Third Reich was muted or took on a new tone, though the specter of National Socialism was never far away.

A piece written by Walther Buhl and the responses to it offer a telling example. Buhl, who later became the head of the Hamburg Police Presidium (1958–64), also served as a regional judicial official during the Third Reich. After the war, he took on the unique job of transforming the former concentration camp at Neuengamme into a model prison in 1948. The construction of a "model facility of humaneness and modern incarceration with an international reputation," Buhl reportedly explained, was intended to "extinguish the gruesome horror of the camp."[12]

Buhl appears to have similarly tried to extinguish traces of Nazi-era abuse—unsuccessfully—in a reflective article published in 1952, on the correctional prison. Buhl could not help but invoke many of the same goals and values that had been informing correctional thinking for decades. Prison, he contended, should awaken the convict's "consciousness of responsibility toward the community and family" and should teach the convict a new sense of self-restraint, self-mastery, and joy in work. Relying on a military metaphor, he asked, "How do we reach the inner workings of people? How do we blow up the armor of defiance, contempt, bitterness, hate, desolation, indifference, despair, and insecurity that envelops the soul of the prisoner?"[13] Buhl's answer to these questions expressed the need for new correctional methods rooted in psychology and pedagogy. The traditional job titles for staff, modeled after the police and military, needed to be replaced, he insisted, and accommodated to the "recovery and resocialization of those socially ill individuals entrusted to us."[14]

Buhl's comments elicited numerous responses from prison staff, who, like Buhl, stepped gingerly around the recent past while arguing for a new beginning. A guard for a work detail at a women's prison, for instance, spoke of the importance of creating an "atmosphere" of trust through gestures of respect and friendliness toward prisoners.[15] An administrator at a youth facility, who likewise emphasized the importance of creating the right atmosphere, argued that the "modern" juvenile prison could not do without the services of a full-time psychologist and a doctor trained in adolescent psychiatry.[16] A chief inspector in Münster reminded readers that all attempts aimed at helping those who fall on hard times were ultimately rooted in "love and empathy."[17]

Others were more willing to make less oblique reference to the legacy of National Socialism. Frankfurt medical officer Joseph Strüder criticized Buhl for being utopian and out of touch with reality (*wirklichkeitsfremd*), given the financial and spatial limitations facing West German prisons at the time. Moreover, Strüder continued, Buhl might hope to reform the inner workings of convicts, but the state and national community (*Volksgemeinschaft*) ask only for an end to their criminal behavior. Citing an article he wrote in 1933, Strüder deplored the waste of time and money implicit in Buhl's plans.

> It contradicts the thinking of eugenics (eugenics is not the achievement of National Socialism), in that it provides better and more for the less valuable person than for someone of full value [*Vollwertige*]. Moreover, it deprives the people [*Volk*] of their right to existence, when it pays all-too-much attention to the less valuable. Whoever among those entrusted to us are capable of and willing to reform should receive our full assistance, but we cannot waste our efforts uselessly.[18]

A prison instructor in Bremen saw things differently. Lamenting what he considered to be the overemphasis on community integration in penology, he warned not to lose sight of individualism.

> This should mean that also the weak personality must appreciate that a unique self [*eigenes Ich*] lives inside it. One must be careful that this [personality] does not become a weak member of society. That can happen all too easily when we simply let impulsive inmates live back in the community. . . . So many people have given up their own self to a wicked society that it has virtually become an epidemic.[19]

Observing Democratically: Inmate Personality Assessment in the 1950s

Writing in 1955, a senior correctional officer working at the Kassel-Wehlheiden Prison observed, "New general, professional, and criminological knowledge has changed the standing of personnel. Earlier, the inmate was a 'criminal' [*Verbrecher*], a term that is already disappearing. It has changed and has been replaced by expressions like lawbreaker, social, and similar ones." The same was true of how prison staff were being encouraged to think about the causes of criminality: "We are also seeing the significance of social circumstances—like poor upbringing, loss of parents, development—in which society recognizes its own culpability for creating offenders. . . . This is influencing and changing the professional interests of personnel, something that finds its expression in a new attitude toward the personality of the prisoner."[20]

To be sure, this writing represented an idealized picture of the attitudes of the prison workforce.[21] Nevertheless, during the 1950s, it was impossible to ignore that virtually everyone involved in the work of criminal justice was being called on to consider new ways of thinking about criminals and convicts. While legal scholars debated just what kind of "image of man" (*Menschenbild*) West Germany's legal order should assume,[22] those working directly with convicts were drawn increasingly to such fields as developmental psychology, psychometrics, social psychology, and personality psychology. This included prison chaplains, who proved remarkably receptive to the methods and findings of the human sciences.[23]

In Hamburg and Lower Saxony, for instance, criminal justice officials established criminal psychology centers soon after the war ended (in 1947 and 1950, respectively). Hamburg's Department of Criminal Psychology was especially pioneering in its approach and ambitions. The department replaced the defunct Nazi-era Criminal Biological Data Collection Center. Historian Imanuel Baumann has stressed the continuity of leadership in the department's postwar administration, but this emphasis neglects the extent to which the new institution marginalized criminal biology.[24] As applied psychologist and director Hans Krüger (d. 1959) explained in 1956, the old criminal biology center proved no longer tenable. "The change in worldview as well as scientific-methodological considerations," he explained, "made it apparent that a new orientation was needed for research on prisoners."[25]

Rehabilitation was the orientation point for the work being done both in Krüger's unit in Hamburg and at the Criminological Investigation Center in Hanover. The goal, Krüger explained, was to give prison staff a "a penal-pedagogically oriented picture of the prisoner's psyche" while also providing judges with useful information to help in their assessment of the convict's personality.[26] In both Hamburg and Hanover, however, personality assessment differed considerably from the way it had been conducted before 1945. Elsewhere, Krüger had warned against essentializing inmate behavior, noting that it often was a response to immediate "penal-psychological" influences.[27] Hamburg and Hanover psychologists observed prisoner reactions to experimental situations; tracked their expressions and social interactions; administered a battery of standardized tests to identify aptitudes, intelligence, and personality traits; and offered psychotherapeutic services to those needing them.[28] Criminal psychologists in Munich and Berlin echoed the view that the behavior of convicts should be understood as varied and contextual, that deterrence was counterproductive, and that psychotherapeutic counseling was essential.[29]

Here, then, was a new psychological outlook—in contrast to the earlier, psychiatric one—on the convict's personality, a point of view that was being applied in other social arenas within postwar West Germany.[30] From this perspective, selfhood took shape and was revealed interpersonally and interactively, with the individual using personal resources to respond situationally to changing circumstances. The psychologist's job involved not only evaluation but also offering supportive and informed guidance. This emerging approach, which drew less from medicine and the life sciences than from experimental psychology and diagnostic testing, represented a deliberate turn toward American sociology and social psychology.[31] As such, the new psychological approach toward prisoners was mostly unfamiliar territory for German penology. Indeed, with only 112 trained psychotherapists working in the three western zones of Germany in 1948,[32] a new cadre of trained specialists was needed, while older staff required retraining.

It is little wonder, then, that training and retraining were a chief focus for criminal justice officials in the early fifties. In Hesse in 1953, the state budgeted for twenty-one new prison caseworkers (*Fürsorger*), trained in social pedagogy, to help counsel inmates about their personal affairs.[33] At the same time, both psychology and sociology figured prominently in the establishment of new training programs for police and prison staff.[34] Since Bonn issued no national mandates, changes in training and continuing education for those working in prisons were left up to individual federal states. While states differed in the length and location of instruction, most curricula in use by mid-decade focused on introducing prison officers to the fields of psychology, pedagogy, sociology, social work, and psychiatry. Visits to criminal trials, orphanages, detention centers, and mental hospitals were commonly included.[35]

The reason behind this shift toward the testing sciences and the helping professions was clear: reforming the reform of convicts presupposed the reform of prison staff. All this was set in motion by two important developments. First, within the international community, legal experts began to distance themselves from criminal biology and punitive sanctions. Organizations like the United Nations, the International Congress of Criminologists, and the International Congress of Social Defense began embracing the idea of humanitarian minimum standards for prisoners and sought to explain criminal behavior by referencing social neglect and low self-esteem.[36] Second and more directly, passage on 4 August 1953 of the Third Criminal Code Amendment gave German judges the ability, for the first time, to grant offenders parole or conditional release, a change that considerably widened the range of cases for which a personality assessment was necessary.[37] In this way, during the 1950s, a new emphasis was placed on gaining insight into the personality of inmates in order to more effectively promote their rehabilitation.

The term for this enterprise was *personality research*, and it was imagined as an eminently collaborative one, requiring rigorous coordination of attendants, instructors, foremen, pastors, doctors, psychologists, and administrators. Proponents insisted that personality research involved more than simply appreciating the role of environmental factors in the lives of prisoners. It required that everyone working in prisons learn new ways of seeing, evaluating, and recording inmate behavior.

Prison psychologist Michael Gallmeier, working in the prison once made famous by Theodor Viernstein, laid out a three-stage process for classifying and prognosing convicts: observing the prisoner, assessing the information, and building a character profile. At each stage, Gallmeier cautioned, the observer needed to guard against drawing hasty or biased conclusions; for instance, he exhorted his readers to report only what they directly witnessed, to be self-reflective, not to get caught up in counting demerits, not to treat all behavior as symptomatic, not to be afraid to award a good prognosis, and to leave the final assessment open to later revision.[38] Expanding on Gallmeier's thoughts, another prison official insisted that the personality profile was something that was never "finished" (*fertig*) but, rather, needed to be constantly revised in the wake of new observations from a variety of perspectives.[39]

These prescriptions for observation represented nothing less than an attempt to institutionalize democratic ideals of tolerance in a postfascist society: respect for the plurality of individual experiences, recognition of difficult social predicaments, adopting self-limiting curbs on overreaching authority, and an acceptance of the life course as an ongoing project.[40] Even with that being the case, however, its reach was limited by circumstances. In fiscally strapped postwar Schleswig-Holstein, for example, there simply were no funds to hire scores of psychologists and pedagogues or to redesign forms. Instead, prisons there relied on Robert Schiedt's 1936 prognostic table and abstained from using personality tests, considering them overly subjective and scientifically unproven.[41]

Nevertheless, an ideal was being established according to which psychodiagnostic tests and trained observation were to be used in guiding and counseling inmates. The casework approach was formalized in the shape of a so-called "prison plan" (*Vollzugsplan*) for each convict. In the Hessian prison at Rockenberg, for instance, the prison plan involved assessing each inmate's "biomedical" and mental health, strengths, and weaknesses, through analysis of records, direct observation of and conversations with the prisoner, and test results.[42] In Mannheim Prison, developing an individual plan was envisioned as a four-step process that began at intake, with conversations between the inmate and a chaplain, a teacher, social workers, and a work supervisor. At the second stage—the "staff conference" (*Beamtenkonferenz*)—the convict met with supervisors, where his character, abilities, interests, interpersonal problems, and work detail were discussed. With good behavior, maintenance of an orderly cell, and a satisfactory work record, the prisoner advanced to the less-supervised, third stage and, finally, to the fourth stage, which served as a transition to release.[43]

By the end of the 1950s, voices of reform—coming first from the Western allies and then from the ranks of academics, regional officials, and prison staff—had succeeded in setting the groundwork for a new, psychologically oriented rehabilitation of convicts. Often without overtly referring to criminal biology or National Socialism, they called on the past, the international community, and an imagined future to inspire change, invoking the penal reform movement of the Weimar Republic, the standards of "civilized nations" (*Kulturnationen*), and the need for modernization.[44] Still, institutional change came only in a segmented and punctuated fashion, with some states, such as Hesse and Baden-Württemberg, pursuing the new agenda more aggressively than others, while living conditions and capacity varied.[45] Even in a reform-minded prison, such as the penal facility at Bruchsal in Baden-Württemberg, where around 30 percent of the inmates in 1955 had previously spent years in concentration camps during the Third Reich, the introduction of personality research and the prison plan did nothing to undercut the focus on prognosis. "The chief task," explained a member of the facility's governing board, "lies in separating the 'wheat' of those still likely to be corrigible from the 'chaff' of the incorrigible and to pave the way for the resocialization of the (former)."[46]

Reforming from Above: Experts and the Law, 1953–76

The Reform of the Criminal Code

In 1953, the Federal Republic took its first steps toward the ambitious reform of its criminal justice system, when Free Democrat (FDP) justice minister

Thomas Dehler began soliciting opinions from seventeen legal experts about making changes to the existing criminal code.[47] In the spring of the following year, Dehler's replacement, Fritz Neumayer (FDP), convened the first meeting of the Large Criminal Law Commission (Große Strafrechtskommission), comprised of Bundestag representatives, civil servants, judges, and legal experts.[48] Over the next fifteen years, the commission and its subcommittees debated and drafted changes intended to modernize criminal law in West Germany. Supported by a succession of federal ministers of justice from the major parties (CSU, 1957–61, 1965–66; FDP, 1961–65; CDU, 1965; SPD, 1966–81), the commission's work inspired a series of legal changes issued piecemeal, starting in June 1969 under the Grand Coalition and ending with the Prison Law of March 1976.

The major political parties generally sought different goals in the reform process. Christian Democrats and Christian Socials (CDU/CSU) mostly took a natural law approach and wished to maintain the punitive and incapacitating functions of punishment, while the Social Democrats (SPD) hoped to decriminalize things such as abortion and to establish rehabilitation as the principal goal of punishment. The FDP looked to find a way to unify the two-track system of criminal sanctions.[49] The results proved to be a victory for supporters of correctional rehabilitation and the expansion of preventive forms of detention.

As we have seen, a therapeutic concept of rehabilitation had been making its way into West German criminal justice without much central direction. Certainly, the policies of the Western allies set the process in motion, but by and large, correctional rehabilitation insinuated itself into the immediate postwar penal system at the initiative of state and local reformers. Most observers, however, believed that real reform could only come with changes at the national level. Officials in Bonn took on a more directive role in 1953, with the Youth Court Law and the Third Criminal Code Amendment of 4 August, which together mandated clinical diagnosis and treatment for an unprecedented number of young and adult offenders. But the establishment of an expert commission to consider the overhaul of the entire criminal justice system expressed the federal government's determination to play a leading role in reshaping a set of eighty-year-old institutions.

Taking on the administrative task of coordinating the commission's work were a number of legal experts, all of whom had been active and rose to prominence during the Third Reich.[50] Josef Schafheutle was head of the department of Criminal Law and Procedures within the Federal Ministry of Justice. Under the National Socialists, he had worked in the criminal law department of the Reich Ministry of Justice. Georg Schwalm, a former member of the National

Socialist German Workers' Party (NSDAP) and a squad leader in the Sturmabteilung (SA) from 1933, was especially involved in the reform of sex crime law in the FRG. Eduard Dreher (1907–96) had been a prosecutor for the Special Court in Innsbruck under the National Socialists, where he had prosecuted political opponents and advocated use of the death penalty. His career in the Federal Ministry of Justice spanned the years 1951–69, and he served as a chief counsel to the criminal law commission. One final key figure was Rudolf Sieverts (1903–80), a specialist in juvenile delinquency, who had taught at the University of Hamburg and had been coeditor, with Franz Exner, of the *Monatsschrift für Kriminalbiologie und Strafrechtsreform* during the Third Reich. Sieverts served as a member of the expert commission that had amended the juvenile criminal law in 1953, after which he was asked to take on a leading role in the criminal law commission as an advising expert, eventually becoming president of the justice ministry's Prison Commission in 1967. Sieverts helped ensure that members of the Working Group for the Reform of the Prison System took part in shaping the new West German criminal code.

The Criminal Sciences, Punishment, and Recidivism in the Fifties

One of the first things taken up by experts was consideration of the extent to which research from the criminal sciences could and should be used by lawmakers as they went about the work of law reform. In April 1953, Eduard Dreher asked a number of elder statesmen in criminology to say whether the criminal sciences could speak to the question of punishment and its effect. The retired law professor Wilhelm Sauer (1879–1962) responded that criminality, like society, was rapidly changing and that commensurately adjusting sentencing guidelines would require up-to-date and accurate diagnostic data. His concern, he added, was that the academic researchers working in the field were too few in number and did not do enough to disaggregate crime statistics.[51] The director of Cologne's Criminal Science Institute, Gotthold Bohne (1890–1957), also voiced reservations about a superficial reliance on existing statistics and spoke of the need for more American-style, collaborative case studies.[52] The controversial law professor Hellmuth von Weber (1893–1970), however, warned that clinical research about the mental effects of incarceration must "avoid degrading criminal human beings into objects of research and causing them new mental damage."[53]

By May 1955, justice official Alfons Wahl concluded that there was ample and reliable research on crime and punishment directly relevant to the work of the reform commission. Despite the fact that many—perhaps most—experts involved in advising the government had careers dating back to the Third Reich, the lesson taken away was that criminology's focus on criminal types over the previous decades was now misguided and should shift to the question of treatment. The "extremely diverse and individually and situationally contingent effects" of incarceration, Wahl noted, made it essential for any research in this area to be done collaboratively.[54]

The Large Criminal Law Commission went about its work by forming three smaller subcommissions to examine specific themes. Members prepared reports on specific topics, tracked international and domestic trends in criminal law, and met intermittently to discuss legal concepts, listen to presentations of outside speakers, and iron out the wording of drafts. One of the early topics considered was recidivism.[55]

Since the 1920s, German policy makers had been especially concerned about "habitual criminals," who had been shown to commit a disproportionately large share of overall crime. The issue was made especially timely by the fact that the Third International Congress on Criminology, held in 1955 in London, made recidivism its focus. Its five working groups qualified a number of the field's long-standing tenets, admitting that criminology had proven far better at describing the symptoms of crime than at identifying its causes. It concluded that recidivism needed to be located on a continuum of behavior and that the tool of social prognosis required further refinement.[56]

In the context of German legal reform, experts were asked to weigh in on two questions. How might the law distinguish between different groups of repeat offenders, and how might specific kinds of punishment and confinement be tailored to these groups? Social prognosis and the rehabilitation of convicts were inextricably bound up with both of these questions.

Sparking a great deal of discussion was a proposal from Rudolf Sieverts to conflate the concepts of the "repeat offender" (*Rückfalltäter*) and the "dangerous habitual criminal" (*Gewohnheitsverbrecher*) under the rubric of "the persistently recidivist" (*beharrlich Rückfälligen*) and to tie preventive detention to this new criminal type. Sieverts's suggestion was an attempt to free judges as much as possible from having to speculate about a convict's long-term psychological inclinations when the judges were deciding on indefinite detention. At the thirty-third meeting of the Large Criminal Law Commission, in October 1955, Eduard Dreher expressed misgivings, noting that a dangerous habitual criminal represented a particular kind of person, that a repeat offender was simply a "case of elevated guilt," and that the two should not be equated with one another.[57] Sieverts, however, expressed the concern of many on the commission that establishing an accused's "guilty way of life" (*Lebensfüh-*

rungsschuld) was impossible in practice. "I have repeatedly found that psychiatric experts themselves have declared their inability to distinguish between which personality elements in a perpetrator are guilty and which are not," he declared, adding, "If you want to work with a stiffer punishment, then, in my opinion, you should tie it to behavior."[58]

Law professor Hans-Heinrich Jescheck agreed with Sieverts and noted that, on average, West German courts committed only about one hundred individuals every year to preventive detention. He explained that judges who were anxious that they did not have enough insight into the convict's circumstances were reluctant to use this authority. To ensure greater use of preventive detention, he argued, criteria needed to be formalized and made objective, along the line of Sieverts's proposal.[59]

A representative from the Bavarian Justice Ministry begged to differ, defending the reliability of social prognosis. He recounted Bavaria's recent experience with preventive detainees. After the war, a number of them were amnestied, under the assumption that no one committed to preventive detention under the National Socialists should remain there. A small percentage proved to do just fine, he explained, but most committed new offenses and landed right back in preventive detention. Arguing that it was therefore wrong to say "that no definitive prognosis about future conduct can be established during imprisonment," the representative concluded, "Unfortunately, the negative prognoses of prisons are virtually 100 percent right."[60]

This debate took another twenty years to resolve, but eventually courts were instructed that their sentencing decisions should take into consideration the "effects that the sentence is likely to have on the future life of the perpetrator" as well as "the perpetrator's previous life, his personal and economic circumstances."[61] The issue of defining recidivism and its legal consequences provides some insight into the many continuities across and within debates about law reform. Legally, the issue seemed to reduce down to whether Germany's two-track system was capable of establishing a consistent legal definition of recidivism. More broadly, however, early and subsequent discussions testified to lawmakers' commitment to considering certain types of people and lives as categorically different from others and thus warranting different treatment. Just how this difference should be determined and characterized was where consensus broke down.

So while the Swiss criminal law scholar Erwin Frey (1906–81) remained wedded to psychopathological explanations for recidivism, drawing on epidemiology to diagnose criminal prodromes among young people, Hellmuth Mayer (1895–1980) drew his inspiration from sociology. He rejected the use of prognostic tables and the attribution of character traits and sought, instead, to identify patterns in the life course of delinquents.[62] The perennial question of the value of social prognosis was never settled. Instead, West German specialists largely accepted that, as one analysis on the state of criminal prognosis in 1960 put it, risk assessment required an interdisciplinary and comprehensive assessment (*Gesamtwürdigung*) based on "criminal-biological and psychological criteria as well as mass statistical findings on crime, with the support of intuition, i.e., knowledge of human nature."[63]

Psychiatry, Psychology, and the Debate over Diminished Capacity, 1954–69

While legal scholars and criminologists dominated the discussion about recidivism, psychiatrists played the pivotal role in negotiations over how to take psychopathologies into account in the new criminal code. Like other legal systems rooted in the notion of free will, modern German law had always treated diminished or lack of mental capacity as a mitigating circumstance in criminal cases. Since 1934, a person was determined to be lacking in or of diminished criminal responsibility (*Schuldfähigkeit*) if, at the time of the crime itself, "due to a disturbance of consciousness, a pathological disturbance of mental activity, or a mental weakness," the individual was unable or significantly disabled in "recognizing the wrongness of the act or in acting on this knowledge."[64] Under the Habitual Offender Law of 1933, those meeting these criteria were not to be released but, instead, were to be placed in a mental hospital, a home for the mentally disabled, or a substance abuse facility and were also eligible for preventive detention.

Since the late nineteenth century, psychiatrists and welfare authorities had complained that the way in which diminished capacity was written into the law did nothing to stop the chronic misplacement of delinquents, criminals, and patients. The reform of the criminal code was believed to offer an opportunity to solve this problem once and for all. Instead, however, the wording of criteria for diminished capacity proved to be one of the most contentious issues taken up in the reform process. Often pitting psychiatrists, psychologists, legal scholars, and politicians at odds with one another, debate especially revealed escalating tensions between psychiatrists, trained in medicine, and psychologists, trained in social science.

While a variety of issues involving diminished capacity divided experts, most of those issues boiled down to the question of how best to handle certain borderline cases. As a committee of the German Chambers of Lawyers determined in the summer of 1956, these marginal cases primarily involved "the affective bouts of psychopaths, neuroses, hereditary conditions (e.g., structural homosexuals), questions of sexual orientation and abnormal sexual drives, deviance and deterioration of personality (senility), drug addiction, etc."[65] The troubling question facing the Large Criminal Law Commission was whether these states of "character deviance, degenerative personality," and "compulsiveness" should be recognized as possible grounds for exculpation. Put more simply, should the law accept that a number of psychopaths, neurotics, homosexuals, and even pedophiles met the criteria for diminished capacity and therefore could not be held responsible for their crimes?

In the years 1955–56, the commission consulted the opinions of a host of prominent "elder statesmen" in West Germany psychiatry, including Konrad Ernst (1903–97), Robert Gaupp (1870–1953, posthumously), Hans Walter Gruhle (1880–1958), Ernst Kretschmer (1888–1964), Vult Ziehen (1899–1975), and Kurt Böhmer (1895–1959). Their reports largely reiterated concerns dating back to earlier in the century: namely, that the notion of diminished capacity needed to be formulated in such a way as to limit its application to repeat and sex offenders and to ensure that disruptive and asocial psychopaths were not committed to psychiatric facilities. When the Society of German Neurologists and Psychiatrists submitted its official position on the matter in early September 1955, it maintained that the key to limiting the inflation of cases was to insist on the proven presence of a pathological (i.e., biological) state.[66]

A change to the intellectual landscape of postwar Germany, however, gave rise to a new set of worries for clinicians. The return of émigré psychologists to the Federal Republic following the war, among other factors, sparked a resurgence of psychoanalysis there.[67] One of the leading and most well-known figures in this renaissance was the analyst Alexander Mitscherlich (1908–82). An outspoken critic of National Socialism, he proved effective in helping to cast psychoanalysis as one of the foremost sources of clinical, social, and cultural criticism in postwar West Germany.[68]

In September 1955, Mitscherlich submitted an opinion paper, on behalf of the German Society for Psychotherapy and Depth Psychology, to the Large Criminal Law Commission. In it, Mitscherlich raised questions about the normative assumption of free will implicit in section 51 of the criminal code. Recognition of the decisive role of unconscious, psychodynamic processes in human thoughts, feelings, and actions, he contended, meant that the idea of diminished capacity could not be limited to purely medical indications of illness. Instead, in any relevant case, the life history and early childhood development of the accused needed to be investigated in order to uncover the extent to which actions were being driven by overwhelming compulsions, emotions, or symbolic expressions.[69]

Mitscherlich's insistence on the need for a biographical approach to clinical cases reflected his more general rejection of objective medicine's attachment to physiological explanation.[70] Other experts from the psychological sciences joined him in criticizing what they viewed as the law's overreliance on a strictly medical perspective on mental capacity. Speaking for the German Society for Psychology, psychologist Friedrich Sander noted that restricting mental incapacity to pathological states ignored the fact "that there can also be exceptional states in mentally normal human beings, in which the capacity to understand and act is so lacking that there is no longer any criminal culpability."[71] Psychiatrists might well prefer bracketing the role of things like emotions, he added, but the state of psychology made a change in criteria essential.

Over the next five years, a subcommittee on diminished capacity held a series of meetings in which they considered virtually every term in section 51. The general consensus of the group was that the new law should retain its combined method of referring to both biological and psychological indicators for diminished capacity (though a somatic etiology was to be presumed). Psychiatrist Werner Villinger and legal scholar Eberhard Schmidt both defended the idea that the law should recognize only three types of states as exculpatory: pathological processes, abnormalities (*Abartigkeit*), and temporary states of unconsciousness.[72] By 1960, debate centered on two proposals. One referred to diminished states of mind resulting from pathological processes or "congenital or acquired severely abnormal mental disturbance," while another referred to pathological processes or those "due to an equivalent mental abnormality."[73]

The new formulations were intended to address the reservations expressed by psychologists and psychiatrists. Yet they proved unsuccessful in satisfying hard-liners in both communities. Psychiatrist and subcommittee member Kurt Schneider (1887–1967), whose work on psychopathy had been canonical since the 1920s, remained a staunch holdout, insisting that only biological criteria should be accepted. In the fall of 1957, he explained to reform commission member Wilhelm Gallas,

> The miserable situation here is simply this. Psychiatry today is so split that it is utterly impossible to unite even just the German university academics on a new version of section 51. . . . But even in my own, well-organized field of psychiatry, there are some gaps, which according to the present state of psychiatry, we simply have to let leave empty. Given the present state of psychiatry, the time is not suitable for a new version of §51.[74]

In a meeting in January 1960, Schneider elaborated on his concerns.

> I am convinced, that this revision will quickly have disastrous consequences for jurisprudence. I am thinking of the legal inequities and, above all, of what is sure to be a form of class justice. Someone who can parade out 3 psychotherapeutic expert witnesses will be much better off than some poor man. The courts will find it difficult to resist such an onslaught and influence.[75]

Many trained in psychology, however, decried the reformulations for not going far enough in accommodating mental factors. An official in the Hessian Ministry of Justice who had completed his dissertation in social psychology in the United States wrote to the Federal Ministry of Justice that German reformers' single-minded devotion to organic causes of mental disorders would strike their American counterparts as odd indeed. Germany would do well, he added, if it followed the Americans in better addressing the environmental aspects of abnormality.[76] In late 1961 and early 1962, the German Society for Psychology added its voice, vehemently rejecting the new wording. The society argued that the subcommittee was continuing to err by measuring criteria by the standards of biology.[77] In March 1964, the director of the psychological institute at the University of Bonn, Hans Thomae (1915–2001), used the weekly newspaper *Die Zeit* to rail against what he referred to as the "exclusion of psychology" in the reform process and to accuse the German psychiatric community of being out of touch with international scholarship.[78]

By the time a draft of the new law was submitted to the Bundestag's Special Committee on Criminal Law Reform in January 1965, the Federal Ministry of Justice had resigned itself to being unable to satisfy all sides in the debate. Still, the criticisms of psychologists clearly had an impact on reformers, pressing them to adopt language that would accommodate different models of personality and opening the door to recognizing the most serious cases of neurosis and psychopathy as candidates for diminished capacity.[79] Just as academic experts had done earlier, committee members in the Bundestag expressed the worry that an overly inclusive set of criteria would lead to an explosion of accused criminals pleading diminished capacity. A change was eventually agreed on, however, and in July 1969, the new formulation was issued. "A person is not culpable," it stated, "if, at the time of the deed, the person is incapable of recognizing the wrongfulness of the deed or is incapable of acting on this knowledge, due to a pathological mental disturbance, due to a severe disturbance of consciousness, or due to feeblemindedness or another severe mental abnormality."[80]

The debate over diminished capacity began as an attempt to ensure that prisons, mental hospitals, units for substance abuse treatment, and juvenile detention centers would no longer be burdened with housing criminal personalities for whom they could offer little to no assistance. It quickly devolved into a battle about the relative merits of psychiatric medicine and psychological science. For the first time since the nineteenth century, academics outside of law were challenging German psychiatry about its role in criminal justice. For its supporters, psychiatry was associated with rigor and objectivity, while detractors accused it of being hopelessly outdated. In turn, proponents of psychology framed their discipline as on the cutting edge, its diverse methods as emblematic of the liberal values underpinning the Federal Republic, while its opponents dismissed the field as naive and lax. In the end, the government was left to broker a compromise that did little to satisfy either side. Moreover, the issue left unresolved the question of how best to deal with the psychopathic, neurotic, and sexually impulsive offenders who, it was agreed, appeared little suited to prisons and mental hospitals. The solution eventually undertaken for that challenge—the building of new social therapeutic facilities—will be taken up in the next chapter.

Penal Reform, Resocialization, and the Treatment Prison, 1967–76

In the summer of 1967, federal minister of justice Gustav Heinemann (SPD) organized what was referred to as the Prison Commission to work out a reform of the adult penal system in West Germany. The commission was composed of legal scholars, criminologists, officials from the justice ministry, members of the Bundestag, judges, doctors, and prison administrators. At its head was criminologist Rudolf Sieverts, a longtime member of the Working Group for the Reform of the Prison System and an advisor to the government on the general reform of the criminal code. From October 1967 until October 1970, members of the commission held a series of meetings in which they listened to presentations from experts, gave reports on focused topics, and debated the provisions of a new law governing prisons. With the work of the commission completed by early 1971, a government draft of the law was first taken up in the Bundestag in October 1973 and was eventually passed in March 1976.

Taken up during the tenure of a succession of Social Democratic ministers of justice and against the backdrop of far-reaching social protest and cultural change, the reform of the prison system proved to be among the most ambitious of all the reforms undertaken by the Federal Republic. With a well-known disciple of the Lisztian school of legal theory as its chairman, the commission was direct and unapologetic about its intent to radically transform punishment in West Germany. The sole purpose of incarceration, it made clear, was "resocialization."

In its first substantive meeting, in December 1967, the Prison Commission signaled that it would be fundamentally rethinking incarceration. Commission members were explicit that, unlike the earlier deliberators on reform, they were seeking inspiration from new directions and critical voices. This included the Alternative Draft of a Penal Code for the Federal Republic of Germany (1962), sketched by progressive critics of the government's first draft of the code. The alternative draft called for the reduction of short sentences, elimination of sanctions against sexual freedom, and an end to the punitive aspects of incarceration.[81] Social psychiatry, with its antiauthoritarian emphasis on eliminating coercion, secrecy, and barriers in mental health care, was another source of ideas.[82] Finally, there was the concept of "the therapeutic community" and its demands for patient participation in facility decision making and for the dissolution of boundaries between institutional and everyday social life.[83]

Over the four days of its first convention, the commission considered international and domestic models and experiments: the transfer of refractory preventive detainees in Denmark and the Netherlands to treatment centers, the American experience with parole, and work with uncooperative inmates at special facilities in Kassel-Wehleiden and Hohenasperg. By the end of its last session, members had agreed on recommending that resocializing goals and activities—group and individual psychotherapy, reorientation of institutional life around pedagogical and therapeutic goals, promotion of inmate contact with the outside world, and integration of prisoners in administrative decision making—should be established in every West German prison. In addition, the commission recommended that workhouses be eliminated and that recidivists and other dangerous delinquents who were deemed "work shy" should be sent to therapeutic facilities to promote their future social integration.[84]

The term *resocialization*, used as early as the 1940s, became a mantra for the commission, with resocialization replacing rehabilitation and correction as the organizing principle of prisoner reform projects. The theme of resocialization was a subject for discussions at the April 1969 meeting of the commission in Bensheim-Auerbach. There, Hessian prison reformer Albert Krebs (1897–1992) and criminologist and government advisor Thomas Würtenberger (1907–89) reinforced a point that had been made by social scientists since the beginning of the decade: namely, that resocialization first required an empirical understanding of the process of "socialization."[85] Würtenberger, who, over the course of the sixties, had become a vocal advocate for a broadly interdisciplinary, multidimensional approach to criminal behavior,[86] stressed the importance of taking seriously the "social" aspect implicit in resocialization.

> When it comes to the impact of prison, the focus of all its efforts has to do with getting the prisoner's relationship toward coexistence with others in order. In this, a belief in an image of humanity is being professed, one that considers the individual no longer in isolation but, rather, within his social connectedness to the group. . . . All efforts at resocialization of prisoners derive from the fact that during his existence, a human being is subject to multiple more or less influential processes of "socialization," by which he increasingly grows from childhood onward into social life. For a human being is a social creature, a creature that at all times is developing with others and adapting to forms of community.[87]

Würtenberger maintained that the lives of many criminals were marked by failures in this socialization process and that prison must therefore serve the function of an "ersatz socialization," informed by scientific and medical knowledge and aimed at three sets of tasks: social adaptation, training and education, and personality formation.[88]

For his part, Albert Krebs emphasized the need for the resocializing prison system to adopt a new vocabulary reflecting its guiding principle, one that is "as much as possible accessible and attention-getting, contemporary and yet timeless."[89] He designated certain terms obsolete, such as "deterrence, reform, correction, adaptation to order and work, legality, morality, moral change, sin, retribution, [and] rearing," while he considered other common terms still useful, such as "work, authority, probation, isolation cell, free time, joint responsibility, legal sensibility, recidivism prevention, security, progressive stage incarceration, therapy, [and] preventive assistance."[90] The watchword for future incarceration, he announced, was "integration," by which he meant the "formation and fortification of the individual personality and its integration into social life."[91]

Turning to research from sociology, pedagogy, and social and developmental psychology, the Prison Commission operated with a decidedly new image of the convict. The "new" inmate was the victim of a failed upbringing, whose deviant behavior required a restorative socialization administered through prisons and informed by cutting-edge science and medicine. Prison was to be a place where prisoners were given the cognitive, emotional, and interpersonal resources and skills to rejoin family, work, and social life.

These ideals of the convict and the prison directed the commission in its work, as it attempted to redesign incarceration by operationalizing these ideals in practice. One of the commission's first tasks along these lines was to outline the nature of treatment within future prisons. Here, it adopted a deliberately political approach. In striking similarity to National Socialist efforts, members stressed the importance of the prison "atmosphere" but turned to the model of the "therapeutic community" to democratize the notion. As criminologist and warden Helga Einsele (1910–2005) announced in the commission's third meeting, in 1968, "the first concrete task is the creation of a democratic atmosphere and, beyond that, a therapeutic milieu."[92] Achieving this goal would require getting rid of authoritarian structures; establishing a dialogic relationship between inmates and staff; reforming the attitudes of both prisoners and personnel; using norms and guidelines, rather than directives, to centrally manage prisons; and working closely with researchers to facilitate the evaluation of the methods being used.[93] Einsele's aims for the personal development of convicts were downright Kantian in their pretense, including "taking down the desocialization, dissocialization, and regressions that the prison environment has caused; moving from correction to self-correction; developing autonomous initiative; awakening a measure of self-consciousness; overcoming antipathy and indifference toward society; [and] dismantling personality disturbances."[94]

From September 1968 to November 1969, the commission went on to consider various facets of the prison experience and how they could be attuned to the new therapeutic ethos. These facets included work, education, recreation, visitation rights, censorship, furlough, the design of buildings, the organization and training of staff, the special needs of female prisoners, and preventive detention. Standing out in the commission's deliberations on these issues is a repeated insistence on the need to take down barriers separating the institutional experience of prison from the outside world, a demand simultaneously being echoed by social psychiatrists in respect to asylums. To this end, the commission concluded, social workers and prison chaplains needed to play a more explicitly social pedagogical role in penal facilities and to facilitate inmates' connections with their friends and family.[95] Prisoners were to be given more, lengthier, and less-monitored visits with relatives and acquaintances. They were to receive training in an appropriate trade or profession.[96] All women's prisons were to create homes for mothers and their children under the age of four, and pregnant inmates were to be given maternity benefits.[97] All prisoners were to retain access to social insurance benefits, in order to be able to support their families.[98] While the commission called for retaining preventive detention as a way "to protect the general public from dangerous lawbreakers," it added that internment should also include "assistance toward integration into social life."[99]

In their final meetings, in the fall of 1970, the members of the commission set to work on a comprehensive draft law to submit to the Federal Ministry of Justice. An early version of the law failed to mention that the purpose of prison was resocialization, sparking debate about the exclusion. While some insisted that resocialization needed to be mentioned up front, others argued that there were indeed other purposes to incarceration, including atonement, retribution, and deterrence. In the end, however, the commission agreed to expressly laying out the goal of treatment in prison, since treatment served as "the core principal of the resocialization prison."[100] This did not resolve the differences in opinion, as some on the commission held that the goal of treatment was an ability to lead a "lawful life," others argued that it was the capacity to lead a "life without crime," and still others considered it to be the "strengthening of a sense of responsibility." In the end, the commission decided to follow the wording put forward by the fortieth Congress of Lawyers:

> Goal and Principles of Treatment
>
> (1) While serving a prison sentence, the prisoner should become capable of living a future life without committing any more crimes (treatment goal).
> (2) Incarceration should be designed in a manner that helps the prisoner integrate himself into a life of freedom.
> (3) Life in the facility should approximate living situations in the outside world as much as possible; the prisoner's sense of responsibility toward society should be reinforced, and the damaging effect of incarceration should be counteracted.[101]

The work of the commission being done, the Brandt government took on the task of drafting its own version of a prison law, completing the job by early 1972 and sending it on for consideration by the Bundesrat. Questions were raised about how these reforms would be funded, and with an absolute majority in the Bundesrat, the CDU/CSU pressed for giving security and deterrence a more prominent place in the new law. In February 1973, the Bundesrat recommended 113 changes to the government's bill, including the insertion of a clause stating that no aspect in the design of the prison system may interfere with the protection of the general public. As a compromise, the government agreed to add to the statement regarding the goals of prison, namely, that the latter also served to protect the general public from future crimes. An alternative version of the law was circulated by a group of German and Swiss law instructors during the summer of 1973, who lobbied for the adoption of an even more ambitiously therapeutic and democratic model referred to as the "problem-solving community."[102] In the end, however, the government's draft enjoyed the support of a majority of the Bundestag, and the law—modeled on the Prison Commission's draft, along with changes demanded by the Bundesrat—was passed in the spring of 1976.

The political hurdles to prison reform had been cleared. There remained, however, other barriers to realizing the ambitions of reformers. Surveys and studies conducted during the years 1969–75 to gauge public opinion about convicts, punishment, and the reform of the prison system showed little support for the ideal of resocialization. A 1969 survey, for instance, found that only 38 percent of West Germans believed that the point of punishment was the "reform and reintegration" of criminals. A survey conducted in 1970 painted an even bleaker picture for therapeutic incarceration in the FRG. When asked about the most important purposes of punishment, 34 percent of respondents cited deterrence; 23 percent, correction; 22 percent, atonement; and 19 percent, the protection of society. Support for deterrence was strongest among those over the age of fifty, CDU followers, the lower middle class, and Catholics, while it enjoyed its least support among the upper class and those with no religious affiliations. In all, a mere 15 percent of those surveyed said they believed it was possible for a criminal to be genuinely reformed. A study conducted in 1975 at the Ruhr University in Bochum, however, provided some room for encouragement for advocates of therapeutic incarceration. It found that, while there remained a fairly widespread lack of sympathy for prisoners, younger people and those with higher education tended to hold decidedly more liberal attitudes about resocialization than their elders.[103]

It was not only the general population who needed convincing about the benefits of correctional rehabilitation. Three studies of attitudes among inmates and prison staff about resocialization published in the years 1970–73 revealed a marked disparity between those working in penal facilities and academic and professional experts. For most personnel, the job was a second career, usually taken up between ages 23–30 and after having first worked for the police or military. Overwhelmingly influencing this choice of career was the opportunity to get a well-paying job with good benefits, not humanitarian or correctional considerations. Within prison itself, there appeared to be other barriers as well to institutionalizing a rehabilitative ethos. The large size of many facilities led to a climate in which officers reported being mostly afraid of inmates and, as a result, felt reduced to the role of "turnkey" or "lackey." Though guards expressed the wish to assume a more supportive, helping role, a majority of surveyed inmates considered staff inadequately trained in pedagogy and psychology and of little help when it came to personal matters.[104]

In the end, the creation of the therapeutic prison in West Germany was a reform from above. To be sure, the catalysts included forces outside of Bonn and traditional criminology and psychiatry: already in the fifties, there were projects developed in individual states and facilities, as well as new antiauthoritarian values and concepts touted by a younger cohort of scholars and students. Still, the reform was carried out and designed by academic experts, longtime federal administrators, and national politicians, who clearly and knowingly operated contrary to the general sentiment of most prison staff and the general population.

Therapy and Its Discontents

The Criminal as Neurotic

As has been detailed, the revamping of the West German criminal code seemed to offer reform-minded researchers and clinicians an opportunity to reintroduce rehabilitation into the penal system. I say *re*introduce, since many of the reformers of the 1950s and early 1960s looked to ideas from the Weimar era for inspiration. In this regard, at least, the Nazi years were largely treated as an interruption, with the Federal Republic providing a chance to finally realize earlier ambitions. Throughout the sixties, however, new concepts and voices from sociology, social psychology, developmental psychology, social psychiatry, and psychoanalysis challenged the notion that one could simply return to the agenda of the 1920s. Over the course of the sixties and seventies, then, concepts such as personality, treatment, therapy, and reintegration assumed new meanings. As was the case in both Nazi and East Germany, the reform of the convict in West Germany was contingent on the reform of punishment, which, in turn, proved to be deeply affected by changes within the human sciences.

Acting as both cause and effect in this pronounced shift was the emergence of a new image of the convict, as a neurotic personality. With the return of psychoanalysis to West Germany after the war and with the increasing equation of treatment in prison with psychotherapy, it certainly made sense to some proponents of rehabilitation to see criminal behavior as a function of neurotic tendencies.[105] As therapist Otto Brink explained to a group of prison officers in Stuttgart in 1963, criminality and delinquency needed to be understood as illnesses.

> The criminal is, in part, developmentally arrested at the stages of childhood. . . . Most are full of mistrust and hate, because they never felt accepted, nurtured, and loved. Many believe they have the right to do something wrong, because they themselves have been wronged. Many were rejected by society already in childhood, berated and chased away as black sheep and scapegoats. Neglect is, for many criminals, the right term. In their youth, they were not properly looked after and supervised, not properly loved. And that is the way it is with our criminals: they are not capable of love.[106]

Helga Einsele made a similar point to fellow members of the Prison Commission in 1968, noting that research showed that failed socialization in childhood could lead to a later descent into neurosis, crime, and mental illness.[107]

More often than not, penology experts in the 1960s and early 1970s, like Brink and Einsele, did not explicitly cite the sources of their views on neurosis. Their thinking, however, was largely in keeping with those of second-generation psychoanalysts like Otto Fenichel and Frankfurt School intellectuals such as Erich Fromm, both of whom emphasized the role of environmental and societal factors in prompting neuroses in individuals. Even if the term *psychoanalysis* was never mentioned, its focus on relationships, feelings, anxieties, and unconscious mechanisms and its language of "sublimation," "projection," and "compensation" often found a place in assessments of convicts.[108]

Admittedly, most treatment specialists working with prisoners were not trained psychoanalysts. Rather, as was the case more generally in the field of abnormal psychology at the time, psychoanalytic concepts and terms were simply folded into an emerging syncretism. What clinical psychologists, psychotherapists, social pedagogues, and social workers in the sixties had to offer to the project of resocialization in prisons was an adaptation of techniques and methods used in other inpatient and outpatient settings—personality testing, group counseling and therapy, autosuggestion, mental training, and music therapy.[109]

Bringing in the Social through Science and Counseling

Together, the increasing decriminalization of minor offenses and the emphasis placed on therapy and secondary socialization brought with them a reassessment of social prognosis. Though always billed as a tool for assigning convicts to an appropriate setting within progressive stage incarceration, social prognosis had been used for decades chiefly as a means to weed out the incorrigible. Now, growing optimism about the effects of therapy and counseling shifted the focus of prognostic evaluation away from personality types and toward "treatment types" (*Behandlungstypen*). This new focus meant, according to Hellmuth Mayer, identifying the correctional, educational, and resocialization needs and relative degrees of motivation presented by inmates.[110] Seeking evidence of a constitutional incorrigibility gave way to understanding the relative corrigibility of convicts on a spectrum and as a function of their personal and interpersonal resources. From this perspective, prognosis was not only an assessment of the individual prisoner but also a reflection on society and the available repertoire of therapeutic treatments.[111] Prognosis still was supposed to serve as a tool for selection, but by the midseventies, its ostensible purpose was matching the convict to a treatment.

The emphasis placed on society as both the cause of and the cure for criminality reflected the ways in which West German sociology and psychology were being combined during the 1960s to question social conventions and hierarchies.[112] Resocialization was an explicitly political project, and its advocates made it abundantly clear that their intent was ideological, contrasting the forms of correction and leadership in authoritarian society with the forms most suited to a pluralist, democratic society. "Penal correction is about not the training of marionette-like creatures conforming to the conceptual requirements of a totalitarian criminal policy," a group of prison guard supervisors were told in 1968, "but, rather, assisting the liberation of an individual capable of making decisions and ready to take responsibility."[113] The goal of correction, pedagogue Hermine Rasch-Bauer explained, was to help form "a mature person," someone who used his or her reason and judgment to find out "where the best possibilities lie for solving tasks and difficulties and for fulfilling his or her own legitimate and emotional needs and the needs of his or her fellow human beings." This goal required a change in the role of the correctional professional, she added: "The correctional officer must take his partner seriously from the start and recognize and acknowledge his uniqueness, which is and remains the unrepeatable and the irreplaceable in his status as the bearer of a human life."[114]

The resocialization of the convict was thus conceived as the mirror image of the socialization of the individual in democratic society at large. At the height of the reform era in the Federal Republic, during the Brandt and Schmidt administrations, West German penology was replete with references to society. Resocialization was not simply a matter of following the Prison Commission's lead in allowing inmates greater access to information and relationships beyond the prison gates. It was also a matter of recognizing the presence of society within prison as well as acknowledging the status of the prisoner within society. The growing attention paid to such topics as foreign inmates, prisoner subcultures, and the social stigma faced by ex-convicts is a reflection of this new emphasis.[115] In 1975, the editors of the leading penology journal signaled their own recognition of this fact by changing its name to *Journal for the Prison System and Ex-Convict Services*.

When, in 1974, a group of specialists published the first textbook on penology in West Germany in twenty years, the book's differences from its predecessor were telling. The 1954 handbook drew mostly on legislation, administrative regulations, legal scholarship, and statistics, to capture a relatively static picture of prison work and the inmate population.[116] By contrast, the new text relied much more on social scientific research and gave more space to competing theories of punishment, therapeutic alternatives, and the interpersonal relationships of convicts.[117] An assessment of the state of international criminology by the director of the Max Planck Institute for Foreign and International Criminal Law in 1975 confirmed that West German research was decidedly empirical in its methods and that treatment was the object of an increasing amount of attention (one-quarter of all research projects at the time). Yet, despite the growing internationalization of the field, there remained regional differences: in central European and Scandinavian states, criminology remained more strongly tied to law and psychiatry faculties, while in the Netherlands, the United Kingdom, and the United States, its intellectual and institutional ties were closer to sociology, psychology, and theory.[118]

By the mid-1970s, the West German prison was becoming a different place, as a host of specially trained helpers and counselors were bringing an array of new methods to the rehabilitation of convicts. Prison pastoral work was increasingly professionalized through the spread of pastoral psychology, giving practitioners tools for carrying out group and individual counseling.[119] The number of prison social workers grew. In Baden-Württemberg, a comparatively wealthy federal state that pursued resocialization aggressively, the number of social work positions doubled between 1962 and 1973, while the number of inmates assigned to each caseworker declined from 173 to 86.[120] The number of psychologists working in the state's prison system rose from two in 1967 to seventeen in 1973, with psychologists working primarily as members of teams whose job was to assign inmates to appropriate facilities, recommend a treatment plan, and track the progress of inmates over time.[121] While records from states with lesser means, like Lower Saxony, show that prison officials there often found it difficult to recruit properly trained psychologists, pedagogues, and trainees, they continued to lobby superiors for more positions.[122]

Even before prison reform was made law, however, some observers sensed still greater challenges ahead for resocialization. Karl Peters (1904–98), a longtime advocate for prison reform, announced already in 1972, "The victory does not allow for much celebration. There is the nagging question of whether the final breakthrough of the resocialization concept did not actually come at a time in which intellectual and ethical changes are taking place that are making resocialization no longer possible due to a weak foundation. The battle might have been won, but the war lost."[123] Three years later, a Bavarian justice official warned an assembly of prison psychologists that economic recession and the steady increase in the inmate population promised to tax the resources and patience of facilities, staff, and convicts alike.[124] An article later that year in the magazine *Der Spiegel* reinforced the point: due to rising unemployment, one in every ten inmates in the Federal Republic could no longer find work, a fact that the magazine article described as a "setback for the resocialization approach, a menace for prison discipline."[125]

Backlash: Efficiency, Indemnity, and Social Training in the Seventies and Eighties

Peters's observation proved to be prophetic. As many have since noted, the great irony of West Germany's penal reform was that it embraced the rehabilitative ideal at the very moment when other states were beginning to abandon it. Already in the early seventies, it was apparent that the same countries that had inspired German reformers in the fifties and sixties were now finding that the treatment model did not work.[126] Returning from a tour of Denmark, Sweden, and Norway in the fall of 1972, two German researchers reported that their counterparts there had resigned themselves to the fact that the recidivism rate for prisoners released from treatment units was no lower than that for prisoners released from traditional facilities. In fact, these same Scandinavian researchers were concluding that the "medical-psychological" perspective implicitly informing therapeutic penology only perpetuated the stigmatization and marginalization of convicts, by attributing their behavior to a static personality. Reform-minded Scandinavian specialists were therefore now focusing their efforts on "humanizing" prison by changing inmate subculture, ensuring better pay for inmates, and awarding more generous furlough and visitation rights.[127] As the Prison Law took effect in 1977, many legal experts, like Albin Eser (1935–), wondered aloud whether resocialization was already in a state of crisis, threatened by a lack of public support and watered down by legalese.[128]

Survey data from 1975 and 1987 confirmed that, similar to citizens in the rest of western Europe and North America, the West German public was growing increasingly more punitive in its outlook on punishment. A comparison of attitudes revealed that 26 percent of respondents in 1975, compared to 44.9 percent in 1987, supported the notion that prison's goal was atonement and deterrence; meanwhile, support for the idea of resocialization declined from 61.2 percent to 47.5 percent. Opposition to resocialization rose particularly among young people aged 18–25 years (from 19.6 to 47.1 percent) and housewives (from 32.1 to 51.5 percent).[129]

Still, the shift in public opinion in the FRG was more ambiguous than it was in other countries. While there was a steep rise in support for the death penalty in the wake of a wave of terrorism in 1976 and 1977, for instance, that support never rose above 45 percent and quickly sunk to below 30 percent by 1980.[130] After Marianne Bachmeier was convicted in 1983 for murder and given a six-year sentence for killing the man who had sexually assaulted and strangled to death her seven-year-old daughter, an Allensbach surveyed found that 25 percent of the public considered the sentence to be too low, 27 percent considered it too high, and 28 percent thought it appropriate.[131] Other surveys in the eighties determined that the West German public was interested more in restitution for victims than in punishment or other responses to crime.[132]

Thus, any change in public attitudes about crime and punishment in West Germany appears to have been less about embracing the value of retribution than reflective of a disenchantment with the rehabilitative ideal. Scholarly circles at the time similarly spoke of an end to the "treatment euphoria" or "resocialization optimism" that had dominated earlier discussions on prison reform. In her 1987 dissertation on contemporary criticisms of the treatment prison, Charlotte Rath identified an array of arguments leveled against therapeutic penology: criminal law arguments questioning the commensurability of involuntary treatment and indefinite sentences with the basic rights of the individual; social and normative arguments dismissing clinical treatment as a stigmatizing, pathologizing, and/or ineffective tool; and third-way arguments offering up alternative sanctions to prison.[133]

How do we account for this sweeping and seemingly sudden change of heart about resocialization in West Germany, and what consequences did it have? Scholars at the time and since then have cited a number of factors behind this turnaround: the politics and economics of austerity, the rise of political conservatism, the appearance of "new groups of offenders" (e.g., organized crime and terrorists), the overcrowding of penal facilities, and the emergence of a victims' rights movement.[134] Social and behavioral scientists in the two decades preceding reunification, however, focused primarily on the failure of treatment to deliver what it had promised: the reform of convicts.

After the sixties and early seventies, which were characterized by correctional experimentation, researchers applied their tools to evaluate the effectiveness of the experiments and innovations from that period. As the renowned criminologist Günther Kaiser (1928–2007) noted in 1977, however, the disillusionment with the treatment model can hardly be explained by its ineffectiveness, since few, if any, empirical studies of resocialization had been conducted before then.[135] Thus, research into the effects of therapeutic treatment on criminals was an effect, not a cause, of the change in attitudes, an institutional response of auditing that became especially prominent across the world of public administration during the 1970s.[136] Put simply, in a climate of both fiscal austerity and public demand for state intervention, public programs were increasingly called on to prove their efficiency.[137]

The result was a decided shift in the focus of criminological research during the 1980s, away from the study of perpetrators and the etiology of crime, toward the effectiveness of sanctions.[138] In particular, two lines of research emerged: on the one hand, organizational analyses revealing administrative shortcomings as well as professional tensions between treatment staff and guards; on the other, evaluations of efficacy measuring personality and behavioral changes among convicts.[139] One of the most ambitious and influential of the latter was conducted by a team at the University of Freiburg and the Max Planck Institute for Foreign and International Criminal Law, under the direction of Helmut Kury (1941–). Tracking both youth and adult offenders from 1976 to 1983, Kury's group concluded that "intramural resocialization approaches up to now have not reached and perhaps cannot reach their goal by and large and, at the very least, to the extent intended." The chief reason for the failure was prison overcrowding: "Practice graphically demonstrates that prison resocialization programs are no longer possible in a situation of overcrowding, such as is the case today in many penal facilities."[140] By the mideighties, social scientific studies made it difficult to overlook that prisons were worlds dominated by "social degradation, malingering, [and] brutal subordination," reducing their inhabitants to adopt simple survival tactics. "The institution 'prison,'" as one specialist put it, "is—looking at its historical development and the objective facts—primarily not an instrument of socialization."[141]

Criticism of the treatment prison was directed not only at its methods and location but also at its target. The 1960s and 1970s witnessed the rise of victim advocacy groups in western Europe and the United States, often taking their cues from movements organized around human rights, feminism, and child protection. In 1976, television journalist Eduard Zimmermann (1929–2009) founded the West German chapter of the White Ring, an international victims' rights group with the mission of giving victims of crime better legal protection and a greater role in legal proceedings. As will be discussed in chapter 6, groups like the White Ring proved effective in gaining media attention and promoting the perception that academic and legal efforts to understand criminals and their social circumstances had led to a softening of criminal justice and a second order of victimization.[142]

The emergence of victim advocacy groups was part of a more general trend in which the victims of crime were given a more prominent role in research (victimology), police work, criminal justice, and international agreements (European Council agreements in 1983, 1985, and 1987; the 1986 United Nations Declaration of Basic Principles of Justice for Victims of Crime and Abuse of Power). A victim compensation law was first put on the books in the Federal Republic in 1976, providing seriously injured victims access to medical and rehabilitative treatment and a pension. This was supplemented by the Victim Protection Law in 1986, allowing the public and, in certain instances, the accused to be excluded from trial proceedings and giving victims rights to compensation from their offenders.[143] In addition, the 1980s witnessed increased use of a form of conflict resolution called "offender-victim mediation." Intended to replace incarceration and generally supervised by a social worker, mediation brings willing victims and their offenders into reconciliatory conversation with another. Subsequent studies, however, have shown that use of offender-victim mediation is relatively rare—utilized in less than 5 percent of cases reported in 2003—with most cases involving domestic conflicts.[144]

Along with the various other intellectual, social, political, and economic changes, the new victim orientation inspired experts to reimagine and reconfigure treatment in prison.[145] Offender-victim mediation, for instance, led one criminologist in 1984 to consider the ways in which reconciliation, not resocialization, might serve as the purpose behind incarceration, by making parole contingent on material restitution, orienting inmate therapy around acknowledging guilt, and using role playing to encourage convicts to imagine the situations of their victims.[146] Ten years after the establishment of resocialization in West German prisons, the situation was less a case of treatment disappearing than of it undergoing a reorientation toward both offering convicts "opportunities" and demanding that they exercise "social responsibility."[147]

In the face of overcrowded facilities, limited funding, and overburdened therapeutic staff, treatment in prison took on a more pragmatic, less contemplative outlook on correction. The adoption of short-term cognitive therapies is one example, employing techniques of self-observation, homework assignments, and the modification of behavioral patterns through the substitution of habitual thoughts.[148] But perhaps most emblematic of this change was the emergence of a new therapeutic intervention: social training.

At the beginning of the 1970s, at the Tegel IV Penal Facility in West Berlin, a group from the Consortium for Empirical Educational Research in Heidelberg developed a curriculum for social training, at the request of the Federal Ministry for Education and Science. The group published its results in 1981. In contrast to the treatment approaches of psychiatrists and psychotherapists, social training was billed as an economic, nonstigmatizing, jargon-free form of group learning that allowed the progress of inmates to be easily measured against real-world tasks. Replacing the medical concepts of pathology and therapy with that of problem solving and social learning, social training shifted the goal of prisoner reform from changing personality to enhancing the chances of success by helping convicts become better at fulfilling daily functions in the outside world.[149] Criminals were thereby understood as beset by certain "deficits" or shortcomings in basic forms of "social competence," such as communication, planning, and conflict resolution.[150]

Though guidelines were refined over time and practices varied across prisons, social training was generally organized around a series of small group sessions (around 1980, this generally meant somewhere between twelve to twenty-two meetings with groups of about five to ten inmates).[151] A professional "trainer," typically a specialist in education, directed group tasks and interactions. Sessions focused on a theme from everyday life, most involving consumption, such as debt management, money, and household spending, as well as job searching and personal relationships. Members first discussed common difficulties associated with the theme, learning goals were set, and various ways of overcoming problems were considered through role playing and other methods.

A survey of programs conducted in 1986 revealed that social training was being used at the time in about 85 percent of West German prisons, with most groups focusing on work-related topics. At the same time, however, administrators reported encountering big challenges in organizing groups. Finding suitable space and financing was often hard to come by, and two-thirds of the respondents admitted that they had problems recruiting participants.[152] Like psychotherapy, social training was also limited by the difficulty inmates had in warming up to the idea of talking about their shortcomings in public.

Conclusions

As with Nazi Germany and East Germany, the Federal Republic linked reform of its society to the reform of both convicts and the punishment they were to receive. In their aspirations for personal and institutional change, West German experts were no less ideological than their fascist and socialist counterparts, imagining correction as a set of scientific and clinical tools judiciously applied by professionalized enablers, suited to the unique individuality of the inmate and aimed at facilitating the realization of his or her potential. As the object of correctional rehabilitation, the West German convict was to be given the idealized goal of becoming a responsible member of a liberal, pluralistic, consumer society. Here, punishment functioned as a form of participatory counseling in democratic and capitalist citizenship, and rehabilitation was redubbed "resocialization."

The technologies and methods used for resocialization in the FRG changed over time, reflecting shifts in both national and international trends. The virtual monopoly that jurists and psychiatrists had held over criminology was, at first, challenged by specialists from subfields of psychology, most with a decidedly American accent, including developmental psychology, psychometrics, social psychology, and personality psychology. A second wave of change came to the field in the 1960s, when practitioners of sociology and psychoanalysis began articulating a more "social" concept of criminality, inspired by Scandinavian and Dutch precedents. Finally, in the decade and a half before reunification, cognitive and behavioral modification and pedagogy came to the fore, stressing the improvement of social, economic, and emotional competencies necessary for success in consumer society.[153] Over time, however, a rather consistent picture was being sketched of the inherently interactive individual, one using personal resources to respond situationally to changing circumstances.

When institutional reform came, it did so slowly, deliberatively, and at the hands of a mostly elderly cohort, many with direct ties to the Nazi era. Drawing on notions of prison reform from the Weimar era, western European and American models, and evolving international standards, these more or less traditional reformers struggled with reimagining correction and constantly drew fire from younger critics. But while the "traditionalists" often still hung on to their increasingly outdated attitudes, concepts, and vocabulary, they also proved receptive to revising their thinking to accommodate new realities. Rudolf Sieverts's career provides a good example of this. Harmonizing the country's system of prisoner resocialization with international practices served the purpose not only of reintegrating the convict within West Germany society but also of reintegrating West German society and science within the international community.

While a good deal of change came at the local level, the reform process was largely a top-down affair. As a result, it exposed many tensions between social scientists, and it left prison staff feeling alienated, while many within the public remained dissatisfied. The cruel irony for advocates of the treatment prison was that while they were trying to dissolve the boundaries separating prisoners from the rest of society, their work also laid open the prison much more to the vagaries of social change. When the economy went into recession and the political climate turned decidedly more conservative, the treatment model quickly lost much of its support and allure. Nevertheless, even in an era dominated by talk of assessment, efficiency, and restitution, West Germany did not abandon the rehabilitative ideal of correction. Instead, the resocialization cause was reduced to a more basic humanitarianism with a set of demands better suited to more liberal sensibilities.

The rise of victim advocacy and victimology in this context is similarly a trend that is more nuanced than is often depicted.[154] Neglected in almost all the scholarly talk about the emergence of victim-oriented justice has been the fact that victim-centered criminal justice appears to have had few, if any, parallels in fascist and communist states. Criminal justice in both Nazi and East Germany laid stress on the damage done to the collective public—the *Volksgemeinschaft*, or socialist society—by criminals. The more recent victim orientation, by contrast, has emphasized individual suffering and compensation, invoking ideals firmly rooted in liberal and Christian democratic traditions, such as family welfare, confession, reconciliation, and the protection of women and children. Victim-oriented justice should be seen, then, not just as part of a "new punitiveness" but also as an effort to extend both treatment and the pathologization of human adversity to the victims of crime, in the name of humanitarianism and restorative civic peace.

CHAPTER 6

The West German Sex Offender as Patient

During the early years of the Federal Republic, many worried that both German infrastructure and German society itself were in a state of catastrophic decay. As noted in the previous chapter, an increase in violent crime and a sense of growing public lewdness following the war raised awareness of sexual crimes. Over the course of the first two decades of the FRG, West German observers first pinned the blame for these developments on the oversexualization of society and on uncontrolled youth. By the mid-1960s, however, anxieties about sex offenders crystallized around sensationalized images of violent and lethal pedophiles.

As had been the case throughout the century, experts and the lay public mostly associated sex offenders with chronic depravity. This meant that considerations about how to best go about handling such criminals were often folded into broader discussions about more effectively incapacitating dangerous incorrigibles. Deliberations over the reform of the criminal justice system became a principal site for debating this issue, which ultimately centered on two main themes: the long-term confinement of psychopaths and the application of castration. In the case of the former, reformers were drawn to precedents in Denmark and the Netherlands, where special treatment units administered an array of therapies to dangerous psychopathic and sexual delinquents. In the case of castration, West German researchers, clinicians, and lawmakers were keen on continuing to rely on the operation, but they sought ways to distance the procedure from its Nazi past. By the mid-1970s, reform deliberations and legal changes led to the creation of new treatment facilities for many sex offenders—so-called social therapeutic facilities—and to the authorization of a system of voluntary castration.

These innovations represented less a change in kind than an intensification of earlier trends. In particular, they built on and further reinforced the medicalization of deviant and dangerous sexualities. Though controversial at the time, the building of social therapeutic facilities and the use of voluntary castration ultimately garnered the approval of lawmakers. Promoted as state-of-the-art, humane, and effective techniques for rehabilitating and incapacitating dangerous sex offenders, social therapy and castration were nevertheless designed on the presumption of a need to distinguish between the corrigible and the incorrigible. As a result, both social therapeutic facilities and preventive detention were increasingly sexualized following reunification, as a growing number of sex offenders were redirected into both institutions.

The Postwar Sexual Crime Wave in Early West Germany

In July 1950, the newspaper *Neue Württembergische Zeitung* published an opinion piece expressing its concern over what it reported was an alarming rise in sex crimes in postwar West Germany. Making the trend even more frightening was the fact that these crimes were geographically closing in on normally serene segments of society. "Whereas in earlier years sexual crime was mostly a phenomenon on the margins of big city life, now there are ever more cases in which the courts of our smaller cities have to adjudicate such sinners," the paper lamented, "individuals who are living not only in these very same small cities but in the countryside as well."[1] Editors at the paper partly blamed a number of recent trends for the disturbing spread of sex offenses—lewd magazines, the pressures of war, the postwar lack of housing and jobs. But they pinned most of the blame on the criminal justice system, which they claimed doled out all-too-mild sentences to juvenile delinquents.

Federal minister of justice Thomas Dehler wrote to the newspaper in the following month to discuss the editors' contentions. He conceded that figures for the British occupation zone following World War II confirmed that western Germany had been experiencing a rise in sexual crimes. While authorities recorded 4,504 sex offenses in the zone in 1947, that figure went up to 8,316 in 1948 and 14,187 in 1949—at the same time that the number of criminal cases in general declined from 1.27 million in 1947 to 717,713 in 1949. Sex offenses against children alone rose 225 percent over this period. But while Dehler agreed that courts needed to be more decisive in how they handled offenders, he added that other factors were playing a role in the sexual crime rate, including malnutrition, alcoholism, and the lack of preventive instruction for children.[2]

Data from other sources confirmed the picture painted by the justice minister. While the general crime rate in western Germany fell by 10 percent between 1948 and 1949, the sexual crime rate rose by almost 50 percent.[3] Political leaders and the general public were especially perturbed by what appeared to be an increase in child molestation, a trend that continued into the early fifties. When asked by the central office of the CDU at the end of 1953 to address the problem, a senior justice official in Bonn tried to place the figures in historical context. The child molestation rate, he pointed out, actually fell after World War II—so low, in fact, that the rate in 1947 (2.5 cases per 100,000 residents) was the lowest since 1882. Nevertheless, the number of cases continued to rise after currency reform in the summer of 1948, through 1952. "It may be that the sentences of the courts do not always match the severity of the crimes in many cases," the official told the CDU, adding, "Nevertheless, I have no influence on the sentences of independent courts."[4]

The increase in sexual crime rates at this time was particularly worrying in light of the polemical atmosphere surrounding both crime and sexuality in the decade following World War II. As Stefan Mörchen has shown, during both the war and the postwar occupation, the mass criminality associated with the black market and property crime was a matter of great concern to authorities and the general public. Attributed primarily to the actions of social rejects and ne'er-do-wells, mass criminality was widely viewed as a seditious breach of existing social norms, one posing not only a legal but a grave moral threat to German society, warranting a firm response.[5]

At the same time, the Catholic Church, the state governments of North Rhine–Westphalia and Rhineland Palatinate, and some members of the CDU led an aggressive campaign aimed at purging Germany of "filth and trash." Sybille Steinbach has demonstrated that this campaign, couched in terms of protecting "decency" (*Sittlichkeit*), took aim at the nudist Freikörperkultur (FKK) movement, the sex shop entrepreneur Beate Uhse, and the film *Die Sünderin*, as emblems of moral decadence. Their sentiments similar to those expressed about the black market, critics of postwar sexual openness believed it to be nothing short of a mortal menace to social harmony and stability.[6]

In reality, of course, the rubric "sex crime" (*Sittlichkeitsverbrechen*) was shorthand for a range of different offenses, including incest, sexual relations with a subordinate, homosexuality, bestiality, prostitution and solicitation, public indecency, and distribution of pornographic literature. Not all of these crimes were on the rise at this time. Over the years 1950–52, convictions for incest remained relatively stable, for instance, while convictions for solicitation, homosexuality, and public indecency increased.[7] An analysis by Hamburg criminologist Rudolf Sieverts in 1960 made the case for a more differentiated understanding of sexual crime in the Federal Republic. National crime statistics, he found, showed that sex offenses made up only between 3.45 and 3.9 percent of all known crimes during the years 1953–56, placing it fifth behind petty larceny (27.95 percent), fraud and forgery (14.56 percent), aggravated larceny (8.66 percent), and embezzlement (4.19 percent). Disturbingly, however, sexual crime convictions for child molestation and statutory rape were the largest in number, constituting almost 38 percent of such convictions in 1955, ahead of homosexuality (20 percent), causing a public nuisance (16 percent), incest (11.5 percent), and rape (3.8 percent).[8]

The general public tended to lump most offenders together when talking about sexual crime, routinely equating it with child molestation and rape. In letters they addressed to politicians in Bonn, individuals and groups complained, time and again, how difficult it had become to protect children and women from the menace of sex offenders. In April 1952, for example, a mother from Braunschweig wrote to Chancellor Konrad Adenauer after her six-year-old son was "indecently harassed" in a nature reserve. Like many other mothers during reconstruction, she explained, her job kept her long hours at work, leaving her no choice but to let "the children be tended to by strangers."[9] Following up with the Ministry of Justice a month later, the woman invoked the language of trauma to describe how the assault on her son left his "mental life shocked" and left her feeling "personally assaulted." It was the government's responsibility, she argued, to ensure "that this hateful crime is atoned for through stiff punishment."[10]

This hard-line message was echoed by a steady stream of citizens angered by reports about the increase in sexual crime during the early years of the Federal Republic. A group of "several fathers and union men," for instance, warned justice officials that Germany was dangerously out of step with other democratic countries like the United States and Canada, where (according to them) all first-time sex offenders were sentenced to castration and hard labor.[11] Similar sentiments were voiced in the spring of 1955 by a group calling themselves the Aachen Women's Committee, who, in response to two recent sexual murders, advocated that sex offenders be given life sentences and only granted clemency on the condition that the convicts submit to castration. In this and comparable cases, justice officials took great pains to remind the public and other government officials that accepted legal procedures simply did not allow for using things like castration and indefinite detention for retributive purposes.[12]

The postwar rise in sex crime garnered the attention of researchers as well, who offered a number of explanations for the increase. The director of Bavaria's Central Office for Criminal Identification and Police Statistics, Franz Meixner, explained in a 1951 textbook on criminal investigation that offenses were often the result of marriage or financial problems. Perpetrators, he noted, frequently described having sexually indifferent or resistant wives who either lay there during sex "like a sack full of grain" or avoided sex altogether out of fear and disgust. In addition, the relatively low income of most German men meant that visiting a prostitute was prohibitively too costly. Both circumstances ultimately led to sexual frustrations, Meixner concluded, "which are oftentimes released explosively in masturbatory or violent attacks on women, molestations of children or subordinates."[13]

While Meixner's argument for seeing sexual crime as an "understandable" outlet for sexual tension likely reflected the sentiments of a number of men at the time, it was not an opinion shared by most experts. Prison psychologist Gustav Nass, for instance, relied on official statistics, court records, and clinical assessments to try to make sense of the disturbingly high number of child molesters in West German prisons (in one prison alone, one-third of its 717 inmates were convicted sex offenders, 90 percent of whom had committed an offense against a minor). The evidence, he concluded, indicated that most sex offenders committed their crimes not because they were incited by erotic objects and fantasies but because they had deficient and unstable psychological abilities.[14] In analyzing 111 incest cases during the years 1945–52, physician Joachim Gerchow took a different approach. A specialist in social medicine, Gerchow conducted an epidemiological analysis of the offenders and their crimes, and he found among their ranks a disproportionately large number of war veterans who spent time as Russian POWs. By and large, the average perpetrator was a man in his forties whose household was characterized by family breakdown and close living quarters.[15]

When it came to treating sex offenders, most specialists remained guardedly hopeful, though dubious. Prison chaplains were among those prison professionals most optimistic about the use of clinical treatments on these convicts, demonstrating an openness to merging religious perspectives stressing virtue with medical approaches emphasizing pathologies.[16] Practitioners were especially drawn to developments in the United States, Denmark, and the Netherlands, where psychiatric treatments, including hormone injections, psychoanalysis, and psychodrama, were being tried with convicted sexual criminals.[17] Forensic physicians remained skeptical, however, that very much could be accomplished with offenders such as violent child abusers, "since little or nothing can be expected by way of 'reforming' these perpetrators."[18]

Managing Sex Offenders by Incapacitating Psychopaths

The pessimism voiced about the relative corrigibility of sex offenders spoke to the distinct status the latter had within German criminology and penology.

Since the late nineteenth century, clinicians and researchers had held to a fairly consistent image of the sexual criminal as the bearer of an abnormal and often pathologically disturbed personality, corrupted by a deviant, regressive, and overpowering sexual drive.[19] Although experts differed as to whether these defects were primarily the result of endogenous or exogenous factors, sex offenders were widely considered to be among the most incorrigible criminals.

It is therefore not altogether surprising to find that scholarly and policy discussions about sex offenders frequently arose within the context of debate over psychopaths and their treatment. As I have described elsewhere[20] and mentioned in previous chapters, psychiatrists first developed the concept of psychopathy at the turn of the twentieth century, to describe a group of individuals who manifested maladjusted personality traits that neither met the criteria for normality nor crossed the threshold for the pathological. From the 1890s through the 1940s, psychopaths were widely referred to by prison, mental health, and welfare professionals as "troublemakers," disruptive residents largely immune to the rehabilitative efforts of their respective facilities. Psychopaths' growing reputation for recalcitrance served to confirm the view that they were a psychopathologically distinct group. With institutions of confinement regularly passing these inmates and patients off on one another, convincing policy makers of the need for separate facilities for these institutionally corrosive influences became the perennial mission for many social reformers in Germany.

The diagnosis of psychopathy hardly mapped neatly onto criminal categories, however. As the Bonn University psychiatrist Hans Gruhle spelled out in 1953, "A psychopathic criminal is not a criminal who happens to be psychopathic but, rather, is a perpetrator who commits his deeds out of psychopathic motivations."[21] In clinical practice, he explained, psychopathic offenders were largely to be found among so-called affect criminals, that is, perpetrators driven by degenerate and relatively uncontrollable passions and feelings. Thus, besides frequently presenting as asocials, vagrants, swindlers, alcoholics, and drug addicts, Gruhle added, psychopaths were often common among particular groups of sex offenders, such as practitioners of bestiality, homosexuals, prostitutes, rapists, and molesters.

Thus, from a criminal justice standpoint, psychopaths presented a heterogeneous population of convicts, difficult to accommodate in any kind of uniform fashion. Though their numbers were believed to be relatively small, their adverse impact on institutional life was considered to be far in excess of their relative size. In addition, they represented a disproportionately large segment of the population institutionalized on the basis of section 42 of the criminal code—about one-third in Baden-Württemberg in the midfifties, for instance.[22] Still, at this time, many psychiatrists remained reluctant to consider medical treatment a viable option in dealing with psychopaths, since "the condition did not constitute a disease."[23]

The problem was hardly unique to Germany. It was reported that psychiatric facilities throughout Europe were also doing their best to resist taking in dangerously incorrigible criminals.[24] But whereas countries like Denmark, Sweden, and Finland were seeking ways to place psychopaths in unconventional, treatment-oriented institutions of confinement, the West Germany of the fifties had only one possibility at its disposal beyond prisons and psychiatric hospitals: preventive detention. As observers at the time noted, however, the postwar courts were proving disinclined to using their authority to consign offenders to preventive detention.[25] Most federal states in West Germany simply adopted the procedure becoming common in East Germany as well: committing these offenders to psychiatric institutions.[26] As at least one hospital in northern Württemberg reported in 1957, the vast majority of those committed to its facility had been convicted of some kind of sexual offense, a statistic testifying to a strong continuity with trends that were in evidence during the Nazi regime.[27]

Critics of the existing system pinned their hopes for reform on the Large Criminal Law Commission convened by the Federal Ministry of Justice. Already by the fall of 1954, the commission was discussing whether to create "special facilities or special units within prisons" for handling psychopaths and dangerous repeat offenders. The issue arose within the context of debate over section 42 of the criminal code, the section regulating the forcible, indefinite commitment of offenders to treatment centers or preventive detention. Over the next two years, a series of prominent mental health experts weighed in on the issue, offering differing opinions: Theodor Ziehen and Alexander Mitscherlich, for instance, supported the creation of new, special facilities for psychopaths; Hans Gruhle and Max Mikorey argued that such individuals should remain in prisons; and Albrecht Langelüddeke expressed support for placing such criminals in forced labor facilities.[28]

Playing a pivotal role in discussions about psychopathic, dangerous repeat offenders was criminologist Rudolf Sieverts (1903–80), whose career, as we have seen, dated back to Weimar and Nazi Germany. Speaking before his fellow commission members in October 1955, Sieverts acknowledged what almost every expert in the field recognized, namely, "that the psychiatric facilities can absolutely not handle a host of psychopathic personality types, because they disrupt the entire atmosphere of such institutions." This being the case, he went on, the commission needed to consider establishing a new kind of facility.

> A distinct kind of accommodation is necessary for deviant personalities, which are not suited for a psychiatric institution but, from a legal standpoint of guilt, either warrant a light sentence or, due to their nature, cannot be treated in a penal facility, nor [do they] meet the prerequisites of other forms of confinement, such as preventive detention or the workhouse.[29]

Sieverts admitted to having in mind something along the lines of Denmark's special facility for psychopathic criminals. Psychiatrist Georg Stürup (1905–88) served as director of the Institution for the Treatment of Criminal Psychopaths at Herstedvester from 1942 to 1972, where he and his staff embarked on an effort at "treating the untreatable."[30] By the midfifties, Herstedvester's psychologists, its teachers, and the 130 members of its support staff were supervising two hundred detainees in three residential houses—most were sex offenders, violent criminals, or white-collar criminals—as well as an additional 350 parolees. Follow-up analysis at the time revealed that less than one-third of sex offenders released from the facility since 1942 had reoffended.[31]

In contrast to criminal biologists, Stürup believed that criminal psychopathy was socially, not biologically, determined, thus opening it up to clinical intervention. The key to treating psychopaths, he contended, was placing them for an indefinite period of time in a closed facility, with a highly regimented treatment plan. While Herstedvester offered individual and family psychotherapy, narcoanalysis, role playing, medications, and even surgery, the main focus of the facility was rehabilitation through immersion in a therapeutic community. In practice, this meant getting staff to coordinate their efforts in treatment teams, encouraging communication from detainees about their problems, and offering detainees alternative, more constructive ways to cope "during emotional moments."[32] Combining elements of discipline, security, surveillance, counseling, and medical treatment, Stürup's institution looked, to West German eyes, like a composite of prison, mental hospital, and preventive detention unit.

In the spring of 1956, Sieverts paid a visit to Stürup and toured the facility at Herstedvester. He was won over immediately and wrote to the Federal Ministry of Justice in enthusiastic terms about the "pioneering work" being done by Stürup and his team.

> The Danes are really the only ones in Europe who not only diagnose psychopathic offenders and place them in special facilities but also treat them

> with truly intensive psychotherapy, group pedagogy, etc. And it is so amazingly interesting here! No one in Germany—including our psychiatrists—has the experience, even at a distance, of what these men here have. And we cannot pass this up but instead need to take advantage of it. There is nothing idealistic going on, but, rather, everything is down to earth and is being realistically seen and carried out.[33]

In July 1956, Stürup was invited to discuss the Herstedvester program with experts associated with the West German Large Criminal Law Commission. His exchanges with these legal specialists reveal the extent to which his German counterparts remained wedded to long-standing psychiatric and administrative assumptions. The director of the psychiatric unit at the Klingelpütz penal facility in Cologne, in particular, did little to conceal his disdain for Stürup's program. Referring to psychopathic criminals as "an especially difficult mass of humanity," the Cologne physician argued that the psychoanalytical emphasis on narratives of life history neglected the importance of congenital abnormalities. "A *psychopathic disposition* is something one can very early on—I would like to say, already as an infant—recognize," he insisted, and he warned his colleagues not to be overly eager in adopting models from foreign countries: "Managing human beings is not something easily exported from one people to another. There are some national characters that are more easily influenced than others."[34]

At the same meeting, CDU politician and jurist Max Güde voiced skepticism that Stürup's approach could be imported to Germany. Herstedvester appeared to him, at least, to be nothing more than a hospital that understood crimes as "symptoms of a disease" and that was designed to treat the curably ill. It was far from clear in his mind that it made sense in the German context to treat convicts as patients. Stürup responded by saying that he considered his charges not ill but, rather, suffering from "personality problems" (*Persönlichkeitsprobleme*). The question that presents itself, he insisted, is "whether we should say that a perpetrator is absolutely lost. . . . One cannot express the judgment 'lost' about these people. When I confront a group, I know that only a portion can be resocialized, but I cannot say which ones they are."[35]

Sieverts and justice ministry officials Josef Schafheutle and Georg Schwalm (see chapter 5) were successful in getting the Large Criminal Law Commission to consider the design of special facilities for dangerous psychopathic offenders in Germany. Initially, the Federal Ministry of Justice supported the idea of establishing a new form of special detention called "institutional commitment" (*Anstaltungsunterbringung*), which itself was to consist of two new forms of confinement, a "sanatorium" (*Heilanstalt*) and a "detention facility" (*Bewahrungsanstalt*), with prison administrators deciding on their appropriateness in individual cases. The detention facility, Schwalm argued, was to take on a role similar to Stürup's Herstedvester facility, offering psychopaths psychiatric and psychological services—personality assessment, education, meaningful work, and group and individual therapy—in a carceral setting.[36]

Subsequent discussions among commission members and advisors largely revolved around the question of how these two facilities differed from one another and from conventional prison and preventive detention. As Schafheutle explained, for assignment to a "detention facility," it would not be enough that a judge determine a convict to be dangerous. Authorities also needed to identify a "pathological mental disturbance" behind the perpetrator's actions. "As a rule, *the detention facility should take only the people who are dangerous due to their abnormal nature*," he emphasized.[37] Thus, while sanatoriums were to cater to mentally ill criminals, the mentally abnormal (*Abartige*) would be directed to the new facilities designated for indefinite detention.

While these subtle distinctions could appear to outsiders to be much ado about nothing, they reveal the extent to which reformers were well aware that they were on the verge of redefining the boundaries of incapacitation and treatment within criminal justice. Whereas preventive detention and preventive custody during the Third Reich served as little more than harsh depositories for those deemed chronically incorrigible, West German authorities in the second half of the fifties were considering extending treatment to these same groups of offenders. This made it necessary not only to establish an effective division of labor between institutions of confinement but also to address the perennial tendency of criminal justice and mental health facilities to "dump" unwanted inmates and patients on one another.[38]

These were not matters that could be resolved quickly. The justice ministry continued to seek the counsel of leading experts, professional groups, and the federal states, in search of some kind of consensus. At the same time, officials recognized that any changes to existing legal practices would have a ripple effect and therefore needed to be coordinated with other reforms being considered. Commission members and representatives from the justice ministry moved cautiously in discussing different aspects of proposals for psychopathic facilities. The definition of dangerousness, the possibility of parole for detainees, and the institutional setting for the new facilities were all topics of debate.

As the decade approached its end, at least one observer could not help expressing the concern that the creation of special facilities for psychopaths was less a response to a public health problem than a quick fix to an administrative inconvenience. Correctional specialist Otto (?) Wilfert told the commission in March 1959 that the clear motivation for constructing the new detention facilities was "to unburden psychiatric facilities of those perpetrators who appear not suited to the possible and conventional methods used there and [who] thus play the role in these facilities of 'disruptives and swallowers of foreign objects.'" While such individuals were being routinely referred to as "psychopaths," he added, little to no attention was being paid to the varieties and degrees of mental disturbances from which they supposedly suffered: epileptics, alcoholics, those with brain damage or learning disabilities, and many others were simply being lumped together. In the end, he insisted, the treatment program at Herstedvester was predominantly medical and psychotherapeutic, treating its detainees as sick individuals not responsible for their actions. Rather than inventing an ostensibly new kind of institution, he concluded, the Federal Republic would be better served learning to make existing prisons and mental hospitals more accommodating to a wider variety of deviants.[39]

The Debate over Castration, 1946–69

While reformers considered creating a new type of treatment facility that would accommodate dangerous, repeat sex offenders, a related debate was raging. As discussed in chapter 2, National Socialism had introduced the compulsory castration of dangerous repeat sex offenders and eventually castrated around twenty-four hundred men. After World War II, Allied Control Council Law Number 11 (30 January 1946) annulled the provision of the criminal code (section 42k) authorizing the procedure.[40] Despite this, neither the Control Council nor the Western military governments occupying Germany invalidated the eugenic hereditary health laws, justifying their decisions on the basis that the regulations were not "typically Nazi" and that similar laws had been enacted domestically by the occupying powers. As a result, there was no uniformity in how the matters of sterilization and voluntary castration were to be handled in postwar western Germany. While Bavaria and Hesse repealed the hereditary health law in 1945 and 1946 respectively, legal confusion remained elsewhere as to whether the voluntary castration of sex offenders was permissible.[41]

In Hamburg in April 1946, for example, the parents of twenty-six-year-old H.G. requested that physicians be allowed to castrate their son. At the time, G. was an involuntary patient in a local asylum, having been transferred there after he was determined to be clinically "feebleminded." Since 1939, G. had been arrested multiple times for initiating sexual contact with young boys and had persisted in this behavior within the asylum as well. Physicians supported the parents' request, stating, "As a result of his feeblemindedness, he is not in the position to marshal the necessary inhibitions against the urges of his sexual pursuits. Castration will likely diminish or extinguish these urges."[42] Records show that prosecutors, justice officials, and health authorities in the British zone of occupation at the time were admittedly unclear as to whether the procedure was allowable. In the end, the president of the Central Justice Office for the British zone rejected the request, fearing that it would give the German public the impression that authorities were setting a precedent for questionable castrations in the name of short-term expedience.[43]

State-Sponsored Research: Albrecht Langelüddeke and the Federal Ministry of Justice

Awareness of the impending reform of the governing criminal code after the founding of the Federal Republic in 1949 provided the spur for experts to more carefully reconsider castration as a criminal policy tool. In July 1951, the chief physician at the psychiatric facility in Marburg-Lahn, Albrecht Langelüddeke, informed the Federal Ministry of Justice of his intention to conduct a thorough empirical study of castration, from both medical and criminal justice perspectives. Arguing that the castration of over two thousand men during the Third Reich offered a kind of natural experiment whose results could be longitudinally and epidemiologically evaluated, he requested that the ministry consider sponsoring his research.[44]

After becoming a *Privatdozent* in 1930, Langelüddeke's career had taken off under the National Socialists. Joining the party and several other party organizations in 1933, he became a professor and director of the state psychiatric facility at Haina in Hesse in 1935. Two years later, he moved to Marburg and became director of the state asylum there, a position he held until 1945. During the Third Reich, Langelüddeke served as a judge on the local superior court overseeing sterilization. While he had to give up his directorship when the war ended, he returned to the position in 1949 and continued to hold it until 1954, after which he served as a regular consultant to West German courts.[45]

Archival records reveal that both the justice and interior ministries supported Langelüddeke's project, considering its data and conclusions useful to judges and legal reformers. Nevertheless, officials privately expressed reservations about having Langelüddeke conduct his research under the auspices of the justice ministry. Interior minister Robert Lehr (CDU) worried that, if done as a government study, it might well encourage the compensation claims being made by men castrated under the Nazi regime. In addition, the proposed study, which was to include follow-up examinations, would provoke widespread resistance from ex-convicts, at the same time that data collection would overly burden courts and government offices.[46] In the end, the justice ministry steered Langelüddeke to the German Research Consortium for funding but instructed state ministries of justice to assist in collecting data and records for the project.[47] The federal states obliged, sending the ministry criminal records on hundreds of castrated convicts, which were passed on to Langelüddeke in installments.[48]

The federal justice ministry's cooperation with Langelüddeke was indicative of one of the major differences between the West and East German states' relationships with experts and the behavioral sciences during the 1950s. Whereas the SED largely distrusted specialists from the human sciences and kept them at a distance from policy-making circles throughout the decade, the Federal Republic, as we have seen, actively solicited expert opinion and encouraged the application of independent research. The justice ministry treated the psychiatrist as an experienced and impartial resource whose research could provide reforms with an unbiased and empirically sound underpinning. In fact, even after publishing the results of his research in 1963, Langelüddeke was regularly asked to comment on specific questions arising in policy discussions. When, in November 1968, the ministry defended the draft of its voluntary castration bill before a special committee of the Bundestag, an official was careful to point out that it was "by and large supported by science," singling out Langelüddeke for special mention. "His work 'The Castration of Sex Offenders' from 1963," he announced, "has been fundamental for subsequent legislative efforts."[49]

In the end, Langelüddeke ended up studying records in 1,036 of what he estimated to be 2,800 cases of men castrated during the Third Reich, tracking criminal records following the operation. In addition, he personally conducted medical examinations and interviews with eighty-nine of the men. His results appeared to offer strong encouragement to supporters of castration. Only twenty-four castrated convicts (2.3 percent) had reoffended following the operation, though the recidivism rate was higher for some groups—for instance, among offenders aged 21–30 (5.3 percent) and homosexual perpetrators (5.9 percent). While he acknowledged ethical reservations about inmates' ability to consent and about the side effects of the procedure, Langelüddeke concluded that surgical castration was especially effective on child molesters, exhibitionists, and rapists. "It is the surest method to avoid recidivism," he insisted, adding, "It is, however, a procedure to be taken seriously and should be used only as *ultimum refugium*."[50]

Considering the Castration of Women

While Langelüddeke's research appeared to provide the medical justification for castrating sex offenders, a decision of the Federal Supreme Court in December 1963 provided key legal support. Reviewing the case of an exhibitionist who requested to be castrated, the court concluded that the operation did not violate Article 2 of the Basic Law (the right to the integrity of one's own body), since its aim and effect were to ameliorate a "degenerate" sexual drive. The judges made it clear, however, that the operation was permissible "insofar as it is the sole medical means to liberate the afflicted of a degenerate sexual drive and insofar as it promises success." They specified the prerequisite that "the afflicted individual voluntarily wishes to undergo the procedure after careful consultation with a physician about the nature and consequences involved."[51]

Thus, by the early 1960s, authoritative voices in West German jurisprudence and clinical research reiterated Nazi-era thinking and designated castration to be a medically indicated, therapeutic intervention first and foremost, only secondarily functioning as a criminal policy tool. Within this framework, the Large Criminal Law Commission and specialists during the late 1950s and 1960s went about considering a specific law governing the use of castration. A number of questions about the parameters of such a law arose within this context. Reservations voiced since the 1930s about the efficacy of castration on homosexual men, for instance, continued to be raised.[52] The federal justice ministry was keen on establishing a minimum age for the operation—it followed Langelüddeke in proposing age twenty-five—owing especially to worries about possible "atypical side effects" in younger men.[53]

Unlike experts during the Third Reich, some in West Germany proposed expanding the reach of the operation to women in the form of ovariectomy. Norwegian and Danish laws made provision for just this very thing, and according to a source from the justice ministry, the Child Protection League (Kinderschutzbund) had suggested the notion of performing ovariectomies on some female offenders as early as 1964.[54] Over the next few years, both the Commission of the German Society for Legal and Social Medicine and the League of Women Physicians voiced their support for the idea.[55]

Debate over the inclusion of women reveals the extent to which clinical and legal experts at the time considered males and females to be similar and different in their relative captivity to their sexual drives. Forensic psychiatrist Siegfried Haddenbrock, director of the psychiatric hospital in Emmendingen since 1954, was the leading voice advocating the extension of "castration" to women. Writing to the Baden-Württemberg Ministry of Interior in the fall of 1967, Haddenbrock contended that, while rare, there were instances in which women committed crimes due to sexual pathology, such as forms of cleptomania. In these instances, he argued, the sexual excitement derived from stealing was so deeply rooted that it made these women incapable of being influenced, resistant to "all therapeutic efforts."[56] A leading official in the Federal Ministry of Justice who later wrote to Haddenbrock explained that he saw little reason for making any special provisions for women, owing to the nature and small number of sex offenses they tended to commit. Noting that only nineteen women were convicted of child molestation in 1965 (compared to 1,195 men), the official pointed out, "If I am seeing this right, sexual pathological crimes by women consistently involve acts with little criminal substance, crimes in which the perpetrator herself suffers more than the victim."[57]

Despite the justice ministry's attitude, Haddenbrock's thinking managed to persuade some in government circles to support the idea of voluntary ovariectomies for female offenders. Both the Plenum of the Bundesrat and the Health Committee of the Bundestag came out in support of the notion. Clinical advisors to the Bundestag's Special Committee for Criminal Law Reform, however, dismissed the idea as ineffective. At a meeting of the special committee in November 1968, both sexuality researcher Werner Krause and endocrinologist Ursula Laschet conceded that women could suffer from hypersexuality and that crimes like shoplifting could be sexually motivated for some female offenders. They emphasized, however, that there was no scientific evidence to support the contention that "castration of women has any kind of influence on cleptomania and other kinds of criminal tendencies."[58] In the end, legislators were persuaded by clinical researchers that removing a woman's ovaries had little bearing on her libido and that, instead, some form of drug treatment promised far more success in treating female shoplifters and arsonists motivated by erotic impulses.[59]

The debate over whether to include women in any new castration law offers interesting insight into the attitudes of reformers toward human biology and psychology during the 1960s. As Anthony Kauders has observed, the prominence of psychoanalysis at the time opened up the possibility for a less materialist reading of human sexuality, one that continued to see sexuality in energetic terms but that was now extended, beyond talk of sex "drives" and "instincts," to include forms of suppressed and sublimated lust.[60] This created a new set of challenges for lawmakers especially, since it upset a long German tradition of jurisprudence—one especially influential in West Germany—that deferred only to somatic explanations of physicians about psychopathologies. Moreover, psychoanalytic thinking appeared to lend credence to the idea that women, too, could be capable of committing sexually violent crimes like rape, a possibility the chairman of the Bundestag's Special Committee on Criminal Law Reform, Max Güde (CDU) considered out of the question.[61] In the end, the castration law of 15 August 1969 excluded women from consideration as recipients of castration (section 1) but mentioned them alongside men (section 4, no. 1) as eligible for medical treatment "of an abnormal sexual drive," which did not aim "to make the genitals nonfunctional on a long-term basis but nevertheless could have just such a result."[62]

The Expansion and Limits of Incapacitation: Public Opinion and the Experts

As reformers and experts weighed the criteria for the voluntary castration of sex offenders during the years 1964–68, two sets of public discussions over the incapacitation of convicts converged on their deliberations. On the one hand, conversations among experts about how broadly to define the probable threat posed by a criminal—a precondition for the operation—led those in reform circles to draw connections between castration and plans for building psychopath facilities. At the same time, via letter-writing campaigns, lobbying groups, and the mass media, an increasingly vocal West German public called on an often resistant federal government to adopt a harder line toward sex offenders. As a result, reformers were led to more deliberately link therapy and incapacitation, to draw out the criminal prevention aspects of clinical treatment.

Well before the Bundestag took up the issue of castration, connections had been drawn between sex offenders, psychopathy, and preventive detention. During its early years, the psychopath facility at Herstedvester had a residential population composed mostly of men convicted of sexual crimes, and under Georg Stürup's direction, the group remained a chief target. As discussed in previous chapters, the German public and officials both during and after the Third Reich frequently sought to use the preventive detention system to incapacitate dangerous repeat sex offenders. Now, in the 1960s, observers were increasingly drawn to portraying sex offenders as psychopaths incapable of being integrated into the conventional system for mental health care.[63]

Many specialists spoke in favor of treating sex offenders as a unique category of convicts, one requiring special attention catered to their peculiar needs.

At a meeting of justice officials in Hamburg in May 1967, for instance, the psychiatric consultants unanimously agreed that existing psychotherapeutic interventions held no promise of success for all but a few perpetrators. In the view of these consultants, the only solution to preventing sex offenders from committing future crimes was incapacitation. This meant, they argued, relying on medical treatment—in the form of castration and new, experimental hormonal preparations—and establishing special facilities solely for sex offenders, where the inmates could be studied and given postoperative treatment.[64]

Arguably the most strident calls for incapacitation came from the West German lay public. In some instances, individual citizens took the opportunity to directly write officials in Bonn to demand that the government adopt a hard line toward sex offenders. In almost every instance, the letter writer explained that he or she had been outraged by news reports about the sexual murder of children. For example, late in the summer of 1962, A.M. cited two recent cases involving "thugs" (*Strolche*) with previous sexual crime convictions, who had raped and murdered a five-year-old girl and a seven-year-old girl respectively. Lamenting the fact that West German law made no provision for handing down death sentences in cases like these, the man called on the government "to issue a law, according to which anyone who is guilty of committing a sex offense, whether old or young, is subject to castration."[65] After being told by the justice ministry that such an operation could only be performed in select cases, owing to the operation's powerful side effects, A.M. insisted that the ministry was out of step with the general public. "Just once, ask the people," he demanded, "and you will discover, esteemed Herr Minister, that 80 percent are for castration of sex offenders against schoolchildren. And why not, since we do live in a democracy, according to which the voice of the people must be heard."[66]

Five and a half years later, the farmer L.S. voiced similar sentiments, albeit in somewhat different terms. Having recently read that federal minister of justice Gustav Heinemann had publicly renounced the death penalty for child molesters, S. wrote to the government, explaining that West Germany's prosperity was in large measure to blame for the reported rise in rape, sexually motivated murders, and child sexual abuse. The problem, he contended, was the "exaggerated sexualization" of public life through girlie magazines and salacious novels and films, which overwhelmed and incited immature and weak-willed persons. He wrote that voluntary castration of sex offenders was far too humane an approach to dissuade such perpetrators. Voicing views reminiscent of criminal biology in the thirties and forties, S. proposed, "In order to protect society, in cases of unimpeachable evidence, compulsory and total castration—meaning removal of the gonads—should be obligatory. Repetition of such a crime as well as the inheritance of criminal constitutions might be prevented in this manner."[67]

The increased public focus on sexual crime during the years when both the Bundestag and the Bundesrat were considering legislation regulating castration was neither spontaneous nor coincidental. From 1964 until the law passed in the summer of 1968, groups that focused on victim advocacy and child protection actively sought to gain the attention of legislators and the mass media. A comparative look at the rhetoric that these actors employed demonstrates how laymen self-consciously offered an image of criminal justice that presented an alternative to the image being crafted by legal reformers and specialists from the human sciences.

On 10 November 1965, for instance, the magazine *Der Spiegel* used the recent case of Cologne resident Richard Strack to publish a lengthy article raising questions about how West German authorities had come to deal with criminals who had committed sex offenses against children. A month earlier, Strack had used a hatchet to murder two eleven-year-old girls, after which he sexually defiled their bodies. On 3 November, *Der Spiegel* had already reported that since 1952, a year had not gone by—with the exception of the year Strack married—during which the man was not convicted of at least one crime (including at least five sex offenses since April 1964).[68] Now, a week later, the magazine linked Strack's case to those of Bruno Pupecka, who committed over twenty-two sexual crimes and seven brutally violent attacks on women and girls in Hamburg in 1958 and 1959, and Peter Pesch, a Duisburg man with a criminal record who had abducted and killed a four-year-old girl during a work break. For the criminals' opportunities to commit these crimes, the magazine placed blame firmly at the feet of lax and inattentive judges, forensic psychiatrists, and politicians.

Referring to a circular from the Freiburg Association for the Prevention and Restitution of Criminal Acts, *Der Spiegel* cited some alarming figures: of sixty-two thousand sex offenses annually in the Federal Republic, eighteen thousand were committed against children, and forty-four thousand were committed against women and girls. Meanwhile, the conviction rate for sexual crimes against minors was actually going down, from 11.1 persons per one hundred thousand residents in 1954 to 7.8 in 1963. Making matters worse, the magazine went on, was the fact that authorities were unwilling to act in those cases involving repeat offenders. It noted that judges were reluctant to sentence sex offenders to preventive detention, due to its associations with National Socialism, and that though the practice of voluntary castration was perfectly legal in a number "democratic countries," the Erhard government was letting a national law simply languish because some federal states feared opposition from the churches.[69]

The justice ministry considered the *Der Spiegel* article riddled with errors and planned to publicly respond to it contentions.[70] The magazine piece gave voice, however, to notions and attitudes that others confirmed were prevalent among the general public.[71] Time and again, citizen groups and media outlets pointed out that sexual assaults on children and women were rising out of control, that jurists were overindulging criminals, and that offenders needed to be dealt with more harshly.

The expressions of public outrage were especially pronounced in the years 1964–67, when coverage of a series of sexual assaults and murders of children—among them were Klaus Lehnert's murder of Timo Rinnelt in early 1964, the Stracker case in the fall of 1965, and the arrest of Jürgen Bartsch in the summer of 1966 for the murder of several boys—sparked a moral panic in West Germany.[72] Lobbying groups such as the German Child Protection League and the Freiburg-based Association for Crime Prevention and Restitution (Verband zur Verhütung und Wiedergutmachung von Straftaten) typically aligned themselves with the suffering of mothers and the welfare of children, while associating the justice system with naïveté and a clinical callousness. In the fall of 1965, for instance, the Freiburg group published a newsletter demanding that victims or their families be heard in all clemency cases and that they receive damages from perpetrators. At the same time, the association called for national registration and castration of all repeat and violent sex offenders and criticized psychiatrists and judges for their "experiment-happy psychologization of criminal law" and for treating criminality like a disease.[73]

Both the German Child Protection League and the Freiburg Association railed against what they termed the new "soft wave" or "psychology wave," which they attributed to postwar West German law.[74] In its place, they offered a more forceful idea of incapacitation. Couched in the vernacular terms of maternal and parental domesticity, it insisted on protection through harsh deterrence and on restricting the influence of scientific and medical expertise.[75]

Women and women's groups took on a leading role in the reaction against therapeutic penology toward sex offenders. In June 1967, the convention of the Women's Consortium (Frauenarbeitsgemeinschaft) of the Christian Social Union (CSU) in Bavaria passed a resolution encouraging the federal minister of justice "to apply more severely and exhaust all punitive means at your disposal" in the state's campaign against sexual crime.[76] In Rhineland-Pfalz, the Women's Circle (Frauenring) in Pirmasen recruited the support of local professionals, police, the Child Protection League, the CDU, and the local newspaper in organizing a petition campaign during the fall of 1967. According to the group, by early October, over ten thousand people had signed a petition that demanded greater protection for children, lifelong imprisonment for sexual criminals, and compulsory castration for all child molesters. "These murderers cannot be cured," commented one angry resident, and almost a quarter of those signing called for the reintroduction of the death penalty.[77] Under the headline "Our Youth Are Not Wild Game! Protect Our Children from Sex Criminals!," the *Pirmasener Zeitung* asked individual readers to pass on their comments to the newspaper.[78] The comments published expressed both a strong retributive current running through public opinion and a remarkable willingness for residents to praise National Socialist crime policy, as the following sampling demonstrates:

> Castration was always the surest way. E.T.
> I am for hanging child molesters. A.S.
> I am for the death penalty and compulsory castration for sex crimes. Dr. M.
> Only the death penalty will help. Castration is too lenient. H.T.
> You would need a Hitler. He would get rid of these people. J.S.
> Categorical sterilization up to death penalty. H.S.
> Chop off their heads! Dr. G.
> For these guys, we need the Hitler Reich back. E.B.[79]

Reactionary statements such as these were far from rare during the second half of the 1960s in West Germany. Kerstin Brückweh has found similar views echoed in letters written by citizens to authorities during the trials of the serial killer Jürgen Bartsch between 1966 and 1971.[80] It would be presumptuous to assume, however, that these expressions of outrage exposed a widespread, latent sympathy for National Socialism. Rather, the linking of the death penalty with compulsory castration revealed that many Germans considered the latter to properly be a form of punishment and incapacitation rather than a therapy.

Officials in the Federal Ministry of Justice at the time understood the public backlash as more or less an overreaction to irrational fears whipped up by the popular press. Time and again, authorities explained to petitioners, the Bundestag, and the media that the statistics thrown around by groups and magazines were demonstrably inflated—the Freiburg group and the then family magazine *Praline* continued to repeat the figures of eighteen thousand child and forty-four thousand female sexual crime victims annually in the FRG. Government statistics at the time did register between sixteen thousand and nineteen thousand police complaints every year about indecency with children during the years 1953–64, but most of these were for minor infractions: only about one in every five cases led to a conviction for sex or attempted sex with a minor. Moreover, the number of cases involving the sexual abuse and killing of a child remained very low, fluctuating between ten and seventeen cases a year from 1961 to 1965.[81]

Justice minister Gustav Heinemann flat out rejected calls for the reimposition of the death penalty, noting, "The human sciences teach that one should not overestimate the deterrent effect of threats of punishment. This also holds true for the death penalty."[82] Officials explained that tougher sentences for child molesters, making it easier to place suspects and convicts in security confinement, the building of detention centers, and more effective supervision of parolees were the measures the government was taking to ensure the public's safety.

Thus, the lobbying efforts of citizens and victims' groups appear to have had only a limited effect on politicians. In part, this was because, by late 1964, many of those involved in the reform process had already expressed their support for augmenting the incapacitating impact of voluntary castration by not requiring the presence of a disease or the commission of a crime in order to approve its use.[83] When, in the fall of 1965, one CDU member of the Bundestag from Düsseldorf put forward the idea of reinstituting compulsory castration for sex offenders, it was rejected by justice ministry officials, who deemed it unconstitutional and ineffective.[84] Still, officials from the justice ministry in Bonn eventually agreed to meet with representatives from the German Child Protection League to discuss their demands. Discussions led to their reaching a consensus to limit the castration of sex offenders to a voluntary basis yet find ways for the criminal justice system and victims' groups to work more closely in actively educating parents and children about sexuality and in attending to the unique plight of child victims.[85]

Don Juan, Casanova, and Androcur: Medicalizing Sexual Crime

By the summer of 1968, virtually all relevant federal and state ministries had come out in support of a new law providing for the voluntary castration of sex offenders (the one exception being the Federal Ministry of Interior, which believed it to be unconstitutional). This left one set of hurdles before a draft bill could be sent to the Bundestag for consideration: ironing out the administrative procedures and the circle of eligible candidates for the operation. As reformers debated a low-end age limit and in what form and under what conditions consent could be granted, concerns continued to be raised over the competing goals of castration—namely, the goals of general crime prevention, on the one hand, and special prevention (equated, in this instance, with medical treatment), on the other.[86]

While virtually all psychiatrists advising the government supported castration as an effective treatment for repeat sexual offenders, some jurists continued to worry that general prevention concerns weighed too heavily in the thinking about criteria for castration in individual cases. For some, at least, it smacked of the kind of eugenic thinking used under the Nazis to justify population policy measures.[87] Against this backdrop, reformers decided to explore another possible treatment for sex offenders: chemical castration.

As discussed in chapter 4, the antiandrogen Androcur was first developed in 1961. While not introduced in East German clinics until 1973, the hormone treatment was already being used in West Germany by the mid-1960s. Rumors about Androcur's potential for reducing the sex drive of men were already circulating at that time in the press and among members of the Bundestag's Special Committee for Criminal Law Reform.[88] Toward the end of 1966, the Federal Ministry of Justice initiated contact with the German clinicians experimenting with the drug, who reported that it was too early to draw any definitive conclusions about its use.[89]

To many involved in crafting a castration law, the prospect of an effective and reversible form of castration seemed to offer a way out of the ethical and legal dilemmas facing lawmakers. So, in the fall of 1968, the Special Committee for Criminal Law invited discussion of the medication and its effects from two clinical researchers who were testing cyproterone acetate on patients: Ursula Laschet (the director of the Psychoendocrinology Department of the Palatinate Psychiatric Clinic) and Werner Krause (a professor and researcher at the Institute for Sexual Research at the University of Hamburg). Laschet informed officials that while surgical castration appeared to be a more invasive procedure, antiandrogen treatment was actually more comprehensive in its effects. Surgical castration solely disabled androgen production in male gonads, she reported, but androgens were also produced by the adrenal cortex, something left untouched by the operation. About treatments using cyproterone acetate, Laschet further explained,

> The function of the adrenal cortex remains completely unchanged, nevertheless androgens produced by the adrenal cortex . . . are made ineffectual via competitive occupation of the receptors with antiandrogen. In this way, the remaining sexuality can also be switched off.[90]

Appearing before the Bundestag's special committee in November 1968, Laschet explained that neither surgical nor chemical castration could be considered a panacea for all forms of sexual deviation. By leaving the adrenal cortex's production of androgen unaffected, the removal of the testicles did not always extinguish a man's libido and potency: indeed, Langelüddeke's study had shown that 35 percent of the men he had examined were still able to be sexually active after the procedure. Moreover, it had been demonstrated that homosexuality did not respond to either form of castration with any reliability. The drug appeared to be especially effective, however, on exhibitionists and compulsive masturbators.[91]

Both Laschet and Werner Krause expressed concerns about relying too heavily on crime prevention indicators for approving castrations of any kind. Laschet pointed out that at her clinic, "around a third of the 80 medically treated men have come for outpatient treatment—Don Juanism."[92] By mentioning Don Juanism (aka Don Juan syndrome), Laschet was referring to satyriasis. The diagnosis of satyriasis, the male counterpart to nymphomania, dates back to ancient times and was historically attributed to certain men who manifested a seemingly irresistible and unbridled lecherousness.[93] As Krause pointed out to the committee, it was critical, from a clinical standpoint, to distinguish between criminal sexual deviations, sexual addictions, and promiscuity. "Don Juanism and promiscuity are not the same thing," Krause emphasized, explaining, "From our perspective, Don Juan was ill; Casanova was simply promiscuous. So, for example, we could not [under the conditions being discussed] treat either one. We could not treat abnormally practiced forms of sexuality that are not violations of the law."[94]

To some extent, the emergence of cyproterone acetate clouded the picture for reformers, making it necessary to recontextualize surgical castration's effectiveness and ethics. For the most part, however, the rise of Androcur helped cement castration's status as a form of medical treatment. In effect, the solution to the reformers' quandary was to medicalize the problem of sexual crime. With German, Dutch, and Scandinavian studies all reporting a recidivism rate between 1 and 3 percent for castrated sex offenders, many reformers shared—whether out of conviction or expedience—the view of forensic psychiatrist W. Mende, that "surgical castration should be primarily a therapeutic intervention, a means to cure a disease, to treat a sex offender."[95] The director of the psychiatric hospital in Eickelborn in Westphalia, whose forensic unit in Rottland-Lippstadt cared for seven hundred patients institutionalized by the courts, made a similar point. The facility had a large number of repeat sex offenders and offered a range of treatment regimens, including surgical and chemical castration (thirty-one castrations were performed there between March 1965 and November 1968). For those sex offenders shown to be truly "sexually addicted," he added, "we feel obligated as physicians to cure and ameliorate a disease, once we have diagnosed it."[96]

When the West German law allowing for the voluntary castration of sex offenders was finalized in August 1969 (first taking effect in 1970), it recognized the procedure solely as a form of treatment "against the effects of an abnormal sex drive."[97] This hardly made it immune from criticism. Surgical castration remained especially controversial, called into question in the aftermath of the death of serial killer Jürgen Bartsch during his operation in 1976 and, more recently, by the European Committee for the Prevention of Torture.[98] All told, from 1970 to 1980, over 770 applications for castration were submitted in the Federal Republic, with about four hundred castrations taking place. Over the course of the 1980s, however, so-called medical castration committees within the individual federal states proved to be increasingly reluctant to grant applications, approving only around five applications a year until 1989.[99]

The Rise, Fall, and Rise of Social Therapeutic Facilities, 1960–89

Writing a Law and Finding a Name

At the same time that voluntary castration was being debated, a parallel and sometimes intersecting series of discussions among experts continued on the topic of finding a way to effectively house dangerous and repeat sex offenders. As was the case with those considering new castration legislation, government officials and reformers carried out their work under the scrutiny of the media and general public. As the 1950s came to an end and the new decade began, victim advocacy groups, religious groups, and parent groups, along with individual citizens, voiced their concerns that lawmakers, acting "out of humanitarian sensitivity," were "giving the protection of criminals more thought than the protection of victims."[100] Calling for tougher prison sentences for those convicted of sexual crimes, the petitions and complaints of these groups tended to follow a similar script: one could not read the newspaper without hearing of another child sexually assaulted and killed; those committing these crimes were amoral, sick degenerates; children and the public deserved to be protected; the most effective way to keep innocent children safe was to reinstate the death penalty and castrate all sex offenders.[101] Justice officials typically responded by reassuring the public that the government took these concerns seriously and was dedicated to using the state's power of indefinite commitment to keep dangerous sexual criminals off the streets.[102]

As noted earlier in this chapter, by 1961, the Federal Ministry of Justice had expressed its support for adding another form of indefinite commitment besides preventive detention and psychiatric hospitalization. While the target of the new institutions of confinement was ostensibly psychopathic repeat offenders, the fact that there was no agreement on what to call these new facilities exposed a general lack of clarity about their mission. Psychiatric and legal specialists bandied about a number of options, including "detention facility" (*Bewahrungsanstalt*), "correctional care and detention facility" (*Heilerziehungs- und Bewahranstalt*), "resocialization facility" (*Resozialisierungsanstalt*), and "medical-pedagogical resocialization facility" (*ärztlich-pädagogische Resozialisierungsanstalt*).[103]

In the meantime, reformers were successful in getting a draft of a bill before committees of both the Bundesrat and the Bundestag by the spring of 1963. Answering a reporter's question about the nature of the new facilities, a leading justice ministry official at the time explained that the idea for them arose out of suggestions from psychiatrists, neurologists, and criminologists and from Danish and Dutch experiences treating psychopaths. The new German detention centers, he added, were to be something between a penitentiary and a psychiatric unit, designed to enhance the "fitness" of those mentally abnormal criminals for whom neither institution was suitable. "In particular," he explained, "we are talking about psychopathic, sexually disturbed, or slightly feebleminded offenders."[104]

As deliberations continued over the course of 1963 and 1964, prominent specialists in social work and psychiatry took the opportunity to urge lawmakers to grant the new custodial facilities a broad mandate. For instance, the head of the Rhineland Landschaftsverband, an organization that oversaw a variety of psychiatric and social services there, pressured the North Rhine–Westphalian minister of justice to support the new legislation, claiming that around 25 percent of the male and 10 percent of the female residents undergoing drug and alcohol rehabilitation alone were wholly unreceptive to conventional correction.[105] A year later, the head of the facility for the criminally mentally ill in Giessen spoke at a public meeting held at the Federal Criminal Office in Wiesbaden and echoed sentiments dating back to at least the Weimar Republic. Most of those abnormal individuals who got in trouble with the law, he insisted, could not be helped by medicine. Out of humanitarian concern for the welfare of treatable patients, such "psychopaths and feebleminded" needed to be removed from psychiatric hospitals like his. "Thus, our demand is: liberate us from the feebleminded and incurable psychopaths, so that we have room and time for the genuinely mentally ill," he proclaimed, adding, "Take the abnormals and criminals out of our facilities and build criminal justice detention facilities for them and for the benefit of the truly mentally ill."[106]

By early 1965, the three major political parties (the CDU/CSU, SPD, and FDP) had reached a consensus in support of constructing therapeutic detention centers for otherwise incorrigible offenders. Nevertheless, differences remained in the functions that each party ascribed to the facilities. This becomes especially clear when examining the divergent ways in which the parties sought to name the new institutions. Members of the SPD were joined by the German Society for Psychiatry and Neurology in wanting to stress the destigmatizing, therapeutic, and pedagogical orientation of the facility and proposed a host of possible names, including "resocialization facility" (*Resozialiseriungsanstalt*), "social pedagogical facility" (*sozialpädagogische Anstalt*), and "therapeutic pedagogical facility" (*heilpädagogische Anstalt*). A CDU/CSU member of the Bundestag's special committee on criminal law, by contrast, suggested the name "psychiatric custodial facility" (*psychiatrische Verwahrungsanstalt*). In his view, the term *Verwahrung* (connoting custody, safekeeping) best conveyed the sense that a resident in the facility was dangerous, like a loaded gun, and therefore needed to be safely kept under lock and key. A representative from the FDP on the same committee, however, spoke in favor of retaining the original label "detention center" (*Bewahrungsanstalt*), since it carried with it a sense, on the one hand, that "the general public is supposed to be protected from this group of people and, on the other, that this group of people is to be protected from committing more criminal acts."[107]

These differences demonstrate just how difficult it continued to be for reformers and policy makers in Weimar, National Socialist, and West Germany to balance the incapacitating and the rehabilitative dimensions of indefinite detention. Striking that balance was not something medical experts or researchers alone could accomplish. Rather, as a matter of weighing the importance of various public values against one another, it was left to the realm of politics. As illustrated by disagreements between the conservative-led Bavarian Ministry of Justice and the SPD-led Federal Ministry of Justice in the years 1966–68, conservatives continued to insist that the purpose of indefinite detention was primarily public safety, while Social Democrats generally argued for the primacy of rehabilitation.[108] In retrospect, it is perhaps not surprising that, by early 1968, West German lawmakers finally found terminology on which most could agree. Naming the facilities by invoking the broadly popular term *social*, the lawmakers settled on calling them "social therapeutic facilities" (*sozialtherapeutische Anstalten*).

The social therapeutic facilities were formally recognized on 4 July 1969 by the Second Criminal Code Reform. Explicitly cited as amendments to the Dangerous Habitual Offender Law first enacted by the National Socialists in 1933, sections 61–65 of the reform established social therapeutic facilities as a fourth possible form of indefinite confinement, alongside psychiatric hospitals, centers for substance abuse treatment, and preventive detention units. Commitment there was to be limited to an offender serving at least a two-year sentence and manifesting "a severe personality disturbance" and to anyone who, "due to a willful criminal act attributable to his sexual drive, is sentenced to at least five years in prison" while "the danger exists that he will commit further significant criminal acts associated with his sexual drive."[109]

The Facilities Imagined

Passage of the Second Criminal Code Reform hardly meant that inmates immediately started being committed to the new institutions. In reality, only one institution that existed in West Germany at the time could claim to be performing the work of a social therapeutic facility (a unit for psychopaths at Hohenasperg in Baden-Württemberg). Thus, by 1970, social therapeutic facilities remained little more than a set of principles and ambitions.

With the convention of the Prison Commission from the fall of 1967 to the fall of 1970, discussions about the scope and nature of social therapeutic facilities were folded into reforms being planned for the entire West German penal system. For many connected to the process of prison reform, the future social therapeutic facility represented two things: (1) a custodial institution that could accept traditionally incorrigible inmates and (2) an emblem of the ideals being projected onto the new treatment prison. When the commission eventually made its recommendations in October 1969, it made it clear that therapeutic interventions were to have priority over disciplinary sanctions in these new institutions of confinement. An inmate's eligibility for commitment to the facility was to be based not on there being an overriding need for the person's incapacitation but, rather, on his or her suitability for the treatment regimen there. Following trends in social psychiatry,[110] personnel were to include psychiatrists, psychotherapists, psychologists, social pedagogues, and social workers, with treatment administered by "teams" offering a variety of individual, group, and work therapies.[111]

Reaffirming the critical importance of the human sciences in this carceral enterprise, the commission also recommended that the new social therapeutic facilities be built in locations directly accessible to institutions of scientific research, particularly those specializing in the fields of psychology, psychotherapy, social pedagogy, and criminology. In the words of a subcommittee on prison reform that was tasked to set up the new system in several states, "the goal must be the trial and application of different kinds of treatment methods in conjunction with research from different fields. In this manner, new scientific research results can then be brought to the professional staff of the social therapeutic facility in short order."[112]

The subcommittee, made up of criminal justice officials from five West German states and the federal justice ministry, began working out the scale and scope of the new detention centers in December 1969. The selection of residents was to be left up to psychiatrists, who would decide on an inmate's suitability on the basis of various factors: length of sentence, age, intelligence, and readiness and aptitude for cooperation. The psychotherapies considered best suited to the work covered the gamut of mainstream offerings: psychoanalysis, depth psychology, group therapy, milieu therapy, behavioral therapy, work therapy, and psychosomatics. All told, the group estimated that demand for the facilities would involve around 13–15 percent of the total prison population and would require about twenty to thirty facilities nationwide with a typical capacity of two hundred beds.[113] Since women were underrepresented among the prison population in general and among sex offenders in particular, the subcommittee estimated that fewer than two hundred beds would be required for them. The notion of a central facility for all qualifying women, however, was rejected on the basis "that, in the case of women, success of therapy is substantially dependent on the maintenance and restoration of personal ties to family, especially children."[114]

While definitive legislation was delayed by negotiations over a general prison law, eager clinicians already set about outlining their visions for what were being touted as "model" social therapeutic facilities. The Berlin-based forensic psychologist Günter Suttinger (b. 1913) sketched his plan for such a facility for the Federal Ministry of Justice in June 1969. Designed to cater to one hundred residents, the facility was intended to be a small campus comprised of three main areas:

- a diagnostic center for intakes and court examinations, with locked doors and barred windows separating offices for eight clinicians and four social workers, twenty-four individual cells, an infirmary, an isolation unit, and rooms for psychotherapy, observation, and instruction;

- a locked unit comprised of two pavilions, providing space for six classrooms, six recreation rooms, four group therapy rooms, an open-stack library, a large sports hall, an outdoor track and field, and a swimming pool; and
- an open-door unit lying outside the outer walls of the facility, with fourteen individual rooms and three double rooms.[115]

Model Facilities, Treatments, and the Question of Corrigibility

Model social therapeutic facilities were established throughout West Germany over the course of the early 1970s, and there were ten by 1975. Most held fewer than forty inmates, in sum representing around 1 percent of the entire prison population by the early1980s.[116] A tour of six of these facilities by the prison psychologist Günter Schmitt (see table 7) showed that, despite some differences, they were being designed in keeping with the "treatment prison" model outlined by the Prison Commission. Emphasis was placed on the use of psychiatric and psychotherapeutic forms of treatment, with an eye toward instilling better decision-making and coping skills for future social integration.

Sex offenders were by no means the only types of convicts targeted for commitment to the new facilities. They were a primary focus, however, and professionals involved in therapeutic penology sought ways to tailor interventions to the rehabilitative challenges sex offenders posed.[117] Admittedly, the talk among forensic experts continued to be of "freeing" men from the force of their deviant "drives." Innovative treatments and technologies, however, were seen as opening up promising new avenues for intervention and social control.

Psychosurgery, in the form of stereotactic hypothalamotomy, was one such option. The surgery involved the deliberate destruction of much of the ventromedial nucleus of the hypothalamus, under the assumption that the latter represented the sexual behavior center of the brain. Proponents touted the procedure for extinguishing libido while leaving a man's genitals fully intact. First performed in West Germany in 1962, around seventy sex offenders underwent the operation by 1979.[118]

A second technology, first making its way into the Federal Republic in the early seventies, was penile plethysmography. Using a device and technique developed by Kurt Freund in Czechoslovakia in the late 1950s and early 1960s,[119] clinicians and researchers could attach a transducer around the penis of a man, measuring the speed, size, intensity, and variations of erections. When used in combination with visual or aural stimuli, it was thought, one could track male sexual arousal and thus test how effective treatments were on dangerous sex offenders.[120]

TABLE 7. Social Therapeutic Facilities in West Germany, 1974

	Hohenasperg	Berlin	Düren	Erlangen	Hamburg	Ludwigshafen
Date of Opening	1 July 1969	19 January 1970	29 April 1971	1 June 1972	1 April 1969	1 February 1972
Location	attached to prison hospital	within Tegel prison	independent facility	independent facility	independent facility	within Ludwigshafen jail
Directors of Facility	prison doctor of hospital and representative of prison director	physician with psychologist as assistant	1 legal and 1 medical director	1 legal and 1 therapeutic (psychologist) director	a prison director and a medical director	team decisions in all therapeutic matters and 1 facility director
Dress of Staff and Inmates	uniform uniform	uniform civilian	civilian civilian	uniform facility clothes	uniform civilian	civilian civilian
Age of Inmates	up to 40	up to 35	22–35	up to 50	up to 50	up to 50
Therapy Methods	analytical psychotherapy, sensitivity training	analytical psychotherapy, nondirective, behavioral, social case work, sensitivity training	nondirective conversational	Rogerian conversational	conversational therapy, group therapy	behavioral
Somatic Treatments	antiandrogens, castration	antiandrogens	sedatives	sedatives	antiandrogens, castration	none
Work	obligatory	obligatory	obligatory	obligatory	obligatory	obligatory
Contact with Outside	30-minute supervised visits, regular leaves	60- to 90-minute observed visits, controlled leaves	2-hour observed visits, normal prison leave policy	30-minute observed visits, normal prison leave policy	1-hour unsupervised visits, one week leave every 6 weeks	unlimited, unsupervised visits, normal prison leave policy
Postrelease Supervision	through social therapeutic center in Stuttgart	through extramural center for released inmates	through social worker for 3–4 months	not yet operational	not yet operational	not yet operational

Source: Table from Günther Schmitt, "Theorie und Praxis der Sozialtherapie im Strafvollzug insbesondere der Verhatlenstherapie," in *Kriminaltherapie heute*, ed. Heinz Müller-Dietz (Berlin: Walter de Gruyter, 1974), 1–9.

While tools like these spurred a measure of therapeutic optimism among forensic clinicians, those working with repeat sex offenders and psychopaths in the 1970s were equally attentive to the many interpersonal, situational, and longitudinal factors inhibiting convicts' receptiveness to treatment.[121] Even with an arsenal of surgical and hormonal treatments at hand, focus continued to be placed on refining the use of forms of custodial psychotherapy.[122] While social therapy's star was rising, it was never assumed to be a universal remedy (one estimate was that it was appropriate for only about 10 percent of the prison population): like other approaches, social therapy divided offenders into the corrigible and the incorrigible.[123]

During the 1970s and 1980s, two social therapeutic facilities and their directors were widely seen as leaders in the field. Already in 1967, the psychiatrist Wilfried Rasch (1925–2000) had laid out his plans for the creation of special detention facilities for psychopaths (among which a significant share would be sex offenders) that placed therapy and openness at the center of its routine.[124] Rasch served as director of the Institute for Forensic Psychiatry at the Free University of Berlin from 1971 to 1993, and he was given the opportunity to apply his ideas after the state of North Rhine–Westphalia opened its model social therapeutic facility in Düren in 1971. During most of the 1970s, Düren was deemed an experimental unit, where various interventions were to be tried on a small number of inmates and evaluated for their relative efficacy. To begin with, volunteers who met the legal requirements for commitment were given standardized medical and psychological examinations: those prisoners with low IQs, drug addictions, brain damage, or signs of psychosis were excluded. The remaining sixty-two inmates were randomly assigned either to the Düren facility or to regular prison, where the latter were to be used as a control group.[125]

Within the social therapeutic facility, inmates were integrated into a comprehensive therapeutic community, in which everyone (both residents and staff) was to take an active part in the treatment and administrative processes, through regular conferences, group activities, and group therapies.[126] Evaluating the program in 1977, Rasch and his colleagues insisted that only treatment indicators based on clinical assessment and psychodiagnostic testing were relevant for making decisions about the fate of residents in social therapeutic facilities. "Therapy does not mean reeducating," Rasch wrote, explaining, "The goal of therapeutic efforts cannot be to treat so-called criminal behavior itself but, rather, the remedy of mental disturbances that determine this behavior."[127]

Well before Rasch helped design the facility at Düren, the psychoanalyst

Gerhard Mauch, along with Rudolf Engell, began using psychotherapeutic techniques on inmates at another facility in the 1950s: the Hohenasperg Prison Hospital near Stuttgart. Relying first only on individual psychotherapy, Mauch and his team expanded into group therapy by the late fifties, eventually establishing an independent psychotherapeutic unit in the hospital in 1963, while also administering castrations and cyproterone acetate treatment. Over time, the unit's emphasis shifted from a focus on psychoanalysis to an emphasis on behavioral, group, and psychodrama therapies.[128] In 1969, Hohenasperg became one of the first social therapeutic facilities to open, with sixty beds to accommodate sex offenders and inmates with personality disorders.[129]

Mauch's ideas about social therapy were similar to Rasch's. Hohenasperg adopted a team approach to treatment, by which staff and residents regularly met to monitor and discuss the progress of the latter. Psychotherapy remained the centerpiece of Mauch's notion of social therapy, combined with work therapy, milieu therapy, group therapy, and behavioral therapy. In contrast to Rasch, however, Mauch awarded greater prominence to psychoanalytic concerns about psychological mechanisms that often hindered social function and interpersonal relations (e.g., projections, identification, rationalizations).[130]

Mauch also went to great trouble to account for and theorize the limits of social therapy. Speaking before the Prison Commission in October 1969, he explained that the social therapeutic approach was oriented toward a specific subset of repeat offenders. For Mauch, the social therapeutic facility's relationship to a criminal was clinical in nature and, thus, was mediated through medical categories, criteria, and procedures. He dubbed repeat offenders "the chronically criminal," individuals characterized by unreliability, instability, a lack of perseverance, and untrustworthiness rooted in a disturbance of personality.[131]

In Mauch's view, an essential part of social therapy was identifying those individuals who could be helped through social therapy and excluding those who could not. This involved two separate but related evaluations of offenders. First, according to Mauch, one was to determine the criminal's "need for treatment" (*Behandlungsbedürftigkeit*). Dealing with criminal actions as symptoms, the evaluating clinician was to uncover the cause behind these actions and to determine the extent to which a treatable personality disorder lay at the root.[132] This evaluation was to be accompanied by an assessment of the offender's "capacity for treatment" (*Behandlungsfähigkeit*), meaning the degree to which the individual possessed features and resources necessary for successful treatment. This, Mauch believed, was a far more difficult determination to make, but he flagged several important criteria for this assessment:

- *Individual characteristics, like personality structure and severity of psychological damage.* Mauch made clear that the severity of the disorder, not the severity of one's crimes, was the main issue here.
- *Age.* From age forty on, the chances of treatment success were considered comparatively low.
- *Intelligence.* Low intelligence, Mauch maintained, correlated with a poor prognosis.
- *Willpower and an ability to withstand mental stress.* Shortcomings in resolve and a relatively low tolerance for frustration made it likelier that treatment would fail.
- *Motivation and the desire to change.* Without feeling a need to change (*Leidensdruck*) and without having a committed attitude toward the therapeutic process, Mauch noted, it was far too easy for offenders to break off treatment.[133]

Nothing better highlights the way in which social therapy sought to reconfigure the carceral relationship in West Germany than the manner in which Mauch and his team set about judging inmates to be among the corrigible or the incorrigible. In a world built around clinical interventions and benchmarks, the social therapeutic facility operationalized corrigibility according to psychotherapeutic measures. Hohenasperg and its counterparts appear, then, to have accomplished something unprecedented in German history: the complete medicalization or therapeutization of carceral correction. Had the prisoner finally become a patient, a client?

A closer look at archival records from the 1970s reveals that clinicians at Hohenasperg were successful in reorienting the assessment of convicts around social therapeutic criteria. Nevertheless, prison authorities, physicians, and psychologists in Baden-Württemberg and Hohenasperg found it difficult, if not impossible, to fully excise security and punitive considerations from their work. Instead, conventional carceral concerns (e.g., escape attempts) were recast as challenges to the therapeutic process, while some conventional psychotherapeutic concerns (e.g., refusing to take part in group therapy) could now be seen as disciplinary problems.

Already by the late 1960s, federal states like Baden-Württemberg had set up commitment review commissions (*Einweisungskommission*)—generally composed of judicial and prison officials, psychologists, work counselors, social scientists, educators, and social workers—whose job was, among other things, to judge the applications of prisoners requesting to be transferred to Hohenasperg for psychotherapeutic treatment. Mauch and his colleagues at the facility played a pivotal role in deciding these cases. Inmates considered viable candidates for the limited number of available slots were typically sent to Hohenasperg, where they were given an examination and observed for a period of time to assess their suitability for admission to the facility. The staff then passed on their recommendations to the commission.

While I was unable to determine how many inmates a year applied and were accepted for social therapy at Hohenasperg during the years 1969–80, it is clear that many inmates considered the facility an improvement over conventional incarceration, with some trying for as many as five years to gain admission.[134] Men petitioning for acceptance to the program often portrayed it as a technology of hope,[135] offering "help" and the "possibility" for a "normal life." Sex offenders frequently spoke of their looking forward to the day they were "liberated" from their pernicious sexual "drives."

In reality, of course, a goodly number of these repeat and dangerous offenders were interested less in self-transformation than in the possibility of being transferred to the potentially more comfortable and relaxed surroundings of a psychotherapeutic unit. Many were more or less adept at mimicking the vocabulary and distinctions of treatment specialists. In a letter to the Hohenasperg director in July 1972 one applicant concluded that only psychotherapy offered him the chance to lead a socially responsible life after release. "My belief is primarily based on the view that severe destructive tendencies are present in my personality," he explained, adding, "Based on my life history, these are attributable to neurotic, and not asocial or wayward, origins."[136] Others, aware of the Hohenasperg unit's psychoanalytic leanings, were even more brazen. Seeking to account for a criminal career that began at age seventeen, thirty-one-year-old G.B. told authorities, in rather awkward German, "I can only clarify that I am an Oedipus complex from earlier childhood or also mentally ill."[137]

Clinicians were well aware of this manipulation and did their best to see through the likely ruse. Not only inmates "gamed" the system, however. Defense lawyers, too, bandied about references to the family conflicts, weak interpersonal skills, and inhibited personality development in their clients' lives.[138] Prison physicians from other facilities who were interested in sending their own charges to Hohenasperg were even more proficient in the idiom of social therapy.[139] Not all of these gestures were disingenuous, but they show the difficult work clinical evaluators faced in identifying what Mauch referred to as those with a need and a capacity for treatment.

Still other challenges faced assessors on the Commitment Review Commission and at Hohenasperg. One of the most common was the perennial problem of inmate "dumping." While social therapeutic facilities had been created, in part, to address the chronic concern with finding an institutional home for those suited neither to prison nor psychiatric care, social therapy specialists made it clear that their facilities were intended for only a small circle of "disruptives" and psychopaths. Following a pattern established already at the beginning of the century, the social therapeutic facility at Hohenasperg and its prison and psychiatric counterparts engaged in the mutual process of passing off especially difficult and disruptive inmates onto other institutions of confinement.[140] As in the case of twenty-two-year-old convicted rapist L.K., who repeatedly threw food, demolished his cell, beat up fellow inmates, attacked guards, and threatened suicide, staff at the facility consistently framed refractory conduct in clinical terms.[141] K.'s behavior was seen by the Commitment Review Commission as a response to a youth spent in institutions, itself the result of a negligent mother who "made no bones about her blatantly hostile contempt for her illegitimate son." The commission's sympathetic reading of K.'s life history only reinforced the sense that K.'s actions in Hohenasperg were only the tip of the iceberg. "Up to now," the commission admitted, "neither correctional nor therapeutic nor punitive interventions have had any influence on his criminogenic underdevelopment, since they end up playing out within a severely abnormal personality development."[142]

I do not mean to imply that security and disciplinary concerns were ultimately behind all decisions regarding commitment to Hohenasperg. Commission members and facility staff proved more than willing to accept even the most recalcitrant and violent of criminals, as long as they met Mauch's criteria for admission. When twenty-six-year-old N.H. applied for social therapeutic treatment in the summer of 1980, for example, he had been convicted on three counts of rape, three counts of attempted rape, a count of attempted sexual assault of a child, one count of attempted rape and sexual assault, five separate counts of rape and sexual assault, and seven other cases involving sexual assault. The Commitment Review Commission found there to be evidence that his actions appeared to be less the result of a deviant sex drive than a function of a deep disturbance of personality. Interviewing H. and concluding that he demonstrated a genuine desire to change, a readiness to cooperate, and a willingness to conform to a long, arduous therapeutic regimen, the commission approved his commitment.[143] Particularly for Mauch, clinical indications—not the severity of the crimes committed—were decisive in considering admissions to Hohenasperg, as indicated by his acceptance of child molesters for castration and treatment with cyproterone acetate.[144]

Rejections, too, followed Mauch's scheme. In the 1978 case of thirty-six-year-old W.G., a man with a record of violent sexual assaults dating back to 1961, a psychologist at the Hohenasperg facility reported that the treatment team found no evidence that G. was properly motivated for undergoing either psychotherapeutic or somatic treatment. Clinicians could find in the man no traces of a sense of guilt about his crimes or of feeling a need to change. "Given motivational prerequisites, which are neither there nor able to be activated in this instance," the psychologist concluded, "the indication for psychotherapeutic or drug treatment cannot be established."[145] In still other cases, admission to the facility was rejected due to the applicant's low intelligence, inability to be self-critical, or ineffective communication skills.[146]

Records from Baden-Württemberg show us, then, the degree to which social therapy was capable of distancing itself from earlier correctional ventures. In contrast to the criminal biology dominating assessment during the years 1930–60, the proponents and administrators of social therapy did not consider the supposed presence of "waywardness" or a psychopathology to indicate irredeemability. For them, neither biology nor upbringing were destiny. Nevertheless, as every generation of specialists before them had done, social therapy experts found it impossible to do away with the distinction between the corrigible and the incorrigible. Social therapeutic facilities may have attempted to blur the boundaries separating their world from society at large, but in seeking to not lock *in* their residents, they invariably locked *out* a great many more.

Conclusions

The social therapeutic facility was seen by its advocates as the epitome of the "treatment prison" system. Like the reform of the West German penal system in general, however, it arrived at the same moment that public opinion was becoming less enamored with therapeutic penology and that state budgets were shrinking. This reality only fed the stigma attached to sex offenders. The Bochum public opinion survey of 1975, for instance, revealed that when individuals were asked to which offenders they were willing to lend a helping hand, sex offenders ranked last (only 4.2 percent), behind murderers (6.2 percent), frauds (18.9 percent), and thieves (55.6 percent).[147]

The low social status of sex offenders served only to hinder the development of social therapy during the 1970s and 1980s. Originally, the creation of a nationwide system of social therapeutic facilities was set to take effect on 1 January 1978, but the deadline was postponed to 1 January 1985. This deadline was also put off, after the original law establishing social therapeutic facilities was rescinded on 20 December 1984, leaving only eleven model facilities still in place, with around 650 spaces (about 1 percent of the prison population), by 1985.[148] Thus, until 2003, social therapeutic facilities in the Federal Republic remained restricted to those convicts who voluntarily agreed to be housed there.

There were a number of reasons beyond public opinion for the failure to develop a comprehensive network of social therapeutic facilities in the Federal Republic. For one, individual states continually resisted central government demands to expand the model facilities that existed, often citing a lack of funding or public support. In addition, jurists and human rights advocates were successful in challenging the clinical benchmarks of the facilities that made therapeutic progress a precondition for release.[149]

By the early 1980s, social therapeutic facilities were drawing criticism from both the political left and right, leading many to wonder aloud whether the project had any future.[150] Assessments of the units' effectiveness conducted during the seventies and early eighties seemed to offer some encouragement for supporters. Studies indicated that inmates undergoing treatment in a social therapeutic facility showed significant improvement in self-esteem and contact with family and friends and had a 14–26 percent lower rate of recidivism than those assigned to control groups. The values of these results remained questionable, however, given that those applying for and gaining admission to a facility were hardly representative of the general prison population.[151]

The upshot of all this was that social therapeutic facilities remained intact but were altered by the same kinds of trends affecting the prison system as a whole. Criminal psychologist Rudolf Egg (b. 1948) captured this shift effectively in his 1984 book *Criminality and Social Therapy*, in which he proposed increasing the capacity of social therapeutic facilities from catering to several hundreds to taking on several thousands of inmates. At the same time, he called for demedicalizing the project by shifting the focus away from individual treatment and toward improving the social situation of inmates, abandoning the reliance on medical benchmarks for assessing progress, and promoting greater personal autonomy by not insisting on conformity to homogeneous norms.[152] Older proponents of social therapy, like Rudolf Engell, expressed concern that treatment of the root causes of criminality was being lost in the name of demedicalization. But like Egg, Engell and his colleagues at Hohenasperg found ways to accommodate new trends in criminal justice and criminology by integrating a victim perspective into inmate therapy.[153]

As a correctional project, the social therapeutic facility began as a proposed solution to the perceived problem of psychopaths, individuals who appeared unsuitable for both prisons and psychiatric hospitals. From the start, sex offenders represented an explicit, yet not the sole, target of social therapy. Unlike in the United States, psychopathy in Germany throughout most of the twentieth century was not considered synonymous with dangerous sexual delinquency.[154] Increasingly, however, the facilities were seen by both the public and experts to be uniquely suited to the confinement of sex offenders. Indeed, just as it did in the case of preventive detention, the West German public consistently expressed surprise at reports that other types of convicts were being treated there.

As social therapy took shape and was institutionalized in the form of social therapeutic facilities over the sixties and seventies, a transformation took place. As critics would later contend, certain convicts were given the chance to become a new kind of patient, the object of psychotherapeutic and somatic experimentation. Their criminal actions were read as symptoms not of a mental illness but, rather, of a disordered personality, a circumstance requiring biopsychosocial intervention. This process of the *medicalization* of punishment, it must be said, was limited in scope, but it was publicly acknowledged and discussed. Far less acknowledged has been the way in which social therapeutic facilities have brought about a *sexualization* of preventive confinement.

This sexualization of preventive confinement was most blatantly affirmed and formalized in January 1998 by the Law to Combat Sex Offenses and Other Dangerous Crimes, officially taking effect in 2003.[155] The law expands the mandate of social therapeutic facilities, ordering that all sex offenders serving prison terms of more than two years and deemed appropriate candidates be committed to a social therapeutic facility for treatment. The law also permits making participation in psychotherapy and other forms of medical treatment a condition of an inmate's eventual release and parole. In effect, the law has transformed the "psychopath" into the "repeat sex offender."

The results have been unmistakable. By March 2012, the capacity of social therapeutic facilities rose to 2,351 beds across sixty-three facilities. Between 1997 und 2012, the number of sex offenders in the facilities grew from 191 to 1,096, a growth accomplished not only by increasing capacity but also by decreasing the number of other types of institutionalized offenders. Over the course of the years 1997–2008, the number of property and economic criminals in social therapeutic facilities decreased around 45 percent, to 201.[156]

The presence of social therapeutic facilities also led to a similar development within preventive detention. As Imanuel Baumann has shown, over 60 percent of those committed to preventive detention in the Federal Republic between 1959 and 1969 had been convicted of theft or robbery, while only around 13–16 percent had committed a sex offense (a distribution that mirrored that of the Third Reich). These figures changed markedly following passage of the law establishing social therapeutic facilities: 31.7 percent of those detained between 1969 and 1979 had committed theft or robbery, while 34 percent had committed a sex offense.[157] This trend, which persisted into the 1990s, indicates that social therapeutic facilities have helped provide a steady supply of "incorrigible" sex offenders for the preventive detention system.

The history of West Germany's approach to sex offenders is a story of an expanding and refining therapeutic impulse. Reformers found in social therapy what they took to be a more effective and humane method to *rehabilitate* dangerous and repeat sexual criminals. As ways were found to introduce therapy into punishment, however, the correctional imagination of reformers led them to simultaneously seek ways to just as effectively *debilitate* and incapacitate convicts. The history of social therapeutic facilities demonstrates that if we wish to speak of a therapeutization of penal correction in West Germany, we must recognize that this process equally involved a carceralization of the therapeutic.

Conclusion

Correctional rehabilitation did not emerge suddenly in Germany, nor has it disappeared. The ideas behind it can be traced back to the early modern workhouse and the penal reformers of the nineteenth and early twentieth centuries. It was institutionalized unevenly, in fits and starts, and has often lacked stability. Despite being criticized and resisted by the public, prison staff, and inmates, it has managed to find a place in every German political system since 1933 and to demonstrate a staying power throughout the twentieth and early twenty-first centuries.

What significance is held by the fact that this particular configuration of the correctional imagination was, to a significant extent, set in motion by National Socialism? To argue that all forms of Nazi criminal policy were solely the reflection of the movement's racist ideology would neglect the historical fact that much of what the Third Reich did realized the ambitions of two generations of self-identified humanitarian penal reformers. If the Dangerous Habitual Offender Law of 1933 served racial hygiene purposes in dividing convicts into the potentially redeemable and the hopelessly unworthy, that dichotomy nevertheless hardly required eugenics. The central organizing principle of the German correctional imagination over time was not eugenics so much as triage, dividing the incarcerated into the corrigible and the incorrigible.

This triage approach to rehabilitation was grounded in the notion that while an indefinite number of convicts could be reformed, resources were limited, and the repertoire of institutions of confinement were insufficient to be uniformly effective. Convicts, particularly repeat offenders, were seen as posing an uncertain threat to public safety. In a word, they were a danger. The menace they presented was not merely to the here and now but, most especially, to the future. This is what both conservative critics and progressive advocates of correctional rehabilitation today often overlook: correctional rehabilitation was not founded out of an unbridled optimism about the capacity of people to change but, rather, arose from a chronic anxiety about the threats posed by others.

It is little wonder, then, that the chief focus of so much of the research on correctional rehabilitation in Germany aimed at contributing not to the design of new therapies but to the refinement of criminal prognosis. Since correction was directed at combating recidivism, the correctional imagination never lost sight of the fact that convicts remained potential future criminals. The human sciences—chiefly, criminology, psychiatry, psychology, pedagogy, sociology, social work, and statistics—provided the invaluable methods, tools, and data to serve special prevention. Modern Germany's secular, clinical form of prisoner reform was built around the claim of researchers and casework professionals that it was possible to know and use the principles and laws governing human thought, motivation, and behavior in order to design remedial interventions.

Germany's two-track system of criminal sanctions (see table 8) was therefore inconceivable without the human sciences and medicine. Admittedly, the second track has catered to a smaller population of convicts than standard prison. Nevertheless, it has historically served as the experimental branch of custodial confinement, testing and refining new methods in rehabilitation for potential mass application.

One might be tempted to treat the existence of the executive measure track as a sign of a German exceptionalism, or *Sonderweg*, but this would be inaccurate. Other European countries have provisions for preventive detention, including Austria, Denmark, the Netherlands, Norway, and Switzerland. Even in nations without such a formal preventive detention system, such as the United States, informal solutions have been found to serve the same function. If anything has distinguished the German approach from many of its foreign counterparts, it has been the resistance of those administering the system to standardized tools of risk assessment. Germany's long-standing practice of institutional deference to academic and professional expertise meant, instead, that clinical evaluation by experienced professionals has been preferred.[1]

Besides legitimating prognostically based detention, the two-track legal system has simultaneously served another function: it has provided an institutional home for confining those deemed dangerous. With rehabilitation being built on the presumption of segregating the corrigible from the incorrigible, a custodial fate needed to be found for the latter. Nazi Germany provided three alternatives: preventive detention, concentration camps, and execution. Whereas both East Germany and West Germany mostly abandoned the latter two,[2] the GDR also dispensed with formal preventive detention, while the FRG retained it. As shown in chapter 4, this repeatedly created dilemmas for the criminal justice system in East Germany, where clinicians and officials were forced to resort to informal workarounds as a way to indefinitely confine those deemed incorrigible. In the meantime, the Federal Republic went about elaborating on preventive detention still further, creating a new set of custodial institutions, social therapeutic facilities. It is perhaps surprising to find, thus, that correctional rehabilitation in Germany was not only linked to but required pre-

TABLE 8. Germany's Two-Track System of Criminal Sanctions (Zweispurigkeit)

	Criminal Punishment (*Strafrecht*)	Executive Measure (*Maßregel*)
Form of State Action	temporally determinate sentence, release upon time served	indeterminate sentence, transfer or release upon improvement
Nature of Sanction	punitive	therapeutic
Institutions of Confinement	penal facilities	preventive detention, psychiatric hospital, center for substance abuse treatment, workhouse (no longer in effect from 1969), social therapeutic facility (since 1969), compulsory castration (1933–45, outlawed in 1945)
Criterion for Commitment	violation of criminal code	deemed to be dangerous repeat offender
Declared Purpose	punish criminal act	protect society
Specific Crime Requirement?	yes: dependent on a person's guilt	no: independent of a person's guilt
Focus of Attention?	The focus is on an "objective" assessment of past conduct relative to the law. The subjectivity of perpetrator may be relevant in particular circumstances (e.g., partial incapacity).	The focus is on a prognostic assessment of future conduct. The subjectivity of the perpetrator is the principal matter.
Basis of Sentence/Commitment Determination	The decision is partly mechanistic, with sentence ranges fixed, though there remains judicial discretion. The judgment is to be made solely on a legal basis.	The decision is individualized, tailored to the individual's requirements, and is altered based on the inmate's ability to reach certain benchmarks (e.g., managing one's impulses). The goals and the methods for reaching these goals are framed in clinical terms based on scientific research and clinical experience.

ventive detention, in that it needed a final destination for those no longer able to be accommodated in other institutions of confinement.

This historically peculiar convergence of rehabilitation, the human sciences, and indefinite detention raises questions about the ways in which the contemporary state has gone about managing crime as a social problem. The work of social theorist Giorgio Agamben furnishes a starting point. The development of Germany's second track of criminal sanctions appears to be a prime instance of what Agamben has identified as the growing expansion and normalization of governance through the state of exception.[3] As a domain of coercive behavioral management that operates on principles outside of those rooted in standard law, the system of executive measures grants a great amount of discretionary power to clinical expertise. At the same time, its emphasis on the prognosis of danger places the convict under a permanent state of suspicion.[4]

National Socialism was increasingly drawn to this form of deterrent governance when it came to crime. From 1938 until the end of the war, the SS and the police assumed ever greater discretionary powers, while projects such as the community alien law and youth detention camps imagined new prophylactic grounds for isolating social deviants. The Third Reich proved far more comfortable with applying brute force than its successor states. Nevertheless, both East Germany and West Germany revealed themselves willing to contravene commitment laws or create new facilities in order to detain those who appeared to fall through the administrative cracks.

Admittedly, the scale of second-track confinement has remained small: even under the National Socialists, for instance, the number of formal preventive detainees never exceeded thirty-eight hundred inmates. But the weight of executive measure commitments has not fallen solely on those they confined. Rather, the very presence of this alternative to criminal punishment established a new set of metrics for judging cases, legitimated the posing of a new range of questions about offenders, and created a new horizon for sovereign intervention.

Once again, this is a process hardly unique to twentieth-century Germany. As Mary Douglas, Michaelis Lianos, and Jonathan Simon have all observed, even in neoliberal, deregulated settings, contemporary societies have increasingly turned to "governing through crime" and "dangerization."[5] Put another way, more and more systems, institutions, and technologies have come to treat all citizens as potential sources of danger whose behavior should be monitored and steered, often through forms of automated control (e.g., CCTV or debit card PIN). Douglas and Lianos, in particular, understand this development as both cause and effect of the public's growing anxieties about victimization: "*Dangerization* is the tendency to perceive and analyze the world through categories of menace. It leads to continuous detection of threats and assessment of adverse probabilities, to the prevalence of defensive perceptions over optimistic ones and to the dominance of fear and anxiety over ambition and desire."[6]

This is not to say that the system of second-track sanctions has been the driving force behind this state of affairs in a place like Germany. Rather, the institution of executive measures represents but another facet of a risk management approach found in multiple settings across contemporary society.[7] These imagined dangers center mostly on biopolitically significant concerns involving life and death: violent crime, health, sexuality, child welfare.

Observing this development in the late twentieth and early twenty-first centuries, Nikolas Rose sees no threat of our repeating the mistakes of the nationalist, statist, and racist eugenics of the first half of the twentieth century. Instead, Rose has argued, the emerging biopolitics of today offer the possibilities of flexibility, choice, debate, autonomy, and activism.[8] For some groups and individuals, this most surely is the case. For convicts, detainees, and those once referred to as "asocials," however, this ideal has been and remains far out of their reach.

It should not be forgotten, however, that prognosis has served not only the general prevention of crime but also special prevention. In fact, rehabilitation was and is the very purpose behind the system of executive measures. This leads to an obvious question: did correctional rehabilitation work?

Viewed from an efficiency standpoint, the results appear to have been equivocal over time. Simply considering sex offenders, for instance, researchers in both Nazi Germany and West Germany made claims that surgical castration reduced the average recidivism rate among sex offenders to under 3 percent. Yet, as investigators also noted, the procedure was not altogether successful in suppressing male sexual function and was accompanied by powerful, irreversible side effects. On the basis of figures from samples of individuals convicted in 1987, 30 percent of West German sex offenders sentenced to a commitment by executive measure subsequently carried out another sexual offense. This rate was higher than that for violent sex offenders (19 percent) and child molesters (22 percent) but appreciably lower than that of East German sex offenders in general (44 percent).[9]

Likewise, recidivism rates for the general convict population have been mixed. A study based on 1994 statistics indicated that only around a third of convicts in unified Germany reoffended within four years. The rate changes considerably, however, when age or gender are considered: both the rate for youth and the rate for males are higher.[10] In any event, the rate in East Germany ten years earlier appears to have been substantially higher (65 percent in 1984).[11]

Most of these figures, of course, may convey little about the relative efficacy of correctional rehabilitation in these German states. Historians—even those studying the twentieth century—are faced with enormous methodological challenges in trying to retroactively determine the success and failure of remedial interventions over time and across multiple regimes. The definition of specific crimes often changed, records and statistics were not consistently reliable, and it is enormously challenging to longitudinally relate independent variables with dependent ones.

Perhaps it makes more sense to ask what functions correctional rehabilitation has served and how successful initiatives were in meeting contemporaneous expectations. What David Garland has said about punishment and prisons holds equally true for correction rehabilitation. "We are too prone to think of punishment as a simple means to a simple end—usually that of crime control—and to treat all other aspects of the institution as minor considerations," he points out, concluding, "Their evaluation thus turns upon measurements of recidivism, of deterrence, and of correlative crime rates rather than judgment of their total worth as social practices."[12] Garland reminds us not just that correctional rehabilitation might or might not work but that it performs work and that the work it performs cannot be wholly captured in terms of technical efficiency.

To understand correctional rehabilitation's work, it is necessary to appreciate the nature of the problem historically placed before it. Crime and its social control represent not simply problems but a case of what George C. Rosenwald once called "human perplexity," by which he was referring to a "process which we grasp partly, but not sufficiently, even after much trying, and which we cannot escape." Rosenwald explained, "Cognitively, we cannot make the pieces add up to a whole or get control of the predicament."[13] Since doing nothing is not an option—particularly in the case of criminal justice—such responses as incarceration, social therapy, castration, and concentration camps represent operationalized interventions that, while far from ideal, seem to provide some leverage on an intractable reality.

As the case of Germany shows, correctional rehabilitation was imagined and realized within the cultural and institutional parameters historically available to those involved. Despite the fact that administrators, researchers, and clinicians tended to treat corrigibility and incorrigibility as ontological states inhering within convicts, the figures of the corrigible and incorrigible could not be divorced from the constraints of custodialism. They were as much artifacts of the institutions that were designed to house them as they were the results of their own actions. Each of the three German penal systems offered a limited repertoire of possible institutional fates and regimes, with each one modeled on an idealized vision of the polity: Nazi Germany tested and spurred the convict's willpower for possible reintegration into the national racial community; East Germany didactically instructed the convict to rejoin the socialist collective; and West Germany invited the convict to take part in a democratic process of speaking, listening, and cooperating toward resocialization.

Sociologist Erving Goffman had a name for this kind of work: "people-work." As he put it, "Perhaps the first thing to say about the staff is that their work, and hence their world, have uniquely to do with people. This *people-work* is not quite like personnel work or the work of those involved in service relationships; the staff, after all, have objects and products to work upon, not services, but these objects and products are people."[14] Across disparate political and social regimes, correctional prisons called on the convict to treat his or her own life as a moral project and become "a particular kind of person who dwells in a particular kind of world."[15] Rehabilitation in German penal facilities operated as a psychagogic enterprise extending beyond prison gates, an attempt to spark self-improvement through discipline and punishment, testing and observation, advice and support.[16] This goal links twentieth-century prisons to the workhouses and penitentiaries of the eighteenth and nineteenth centuries.

It is difficult to look at the scope and scale of the German rehabilitative project and not conclude that repeated individual failure was bound to be inevitable. Yet it is often overlooked that the professionals and experts involved were not blind to this fact. Consistently, their aspirations were tempered, the impact of new methods was limited, and expectations for change were lowered. The prominence of criminal prognosis testifies that the history of the correctional imagination has been as much about expected failure and resigned acceptance as about promise and innovation. This fact was better understood by those in the field than by policy makers.

As historian Steven Walton points out, technologies in use tend not necessarily toward efficiency but, rather, toward sufficiency.[17] Correctional tools and techniques utilized in Germany in the twentieth century generally did not operate on the model of command and control. Some scientists and officials were, of course, interested in standardizing procedures and methods. On the whole, however, administrators of things like the "pedagogical atmosphere" during the Third Reich, "correction" in East Germany, or "social therapy" in West Germany had a high degree of interpretive flexibility.[18] The closer one got to "ground level," to the world of everyday interactions with inmates, the more the executors of policy were satisfied with simply "good enough." This irrational aspect of social disciplinary power is one that Foucault never seemed to grasp.

Linked, as it has been, with the rise of the criminal sanctions by executive measures, correctional rehabilitation in Germany has demonstrated the potential to be not only understanding, caring, and supportive but also peremptory, ruthless, and lethal. It is perhaps tempting to see this fact as confirmation of Agamben's contention that the concentration camp offers an emblematic vision of modern biopolitics. The history of the German correctional imagination would indicate that while the camp did indeed arise out of the same gesture of executive exception as the Dangerous Habitual Offender Law, the latter cannot be reduced to the former.

In a recent essay, legal scholar Hans-Jörg Albrecht has noted a relative moderation and stability in judicial sentencing in Germany over the past four decades. In trying to account for this, Albrecht has found plausible evidence to indicate that the second track of criminal sanctions has served as a kind of safety valve "exerting restraint on resorting to long prison sentences."[19] In short, by diverting the question of dangerousness to the circumscribed world of executive measures, contemporary German criminal justice may well have made it easier for the main body of criminal law to function in a rule-bound manner and unencumbered by concerns over public safety. Perhaps, then, there is no choice but to concede that the legacy of correctional rehabilitation in Germany is an equivocal one, offering reason for both worry and hope.

Notes

CHAPTER 1

1. Robert Martinson, "What Works? Questions and Answers about Prison Reform," *Public Interest* 35 (1974): 25.

2. Roy Walmsley, "Global Incarceration and Prison Trends," *Forum on Crime and Society* 3 (2003): 65–78; David Garland, *The Culture of Control: Crime and Social Order in Contemporary Society* (Chicago: University of Chicago Press, 2001).

3. Jonathan Simon, *Governing through Crime: How the War on Crime Transformed American Democracy and Created a Culture of Fear* (New York: Oxford University Press, 2007); Marie Gottschalk, *The Prison and the Gallows: The Politics of Mass Incarceration in America* (Cambridge: Cambridge University Press, 2006).

4. Laura Mansnerus, "Time Served: Zoning Laws That Bar Pedophiles Raise Concerns," *New York Times*, 27 November 2006, accessed 20 March 2013, http://www.nytimes.com/2006/11/27/nyregion/27sex.html; Eric S. Janus, "Sexual Predator Commitment Laws: Lessons for Law and the Behavioral Sciences," *Behavioral Sciences and the Law* 18 (2000): 5–21.

5. David Garland, *Peculiar Institution: America's Death Penalty in an Age of Abolition* (Cambridge, MA: Belknap Press of Harvard University Press, 2010); James Q. Whitman, *Harsh Justice: Criminal Punishment and the Widening Divide between America and Europe* (Oxford: Oxford University Press, 2003); David Downes, "The *Macho* Penal Economy: Mass Incarceration in the United States—a European Perspective," *Punishment and Society* 3 (2001): 1–80.

6. Christian Pfeiffer, "Weniger Verbrecher, mehr Panikmache," *Die Zeit*, 2 June 2005, 9.

7. "Kritik an Karlsruher Urteil," *Frankfurter Allgemeine Zeitung*, 5 May 2011, accessed 20 March 2013, http://www.faz.net/aktuell/politik/staat-und-recht/sicherungsverwahrung-kritik-an-karlsruher-urteil-1639499.html; Herbert R. Steinböck, "New Developments in Preventive Detention in Germany," *Current Opinion in Psychiatry* 22 (2009): 488–91; Gerhard Stolpmann, "Psychiatrische Maßregelbehandlung," *Aus Politik und Zeitgeschichte* 60 (2010): 28–33.

8. S. Snacken, K. Beyens, and H. Tubex, "Changing Prison Populations in Western Countries: Fate or Policy?," *European Journal of Crime, Criminal Law, and Criminal Justice* 3 (1995): 18–53.

9. Tapio Lappi-Seppälä, "Penal Policies in the Nordic Countries 1960–2010,"

supplement, *Journal of Scandinavian Studies in Criminology and Crime Prevention* 13 (2012): 85–111; Nils Christie, *Limits to Pain* (Oxford: Martin Robertson, 1982).

10. Francis A. Allen, *The Decline of the Rehabilitative Ideal* (New Haven: Yale University Press, 1981).

11. Tony Ward and Shadd Maruna, *Rehabilitation* (London: Routledge, 2007); Bernard E. Harcourt, "From the Ne'er-Do-Well to the Criminal History Category: The Refinement of the Actuarial Model in Criminal Law," *Law and Contemporary Problems* 66 (2003): 99–150; John Pratt, *Punishment and Civilization: Penal Tolerance and Intolerance in Modern Society* (London: Sage, 2002); Philip Jenkins, *Moral Panic: Changing Concepts of the Child Molester in Modern America* (New Haven: Yale University Press, 1998).

12. In using the term *configuration*, I borrow heavily from the figurational sociology associated with Norbert Elias, which emphasizes the primacy of process in social relations. In this context, then, I take correctional rehabilitation to be a relatively stable social enterprise serving as both cause and effect of "power, behavior, emotions, and knowledge." See Stephen Mennell, "Figurational Studies: Some Concepts, Principles, and Major Research Areas," accessed 21 March 2013, http://www.norberteliasfoundation.nl/network/concepts.php.

13. Garland, *Culture of Control*, 35–41.

14. G. Geltner, *The Medieval Prison: A Social History* (Princeton: Princeton University Press, 2008); Herman Roodenburg and Pieter Spierenburg, eds., *Social Control in Europe, 1500–1800* (Columbus: Ohio State University Press, 2004); Jean Dunbabin, *Captivity and Imprisonment in Medieval Europe, 1000–1300* (Basingstoke: Palgrave Macmillan, 2002); Edward M. Peters, "Prison before the Prison: The Ancient and Medieval Worlds," in *The Oxford History of the Prison*, ed. Norval Morris and David J. Rothman (New York: Oxford University Press, 1995), 3–47.

15. Pieter Spierenburg, *The Prison Experience: Disciplinary Institutions and Their Inmates in Early Modern Europe* (Amsterdam: Amsterdam Academic Archive, 2007).

16. Sabine Pitscheider, "'Biz zur Besserung': Die Praxis von Einweisung, Anhaltung, und Entlassung im Provinzialzwangsarbeitshaus Schwaz/Innsbruck 1825 bis 1860," in *Orte der Verwahrung: Die innere Organisation von Gefängnissen, Hospitälern, und Klostern seit dem Spätmittelalter*, ed. Gerhard Ammerer, Arthur Brunhart, Martin Scheutz, and Alfred Stefan Weisse (Leipzig: Leipziger Universitätsverlag, 2010), 131–48; Gerhard Ammerer and Alfred Stefan Weiss, "Zucht- und Arbeitshäuser in Österreich um 1800—Recht, Konzepte, und Alltag," in *Gefängnis und Gesellschaft: Zur (Vor-)Geschichte der strafenden Einsperrung*, ed. Gerhard Ammerer, Falk Bretschneider, and Alfred Stefan Weiss (Leipzig: Leipziger Universitätsverlag, 2003), 149–76.

17. Sylvia Kesper-Biermann, *Einheit und Recht: Strafgesetzgebung und Kriminalrechtsexperten in Deutschland vom Beginn des 19. Jahrhunderts bis zum Reichsstrafgesetzbuch von 1871* (Frankfurt: Vittorio Klostermann, 2009).

18. Falk Bretschneider, "Die glückliche Verdrängung des mittelalterlichen Strafvollzugs?," in *Verbrechen im Blick: Perspektiven der neuzeitlichen Kriminalitätsgeschichte*, ed. Rebekka Habermas and Gerd Schwerhoff (Frankfurt: Campus, 2009), 108–47.

19. Karl Härter, "Die Entwicklung des Strafrechts in Mitteleuropa 1770–1848," in Haberman and Schwerhoff, *Verbrechen im Blick*, 71–107. See also Thomas Vormbaum, *Einführung in die moderne Strafrechtsgeschichte* (Heidelberg: Springer, 2011), 107–13; Hinrich Rüping, *Von der Aufklärung bis zur doppelten Staatsgründung*, vol. 2 of *Studien- und Quellenbuch zur Geschichte der deutschen Strafrechtspflege*, ed. Wolfgang Sellert and Hinrich Rüping (Darmstadt: Scientia Verlag Aalen, 1994), 34–112.

20. Martina Henze, "Netzwerk, Kongressbewegung, Stiftung: Zur Wissenschaftsgeschichte der internationalen Gefängniskunde 1827 bis 1951," in *Verbrecher im Visier der Experten: Kriminalpolitik zwischen Wissenschaft und Praxis im 19. und frühen 20. Jahrhundert*, ed. Desiree Schauz and Sabine Freitag (Stuttgart: Franz Steiner, 2007), 55–77; Sylvia Kesper-Biermann, "Internationalisierung in der Geschichte der Strafrechtwissenschaft und Kriminalpolitik (1870–1930): Deutschland im internationalen Kontext," in *Die Internationalisierung von Strafrechtswissenschaft und Kriminalpolitik (1870–1930): Deutschland im Vergleich*, ed. Sylvia Kesper-Biermann and Petra Overath (Berlin: Berliner Wissenschafts-Verlag, 2007), 3–16.

21. General prevention refers to sanctions intended to deter overall criminality, while special prevention refers to sanctions intended to deter the criminal behavior of a specific delinquent.

22. Martina Henze, *Strafvollzugsreformen im 19. Jahrhundert: Gefängniskundlicher Diskurs und staatliche Praxis in Bayern und Hessen-Darmstadt* (Darmstadt: Hessische Historische Kommission und Historische Kommission für Hessen, 2003).

23. Sean McConville, *A History of English Prison Administration*, vol. 1, *1750–1877* (London: Routledge and Kegan Paul, 1981), 400–404.

24. Christina Schenk, *Bestrebungen zur einheitlichen Regelung des Strafvollzugs in Deutschland von 1870 bis 1923* (Frankfurt: Lang, 2001), 181.

25. Herbert Schattke, *Die Geschichte der Progression im Strafvollzug und der damit zusammenhängenden Vollzugsziele in Deutschland* (Frankfurt: Lang, 1979), 69–195.

26. Michel Foucault, *Discipline and Punish: The Birth of the Prison* (New York: Vintage, 1995).

27. David Garland, *Punishment and Modern Society: A Study in Social Theory* (Chicago: University of Chicago Press, 1990), 157–75.

28. Thomas Nutz, *Strafanstalt als Besserungsmaschine: Reformdiskurs und Gefängniswissenschaft, 1775–1848* (Munich: Oldenbourg, 2001); Wolfgang Dressen, *Die pädagogische Maschine: Zur Geschichte des industrialisierten Bewußtseins in Preußen/Deutschland* (Frankfurt: Ullstein, 1982).

29. Falk Bretschneider, *Gefangene Gesellschaft: Eine Geschichte der Einsperrung in Sachsen im 18. und 19. Jahrhundert* (Konstanz: UVK, 2008), 490–521.

30. Ylva Greve, *Verbrechen und Krankheit: Die Entdeckung der "Criminalpsychologie" im 19. Jahrhundert* (Cologne: Böhlau, 2004).

31. Eric J. Engstrom, "Die Psychologie als Argument für die Abschaffung des Strafmasses," in *Psychologie als Argument in der juristischen Literatur des Kaiserreichs*, ed. Mathias Schmoeckel (Baden-Baden: Nomos, 2009), 43–55; Silviana Galassi, *Kriminologie im deutschen Kaiserreich: Geschichte einer gebrochenen Verwissenschaftlichung* (Stuttgart: Franz Steiner, 2004); Christian Müller, *Verbrechensbekämpfung im Anstaltsstaat: Psychiatrie, Kriminologie und Strafrechtsreform in Deutschland, 1871–*

1933 (Göttingen: Vandenhoeck und Ruprecht, 2004); Richard F. Wetzell, *Inventing the Criminal: A History of German Criminology, 1880–1945* (Chapel Hill: University of North Carolina Press, 2000).

32. Lutz Raphael, "Die Verwissenschaftlichung des Sozialen als methodische und konzeptionelle Herausforderung für eine Sozialgeschichte des 20. Jahrhunderts," *Geschichte und Gesellschaft* 22 (1996): 165–93. For a recent example of what Raphael has inspired, see Schauz and Freitag, *Verbrecher im Visier der Experten*.

33. Therese Stäcker, *Die Franz von Liszt-Schule und ihre Auswirkungen auf die deutsche Strafrechtsentwicklung* (Baden-Baden: Nomos, 2012), 19–77.

34. "Vereinbarung der Landesregierungen über Grundsätze für den Vollzug von Freiheitsstrafen vom 7. 6. 1923," in, *Von der Aufklärung bis zur doppelten Staatsgründung*, ed. Hinrich Rüping, vol. 2 of *Studien- und Quellenbuch zur Geschichte der deutschen Strafrechtspflege*, ed. Wolfgang Sellert and Hinrich Rüping (Darmstadt: Scientia Verlag Aalen, 1994), 199.

35. Jürgen Simon, *Kriminalbiologie und Zwangssterilisation: Eugenischer Rassismus, 1920–1945* (Münster: Waxmann, 2001), 97–152.

36. Theodor Viernstein, "Die Einführung eines Stufensystems in den bayrischen Strafanstalten," *Zeitschrift für Medizinalbeamte* 35 (1922): 538–53.

37. Müller, *Verbrechensbekämpfung im Anstaltsstaat*, 236–66.

38. Thomas Kailer, *Vermessung des Verbrechers: Die kriminalbiologische Untersuchung in Bayern, 1923–1945* (Bielefeld: Transcript, 2011), 248.

39. Simon, *Kriminalbiologie und Zwangssterilisation*, 106.

40. These came in the form of the Reich Juvenile Court Law of 16 February 1923 and the so-called Principles for Criminal Incarceration of 7 June 1923.

41. Nikolaus Wachsmann, "Between Reform and Repression: Imprisonment in Weimar Germay," *Historical Journal* 45 (2002): 416–17; Schattke, *Die Geschichte der Progression im Strafvollzug*, 69–195.

42. Some transitional assistance was provided by welfare associations and social court assistance. See Warren Rosenblum, *Beyond the Prison Gates: Punishment and Welfare in Germany, 1850–1933* (Chapel Hill: University of North Carolina Press, 2008), 165–99; Desiree Schauz, *Strafen als moralische Besserung: Eine Geschichte der Straffälligenfürsorge, 1777–1933* (Munich: Oldenbourg, 2008), 333–76.

43. As discussed in chapter 3, East Germany repealed much of the law's provisions, but the law continued to have an impact there through administrative measures and work-arounds.

44. Albin Eser, "Zur Entwicklung von Maßregeln der Besserung und Sicherung als zweite Spur im Strafrecht," in *Grundfragen staatlichen Strafens*, ed. Guido Britz (Munich: C. H. Beck, 2001), 213–36.

45. Christian Müller, *Das Gewohnheitsverbrechergesetz vom 24. November 1933: Kriminalpolitik als Rassenpolitik* (Baden-Baden: Nomos, 1997).

46. Immanuel Baumann, *Dem Verbrechern auf der Spur: Eine Geschichte der Kriminologie und Kriminalpolitik in Deutschland 1880 bis 1980* (Göttingen: Wallstein, 2006).

47. See, for instance, Joachim Vogel, *Einflüsse des Nationalsozialismus auf das Strafrecht* (Berlin: Berliner Wissenschafts-Verlag, 2004).

48. M.-P. Drost, "Sartre's Concept of a Person as a Project," *Dialogos* 23 (1988): 97–108.

49. Greg Eghigian, Andreas Killen, and Christine Leuenberger, eds., *The Self as Project: Politics and the Human Sciences*, Osiris 22 (Chicago: University of Chicago Press, 2007).

50. Margrit Szöllösi-Janze, "Wissensgesellschaft in Deutschland: Überlegungen zur Neubestimmung der deutschen Zeitgeschichte über Verwissenschaftlichungsprozesse," *Geschichte und Gesellschaft* 30 (2004): 277–313; Jakob Vogel, "Von der Wissenschafts- zur Wissensgeschichte: Für eine Historisierung der 'Wissensgesellschaft,'" *Geschichte und Gesellschaft* 30 (2004): 639–60.

51. Cornelius Castoriadis, *The Imaginary Institution of Society* (Cambridge, MA: MIT Press, 1987).

52. Charles Taylor, "Modern Social Imaginaries," *Public Culture* 14 (2002): 91–124.

53. Claudia Strauss, "The Imaginary," *Anthropological Theory* 6 (2006): 322–44.

54. Joseph R. Gusfield, *The Culture of Public Problems: Drinking-Driving and the Symbolic Order* (Chicago: University of Chicago Press, 1980), 5. See also Erving Goffman, *Stigma: Notes on the Management of a Spoiled Identity* (New York: Simon and Schuster, 1986); Edward Sutherland, "The Diffusion of Sexual Psychopath Laws," *American Journal of Sociology* 56 (1950): 142–48.

55. Michel Foucault, *Abnormal: Lectures at the Collège de France, 1974–1975* (New York: Picador, 2003). I share Pieter Spierenburg's reservations about Foucault's reifying conception of power. See Petrus Cornelis Spierenburg, "Punishment, Power, and History: Foucault and Elias," *Social Science History* 28 (2004): 607–36.

56. Michel Foucault, *The History of Sexuality: An Introduction*, vol. 1 (New York: Vintage, 1990), 139.

57. Thomas Lemke, *Biopolitics: An Advanced Introduction* (New York: New York University Press, 2011), 5.

58. Georges Vigarello, *A History of Rape: Sexual Violence in France from the 16th to the 20th Century* (Cambridge: Polity, 2001).

59. Brigitte Kerchner, "'Sexualdiktatur': Macht und Gewalt in Gerichtsverfahren der Weimarer Republik," in *Unzucht—Notzucht—Vergewaltigung: Definitionen und Deutungen sexueller Gewalt von der Aufklärung bis heute*, ed. Christine Künzel (Frankfurt: Campus, 2003), 137–63; Tanja Hommen, *Sittlichkeitsverbrechen: Sexuelle Gewalt im Kaiserreich* (Frankfurt: Campus, 1999).

60. Robert Beachy, "The German Invention of Homosexuality," *Journal of Modern History* 82 (2010): 801–38.

61. Francisca Loetz, "Sexualisierte Gewalt in Europa 1520–1850: Historisierung von 'Vergewaltigung' und Missbrauch,'" *Geschichte und Gesellschaft* 35 (2009): 561–602.

62. Sue Rodmell, "Men, Women, and Sexuality: A Feminist Critique of the Sociology of Deviance," *Women's Studies International Quarterly* 4 (1981): 145–55.

63. Mark Fenemore, "The Recent Historiography of Sexuality in Twentieth-Century Germany," *Historical Journal* 52 (2009): 763–79.

64. Sabine Maasen, *Genealogie der Unmoral: Zur Therapeutisierung sexueller Selbste* (Frankfurt: Suhrkamp, 1998).

65. Historians of deviance in the USSR and East Germany have been especially effective in drawing attention to this fact. See Brian LaPierre, *Hooligans in Khrushchev's Russia: Defining, Policing, and Producing Deviance during the Thaw* (Madison: Uni-

versity of Wisconsin, 2012); Sandrine Kott, "Die Unerreichbaren der sozialistischen Gesellschaft: Die Arbeiterjugend in der DDR (1970–1989)," in *Der Schein der Stabilität: DDR-Betriebsalltag in der Ära Honecker*, ed. Renate Hürtgen and Thomas Reichel (Berlin: Metropol, 2001), 229–48.

CHAPTER 2

1. Nikolaus Wachsmann, *Hitler's Prisons* (New Haven: Yale University Press, 2004).

2. Heinz Faulstich, *Hungersterben in der Psychiatrie 1914–1949: Mit einer Topographie der NS-Psychiatrie* (Freiburg: Lambertus, 1998); Michael Burleigh, *Death and Deliverance: "Euthanasia" in Germany, c. 1900–1945* (New York: Cambridge University Press, 1994); Hans-Walter Schmuhl, *Rassenhygiene, Nationalsozialismus, Euthanasie: Von der Verhütung zur Vernichtung "lebensunwerten Lebens," 1890–1945* (Göttingen: Vandenhoeck und Ruprecht, 1992).

3. Paul Weindling, *Epidemics and Genocide in Eastern Europe, 1890–1945* (New York: Oxford University Press, 2000); Michael Burleigh and Wolfgang Wippermann, *The Racial State: Germany 1933–1945* (New York: Cambridge University Press, 1991).

4. Nikolaus Wachsmann, "From Indefinite Confinement to Extermination: 'Habitual Criminals' in the Third Reich," in *Social Outsiders in Nazi Germany*, ed. Robert Gellately and Nathan Stoltzfuss (Princeton: Princeton University Press, 2001), 165–91; Lisa Pine, "Hashude: The Imprisonment of 'Asocial' Families in the Third Reich," *German History* 13 (1995): 182–97; Norbert Emmerich, "Die forensische Psychiatrie 1933–1945: Das Schicksal der wegen einer Straftat eingewiesenen Kranken," in *Totgeschwiegen 1933–1945*, ed. Arbeitsgruppe zur Erforschung der Geschichte der Karl-Bonhoeffer-Nervenklinik (Berlin: Edition Hentrich, 1989), 105–23.

5. Heiko Stoff, *Ewige Jugend: Konzepte der Verjüngung vom späten 19. Jahrhundert bis ins Dritte Reich* (Cologne: Böhlau, 2004).

6. Wachsmann, *Hitler's Prisons*, 59–64.

7. Thierack, "Der Strafvollzug im Dienste der Volksgemeinschaft," *Monatsblätter für Gerichtshilfe, Gefangenen- und Entlassenenfürsorge* (hereafter *MfGGE*), 11 (1936): 209–15, quote from 214.

8. Gellately and Stoltzfus, eds., *Social Outsiders in Nazi Germany*.

9. Müller, *Verbrechensbekämpfung im Anstaltsstaat*; Burleigh and Wippermann, *The Racial State*; Robert N. Proctor, *Racial Hygiene: Medicine under the Nazis* (Cambridge, MA: Harvard University Press, 1988).

10. Wetzell, *Inventing the Criminal*, 179–85.

11. See, for instance, the praise showered on early Nazi reforms by the president of the Association of German Prison Staff, Otto Weissenrieder, in "Vorwort," *Blätter für Gefängniskunde* (hereafter *BfG*) 64 (1933): 113–17.

12. This point is brought home particularly well by Robert Proctor in *The Nazi War on Cancer* (Princeton: Princeton University Press, 1999).

13. David Bankier, *The Germans and the Final Solution: Public Opinion under Nazism* (Oxford: Blackwell, 1992).

14. Simon, *Kriminalbiologie und Zwangssterilisation.*

15. Richard F. Wetzell, "Criminology in Weimar and Nazi Germany," in *Criminals and Their Scientists: The History of Criminology in International Perspective*, ed. Peter Becker and Richard F. Wetzell, (New York: Cambridge University Press, 2006), 401–23.

16. Franz Exner, "Aufgaben der Kriminologie im neuen Reich," *Monatsschrift für Kriminalpsychologie und Strafrechtsreform* (hereafter *MfKuS*) 27 (1936): 3–17. The journal *Monatsschrift für Kriminalpsychologie und Strafrechtsreform* changed its name to *Monatsschrift für Kriminalbiologie und Strafrechtsreform* in 1937. After the war, in 1953, it was redubbed the *Monatsschrift für Kriminologie und Strafrechtsreform.*

17. Kailer, *Vermessung des Verbrechers*,174–75; Oliver Liang, "The Biology of Morality: Criminal Biology in Bavaria, 1924–1933," in Becker and Wetzell, *Criminals and Their Scientists*, 425–46; Wolfgang Burgmair, Matthias M. Weber, and Nikolaus Wachsmann, "'Die soziale Prognose wird damit sehr trübe . . .'—Theodor Viernstein und die Kriminalbiologische Sammelstelle in Bayern," in *Polizeireport München, 1799–1999*, ed. Michael Farin (Munich: Belleville, 1999), 250–87.

18. Bundesarchiv (hereafter BArch), R 3001/alt R 22/1451, Reisebericht, Reichministerium der Justiz, undated [ca. December 1934/January 1935], S. 63–67.

19. See Richard F. Wetzell, "From Retributive Justice to Social Defense: Penal Reform in Fin-de-Siécle Germany," in *Germany at the Fin-de-Siécle: Culture, Politics, and Ideas*, ed. Suzanne Marchard and David Lindenfeld (Baton Rouge: Louisiana State University, 2004), 59–77.

20. Franz von Liszt, "Der Zweckgedanke im Strafrecht," *Zeitschrift für die gesamte Strafrechtswissenschaft* (hereafter *ZfdgS*) 3 (1883): 1–47, quote from 36.

21. Geril Thulfaut, *Kriminalpolitik und Strafrechtslehre bei Edmund Mezger (1883–1962)* (Baden-Baden: Nomos, 2000), 108–17; Versammlungsbericht, Juristisch-medizinische Gesellschaft zu Leipzig, Edmund Mezger, "Arbeitsmethode und Bedeutung der kriminalbiologischen Untersuchungsstellen für Strafrechtspflege," *MfKuS* 23 (1932): 415–16; Edmund Mezger, "Die Behandlung der gefährlichen Gewohnheitsverbrecher," *MfKuS* 14 (1923): 135–75.

22. Matthias Willing, *Das Bewahrungsgesetz (1918–1967): Eine rechtshistorische Studie zur Geschichte der deutschen Fürsorge* (Tübingen: Mohr Siebeck, 2003), 9–119. For a comparatively more generous interpretation of welfare advocates at this time, see Rosenblum, *Beyond the Prison Gates*, 141–99.

23. Benedikt Hartl, *Das nationalsozialistische Willensstrafrecht* (Berlin: Weissensee, 2000), 37.

24. Ibid., 66–126.

25. "Gesetz gegen gefährliche Gewohnheitsverbrecher und über Maßregeln der Sicherung und Besserung vom 24. November 1933," *MfKuS* 25 (1934): 261–65.

26. Prussian police were awarded similar powers a few days before the Dangerous Habitual Offender Law was announced. A Prussian decree from 13 November 1933 gave police there the right to place suspects in indefinite "preventive custody," independent of the judiciary. This became the legal precedent for the internment of the regime's political and racial enemies in concentration camps. All told, from 1933 to 1943, the German police (Kripo) preventively deported around seventy thousand to eighty thou-

sand people to concentration camps on this basis. See Thomas Roth, *"Verbrechensbekämpfung" und soziale Ausgrenzung im nationalsozialistischen Köln* (Cologne: Emons, 2010), 64.

27. Müller, *Das Gewohnheitsverbrechergesetz vom 24. November 1933*, 60.

28. Franz Zeugner, "Zur Kritik der Erziehungsmethoden im Strafvollzug," *MfKuS* 26 (1935): 267–70; Fink, "Der zukünftige Strafvollzug," *MfKuS* 26 (1935): 537–40.

29. Josef Schafheutle and Fritz Hauptvogel, "Sicherungsverwahrung," in *Handwörterbuch der Kriminologie und der anderen Strafrechtlichen Hilfswissenschaften*, vol. 2, ed. Alexander Elster and Heinrich Lingemann (Berlin: Walter de Gruyter, 1936), 597–610, quote from 605.

30. Franz Kapp, "Über die Beobachtungsabteilungen bei den Gefangenenanstalten der Justizverwaltung," *Zeitschrift für psychische Hygiene* 10 (1937): 3–15.

31. Georg Steigertahl, "Die Zusammenhänge zwischen Zwangsfürsorge und Maßregeln der Sicherung und Besserung in Hamburg," *MfKuS* 28 (1937): 128–40.

32. BArch, R 3001/alt R 22/1334, Reichsministerium der Justiz, "Übersicht über den Vollzug der Maßregeln der Sicherung und Besserung in den einzelnen Ländern," undated [ca. 15 November 1934], S. 8–30.

33. BArch, R 3001/alt R 22/1334, Dr. Jung, Generalstaatsanwalt bei dem Kammergericht an Reichsminister der Justiz, 4 April 1935, S. 39–42; 25 April 1935, S. 42–44. In 1937, Hans Mayr reported that of 581 men held in preventive detention during the first year of operation of the facility in Straubing, forty were released. Hans Mayr, "Die Entlassung aus der Sicherungsverwahrung: Bisherige süddeutsche Erfahrungen," *MfKuS* 28 (1937): 84–86.

34. Section 42 provided the legal justification for committing someone to a psychiatric facility on the grounds that the person was a danger to himself or herself and/or to others. Section 51 provided for the commitment of an individual due to his or her diminished capacity to be held responsible for his or her crimes (*Unzurechnungsfähigkeit* or *verminderte Zurechnungsfähigkeit*).

35. W. Creutz, "Psychiatrische Erfahrungen mit §§ 42b und 42c des Gesetzes gegen gefährliche Gewohnheitsverbrecher und über Maßregeln der Sicherung und Besserung vom 24. November 1933," *Allgemeine Zeitschrift für Psychiatrie und ihre Grenzgebiete* 111 (1939): 137–68; Ferdinand Hürten, "Die ersten Hundert auf Grund des Gesetzes vom 24. November 1933 in der westfälischen Prov.-Heilanstalt Eickelborn untergebrachten geistig abnormen Rechtsbrecher," *Allgemeine Zeitschrift für Psychiatrie und Psychisch-Gerichtliche Medizin* 106 (1937): 255–338.

36. Hans Trunk, "Unterbringung in Heil- und Pflegeanstalten als Sicherheitsmaßnahme," *Zeitschrift für psychische Hygiene* 9 (1936): 120–26.

37. Emmerich, "Die forensische Psychiatrie 1933–1945."

38. Johannes Schottky, "Psychiatrische und kriminalbiologische Fragen bei der Unterbringung in einer Heil- und Pflegeanstalt nach § 42b und c des Strafgesetzbuches," *Allgemeine Zeitschrift für Psychiatrie und ihre Grenzgebiete* 117 (1941): 287–355, quote from 336.

39. Werner Gerecke, "Eindrücke vom Strafvollzug im Staate New York," *BfG* 68 (1937–38): 379–83; Leopold Quentin and Rudolf Sieverts, "Die Behandlung der jungen Rechtsbrecher im Alter von 17 bis 23 Jahren in England unter besonderer Berücksichtigung des Borstal-Systems," *BfG* 68 (1937): 165–239; Review of "Die Anthropologie

im Vollzug (L'anthropologia Correzionale) von Quintiliano Saldana," by Schwab, *BfG* 67 (1936): 348–51; H. Gummersbach, "Die Neugestaltung des italienischen Strafvollzugs im Vergleich mit den deutschen Reformen," *MfKuS* 25 (1934): 369–82; Erik Kampmann, "Das Gefängniswesen in Dänemark nach dem neuen Strafgesetz von 1930," *BfG* 65 (1934): 95–118; Bruno Steinwallner, "Faschistischer Strafvollzug: Die italienische Strafvollzugsverordnung von 1931," *BfG* 65 (1934): 191–200; Reinhart Maurach, "Der neue Strafvollzug in Sowjetrußland," *MfKuS* 24 (1933): 705–19.

40. Franz Exner, *Kriminalistischer Bericht über eine Reise nach Amerika* (Berlin: Walter de Gruyter, 1935), 26–52.

41. Ibid., 72–82.

42. Otto Weissenrieder, Review of *Kriminalistischer Bericht über eine Reise nach Amerika*, by Franz Exner *BfG* 66 (1935): 183–86; Exner, *Kriminalistischer Bericht*, 82.

43. Franz Exner, "Das System der sichernden und bessernden Maßregeln nach dem Gesetz v. 24. November 1933," *ZfdgS* 53 (1934): 629–65, specific references from 637 and 639.

44. Schafheutle and Hauptvogel, "Sicherungsverwahrung," 600.

45. Simon, *Kriminalbiologie und Zwangssterilisation*, 129–52.

46. Kailer, *Vermessung des Verbrechers*, 241.

47. BArch, R 3001/alt R 22/1451, Zentralstelle für kriminalbiologische Untersuchungen an den Preußischen Gefangenanstalten, Fragebogen, undated [ca. 1933], S. 1–17.

48. Staatsarchiv Hamburg (hereafter StAHH), Bestand 241-1 I/2830, Ministerialrat Dr. Viernstein, "Kriminalbiologie und Erneuerung der Rechtsordnung: Denkschrift," 1933.

49. E. Hacker, "Beiträge zum Problem der rückfälligen und unverbesserlichen Verbrecher," *MfKuS* 26 (1935): 247–53; Strüder, "Gedanken über die Erziehbarkeit der Zuchthausgefangenen," *MfKuS* 24 (1933): 519–25.

50. Friedrich von Rohden, "Gibt es unverbesserliche Verbrecher?," *MfKuS* 24 (1933): 74–92.

51. Karl Schnell, *Anlage und Umwelt bei 500 Rückfallsverbrechern: Ein Beitrag zum Problem des Gewohnheitsverbrechertums erarbeitet an einem Material der Bayerischen Kriminalbiologischen Sammelstelle* (Leipzig: Ernst Wiegandt, 1935), 117–18.

52. Burgmair, Weber, and Wachsmann, "Die soziale Prognose," 273–77.

53. Robert Schiedt, *Ein Beitrag zum Problem der Rückfallsprognose* (Munich: Münchener Zeitungs-Verlag, 1936), 7–10. For his study, Schiedt examined the prognostic value of twenty-one factors, finding that only fifteen could reliably be associated with recidivism.

54. Albert J. Harno, Andrew A. Bruce, Ernest W. Burgess, and John Landesco, *The Workings of the Indeterminate-Sentence Law and the Parole System in Illinois* (Chicago: State of Illinois, 1928).

55. Sheldon Glueck and Eleanor Glueck, *500 Criminal Careers* (New York: Knopf, 1930).

56. All subjects were released in 1931. Their criminal records were checked again in 1935, to see if they had committed a new offense since being released.

57. Schiedt, *Ein Beitrag*, 69.

58. Ibid., 31–62, 68.

59. Franz Exner, "Über Rückfall-Prognosen," *MfKuS* 27 (1936): 401–9.

60. Hans Trunk, "Soziale Prognose an Strafgefangenen," *MfKuS* 28 (1937): 209–27, data from 223–24.

61. Franz Exner, "Bemerkungen zu dem vorstehenden Aufsatz von Dr. H. Trunk über 'Soziale Prognose an Strafgefangenen,'" *MfKuS* 28 (1937): 227–30.

62. Wilhelm Meywerk, "Beitrag zur Bestimmung der sozialen Prognose an Rückfallsverbrechern," *MfKuS* 29 (1938): 422–44, quote from 443.

63. Ferdinand von Neureiter, *Kriminalbiologie* (Berlin: Carl Heymann, 1940); Fritz Schwaab, *Die soziale Prognose bei rückfälligen Vermögensverbrechern* (Leipzig: Ernst Wiegandt, 1939); Werner Gerecke, "Zur Frage der Rückfallprognose," *MfKuS* 29 (1939): 35–38; Heinz Möller, *Die Entwicklung und Lebensverhältnisse von 135 Gewohnheitsverbrechern* (Leipzig: Ernst Wiegandt, 1939); Wilhelm Polligkeit, "Menschen und Schicksale: Aus Lebensläufen von Landstreichern," in *Der nichtseßhafte Mensch: Ein Beitrag zur Neugestaltung der Raum- und Menschenordnung im Großdeutschen Reich*, ed. Bayerischer Landesverband für Wanderdienst, München (Munich: C. H. Beck, 1938), 371–428.

64. Exner, *Kriminalistischer Bericht*, 84.

65. Patrick Wagner, *Volksgemeinschaft ohne Verbrecher: Konzeptionen und Praxis der Kriminalpolizei in der Zeit der Weimarer Republik und des Nationalsozialismus* (Hamburg: Christians, 1996), 258–98; Lothar Gruchmann, *Justiz im Dritten Reich 1933–1940: Anpassung und Unterwerfung in der Ära Gürtner* (Munich: Oldenbourg, 1988), 719–45.

66. Friedrich Schaffstein, "Vorbeugungshaft, Verwahrung, und Bewahrung," *ZfdgS* 58 (1939): 307–13.

67. Rudolf Sieverts, "Die strafrechtlichen Behandlung der Frühkriminellen," in Bayerischer Landesverband für Wanderdienst, München, *Der nichtseßhafte Mensch*, 231–39.

68. Sigmund Silbereisen, *Die spätere Straffälligkeit jugendlicher Rechtsbrecher: Eine Nachuntersuchung über die im Jahre 1928 in München verurteilten Jugendlichen* (Leipzig: Ernst Wiegandt, 1940).

69. Roland Freisler, "Ein Querschnitt durch die Fragen der Sicherungsverwahrung," in *Dringende Fragen der Sicherungsverwahrung, Gemeinschaftsarbeit aus der Praxis für die Praxis*, ed. Roland Freisler et al. (Berlin: R. von Decker's Verlag, 1938), 7–14, quote from 7.

70. Michael Berkowitz, *The Crime of My Very Existence: Nazism and the Myth of Jewish Criminality* (Berkeley: University of California Press, 2007).

71. Werner Villinger, "Welche Merkmale lassen am jugendlichen Rechtsbrecher den künftigen Gewohnheitsverbrecher voraussehen?," in Bayerischer Landesverband für Wanderdienst, München, *Der nichtseßhafte Mensch*, 213–30, quote from 225.

72. Ludwig Lotz, *Der gefährliche Gewohnheitsverbrecher* (Leipzig: Ernst Wiegandt, 1939), 14.

73. BArch, R 3001/alt R 22/845, Strafsache gegen T.E. wegen gewerbmäßiger Abtreibung, Reichsgericht, 1. Strafsenat, 24 March 1942, S. 576–79.

74. As the renowned psychiatrist Kurt Schneider defined it, volition is "the possibility to decide between two or more different strivings." Kurt Schneider, *Pathopsychologie der Gefühle und Triebe: Ein Grundriss* (Leipzig: Georg Thieme, 1935), 26.

75. Evidence of a good faith effort and willpower to reform was also critical in clemency cases. See Roth, *Verbrechensbekämpfung*, 482–88.

76. Landesarchiv Berlin (hereafter LAB), A Rep. 369, Nr. 283, Führungsbericht, Strafgefängnis Plötzensee, 30 August 1943.

77. LAB, A Rep. 369, Nr. 144, Berlin-Plötzensee, Führungsbericht, 2 November 1944.

78. See, for instance, BArch, R 3001/alt R 22/1334, Dr. Sturm, Generalstaatanwaltschaftschaft an Reichsminister der Justiz, Breslau, 25 April 1935, S. 42–44.

79. BArch, R 3001/alt R 22/1334, Dr. Jung, Generalstaatsanwaltschaft bei dem Kammergericht an Reichsminister der Justiz, Berlin, 4 April 1935, S. 39–42.

80. Henry Werlinder, *Psychopathy: A History of the Concepts; Analysis of the Origin and Development of a Family of Concepts in Psychopathology* (Stockhom: Almqvist och Wiksell International, 1978).

81. Michael Cowen, *Cult of the Will: Nervousness and German Modernity* (University Park: Pennsylvania State University Press, 2008), 69–198.

82. George Mosse, *The Image of Man: The Creation of Modern Masculinity* (New York: Oxford University Press, 1996), 155–80; Jay W. Baird, *To Die for Germany: Heroes in the Nazi Pantheon* (Bloomington: Indiana University Press, 1992).

83. Adolf Lenz, "Persönlichkeitsaufbau," and Karl Birnbaum, "Persönlichkeitsforschung," in Elster and Lingemann, *Handwörterbuch der Kriminologie*, 263–68, 268–80.

84. Walter Betzendahl, "Über maskierte Verrücktheit und ihre sozialen Folgen," *Allgemeine Zeitschrift für Psychiatrie und psychisch-gerichtliche Medizin* 100 (1933): 141–85.

85. Hans Schneickert, "Die Schwierigkeit der Charakterbestimmung," *Archiv für Kriminalpsychologie* 111 (1942): 86–91.

86. Schläger, "Abartige Geisteszustände und die Rechtsprechung," *Allgemeine Zeitschrift für Psychiatrie und ihre Grenzgebiete* 123 (1944): 112–21; Hegemann, "Zu der Frage nach Überlegung bei einer Anklage auf Mord," *Allgemeine Zeitschrift für Psychiatrie und ihre Grenzgebiete* 118 (1941): 380–91.

87. Stettner, "Die Erziehung im deutschen Strafwesen, von der Strafentlassenenfürsorge aus gesehen," *Monatsblätter des Deutschen Reichszusammenschlusses für Gerichtshilfe, Gefangenen- und Entlassenenfürsorge der freien Wohlfahrtspflege* 9 (January–February 1934): 40–64.

88. Friedrich Schaffstein, "Die Bedeutung des Erziehungsgedankens im neuen deutschen Strafvollzug," *ZfdgS* 55 (1936): 275–90, quote from 277.

89. Heinz Vogelsang, "Organisatorischer Aufbau und Zielsetzung der neuen deutschen Straffälligenfürsorge," *MfGGE* 10 (1935): 152–57.

90. Wachsmann, *Hitler's Prisons*, 67–111.

91. Karola Fings, "The Public Face of the Camps," in *Concentration Camps in Nazi Germany: The New Histories*, ed. Jane Caplan and Nikolaus Wachsmann (London: Routledge, 2010), 108–26; Carina Baganz, *Erziehung zur "Volksgemeinschaft": Die frühen Konzentrationslager in Sachsen 1933–1934/37* (Berlin: Metropol, 2005), 155–93.

92. Petra Götte, *Jugendstrafvollzug im "Dritten Reich": Diskutiert und realisiert—erlebt und erinnert* (Bad Heilbrunn: Julius Klinkhardt, 2003), 107–33; Frank Kebbedies,

Außer Kontrolle: Jugendkriminalität in der NS-Zeit und der frühen Nachkriegszeit (Essen: Klartext, 2000); Ulrike Jureit, *Erziehen, Strafen, Vernichten: Jugendkriminaliät und Jugendstrafrecht im Nationalsozialismus* (Münster: Waxmann, 1995).

93. Christian Goeschel and Nikolaus Wachsmann, "Before Auschwitz: The Formation of the Nazi Concentration Camps, 1933–9," *Journal of Contemporary History* 45 (2010): 515–34.

94. W. Bormann, "Die Wiedereingliederung des politischen Gefangenen in die Volksgemeinschaft," *MfGGE* 10 (1935): 129–30; Otto Weissenrieder, "Selbsterziehung eines 'Unverbesserlichen,'" *BfG* 66 (1935): 391–97.

95. StAHH, Bestand 241-1 I, Justizverwaltung I, 2514, "Niederschrift über die Konferenz der Strafvollzugsreferenten in Darmstadt vom 5. und 6. Oktober 1933," Berlin, 21 September 1933.

96. StAHH, Bestand 241-1 I, Justizverwaltung I, 2514, "Richtlinien für den Strafvollzug in Stufen," undated [ca. 1934].

97. E. Schmidt, "Sinn und Zweck des Strafvollzugs," *BfG* 68 (1937): 42–52; Fink, "Der zukünftige Strafvollzug."

98. BArch, R 3001/alt R 22/1259, Reichsminister der Justiz an Reichsminister der Finanzen, 8 January 1939, S. 18–21.

99. Franz Böttcher, "Erziehung und praktische Auslesearbeit in der Gefangenenanstalt," *Die deutsche Sonderschule* 6 (1939): 567–70; Schaffstein, "Die Bedeutung des Erziehungsgedankens," 288.

100. Zeugner, "Zur Kritik der Erziehungsmethoden." For a contrary position, see Konrad Dra, "Was heißt Besserung im Strafvollzug?," *BfG* 70 (1939): 44–48.

101. One notable exception was Franz Kapp, a prison physician in Cologne. Nevertheless, Kapp believed that psychotherapy was limited in its usefulness, needing to be combined with ethical instruction, pedagogy, and social intervention in order to be truly effective in reorienting the criminal will. See Franz Kapp, "Kriminalpsychotherapeutische Einzelfälle," part 1, "Ein Neurotiker mit Mordphantasien," and part 2, "Ein Neurotiker mit vielseitigen (polytropen) verbrecherischen Neigungen," *Allgemeine Zeitschrift für Psychiatrie und psychisch-gerichtliche Medizin* 103 (1935): 1–25.

102. Finke, "Anlage und Umwelt als kriminalpädagogisches Problem," *MfGGE* 10 (1935): 67–69, quote from 68. See also Fink, "Der zukünftige Strafvollzug"; Zeugner, "Zur Kritik der Erziehungsmethoden," 270.

103. H. Gummersbach, "Die Erziehung zur Lebenstauglichkeit als Strafvollzugsziel der Reformen," *Monatsblätter des Deutschen Reichszusammenschlusses für Gerichtshilfe, Gefangenen- und Entlassenenfürsorge der freien Wohlfahrtspflege* 9 (January–February 1934): 11–17, quote from 13. See also Wilhelm Bleidt, "Strafvollzug als Erziehungsgelegenheit," in Elster and Lingemann, *Handwörterbuch der Kriminologie*, 712–15.

104. W. Dziembowski, "Strafvollzug im nationalsozialistischen Staate und Erziehungsmöglichkeiten an Strafgefangenen durch den Anstaltspädagogen," *BfG* 67 (1936): 142–59, quote from 157–58.

105. Wilhelm Narr, "Der Erziehungsgedanke und seine Verwirklichung im Strafvollzug," *Die deutsche Sonderschule* 2 (1936): 933–35.

106. Martin Stahlmann and Jürgen Schiedeck, *"Erziehung zur Gemeinschaft—*

Auslese durch Gemeinschaft": Zur Zurichtung des Menschen im Nationalsozialismus (Bielefeld: Karin Böllert/KT-Verlag, 1991).

107. Catherine Fussinger, "'Therapeutic Community,' Psychiatry's Reformers, and Antipsychiatrists: Reconsidering Changes in the Field of Psychiatry," *History of Psychiatry* 22 (2011): 146–63.

108. A. Kothe, "Der Wert der Persönlichkeit im Strafvollzuge," *MfKuS* 24 (1933): 602–9.

109. A. Kothe, "Zum künftigen Strafvollzug," *MfKuS* 26 (1935): 127–35, quote from 135.

110. Käte Schmitz, "Soziale Stellung—äußere Faktoren in ihrer Bedeutung für die Beurteilung der rechtsbrecherischen Frau," *Monatsblätter für Straffälligenbetreuung und Ermittlungshilfe* 13 (1938): 129–32.

111. Günther Kersten, "Besonderheiten in der Betreuung weiblicher Strafgefangener," *Monatsblätter für Straffälligenbetreuung und Ermittlungshilfe* 14 (1939): 49–56. See also Sandra Leukel, "Reforming Women's Prisons in Imperial Germany," in *Crime and Criminal Justice in Modern Germany*, ed. Richard F. Wetzell (New York: Berghahn, 2014), 86–111.

112. Else Voigtländer, "Über den Strafvollzug an Frauen," *BfG* 68 (1937): 268–78.

113. Franz Weber, "Erfahrungen in der Sicherungsanstalt," *BfG* 68 (1938): 429–48, here 442–43); Schiefer, "Der Verwahrungsvollzug in der Sicherungsanstalt Waldheim," *BfG* 68 (1938): 448–65, here 453.

114. Hans Eichler, "Die Entlassung aus der Sicherungsverwahrung," *BfG* 69 (1938): 265–83; Weber, "Erfahrungen in der Sicherungsanstalt," 430–41; Schiefer, "Der Verwahrungsvollzug," 458–59.

115. StAHH, Bestand 241-1 I/2470, Dr. Bertram to Amtsgerichtsdirektor Korn, 21 December 1935.

116. Roth, *Verbrecherbekämpfung*, 207.

117. Wachsmann, *Hitler's Prisons*, 138.

118. LAB, A Rep. 369, Nr. 349, Vermerk über die Erörterung von Tat und Vorleben und über den dabei gewonnenen Eindruck, 20 November 1942; Nr. 60, Vorstand des Strafgefängnisses Plötzensee, Führungsbericht, 29 June 1942.

119. LAB, A Rep. 369, Nr. 283, Vorstand des Strafgefängnisses Plötzensee, Führungsbericht, 30 August 1943.

120. LAB, A Rep. 369, Nr. 355, Strafgefängnis Plötzensee to Kriminalpolizeistelle Hamburg, no day, September 1942.

121. LAB, A Rep. 369, Nr. 128, Vorstand des Gefängnisses Plötzensee, Führungsbericht, 4 August 1943.

122. LAB, A Rep. 369, Nr. 144, Berlin-Plötzensee, Führungsbericht, 2 November 1944.

123. Lewark, "Resozialisierungsmaßnahmen," *MfGGE* 10 (July 1935): 139–41, quote from 140.

124. Vogelsang, "Organisatorischer Aufbau," 156.

125. Schauz, *Strafen als moralische Besserung*, 359–66.

126. Eva Lemke, "Hausbesuch und Familienforschung, eine wichtige Vorarbeit zweckmäßiger Gefangenen- und Entlassenenfürsorge," *MfGGE* 11 (1936): 164–69.

127. Büttner, "Die Zusammenarbeit der NSV mit den Kreisstellen der Sächsischen

Straffälligenbetreuung und Ermittlungshilfe," *MfGGE* 13 (1937–38): 44–45; Bormann, "Ein Beitrag zur Selbshilfe der Gefangenen," *MfGGE* 11 (1936): 182–97.

128. Rupperath, "Individuelle Behandlung der Gefangenen," *MfGGE* 12 (1937): 115–20.

129. LAB, A Rep. 003-02, Nr. 63/1, Kapp, "Die Kriminalbiologie und ihre Beziehungen zur Ermittlungshilfe und Entlassenenfürsorge," *Monatsblätter für Straffälligenbetreuung und Ermittlungshilfe* 14 (1939), S. 5–6.

130. Sieber, "Die Ehre als Schnittpunkt in der Tendenz des Strafvollzuges, der Straffälligenbetreuung und Strafanstaltsseelsorge," *BfG* 71 (1940): 53–60.

131. BArch, R 160/68, Staatliche Kriminalpolizeistelle Aachen an Kriminalbiologisches Institut des Reichsgesundheitsamtes, 17 August 1942, S. 13; J.D., undated, S. 17–24, K.L., undated, S. 60–69, Erb- und lebensgeschichtlicher Fragebogen.

132. BArch, R 160/68; P.B., undated, S. 8–11, P.G., undated, S. 32–40, J.H., undated, S. 50–55, J.M., undated, S. 70–76, P.M., undated, S. 82–93, K.T., undated, S. 158–70, Erb- und geschichtlicher Fragebogen.

133. StAHH, Bestand 242-4/V23, Kriminal-Sekretär Hildesheim an Kriminalbiologische Sammelstelle bei der Untersuchungshaftanstalt Hamburg-Stadt, 2 September 1943.

134. Schwaab, *Die soziale Prognose bei rückfälligen Vermögensverbrechern*, 54.

135. Herbert Linden, "Bekämpfung der Sittlichkeitsverbrechen mit ärztlichen Mitteln," *Allgemeine Zeitschrift für Psychiatrie und ihre Grenzgebiete* 112 (1939): 405–23, quote from 415.

136. Ferdinand Wiethold, "Sittlichkeitsverbrechen," in Elster and Lingemann, *Handwörterbuch der Kriminologie*, 615–27.

137. Franz Rattenhuber, *Der gefährliche Sittlichkeitsverbrecher* (Bottrop: Wilhelm Postberg, 1939), 77–79.

138. Rudolf Koch, *Über Sittlichkeitsverbrecher* (Leipzig: Ernst Wiegandt, 1940), 13–14. One contributing reason for the increase has to do with the fact that the government began, in December 1934, to categorize as sex offenders those who exhibited themselves to children.

139. Ibid., 24–79.

140. Gerhard Wessel, *Das Delikt der Kinderschändung im Landgerichtsbezirk Bonn* (Düsseldorf: Dissertations-Verlag G. H. Nolte, 1939), 27–29, 40.

141. Herbert Krempler, *Die Sittlichkeitsdelikte im Bezirk des Landgerichts Eisenach in den Jahren 1905–1936* (Jena: Frommann, 1939), 65; Albert Günter Hess, *Die Kinderschändung: Unter besonderer Berücksichtigung der Tatsituation* (Leipzig: Ernst Wiegandt, 1934), 37.

142. Heiko Stoff, "Degenerierte Nervenkörper und regenerierte Hormonkörper: Eine kurze Geschichte der Verbesserung des Menschen zu Beginn des 20. Jahrhunderts," *Historische Anthropologie* 11 (2003): 224–39.

143. Otto Striehn, *Kastration nach § 14 II des Gesetzes zur Verhütung erbkranken Nachwuchses und nach § 42 k des Reichsstrafgesetzbuches unter Berücksichtigung der an der Kreis-Heil- und Pflegeanstalt zu Frankenthal vorhandenen Fälle* (Bleicherode: Carl Nieft, 1938), 51–52.

144. Albrecht Böhme, *Psychotherapie und Kastration: Die Bedeutung der Psychotherapie als Erziehungs- und Ausscheidungsmethode für sexuell Abwegige und Sittlich-*

keitsverbrecher, dargestellt an Fällen aus der Kriminalpraxis, unter Heranziehung der Graphologie als Hilfswissenschaft (Munich: J. F. Lehmanns Verlag, 1935), 48–64.

145. Fritz Reuter, *Aufartung durch Ausmerzung* (Berlin: Reimar Hobbing, 1936), 87–94; Siegfried Mallow, *Beitrag zur Kastration von Sexualverbrechern* (Leipzig: August Hoffmann, 1933), 503.

146. Georg Xingas, *Die Kastration als Sicherungsmaßnahme gegen Sittlichkeitsverbrecher* (Berlin: R. Pfau, 1937), 30–36.

147. Rattenhuber, *Der gefährliche Sittlichkeitsverbrecher*, 18–19.

148. Rodewald, "Entmannung und Entmannungsuntersuchungen: Text und Erläuterung der AV des Reichsjustizministers vom 10. Okt 1936," *MfKuS* 28 (1937): 3–11.

149. StAHH, Bestand 242-4/V8, "Einrichtung eines kriminalbiologischen Dienstes im Bereich der Reichsjustizverwaltung AV des Reichsjustizministeriums vom 30. November 1937," Abschrift aus der Zeitschrift Deutsche Justiz, Ausgabe A, Nr. 48, S. 1872–74.

150. StAHH, Bestand 242-4/V8, Leiter, Gerichtsobermedizinalrat Dr. Rodewald, Kriminalbiologische Sammelstelle Leipzig an Reichsminister der Justiz, Leipzig, 21 March 1939; Dr. Dallinger, Besprechung mit den Leitern der kriminalbiologischen Sammelstellen im Reichsjustizministerium am 8. Feb 1938, 24 February 1938.

151. Christiane Rothmaler, "Von 'haltlosen Psychopathinnen' und 'konstitutionellen Sittlichkeitsverbrechern': Die Kriminalbiologische Untersuchungs- und Sammelstelle der Hamburgischen Gefangenenanstalten 1926 bis 1945," in *Wissenschaftlicher Rassismus: Analysen einer Kontinuität in den Human- und Naturwissenschaften*, ed. Heidrun Kaupen-Haas and Christian Saller, (Frankfurt: Campus, 1999), 257–303; StAHH, Bestand 242-4/V8, Dr. Meywerk, Kriminal-Biologische Abteilung der Hamburgischen Gefangenenanstalten Hamburg, "Bericht," 4 December 1936.

152. StAHH, Bestand 241-1 I/2469, Generalstaatanwaltschaft, Drescher an Reichsminister der Justiz, 13 May 1935.

153. StAHH, Bestand 242-4 V21, Dr. Schaedel, 25 November 1935.

154. Wilhelm Meywerk, "Resozialisierung durch Entmannung," *MfKuS* 34 (1943): 1–61, data from 5–8.

155. Ibid., 27–33, quote from 27.

156. Langelüddeke, "Resozialisierung durch Entmannung: Bemerkungen zu der gleichnamigen Arbeit von W. Meywerk," *MfKuS* 34 (1943): 148–53.

157. Helmut Wolf, *Beitrag zur Frage der Kastration unter Berücksichtigung von Fällen der Heil- und Pflegeanstalt Göttingen* (Göttingen: MartinSass, 1941).

158. StAHH, Bestand 242-4/150, Strafregisterführer, R.C., 23 October 1940.

159. StAHH, Bestand 242-4/85, Landgericht Hamburg, Urteil, 11 March 1943; Dr. Reuss, Medizinalrat an Oberstaatsanwalt Landgericht Hamburg, 18 December 1942.

160. StAHH, Bestand 242-4/3, Amtsarzt [Dr. Radmann], Leiter des Gesundheitsamtes des Stadt- und Landkreises Güstrow, Gerichtsärztliches Gutachten, 7 October 1942.

161. StAHH, Bestand 242-4/354, Polizeipräsidium Berlin, Abt. V an Krim.Biolog. Sammelstelle Hamburg, 8 July 1941; Amtsarzt und Leiter des Gesundheitsamts Kreuzberg, Mag. Obermedizinalrat an Krim.Biolog.Sammelstelle Hamburg, 30 August 1939; StAHH, Bestand 242-4/39, Nachuntersuchung, Regierungsmedizinalrat, Strafgefängnis Wolfenbüttel, 23 August 1938; StAHH Bestand 242-4/63, Nachuntersuchung, 22 December 1937.

162. Franz Bunsmann, *Überblick über die Entwicklung der Entmannung sowie Beobachtungen an 30 auf Grund des Gesetzes vom 24.11.1933 entmannten Sittlichkeitsverbrechern* (Würzburg: Richard Mayr, 1938), 25.

163. Bunsmann, *Überblick*, 28.

164. StAHH, Bestand 242-4/226, Ortspolizeibehörde, Kriminalpolizei an Leiter der Kriminalbiologischen Sammelstelle Hamburg, 26 July 1943.

165. Waschsmann, *Hitler's Prisons*, 400–401.

166. BArch, B 141/18991, Horstkotte, Vermerk, 24 January 1966.

167. Nikolaus Jensch, *Untersuchungen an entmannten Sittlichkeitsverbrechern* (Leipzig: Georg Thieme, 1944), 53.

168. Walter Wagner, *Der Volksgerichtshof im nationalsozialistischen Staat* (Munich: Oldenbourg, 2011), 284–396, 832–44; Wachsmann, *Hitler's Prisons*, 218; Kebbedies, *Außer Kontrolle*, 123–84.

169. Gruchmann, *Justiz im Dritten Reich*, 740–45.

170. Ibid., 63–83.

171. Sarah Schädler, *"Justizkrise" und "Justizreform" im Nationalsozialismus: Das Reichsjustizministerium unter Reichsjustizminister Thierack (1942–1945)* (Tübingen: Mohr Siebeck, 2009), 7–55, 160–69.

172. Wachsmann, *Hitler's Prisons*, 223.

173. Franz Exner, "Wie erkennt man den gefährlichen Gewohnheitsverbrecher?," *Deutsche Justiz* 11 (6 August 1943): 377–79.

174. Adalbert Gregor and Albert Zink, "Soziale Eingliederung und Prognose aus dem Jugendgefängnis Entlassener," *BfG* 72 (1942): 241–91.

175. LAB, A Rep. 62, Nr. 168, Obergerichtsvollzieher, Ermittlungsbericht für die Kurhess. Straffälligenbetreuung und Ermittlungshilfe e. V. Kasse über den Strafgef. G.K., 23 October 1943, S. 35–36; Kretschmar, "Die Sächsische Straffälligenbetreuung," *Monatsblätter für Straffälligenbetreuung und Ermittlungshilfe* 17 (1942): 60–62; Hilgenfeldt, "Kriegsaufgaben der Straffälligenbetreuung," *Monatsblätter für Straffälligenbetreuung und Ermittlungshilfe* 17 (1942): 1–5; Fritz Krüger, "Die Aufgaben der Gefangenenfürsorge im Kriege," *Monatsblätter für Straffälligenbetreuung und Ermittlungshilfe* 16 (1940): 4–6.

176. See, for instance, records of the Criminal Biological Research Office (BArch, R 160/68), the Reich Ministry of Justice (BArch, R 3001/alt R 22/1334), the Youth Penitentiary at Plötzensee (LAB, A Rep. 369), and the Office of the Magistrate of Berlin (LAB, A Rep. 003-02, Nr. 63/1; A Rep. 003-04/1, Nr. 105).

177. BArch, R 3001/alt R22/970, Martin Bormann, Leiter der NSDAP-Kanzlei an Richsminister der Justiz, Dr. Thierack, 21 September 1942, S. 107–10.

178. Roland Freisler, "Wiedereingliederung—Abschlußteil des Strafrechts," *Monatsblätter für Straffälligenbetreuung und Ermittlungshilfe* 17 (1942): 6–10.

179. Peter Longerich, *Heinrich Himmler: A Life* (New York: Oxford University Press, 2012), 634–37; Jürge Zarusky, "Von der Sondergerichtsbarkeit zum Endphasenterror: Loyalitätserzwingung und Rache am Widerstand im Zusammenbruch des NS-Regimes," in *Terror nach Innen: Verbrechen am Ende des Zweiten Weltkrieges*, ed. Cord Arendes, Edgar Wolfrum, and Jörg Zedler (Göttingen: Wallstein, 2006), 103–21.

180. Ernst Kühn, "Kriminalpsychiatrische Untersuchungen an geistig abnormen politischen Rechtsbrechern," *Allgemeine Zeitschrift für Psychiatrie und ihre Grenzgebiete* 120 (1942): 158–85, quote from 163.

181. Schläger, "Abartige Geisteszustände"; Werner Eberhard, "Ein Beitrag zur Frage der Beziehungen zwischen Krankheit und Verbrechen," *BfG* 73 (1942–43): 107–14.

182. BArch, R 3001/alt R 22/845, "Gesetz zur Änderung des Reichsstrafgesetzbuchs vom 4. Sept. 1941," *Reichsgesetzblatt* 1, no. 101 (8 September 1941): 549–50.

183. Roland Freisler, "Gedanken über das Gesetz zur Änderung des Reichsstrafgesetzbuches," *Deutsche Justiz, Rechtspflege und Rechtspolitik* 103 (26 September 1941): 929–38.

184. BArch, R 3001/alt R 22/845, Prof. Dr. Lange, "Krieg und Strafrecht: Zur Strafgesetznovelle vom 4. September 1941," *Berliner Dienst: Zeitungsdienst Graf Reischack*, 3 November 1941, S. 529–32.

185. BArch, R 3001/alt R 22/845, Strafsache gegen T. E., Reichsgericht, 24 March 1942, S. 576–79.

186. Admittedly, these arguments were of little concern to the likes of Hitler and Himmler, who exhibited little patience for lawyers and judicial process.

187. Wagner, *Volksgemeinschaft ohne Verbrecher*, 376–84.

188. Joachim S. Hohmann, *Robert Ritter und die Erben der Kriminalbiologie: "Zigeunerforschung" im Nationalsozialismus und in Westdeutschland im Zeichen des Rassismus* (Frankfurt: Lang, 1991).

189. Robert Ritter, "Die Artung jugendlicher Rechtsbrecher," *Deutsches Jugendrecht* 4 (1942): 33–60, quote from 33.

190. A third camp was established in Lodz for Polish youth.

191. Brandenburgisches Landeshauptamt, Pr.Br. Rep. 55, Provinzialverband Abt. VIIa, Nr. 218, Bl. 4, Besprechung im Reichskriminalpolizeiamt am 11. Juni 1941, copy in Landesjugendamt Brandenburg, *"Wir hatten noch gar nicht angefangen zu leben": Materialien zur Ausstellung über die Jugendkonzentrationslager Moringen und Uckermark*, ed. Landesjugendamt Brandenburg (Bernau: Landesjugendamt, 1996), 12–13.

192. "Mitwirkung des Landesjugendamtes Mark Brandenburg bei der Unterbringung männlicher und weiblicher Minderjähriger in Jugendschutzlagern," in Landesjugendamt Brandenburg, *Wir hatten noch gar nicht angefangen zu leben*, 7.

193. Brandenburgisches Landeshauptamt, Pr.Br. Rep. 55, Provinzialverband Abt. VIIa, Nr. 218, Bl. 1, Landesrat Fink, Potsdam, 11 January 1941, copy in Landesjugendamt Brandenburg, *Wir hatten noch gar nicht angefangen zu leben*, 10–11.

194. Manuela Neugebauer, *Der Weg in das Jugendschutzlager Moringen* (Mönchengladbach: Forum, 1997), 30.

195. B Block (around 25 percent of the inmate population in the fall of 1943) was for the observation of new admissions; U Block (7.4 percent) for the mentally disabled, who were to be transferred to psychiatric and long-term care facilities; S Block (7.4 percent) for particularly disruptive malcontents; D Block (11.7 percent) for the lazy and unambitious; G Block (11.5 percent) for inhibited, needy, and frivolous types; F Block (23.7 percent) for those youths believed to be potentially receptive to correction; E Block (6 percent) for those deemed corrigible and for whom release could be expected; and ST Block (7.4 percent) for political criminals committed by the Gestapo. See Paul Werner, "Die Einweisung in die polizeilicher Jugendschutzlager," *Deutsches Jugendrecht* 4 (1944): 95–106, here 99–100.

196. Ibid., 101.

197. Stadtarchiv Frankfurt am Main, Personalakten, 18.576, C.S., Moringen, 30 April 1946, S. 22–23, and G.S. an Dr. Paul Wiedel, Höxter, 6 May 1946, S. 25–26;

Bericht des Oberregierungsrats Hermann Schmidhäuser an den Ministerialrat im Reichsjustizministerium Dr. Johann Eichler, 31 July 1943, in *"Gemeinschaftsfremde": Quellen zur Verfolgung von "Asozialen" 1933–1945*, ed. Wolfgang Ayass (Koblenz: Bundesarchiv, 1998), 352–59.

198. Gesellschaft für christlich-jüdische Zusammenarbeit Göttingen e.V. und dem evangelisch-lutherischen Pfarramt Moringen, ed., *KZ Moringen: Männerlager, Frauenlager, Jugendschutzlager* (Göttingen: Steidl, 1983), 53.

199. Manfred Kappeler, "Verstrickung und Komplizienschaft—Die Beteiligung von Jugendbehörden an der nationalsozialistischen Bevölkerungspolitik 1933–1945," in Landesjugendamt Brandenburg, *Wir hatten noch gar nicht angefangen zu leben*, 29–51.

200. Schreiben des SS-Standartenführers und Obersten der Polizei im Reichskriminalpolizeiamt Paul Werner an den Ministerialdirigenten im Reichsjustizministerium Fritz Gau, 17 March 1944, in Ayass, *Gemeinschaftsfremde*, 366–78.

201. Schädler, *"Justizkrise" und "Justizreform,"* 265, 289, quote from 265.

202. Ibid., 284–92.

203. Nikolaus Wachsmann, "The Policy of Exclusion: Repression in the Nazi State, 1933–1939," in *Nazi Germany*, ed. Jane Caplan (Oxford: Oxford University Press, 2008), 122–45.

204. Steven A. Barnes, *Death and Redemption: The Gulag and the Shaping of Soviet Society* (Princeton: Princeton University Press, 2011); Golfo Alexopoulos, "Amnesty 1945," *Slavic Review* 64 (2005): 274–306; J. Arch Getty, Gábor T. Rittersporn, and Viktor N. Zemskov, "Victims of the Soviet Penal System in the Pre-War Years: A First Approach on the Basis of Archival Evidence," *American Historical Review* 98 (1993): 1017–49.

205. Petra Gödecke, "Criminal Law after National Socialism: The Renaissance of Natural Law at the Beginning of Penal Reform in West Germany," in Wetzell, *Crime and Criminal Justice in Modern Germany*, 270–301; Detlev Peukert, *Grenzen der Sozialdisziplierung: Aufstieg und Krise der deutschen Jugendfürsorge von 1878 bis 1932* (Cologne: Bund-Verlag, 1986).

206. Roth, *Verbrechensbekämpfung*, 613.

207. Vogel, *Einflüsse des Nationalsozialismus auf das Strafrecht*.

CHAPTER 3

1. See, for instance, Jörg Morré, "Vom Niedergang des Erziehungsgedankens im Strafvollzug der DDR," in *Hinter Gittern: Zur Geschichte der Inhaftierung zwischen Bestrafung, Besserung und politischem Ausschluss vom 18. Jahrhundert bis zur Gegenwart*, ed. Silke Klewin, Herbert Reinke, and Gerhard Sälter (Leipzig: Leipziger Universitätsverlag, 2010), 241–54.

2. Werner Gentz, "Der moderne Strafvollzug," *ZfdgS* 46 (1925): 132–33.

3. Quoted in W. Heinrich, "Zuchthaus und Gefängnis oder Einheitsstrafe?," *Neue Justiz* 1 (1947): 32.

4. Werner Gentz, "Straffälligen-, Gefangenen-, und Entlassenenfürsorge," *Neue Justiz* 2 (1948): 72.

5. Werner Gentz, "Reform des Stravollzuges," in *Beiträge zur Demokratisierung der Justiz*, ed. Max Fechner (Berlin: Dietz, 1948), 231–57.

6. Walther Hoeniger, "Bewährungseinsatz statt Strafvollzug," *Neue Justiz* 1 (1947): 178.

7. Ibid., 178–80.

8. Walther Hoeniger, "Über das richtige Strafmaß und verwandte Probleme," in Fechner, *Beiträge zur Demokratisierung der Justiz*, 211–28, figures cited on 222.

9. Petra Weber, *Justiz und Diktatur: Justizverwaltung und politische Strafjustiz in Thüringen 1945–1961* (Munich: Oldenbourg, 2000), 51–59.

10. Bettina Greiner, *Verdrängter Terror: Geschichte und Wahrnehmung sowjetischer Speziallager in Deutschland* (Hamburg: Hamburger Edition, 2010); Bodo Ritscher, "Die Abteilung Spezlager: Anmerkungen zur Struktur und zum Funktionsbereich einer NKWD/MWD-Behörde in Deutschland," in *Das Torgau-Tabu*, ed. Norbert Haase and Brigitte Oleschinski (Leipzig: Forum, 1993), 135–45; Brigitte Oleschinski, "'Nur für den Dientgebrach?' Das Tabu Strafvollzug in der DDR," in *Verriegelte Zeiten: Vom Schweigen über die Gefängnisse in der DDR*, ed. Rolf Hanusch (Tutzing: Evangelische Akademie, 1993), 7–13, figures cited on 9.

11. Petra Weber, *Justiz und Diktatur: Justizverwaltung und politische Strafjustiz in Thüringen 1945–61* (Munich: Oldenbourg, 2000), 218.

12. Ibid., 369–98.

13. Leonore Ansorg, *Politische Häftlinge imn Strafvollzug der DDR: Die Strafvollzugsanstalt Brandenburg* (Berlin: Metropol, 2005), 32–33.

14. Morré, "Vom Niedergang"; Ansorg, *Politische Häftlinge*, 11–13.

15. See, for instance, Anne Krutoff, "Ein sozialhygienischer Beitrag zum Strafvolzugsproblem" (MD diss., Humboldt University of Berlin, 1951).

16. B. Gertig and R. Schädlich, *Lehrbuch für Kriminalisten: Die allgemeinen Verfahren und Arbeitsmethoden der Kriminalistik* (Berlin: Verlag für Fachliteratur der Volkspolizei, 1955), 3.

17. Greg Eghigian, "Was There a Communist Psychiatry? Politics and East German Psychiatric Care, 1945–1989," *Harvard Review of Psychiatry* 10 (2002): 364–68; Kitty Dumont, *Die Sozialpsychologie der DDR: Eine wissenschaftshistorische Untersuchung* (Frankfurt: Lang, 1999), 21–54.

18. K. Jarosch, "Zur Psychopathologie einzelner Deliktformen," *Psychiatrie, Neurologie, und medizinische Psychologie* (hereafter *PNumP*) 12 (1960): 266–73; "Protokoll über die Tagung der Medizinisch-wissenschaftlichen Gsellschaft für Psychiatrie und Neurologie an der Karl-Marx-Universität Leipzig am 6. und 7. Dezember 1957 in Leipzig," *PNumP* 10 (1958): 366–72; Helmut Rennert, "Psychiatrische Betrachtungen zum Inzest und seiner Verbreitung," *PNumP* 6 (1954): 80–87.

19. "Oberstes Gericht, Urteil vom 23. Dezember 1952," *Neue Justiz* 7 (1953): 54–55.

20. This is evident in two prominent studies of the early fifties: Arthur von der Heydt, *Querulatorische Entwicklungen* (Halle: Marhold, 1952); H. v. Keyserlingk, "Psychopathische Persönlichkeiten, ihre Kriminalität und ihre Stellung vor dem Gesetz," *PNumP* 3 (1951): 180–90, 207–22.

21. Institut für Geschichte der Medizin, Berlin (hereafter IGM), Charité Forensik, Case 165, 1952.

22. IGM, Charité Forensik, Case 155, 1952, S. 9, 16.

23. IGM, Charité Forensik, Case 2, 1950, S. 10.

24. IGM, Charité Forensik, Case 253, 1953, S. 4.

25. Forel's concept of blastophthoric degeneration held that "a deterioration of the germ" can occur as the result "of all direct pathogenic or disturbing action, especially that of certain intoxications, on the germinal cells, whose hereditary determinants are thus changed. Blastophthoria thus acts on germs not yet conjugated, through the medium of their bearers, and creates at their origins *hereditary stigmata* of all kinds." Auguste Forel and Charles Frederic Marshall, *The Sexual Question* (New York: Rebman, 1908), 36. On the reception of Forel's idea during the Third Reich, see Kurt Pohlisch, "Alkoholismus," in *Die psychiatrischen Aufgaben bei der Ausführung des Gesetzes zur Verhütung erbkranken Nachwuchses*, ed. Karl Bonhoeffer (Berlin: S. Karger, 1934), 78–87.

26. Sven Korzilius, *"Asoziale" und "Parasiten" im Recht der SBZ/DDR* (Cologne: Böhlau, 2005).

27. To this extent, Thomas Lindenberger is quite correct that "real existing socialism" did not divest the implicit racialized content from the concept of asociality. Thomas Lindenberger, "'Asociality' and Modernity: The GDR as a Welfare Dictatorship," in *Socialist Modern*, ed. Katherine Pence and Paul Betts (Ann Arbor: University of Michigan Press, 2008), 211–33.

28. IGM, Charité Forensik, Case 27, 1950, S. 8 (italics in original).

29. Mitchell G. Ash, "Kurt Gottschaldt and Psychological Research in Nazi and Socialist Germany," in *Science under Socialism*, ed. Kristie Macrakis and Dieter Hoffmann (Cambridge, MA: Harvard University Press, 1999), 286–301; Mitchell G. Ash, "Verordnete Umbrüche—Konstruierte Kontinuitäten: Zur Entnazifizierung von Wissenschaftlern und Wissenschaften nach 1945," *Zeitschrift für Geschichtswissenschaft* 43 (1995): 903–23.

30. Andreas von Arnauld, *Rechtssicherheit: Perspektive Annäherungen an eine idée directrice des Rechts* (Tübingen: Mohr Siebeck, 2006), 55–60. Some modifications to the concept of socialist lawfulness were made during the second half of the 1970s, with the individual given a more prominent role in legal theory, primarily as an object to be protected and educated.

31. BArch, DP 1, VA/5873, Direktor, Kreisgericht Grimmen, Urteileinschätzungsbogen—H. F., 8 November 1962; Kreisgericht Halle, Stadtbezirk Ost, Urteil in dem Strafverfahren gegen G. W. E., 14 March 1959; "In Jugendsachen ist größte Sorgfalt darauf zu verwenden, die Persönlichkeit des Jugendlichen und seine Motive zu erkennen," *Neue Justiz* 8 (1954): 252.

32. Korzilius, *"Asoziale" und "Parasiten,"* 195–96.

33. Tobias Wunschik, "Der Strafvollzug als Aufgabe der Deutschen Volkspolizei in den fünfziger Jahren," *Archiv für Polizeigeschichte* 8 (1997): 74–91.

34. Ansorg, *Politische Häftlinge*, 10–36.

35. Jens Borchert, *Erziehung im DDR-Vollzug: Theoretische und gesetzliche Grundlagen sowie die Durchführung in der Strafvollzugseinrichtung Torgau* (Herbolzheim: Centaurus, 2002), 26. This is evidence that during the second half of the decade, prisoners began to be segregated according to sentence and type of crime. See Wunschik, "Strafvollzug," 83.

36. Christian Rode, *Kriminologie in der DDR* (Freiburg: Edition Iuscrim, 1996), 25–74; Günther Sander, *Abweichendes Verhalten in der DDR: Kriminalitätstheorien in einer sozialistischen Gesellschaft* (Frankfurt: Campus, 1979), 48–54.

37. Hedwig Scholz, *Sie sollen wieder vollwertige Menschen werden: Über den demokratischen Strafvollzug in der Deutschen Demokratischen Republik* (Berlin: Verlag Kultur und Fortschritt, 1953), 13.

38. Herbert Kern, *Die Erziehung im Strafvollzug* (Berlin: VEB Deutscher Zentralverlag, 1958), 42–43.

39. Ibid., 79.

40. Heinrich Mehner, "Aspekte zur Entwicklung des Straf- und Untersuchungshaftvollzugs in der ehemaligen sowjetischen Besatzungszone Deutschland (SBZ) sowie in den Anfangsjahren der DDR," *Zeitschrift für Strafvollzug und Straffälligenhilfe* 41 (1992): 91–98.

41. "Hausordnung der Strafvollzugsanstalt Bautzen, 4 November 1957," in *Humaner Strafvollzug und politischer Mißbrauch*, ed. Karl Wilhelm Fricke (Dresden: Sächsischer Staatsministerium der Justiz, 1999), 174–84.

42. See the reports from the years 1955–60 in Bundesbeauftragte für Stasiunterlagen (hereafter BStU), MfS AS 137/63 and MfS AU 248151 Bd. 3.

43. BArch, DO 1/3809, 3809, Führungsberichte des Haftsarbeitskommando II/b, 1954.

44. Morré, "Vom Niedergang," 251–52.

45. Kern, *Erziehung*, 104.

46. Rode, *Kriminologie*, 74–111; Sander, *Abweichendes*, 58–64.

47. Raymond G. Stokes, *Constructing Socialism: Technology and Change in East Germany, 1945–1990* (Baltimore: Johns Hopkins University Press, 2000), 37.

48. Manfred Bierwisch, "Wissenschaft im realen Sozialismus," *Kursbuch* 101 (1990): 112–23; Peter Altner and Günter Kröber, eds., *KPD und Wissenschaftsentwicklung, 1919–1945* (Berlin: Dietz, 1986).

49. Hansgünter Meyer, "Wissenschaftspolitik, Intelligenzpolitik: Das Personal für Wissenschaft, Forschung, und Technik in der DDR," in *Intelligenz, Wissenschaft, und Forschung in der DDR*, ed. Hansgünter Meyer (Berlin: Walter de Gruyter, 1990), 1–51.

50. Eghigian, "Was There a Communist Psychiatry?"; Anna-Sabine Ernst, *"Die beste Prophylaxis ist der Sozialismus": Ärzte und medizinische Hochschullehrer in der SBZ/DDR, 1945–1961* (Münster: Waxmann, 1997).

51. Ash, "Verordnete Umbrüche—Konstruierte Kontinuitäten"; Meyer, "Wissenschaftspolitik," 16.

52. Andreas Malycha, "Frost nach dem Tauwetter: Wissenschaft und Politik in der DDR in den fünfziger Jahren," *Deutschland Archiv* 35 (2002): 237–52; Mitchell G. Ash, "Wissenschaft, Politik, und Modernität in der DDR: Ansätze zu einer Neubetrachtung," in *Wissenschaft und Politik: Genetik und Humangenetik in der DDR (1949–1989)*, ed. Karin Weismann, Peter Kröner, and Richard Toellner (Münster: LIT, 1997), 1–25; Hubert Laitko, "Wissenschaftspolitik," in *Die SED: Geschichte—Organisation—Politik; Ein Handbuch*, ed. Andreas Herbst, Gerd-Rüdiger Stephan, and Jürgen Winkler (Berlin: Dietz, 1997), 405–20.

53. Konstantin Ivanov, "Science after Stalin: Forging a New Image of Soviet Science," *Science in Context* 15 (2002): 317–38, quote from 318.

54. Corey Ross, *Constructing Socialism at the Grass-Roots: The Transformation of East Germany, 1945–1965* (New York: St. Martin's, 2000).

55. See, for example, BArch, DP 1, VA/5873, Bezirksgericht Suhl in Meiningen, 2. Strafsenat, Strafsache gegen F. B., Beschluß, 4 February 1959.

56. John Rodden, *Repainting the Little Red School House: A History of Eastern German Education, 1945–1995* (New York: Oxford University Press, 2002), 44–110.

57. Gesine Obertreis, *Familienpolitik in der DDR 1945–1980* (Opladen: Leske und Budrich, 1986), 48–88, 140–70.

58. Anna-Sabine Ernst, "Vom 'Du' zum 'Sie': Die Rezeption der bürgerlichen Anstandsregeln in der DDR der 1950er Jahre," *Mitteilungen aus der kulturwissenschaftlichen Forschung* 16, no. 33 (1993): 190–209.

59. Monika Kaiser, "Reforming Socialism? The Changing of the Guard from Ulbricht to Honecker during the 1960s," in *Dictatorship as Experience: Towards a Socio-Cultural History of the GDR*, ed. Konrad H. Jarausch (New York: Berghahn, 1999), 325–39; Ash, "Wissenschaft, Politik, und Modernität in der DDR"; Jeffrey Kopstein, "Ulbricht Embattled: The Quest for Socialist Modernity in the Light of New Sources," *Europe-Asia Studies* 46 (1994): 597–615; Jörg Roesler, "Die Wirtschaftsreform der DDR in den sechziger Jahren: Einstieg, Entwicklungsprobleme, und Abbruch," *Zeitschrift für Geschichtswissenschaft* 38 (1990): 979–1003.

60. Peter Christian Ludz, "Soziologie und empirische Sozialforschung in der DDR," in "Studien und Materialien zur Soziologie der DDR," ed. Peter Christian Ludz, special issue, *Kölner Zeitschrift für Soziologie und Sozialpsychologie* 8: 327–418.

61. Ina Merkel, *Utopie und Bedürfnis: Die Geschichte der Konsumkultur in der DDR* (Cologne: Böhlau, 1999), 133–50; Heinz Niemann, *Hinterm Zaun: Politische Kultur und Meinungsforschung in der DDR; Die geheimen Berichte an das Politbüro der SED* (Berlin: Edition Ost, 1995); Horst Laatz, *Klassenstruktur und soziales Verhalten: Zur Entstehung der empirischen Sozialstrukturforschung in der DDR* (Cologne: Wissenschaft und Politik, 1990).

62. Stefan Busse, "'Von der Sowjetwissenschaft lernen': Pawlowismus und Psychologie," *Psychologie und Geschichte* 8 (1998): 150–73.

63. Joachim Siebenbrodt, ed., *Bericht über den 2. Kongreß der Gesellschaft für Psychologie in der DDR* (Berlin: Deutscher Verlag der Wissenschaften, 1969); Vorstand der Gesellschaft für Psychologie in der DDR, ed., *Psychologie als gesellschaftliche Prodkuktivkraft: Bericht über den 1. Kongreß der Gesellschaft für Psychologie in der DDR vom 21.–23. Mai 1964 in Dresden* (Berlin: Deutscher Verlag der Wissenschaften, 1965).

64. Uta G. Poiger, *Jazz, Rock, and Rebels: Cold War Politics and American Culture in a Divided Germany* (Berkeley: University of California Press, 2000); Peter Skyba, *Vom Hoffnungsträger zum Sicherheitsrisiko: Jugend in der DDR und Jugendpolitik der SED 1949–1961* (Cologne: Böhlau, 2000); Dorothee Wierling, "Die Jugend als innerer Feind: Konflikte in der Erziehungsdiktatur der sechziger Jahre," in *Sozialgeschichte der DDR*, ed. Hartmut Kaelble, Jürgen Kocka, and Hartmut Zwahr (Stuttgart: Klett-Cotta, 1994), 404–25.

65. Gerrit Bratke, *Die Kriminologie in der Deutschen Demokratischen Republik und ihre Anwendung im Bereich der Jugenddelinquenz: Eine zeitgeschichtlich-kriminologische Untersuchung* (Münster: LIT, 1999), 36, 116–25.

66. Dorothee Wierling, "Über die Liebe zum Staat—der Fall der DDR," *Historische Anthropologie* 8 (2000): 236–63.

67. Dumont, *Die Sozialpsychologie der DDR*, 77–129; Hans-Dieter Schmidt, *Allgemeine Entwicklungspsychologie* (Berlin: Deutscher Verlag der Wissenschaften, 1970).

68. On the history of the concept of personality in general, see Giovanni Pietro Lombardo and Renato Foschi, "The Concept of Personality in 19th-Century French and 20th-Century American Psychology," *History of Psychology* 6 (2001): 123–42; David G. Winter and Nicole B. Barenbaum, "History of Modern Personality Theory and Research," in *Handbook of Personality: Theory and Research*, ed. Lawrence A. Pervin and Oliver P. John (New York: Guilford, 1999), 3–27.

69. Karl-Heinz Günther, "Begrüßungsansprache," in *Psychologische Probleme der Entwicklung sozialistischer Persönlichkeiten*, ed. Akademie der Pädagogischen Wissenschaften der DDR and Akademie der Pädagogischen Wissenschaften der UdSSR (Berlin: Volk und Wissen, 1972), 9.

70. Verena Zimmermann, *"Den neuen Menschen schaffen": Die Umerziehung von schwererziehbaren und straffälligen Jugendlichen in der DDR (1945–1990)* (Cologne: Böhlau, 2004), 187–93.

71. International Society for Criminology, *4th International Criminological Congress* (Hague: CIC, 1960), 563.

72. BArch, DP 3/1054, Prof. A. S. Schljapochnikov, *Die sowjetische Kriminologie in der gegenwärtigen Etappe (Sovetskaja Kriminologija na sovremennem etape)*, Moskau, 1973.

73. "Gesprächsprotokoll vom 15.2.1995 mit Herrn Prof. Buchholz in Berlin," in Rode, *Kriminologie*, A12.

74. BArch, DO 1/3668, Oberst Kohoutek (Leiter der Verwaltung Strafvollzug) an 1. Stellvertr des Ministers Staatssekretär Generalleutnant Grünstein, Berlin, 24 April 1964.

75. BArch, DO 1/3668, Generalleutnant Grünstein an Harrland, Berlin, 20 December 1967.

76. BArch, DP 1/VA 2497, Generalstaatsanwalt, Abteilung IX, Kurzprotokoll über die gemeinsame Beratung mit den Leitern der zentralen Rechtspflegeorgane und den Vertretern der Strafrechtswissenschaft am 22. Dezember 1964.

77. BArch, DP 1/VA 2497, Generalstaatsanwalt, Abteilung IX, Vorläufige Zusammenstellung der geplanten Themen für die Kriminalitäts- und Strafrechtswissenschaftliche Forschung in der DDR (1965–70), 18 January 1965.

78. BArch, DP 1/VA 2497, Generalstaatsanwalt, Abteilung IX, Vorschläge für das Herangehen an die Ausarbeitung eines perspektivischen Programme der Kriminalitätsforschung in der DDR, 15 March 1965.

79. BArch, DP 3/91, Generalstaatsanwalt der DDR, Bericht der Arbeitsgruppe zur Verallgemeinerung der Ergebnisse der Kriminalitätvorbeugungsprogramme, 20 July 1967. See also Zimmermann, *Den neuen Menschen schaffen*, 193–238.

80. Hanns Schwarz, ed., *Das milieubeschädigtes Kind* (Jena: Gustav Fischer, 1961).

81. Stefan Orlob, "War der deutsche forensische Psychiater Hans Szewczyk der erste moderne Profiler?," *Archiv für Kriminologie* 207 (2001): 65–72.

82. "Symposion über aktuelle Fragen der Gerichtspsychiatrie in der Charité, Berlin am 8. und 9. März 1963," *PNumP* 16 (1964): 120.

83. Hans Szewczyk, "Die künftigen Aufgaben des Psychiaters in der Rechtspflege," in *Die Gerichtspsychiatrie in der neuen Rechtspflege: Bericht über das Symposion*

"Über aktuelle Fragen der Gerichtspsychiatrie," 8. und 9. März 1963, Charite zu Berlin, ed. Hans Szewczyk (Jena: Gustav Fischer, 1964), 23–36.

84. See the papers in Szewczyk, *Die Gerichtspsychiatrie in der neuen Rechtspflege.*

85. Hans Szewczyk, ed., *Die Begutachtung und Behandlung erwachsener und jugendlicher Täter: Bericht über das III. Internationale Symposion "Über aktuelle Fragen der Gerichtspsychiatrie," 21. bis 23. 9. 1964, Charité zu Berlin* (Jena: Gustav Fischer, 1966), 13.

86. This was likely due to the fact that since arriving in East Germany in 1955, Leonhard had made it clear to authorities that he intended to return one day to the Federal Republic to assume the post of his mentor in Frankfurt. BArch DO 1/3795, Kohoutek to Generalleutnant Grünstein, 23 January 1963.

87. BArch DO 1/3795, Kohoutek to Generalleutnant Seifert über Oberst Weidlich, 9 March 1963.

88. BArch, DP 3/197, Protokoll über die Sitzung des Wissenschaftlichen Beirats für Kriminalitätsforschung beim Generalstaatsanwaltschaft der DDR am 17. Oktober 1967.

89. Wolfgang Seifart, "Zur Rolle der Information und Dokumentation bei der prognostischen Tätigkeit der Rechtspflegeorgane," *Neue Justiz* 22 (1968): 13–14, quote from 14.

90. Gerhard Stiller, "Zur Rolle der Prognose in der bürgerlichen Kriminologie," *Neue Justiz* 22 (1968): 599–601, quote from 601.

91. Richard Hartmann, "Möglichkeit und Notwendigkeit der Gemeinschaftsarbeit bei der Erforschung der Jugendkriminalität," in Szewczyk, *Die Gerichtspsychiatrie in der neuen Rechtspflege*, 129.

92. Gerhard Stiller, "Theoretische und methodologische Grundlagen der kriminologischen Forschungen in der Deutschen Demokratischen Republik" (Habilitationsschrift, Wiss. Rat des Institutes für staats- und rechtswissenschaftliche Forschung der Deutschen Akademie für Staats- und Rechtswissenschaft "Walter Ulbricht" in Potsdam-Babelsberg, 1965), 87. See also H. Blüthner and H. Kerst, "Ursachen und Vorbeugung bei Eigentumsstraftaten im Bauwesen," in *Kriminalitätsursachen und ihre Überwindung*, ed. Gerhard Stiller (Berlin: Staatsverlag der Deutschen Demokratischen Republik, 1964), 57–110.

93. See, for instance, Gerhard Wagner, "Zur Motivation der Brandstiftung," *PNumP* 26 (1974): 155–64; H. Szewczyk, "Die 'seelische Notlage' als Motiv für Tötungsdelikte," *PNumP* 21 (1969): 262–65; J. Greger and E. Popella, "Zur forensisch-psychiatrischen Beurteilung motivisch unklarer Diebstähle," *PNumP* 20 (1968): 302–12.

94. By the end of 1960, there were 18,109 prisoners (*Strafgefangene*) in the GDR. This figure rose to 30,124 by the end of 1961. Wilhelm Heinz Schröder and Jürgen Wilke, "Politische Strafgefangene in der DDR: Versuch einer statistischen Beschreibung," *Historical Social Research* 23 (1998): 64.

95. BArch, DO 1/3746, Taube [Ministerium des Innern], 19 May 1962.

96. Staatsrat der Deutschen Demokratischen Republik, *Rechtpflegeerlaß—bedeutsame Weiterentwicklung unserer sozialistischen Demokratie* (Berlin: Staatsverlag der Deutschen Demokratischen Republik, 1963), 159–60.

97. BArch, DO 1/3746, Verwaltung Strafvollzug, Abt. I/1. "Konzeption für die Einweisung der Strafgefangenen nach Kategorien," 24 October 1963.

98. BArch, DO 1/3746, Grünstein (Verwaltung Strafvollzug) an Vizepräsident, Oberstes Gericht, 1 April 1964.

99. BArch, DO 1/3746, Ministerium des Innern (Verwaltung Strafvollzug), Entwurf: Instruktion des Leiters der Verwaltung Strafvollzug über die Einweisung Strafgefangener in die Strafvollzugseinrichtungen, 1965 [first half].

100. BArch, DO 1/3668, Oertel to Grünstein, 13 April 1966.

101. BArch, DO 1/3403, Major des SV, [Überweisungsbericht K.B.] to Tunnat, 8 August 1968.

102. BArch, DO 1/3403, Tunnat, Vollzugsentscheidung Nr. 14/68, 20 September 1968.

103. BArch, DO 1/3403, [Überweisungsbericht F.S.] to Tunnat, 8 August 1968.

104. See, for example, BArch, DO 1/3403, Major Hakner (Leiter, Strafvollzugsanstalt Bützow) and Ministerium des Innern, Strafvollzug, 4 October 1968.

105. BArch, DO 1/31178, Ministerium des Innern, Instruktion Nr. 10/67 des Leiters der Verwaltung Strafvollzug, no day or month, 1967.

106. BArch, DO 1/31178, Heidler (Hauptmann), SV Görlitz to Ministerium des Innern, Verwaltung SV, 23 November 1966.

107. See, for instance, BArch, DO 1/31178, Pokorny (Hauptmann), Leiter des StVA Bautzen II, an Ministerium des Innern, Leiter der Verwaltung SV, 18 October 1966; Friedrich (Major), StVA Leipzig an Ministerium des Innern, Verwaltung SV, 2 December 1965.

108. BArch, DO 1/31178, Kunze, Generalstaatsanwalt, SV Aufsicht an Ministerium des Innern, Verwaltung SV, 15 February 1966; Ahlborn (Obersleutnant), StVA Bützow-Dreibergen an Ministerium des Innern, Verwaltung SV, 27 November 1965.

109. BArch, DO 1/31178, Ärztlicher Abschlußbericht, Dr. med. Ochernal, 17 May 1966.

110. See, for example, BArch, DO 1/31178, Ärztlicher Abschlußbericht, Drs. Ochernal und Hillmann, 24 and 30 November 1966; Ärztlicher Abschlußbericht, Dr. med. Ochernal, 1 August 1966.

111. BArch, DO 1/31178, Ärztlicher Abschlußbericht, Drs. Ochernal und Hillmann, 9 September 1966.

112. BArch, DP 3/1059, Prof. Dr. Buchholz, "Zur Erforschung der gesellschaftlichen und individuellen Wirksamkeit der Strafe," 1966.

113. BArch, DP 3/197, Generalstaatsanwalt der DDR, Arbeitsgruppe Leuna, "1. Auswertungsbericht der gemeinsamen Arbeitsgruppe," 26 November 1966.

114. Ministerium des Innern [Alfred Meyer, Otto Adam, and Lothar Bohmüller], *Die Wiedereingliederung Strafentlassener in das gesellschaftliche Leben und die Erziehung kriminell gefährdeter Bürger* (Berlin: Ministerium des Innern, 1970); Heinz Szkibik, *Sozialistischer Strafvollzug: Erziehung durch Arbeit* (Berlin: Staatsverlag der Deutschen Demokratischen Republik, 1969).

115. Harry Dettenborn and Hans-H. Fröhlich, *Psychologische Probleme der Täterpersönlichkeit* (Berlin: VEB Deutscher Verlag der Wissenschaften, 1971); Hans Hiebsch and Reiner Werner, "Aufgaben der forensischen Psychologie," *Neue Justiz* 22 (1968): 713–15.

116. W. F. Piroshkov, "Der Gegenstand, die Aufgaben und die Methoden der sowjetischen Strafvollzugspsychologie," in *Beiträge zur Strafvollzugspsychologie*, vol. 3, [ed. Ministry of Interior of the USSR] (Berlin: Ministerium des Innern, 1972), 13–59; Imre

Kertész, "Zu einigen Problemen der kriminalpsychologischen Methodologie," *Kriminalistik und forensische Wissenschaft* 1 (1970): 63–68; A. R. Ratinow, *Forensische Psychologie für Untersuchungsführer* (Berlin: Ministerium des Innern, 1970).

117. Oleg Kharkhordin, *The Collective and the Individual in Russia: A Study of Practices* (Berkeley: University of California Press, 1999), 75–122.

118. Adolf Kossakowski, "Die pädagogische Psychologie der DDR im Spannungsfeld zwischen kindorientierter Forschung und bildungspolitischen Forderungen," in *Pädagogik in der DDR*, ed. Ernst Cloer and Rolf Wernstedt (Weinheim: Deutscher Studien, 1994), 205–18; Alex Kozulin, "The Concept of Activity in Soviet Psychology," *American Psychologist* 41 (1986): 264–74.

119. E. Erlebach, U. Ihlefeld, and K. Zehner, *Psychologie für Lehrer und Erzieher* (Berlin: Volk und Wissen, 1971), 397.

120. A. D. Glototschkin and W. F. Piroshkov, "Die Psychologie des Strafgefangenenkollektivs," in [Ministry of Interior of the USSR], *Beiträge zur Strafvollzugspsychologie*, 1: 67–106.

121. Heinrich Mehner, Gerhard Meier, and Hermann Bodenburg, *Die Erziehung der Strafgefangenen zu Ordnung und Disziplin: Anerkennungen, Disziplinar- und Sicherungsmaßnahmen* (Berlin: Ministerium des Innern, 1972); A. D. Glototschkin and W. F. Piroshkov, "Psychologische Grundfragen des Regimes," in [Ministry of Interior of the USSR], *Beiträge zur Strafvollzugspsychologie*, 1: 41–66.

122. [Ministry of Interior of the USSR], *Lehrbuch der Strafvollzugspädagogik* (Berlin: Ministerium des Innern, 1970), 59–60.

123. W. F. Piroshkov, "Der Charakter," in [Ministry of Interior of the USSR], *Beiträge zur Strafvollzugspsychologie*, 4: 9–48; [Ministry of Interior of the USSR], *Lehrbuch der Strafvollzugspädagogik*, 65.

124. BArch, DO 1/3552, Hakner, Leiter, Strafvollzugsanstalt Bützow an Verwaltung Strafvollzug, 1. Stellvertreter Gen. Oberst Schmidt-Bock, 13 October 1970.

125. The following summary and quotes come from BArch, DO 1/3552, BDVP Potsdam, Abteilung K, Dez. II, Vernehmungsprotokoll mit M.S., 21 July 1970.

126. BStU, MfS, HA XX/AKG 926, Detlef Brüggemann, "Die Zusammenarbeit des Rates der Stadt Magdeburg mit den Betrieben bei der Vorbereitung und Realisierung gemeinsamer Maßnahmen zur Wiedereingliederung Strafentlassener in das gesellschaftliche Leben," Fachschulabschlußarbeit, submitted 6 April 1978, S. 4–59.

127. Brandenburgisches Landeshauptarchiv, Rep. 601, Nr. 2653, Gemeinsame Beratung über weitere Maßnahmen der Bekämpfung von Asozialität und debilen Personen, 6 June 1973. For more on this episode, see Sonja Süss, *Politisch mißbraucht? Psychiatrie und Staatssicherheit in der DDR* (Berlin: Ch. Links, 1999), 523–34.

128. Ansorg, *Politische Häftlinge*, 210–19; Johannes Raschka, *Justizpolitik im SED-Staat: Anpassung und Wandel des Strafrechts während der Amtszeit Honeckers* (Cologne: Böhlau, 2000).

129. Jens Gieseke, *Mielke-Konzern: Die Geschichte der Stasi, 1945–1990* (Stuttgart: Deutsche Verlags-Anstalt, 2001), 72–73. The number of those working for the Stasi rose from 20,000 in 1961 to 81,500 in 1982.

130. Matthias Wanitschke, *Methoden und Menschenbild des Ministeriums für Staatssicherheit der DDR* (Cologne: Böhlau, 2001), 187–88.

131. Sandra Pingel-Schliemann, *Zersetzen: Strategie einer Diktatur* (Berlin: Robert-

Havemann-Gesellschaft, 2003); Jörn Mothes, Gundula Fienbork, Rudi Pahnke, Renate Ellmenreich, and Michael Stognienko, ed., *Beschädigte Seelen: DDR-Jugend und Staatssicherheit* (Bremen: Edition Temmen, 1996); Klaus Behnke and Jürgen Fuchs, ed., *Zersetzung der Seele: Psychologie und Psychiatrie im Dienste der Stasi* (Hamburg: Rotbuch, 1995).

132. Beatrix Bouvier, *Die DDR—ein Sozialstaat? Sozialpolitik in der Ära Honecker* (Bonn: Dietz, 2002), 68–77; Sebastian Pfau, Burkhard Raue, and Sascha Trültzsch, "Der Traum vom neuen Menschen: Sozialistisches Menschenbild und Familienleitbilder in der DDR," in *Die Liebenswürdigkeit des Alltages: "Die Familienserie Rentner haben niemals Zeit,"* ed. Reinhold Viehoff (Leipzig: Leipziger Universitätverlag, 2003), 47–90.

133. Dorothee Wierling, "Das weiblich-proletarische Tüchtigkeitsideal der DDR," in *Arbeiter in der SBZ-DDR*, ed. Peter Hübner and Klaus Tenfelde (Essen: Klartext, 1999), 831–48; Susanne Diemer, *Patriarchalismus in der DDR: Strukturelle, kulturelle, und subjektive Dimensionen der Geschlechterpolarisierung* (Opladen: Leske und Budrich, 1994), 72–82.

134. Gunilla-Friederike Budde, "Heldinnen der Arbeit: Öffentliche Fremd- und Selbstdarstellungen von Arbeiterinnen in der DDR der 50er und 60er Jahre," in Hübner and Tenfelde, *Arbeiter in der SBZ-DDR*, 849–66.

135. Wolfgang Lassleben, "Zur Rehabilitierung von Verurteilungen nach § 249 StGB/DDR," *Horch und Guck* 60 (2008): 42–45.

136. "Gemeinsamer Standpunkt zur wirksamen Bekämpfung kriminellen asozialen Verhaltens, Generalstaatsanwalt der DDR, Minister des Innern, Oberstes Gericht der DDR, Minister der Justiz v. 11. Juni 1980," *Informationen des Obersten Gerichts der DDR* 4 (1980): 2–9.

137. As Inga Markovits notes, from this point on, authorities in Berlin insisted that local judges and administrators rely more concertedly on social welfare and collectives to shepherd "asocials," rather than on incarceration. Inga Markovits, *Justice in Lüritz: Experiencing Socialist Law in East Germany* (Princeton: Princeton University Press, 2010), 126–29.

138. BStU, MfS Arbeitsbereich Neiber 239, Leiter, Hauptabt VII an Generalmajor Neiber, Information über Ergebnisse des Jahres 1981 und perspektivische Vorhaben des MdI bei der Bekämpfung der kriminellen Asozialität, 7 April 1982, S. 4–5.

139. Ibid, S. 6–10.

140. BStU, MfS Arbeitsbereich Neiber 239, Ministerium für Gesundheitswesen, "Beschluß zur Betreung und Unterbringung straffällig gewordener und krimineller gefährdeter Bürger, die psychisch geschädigt und zugleich asozial sind," unsigned and undated [ca. December 1982], S. 41–48.

141. Markovits, *Justice in Lüritz*, 128–29.

142. Erich Buchholz, "Ein—unbeabsichtigtes—Loblied auf die DDR-Justiz," *Informationen der Gesellschaft zur rechtlichen und humanitären Unterstützung* 5 (2007), accessed 14 June 2011, http://www.grh-ev.org/html/body_information_5_07.html.

143. BStU, MfS HA VII 2749, Hauptabteilung VII, Abt. 9, "Information über einige aktuelle Probleme der Bekämpfung der Rückfallkriminalität und Asozialität der volkspolizeilichen Personenkontrolle, der Wiedereingliederung strafentlassener Personen sowie der Arbeit mit kriminell Gefährdeten," 29 October 1985, S. 132

144. Alfred Meyer, Franz Irro, and Rudi Rödszus, "Informatischer Bericht über die Tätigkeit von Expertengruppen zur Bekämpfung der Rückfallkriminalität und Erziehung kriminell Gefährdeter und die Möglichkeiten der Psychiater, dabei wirksam mitzuhelfen," *PNumP* 26 (1974): 98–103.

145. Volker Saupe and Brigitte Wende, "Gruppengesprächstherapie mit ausgewählten forensisch-psychiatrischen Patienten (Dissoziale Fehlentwicklung)," *PNumP* 37 (1985): 300–304; Ewald Heinz Strauss and Jürgen Mehl, "Zu einigen neueren Problemen und Ergebnissen der Verhaltenstherapie," *PNumP* 29 (1977): 705–11; J. Burmeister, H. Dettenborn, and H.-H. Fröhlich, "Zur Kritik bürgerlicher Sozialtherapie im Strafvollzug," *Kriminalistik und forensische Wissenschaften* 21 (1975): 153–89.

146. Heinz Albrecht, Lothar Blei, and Erich Weber, *Handbuch für Betriebsangehörige* (Berlin: Ministerium des Innern, 1982).

147. Karen Essig, *Die Entwicklung des Strafvollzuges in den neuen Bundesländern* (Mönchengladbach: Forum Verlag Godesberg, 2000), 68–83.

148. Lothar Kolb, *Mitwirkung Strafgefangener im Erziehungsprozeß* (Berlin: Ministerium des Innern, 1979), 50–63.

149. Ansorg, *Politische Häftlinge*, 261–81; Jürgen Fuchs, "'Zelleninformatoren': Über die 'Inoffiziellen Mitarbeiter' des MfS im Strafvollzug," in *Verriegelte Zeiten: Vom Schweigen über die Gefängnisse in der DDR*, ed. Rolf Hanusch (Tutzing: Evangelische Akademie, 1993), 24–27; Torsten Heyme and Felix Schumann, *"Ich kam mir vor wie'n Tier"—Knast in der DDR* (Berlin: BasisDruck, 1991).

150. Heyme and Schumann, *Ich kam mir vor wie'n Tier*, 222. A 1975 study by the Penal Administration in the Ministry of Interior revealed that many prison staff members did not have even this much training. The ministry's report stated that almost half of all those in leadership positions, 33 percent in midlevel posts, and around 54 percent of guards had not yet completed the appropriate training. BArch, DO 1/3767, Verwaltung Strafvollzug, Einschätzung der Lage in den Vollzugseinrichtungen des Organs Strafvollzug, 8 May 1975.

151. Heyme and Schumann, *Ich kam mir vor wie'n Tier*, 222–45.

152. BArch, DP 2/467, Stadtgericht Berlin, 1. Strafsenat, "Bericht zur Wirksamkeit der Wiedereingliederungsmaßnahmen aus den §§ 47, 48, 249 Abs. 5 StGB sowie der Aufenthaltsbeschränkung im Kampf gegen kriminelles asoziales Verhalten," Berlin, 12 March 1984; BArch, DP 2/578, 3. Strafsenat, "Probleme der Rechtsprechung zu § 249 StGB," no day, February 1980; BStU, MfS HA VII MfS AS 110/88, S. 54–58, 95–97; MfS AS 33/86, S 168–72; MfS AS 104/88, S. 37–41, 170, 178–79; MfS AS 103/88, S. 52–53; MfS HA VII 3325, Baier to Spange, 6 Sept. 1979, S. 6–26.

153. BStu, MfS HA VII 5686, untitled, unsigned, undated report on socialization and reintegration [ca. second half of 1980], S. 1–25. This Stasi investigation found that every third released prisoner with more than one previous conviction never made it beyond six months after release without reoffending. In a survey of recidivists, 44.8 percent cited a failed reintegration transition as the cause for the commission of a new crime.

154. BStU, MfS HA II 40774, HA II AKG, "Meinungsäußerungen im Zusammenhang mit der allgemeinen Amnestie," 1987.

155. BStU, MfS HA VII 2965, HA Kriminalpolizei, Abt. VI. Berichterstattung Amnestie—Stand: 30. 12. 1987, 30 December 1987, S. 106–9.

156. Pingel-Schliemann, *Zersetzen*; Hubertus Knabe, "'Weiche' Formen der Verfol-

gung in der DDR: Zum Wandel der repressiven Strategien in der Ära Honecker," *Deutschland Archiv* 30 (1997): 709–19.

CHAPTER 4

1. BArch, DP 1/VA 5873, Kreisgericht Neuruppin, Strafsache P.G., 8 June 1961.

2. BArch, DP 1/VA 5873, Justizverwaltungsstelle, Abt. Recht to Richter, Ministerium der Justiz, HA II, 26 June 1961; [internal memo, Verwaltungsstelle], 27 June 1961.

3. On communist subjectivity, see Jochen Hellbeck, *Revolution in My Mind: Writing a Diary under Stalin* (Cambridge, MA: Harvard University Press, 2006).

4. BArch, DP 1/VA 5873, Strafsache P.G.

5. Dagmar Herzog, *Sexuality in Europe: A Twentieth-Century History* (Cambridge: Cambridge University Press, 2011).

6. Mark Fenemore, *Sex, Thugs, and Rock 'n' Roll: Teenage Rebels in Cold-War East Germany* (New York: Berghahn, 2007); Skyba, *Vom Hoffnungsträger zum Sicherheitsrisiko*; Wierling, "Die Jugend als innerer Feind."

7. I use the term *civilization* here as historian Pieter Spierenburg does when he speaks of so-called civilization offensives, that is, "the more or less conscious efforts by powerful groups to change the norms and conduct of others in the direction of the former's standards of civilized behavior." Pieter Spierenburg, "Social Control and History: An Introduction," in *Social Control in Europe*, vol. 1, *1500–1800*, ed. Herman Roodenburg and Pieter Spierenburg (Columbus: Ohio State University Press, 2004), 16. See also Pratt, *Punishment and Civilization*.

8. The exception to this was the Nazi compulsory sterilization law of 14 July 1933. The Soviet Military Administration in Germany nullified the law with Order Number 6 on 8 January 1946. In the Federal Republic, the Nazi law was only first declared to be "no longer in force" on 18 June 1974. Hubert Rottleuthner, "Die strafrechtliche Verfolgung von DDR-Systemunrecht und NS-Verbrechen im Vergleich," in *Transformation des Rechts in Ost und West*, ed. Dirk Fischer (Berlin: Berliner Wissenschafts-Verlag, 2006), 425.

9. Keyserlingk, "Psychopathische Persönlichkeiten."

10. IGM, Charité Forensik, Case 24, 1950.

11. IGM, Charité Forensik, Case 35, 1950.

12. IGM, Charité Forensik, Case 44, 1955.

13. I have discussed this elsewhere in some detail. See Greg Eghigian, "Der Kalte Krieg im Kopf: Ein Fall von Schizophrenie und die Geschichte des Selbst in der sowjetischen Besatzungszone," *Historische Anthropologie* 11 (2003): 101–22.

14. Wolfgang Schivelbusch, *In a Cold Crater: Cultural and Intellectual Life in Berlin, 1945–1948* (Berkeley: University of California Press, 1998), 1–18; Klaus R. Scherpe, "Erzwungener Alltag: Wahrgenommene und gedachte Wirklichkeit in der Reportageliteratur der Nachkriegszeit," in *Nachkriegsliteratur in Westdeutschland 1945–1949*, vol. 1, *Schreibweisen, Gattungen, Institutionen*, ed. Jost Hermand, Helmut Peitsch, Klaus R. Scherpe (Berlin: Argument, 1982), 35–102.

15. See Rolf Schörken, *Jugend 1945: Politisches Denken und Lebensgeschichte* (Frankfurt: Fischer, 1995).

16. Svenja Goltermann, *Die Gesellschaft der Überlebenden: Deutsche Kriegsheim-*

kehrer und ihre Gewalterfahrungen im Zweiten Weltkrieg (Munich: Deutsche Verlags-Anstalt, 2009).

17. IGM, Charité Forensik, Case 173, 1952.

18. Josie McLellan, *Love in the Time of Communism: Intimacy and Sexuality in the GDR* (Cambridge: Cambridge University Press, 2011); Dagmar Herzog, *Sex after Fascism: Memory and Morality in Twentieth-Century Germany* (Princeton: Princeton University Press, 2005), 194–99.

19. IGM, Charité Forensik, Case 20, 1955.

20. IGM, Charité Forensik, Case 27, 1955.

21. IGM, Charité Forensik, Case 260, 1953.

22. Gerhard Feix, *Die Bekämpfung von Sexualverbrechen an Kindern* (Berlin: Verlag des Ministeriums des Innern, 1961), 12, 21, 56–60.

23. Ibid., 11–12, 32–33, quote from 39.

24. Ibid., 29.

25. The figures are derived from Wilhelm Heinz Schröder and Jürgen Wilke, *Politische Gefangene in der DDR—eine quantitative Analyse*, Wissenschaftliche Expertise für die Enquete-Kommission des Deutschen Bundestages "Überwindung der Folgen der SED-Diktatur im Prozeß der deutschen Einheit" (Cologne: Zentralarchiv fur Empirische Sozialforschung, 1997), 61.

26. IGM, Charité Forensik, Case 401, 1956.

27. See IGM, Charité Forensik, Case 118, 1956.

28. Joachim Gerchow, *Die ärztlich-forensische Beurteilung von Kindesmörderinnen* (Halle: Carl Marhold, 1957).

29. IGM, Charité Forensik, Case 387, 1958.

30. See, for instance, IGM, Charité Forensik, Case 374, 1958.

31. BArch, DP 1, VA/5873, Kreisgericht Halle, Stadtbezirk Ost, Urteil in dem Strafverfahren gegen den G.E., 14 March 1959.

32. BArch, DP 1, VA/5873, Bezirksgericht Suhl in Meiningen, 2. Strafsenat, Strafsache gegen B.F., 4 February 1959.

33. BArch, DP 1, VA/2497, Ministerium der Justiz, Hauptabteilung Gesetzgebung an Ministerium für Gesundheitswesen, Stationäre u. ambulatorische Krankenversorgung, 8 March 1956; Dr. Krüger, Ministerium für Arbeit und Gesundheitswesen an Landesheilanstalt Altscherbitz, 11 February 1950.

34. Jarosch, "Zur Psychopathologie einzelner Deliktsformen," 266.

35. See the cases of two child molesters: Charité Forensik, Case 265, 1953; Case 168, 1952.

36. Keyserlingk, "Psychopathische Persönlichkeiten," 221.

37. See, for example, IGM, Charité Forensik, Case 35, 1950.

38. H. J. Bochnik, "Erinnerung an Professor Dr. med. Karl Leonhard," *Hessisches Ärzteblatt* 3 (2004): 158–59; Hans-Walter Leonhard, "Psyche und Psychosen: Zum wissenschaftlichen Werk von Karl Leonhard," n.d., accessed 3 March 2011, http://www.menschenkunde.net/artikel/kl-werk.htm.

39. Karl Leonhard, *Aufteilung der endogenen Psychosen* (Berlin: Akademie-Verlag, 1957); *Grundlagen der Psychiatrie* (Stuttgart: Ferdinand Enke, 1948), 3–47.

40. Karl Leonhard and Sieglinde von Trostorff, *Prognostische Diagnose der endo-*

genen Psychosen (Jena: Gustav Fischer, 1964). Catamnesis refers to following up on patients released from care.

41. His treatment method, he said, focused on four things: diversion, stress, acclimation, and correction (*Ablenkung, Belastung, Gewöhnung, Umerziehung*). Karl Leonhard, *Individualtherapie der Neurosen* (Jena: Gustav Fischer, 1963), 16–26.

42. Karl Leonhard, *Instinkte und Urinstinkte in der menschlichen Sexualität* (Stuttgart: Ferdinand Enke, 1964), 1–15.

43. Marga Vicedo, *The Nature and Nurture of Love: From Imprinting to Attachment in Cold War America* (Chicago: University of Chicago Press, 2013).

44. Leonhard, *Instinkte und Urinstinkte*, 15–110.

45. IGM, Charité Forensik, Case 7, 1964.

46. K. Liebner, "Das EEG bei Psychopathen," *PNumP* 21 (1969): 373–76; H. Schulz and G. Mainusch, "Beitrag der klinischen Elektroencephalographie zur forensischen Begutachtung," *PNumP* 21 (1969): 266–75.

47. Ulrich Roehl and Hans Szewczyk, "Die schwerwiegende abnorme Entwicklung einer Täterpersönlichkeit mit Krankheitswert," in *Kriminalität und Persönlichkeit: Psychiatrisch-psychologische strafrechtliche Aspekte*, ed. Hans Szewczyk (Jena: Gustav Fischer, 1972), 132.

48. Jürgen Mehl, "Über den gegenwärtigen Stand des Problems klinischer und statistischer Vorhersage," in *Persönlichkeitsdiagnostik: Probleme und Ergebnisse persönlichkeitsdiagnostischer Forschungen in der klinischen Psychologie der DDR*, ed. Hans-Dieter Rösler, Hans-Dieter Schmidt, and Hans Szewczyk (Berlin: Deutsche Verlag der Wissenschaften, 1970), 24–36.

49. Hans Szewczyk, "Zur Validität der Exploration in der klinischen Psychologie," in Rösler, Schmidt, and Szewczyk, *Persönlichkeitsdiagnostik*, 199–217.

50. An example of a filled-out questionnaire can be found in IGM, Charité Forensik, Case 344a, 1966.

51. A. R. Jensen, "The Maudsley Personality Inventory," *Acta Psychologica* 14 (1958): 314–25.

52. IGM, Charité Forensik, Case 8, 1964.

53. IGM, Charité Forensik, Case 152, 1962.

54. Hans Szewczyk, "Untersuchungen zur kriminellen Entwicklung Jugendlicher," in Szewczyk, *Kriminalität und Persönlichkeit*, 28.

55. IGM, Charité Forensik, Case 166, 1962.

56. In the early 1970s, psychologist Arnold P. Goldstein conducted research, subsequently confirmed, finding that therapists tended to favor clients who had the so-called YAVIS characteristics, that is, who were young, attractive, verbal, intelligent, and successful. See A. P. Goldstein, *Structured Learning Therapy: Toward a Psychotherapy for the Poor* (New York: Academic, 1973).

57. IGM, Charité Forensik, Case 8, 1964.

58. IGM, Charité Forensik, Case 150, 1967.

59. IGM, Charité Forensik, Case 138, 1961.

60. IGM, Charité Forensik, Case 154, 1967. On the rise of social therapeutic facilities in the Federal Republic, see chapter 6 in the present study.

61. Szewczyk discussed this issue in IGM, Charité Forensik, Case 345, 1966.

62. See, for instance, IGM, Charité Forensik, Case 154, 1967.

63. IGM, Charité Forensik, Case 16, 1964.

64. Owen Whooley, "Diagnostic Ambivalence: Psychiatric Workarounds and the Diagnostic and Statistical Manual of Mental Disorders," *Sociology of Health and Illness* 32 (2010): 456. See also Geoffrey C. Bowker and Susan Leigh Star, *Sorting Things Out: Classification and Its Consequences* (Cambridge, MA: MIT Press, 2000).

65. See, for example, BArch, DP 1/VA 1398, Jochen Quandt, Ärztlicher Direktor, Besirkskrankenhaus für Psychiatrie und Neurologie Bernburg an Toeplitz, Präsident, Oberstes Gericht, 7 November 1966.

66. BArch, DP 3/1194, Plath, Generalstaatsanwaltschaft, Abt. Jugendkriminalität to Ministerium für Gesundheitswesen, Dr. Barleben, 24 June 1974.

67. BArch, DP 3/1194, memo, Generalstaatsanwaltschaft, [ca. summer] 1974.

68. Süss, *Politisch mißbraucht*, 523–34; Klaus-Peter Dahle, *Zur Versorgung forensisch-psychiatrischer Patienten in den neuen Bundesländern: Bestandaufnahme und Empfehlungen* (Baden-Baden: Nomos, 1995); C. Gold and R. Gold, "Zur Problematik der befristeten ärztlichen Einweisung durch Anordnung bei Alkoholismus: Ein kritischer Beitrag zur Anwendung des Gesetzes über die Einweisung in stationäre Einrichtunge für psychisch Kranke vom 11. Juni 1968" (MD diss., Akademie für Ärztliche Fortbildung der DDR, 1980); BArch, DP 3/1194, internal memo, Generalstaatsanwaltschaft, ca. 1974; Prof. Dr. sc. med. Mecklinger, Ministerium für Gesundheitswesen, "Vorschläge für die ständige Betreuung sozial und kriminell gefährdeter Debiler und Psychopathen," 2 August 1974. Particularly instructive in this regard are the dissertations of Gertraude Weissheit and Sabine Scholz, both of whom examined commitment records of the District Psychiatric Facility in Brandenburg following the introduction of the new psychiatric commitment law in June 1968. See Sabine Scholz, "Die Einweisung und Unterbringung gerichtspyschiatrischen Patienten in der DDR am Beispiel der Bezirksnervenklinik Brandenburg" (MD diss., Medizinische Fakultät der Humboldt-Universität Berlin, 1996); Gertraude Weissheit, "Erfahrungen der Bezirksnervenklinik Brandenburg mit der Einweisung von Patienten nach § 6 des Gesetzes über die Einweisung in stationäre Einrichtungen für psychisch Kranke vom 11. 6. 1968" (MD diss., Akademie für Ärztliche Fortbildung der DDR, 1986).

69. Vigarello, *History of Rape*.

70. Brigitte Kerchner, "'Unbescholtene Bürger' und 'gefährliche Mädchen' um die Jahrhundertwende," *Historische Anthropologie* 6 (1998): 1–32.

71. Brigitte Kerchner, "Kinderlügen? Zur Kulturgeschichte des sexuellen Mißbrauchs," in *Mißhandlung, Vernachlässigung und sexuelle Gewalt in Erziehungsverhältnissen*, ed. Urte Finger-Trescher and Heinz Krebs (Giessen: Psychosozial, 2000), 15–41.

72. IGM, Charité Forensik, Case 86, 1959.

73. IGM, Charité Forensik, Case 374, 1958.

74. All material about S.F.'s case comes from IGM, Charité Forensik, Case 344b, 1966.

75. IGM, Charité Forensik, Case 334a, 1966.

76. All material about J.P.'s case comes from IGM, Charité Forensik, Case 17, 1964.

77. Hans Szewczyk, "Besondere Probleme der Begutachtung außerhalb der Zurechnungs- und Schuldfähigkeit," in Szewczyk, *Kriminalität und Persönlichkeit*, 107–26.

78. Rolf Jakuszek and Gerhard Rosenfeld, "Die Berücksichtigung psychologischer Analysen des Erziehungsprozesses in der forensischen Gutachtertätigkeit," in Rösler, Schmidt, and Szewczyk, *Persönlichkeitsdiagnostik*, 193–204.

79. Jennifer V. Evans, "Decriminalization, Seduction, and 'Unnatural Desire' in East Germany," *Feminist Studies* 36 (2010): 553–77.

80. BArch, DQ 1/135, Dr. Krüger, Min. f. Arbeit und Gesundheitswesen an Landesheilanstalt Altscherbitz, 11 February 1950, S. 358.

81. BArch, DP 1, VA-2497, Ministerium der Justiz, Hauptabt. Gesetzgebung an Ministerium für Gesundheitswesen, Stat. u. amb. Krankenversorgung, 8 March 1956.

82. Examples of these requests can be found in BArch, DQ 1/12006.

83. BArch, DQ 1/12006, Abt. Recht, Minister für Gesundheitswesen an Dr. med. G. Kollmorgen, Direktor, Zentralstelle für ärztliches Begutachtungswesen, 7 January 1975.

84. BArch, DQ 1/12953, Mandel, Abt. Recht, Beratung zu Fragen der "Kastration" am 11. September 1981.

85. G. Vietze, "Indikationen, Kontraindikationen, und rechtliche Problematik bei der Antiandrogen-Behandlung," *PNumP* 28 (1976): 684–89.

86. Mahnolf Rossner, "Zur Frage der operativen Kastration von Sexualdelinquenten—Aktuelle Literaturübersicht und der Ansatz einer Meinungsbildung," *PNumP* 31 (1979): 321–29.

87. Carsta Drillisch and Gerhard Schott, "Antiandrogene zur Behandlung bestimmter Triebperversionen," in Szewczyk, *Kriminalität und Persönlichkeit*, 215–22.

88. Rudolf Burian, "Über eine durch sexuelle Prägung entstandene Form der Pädophilie," *PNumP* 22 (1970): 249–53; Karl Leonhard, "Was ist eine Sexualstörung," *PNumP* 20 (1968): 1–3.

89. Karl Müller, "Über das Suchtproblem bei sexuellen Deviationen," *PNumP* 23 (1971): 267–73.

90. Hans-H. Fröhlich, "Zur Konzeption und Methodik der Behandlung funktioneller Sexualstörungen—Erfahrungen und Probleme," *PNumP* 34 (1982): 554–62; Werner Dummer and Diether Rudolf Burian, "Eine Behandlungskonzept für sexuelle Deviationen (Methodik und bisherige Ergebnisse)," *PNumP* 39 (1978): 599–607; Hansgeorg Schmieschek, "Verhaltenstherapie bei sexuellen Deviationen," *PNumP* 29 (1977): 725–31; Jadwig Kozarska-Dworska, "Die Rehabilitation von Psychopathen im Strafvollzug," *Kriminalistik und forensische Wissenschaften* 8 (1972): 57–71.

91. Evans, "Decriminalization"; Herzog, *Sex after Fascism*, 202–16.

92. Lykke Aresin, "Ehe- und Sexualberatungsstellen und Familienplanung in der DDR," in *Sexuologie in der DDR*, ed. Joachim S. Hohmann (Berlin: Dietz, 1991), 72–94.

93. Peter Hesse et al., ed., *Sexuologie: Geschlecht, Mensch, Gesellschaft*, 3 vols. (Leipzig: Hirzel, 1974–78). See also Siegfried Schnabl, *Intimverhalten, Sexualstörungen, Persönlichkeit* (Berlin: Deutscher Verlag der Wissenschaften, 1972).

94. Kurt Richard Bach, "Zur Entwicklung der Sexualpädagogik in der DDR" and "Grundpositionen und Ziele der Sexualerziehung in der DDR," in Hohmann, *Sexuologie in der DDR*, 228–38, 239–61.

95. Hans Szewczyk, "Die Bedeutung sexueller Erlebnisse für die Persönlichkeits- und Sexualentwicklung von Kindern und Jugendlichen," in *Sexualität: Fakten, Normen,*

gesellschaftliche Verwantwortung, ed. Hans Szewczyk and Horst Burghardt (Berlin: Verlag Volk und Gesundheit, 1978), 192–202; Paul Fehlow, "Der weibliche Sexualstraftäter," *PNumP* 27 (1975): 612–18; Hanns Schwarz, ed., *Kriminalität der Frau—Alterskriminalität—Psychiatrische Begutachtungsfrage im Zivilrecht* (Jena: Gustav Fischer, 1971).

96. Eckhard Littmann, "Victimologische Untersuchungen an sexuell mißbrauchten Kindern und Jugendlichen," in *Kriminalpsychologie und Kriminalpsychopathologie*, ed. Heide-Ulrike Jähnig and Eckhard Littmann (Jena: Gustav Fischer, 1985), 88–129; K.-H. Röhner, "Bedeutung und Rolle einer ungenügenden Sexualerziehung für die Begehung gewaltsamer Sexualstraftaten durch Jugendliche," *Kriminalistik und forensische Wissenschaften* 45 (1982): 101–6; E. Fikentscher, H. Hinderer, K. Liebner, and H. Rennert, "Sexualstraftaten an Kindern und Jugendlichen unter Berücksichtigung latenter Kriminalität," *Kriminalistik und forensische Wissenschaften* 33 (1978): 67–82.

97. Paul Fehlow, "Pädophil-voyeuristisches Verhalten," *PNumP* 41 (1989): 109–11; Michael Heim and Joachim Morgner, "Der pädophile Straftäter," *PNumP* 37 (1985): 107–12; Heide-Ulrike Jähnig, "Psychiatrische Beiträge bei der Ermittlung von Sexualdelikten," in Jähnig and Littmann, *Kriminalpsychologie und Kriminalpsychopathologie*, 130–46; Paul Fehlow, "Zur Persönlichkeit des Notzuchtstraftäters," *PNumP* 32 (1980): 164–69.

98. H.-H. Fröhlich, "Die Sexualkriminalität im Blickwinkel menschlicher Sexualität und sexueller Normen," *Kriminalistik und forensische Wissenschaften* 41 (1980): 43–54, quote from 51.

99. Eckhard Littmann, "Zur Persönlichkeitsstruktur forensisch begutachteter Sexualstraftäter," in Jähnig and Littmann, *Kriminalpsychologie und Kriminalpsychopathologie*, 147–65, quote from 163.

100. Joachim Morgner, "Exhibitionistische sexuelle Fehlentwicklungen," *Kriminalistik und forensische Wissenschaften* 30 (1977): 105–8, quote from 105.

101. Simon A. Cole, "From the Sexual Psychopath Statute to 'Megan's Law': Psychiatric Knowledge in the Diagnosis, Treatment, and Adjudication of Sex Criminals in New Jersey, 1949–1999," *Journal of the History of Medicine and Allied Sciences* 55 (2000): 292–314, quote from 293.

102. Robert A. Williams Jr., *Savage Anxieties: The Invention of Western Civilization* (New York: Palgrave Macmillan, 2012).

103. Joachim S. Hohmann, introduction to Hohmann, *Sexuologie in der DDR*, 45.

CHAPTER 5

1. Karl S. Bader, *Soziologie der deutschen Nachkriegskriminalität* (Tübingen: J. C. B. Mohr, 1949).

2. Josef Georg Wilhelm, ed. *Einführung in die praktische Kriminalistik* (Stuttgart: W. Kohlhammer, 1946), 17.

3. Niedersächsisches Hauptstaatsarchiv Hannover (hereafter HStAH), Hann. 173a, Nds. 711, Acc. 6/95, Nr. 153, Niederschrift über die Tagung der Generalstaatsanwälte der Britischen Zone in Bad Pyrmont am 22. Nov 1945, S. 26.

4. "Stellungnahme des Rechtsunterausschusses der Britischen Zone vom 26. 7.1946 zur Weitergeltung der Sicherungsverwahrung," in *Von der Aufklärung bis zur doppelten Staatsgründung*ed. Hinrich Rüping, vol. 2 of *Studien- und Quellenbuch zur Geschichte der deutschen Strafrechtspflege*, ed. Wolfgang Sellert and Hinrich Rüping (Darmstadt: Scientia Verlag Aalen, 1994), 338–39.

5. HStAH, Hann. 173a, Nds. 711, Acc. 6/95, Nr. 153, Generalstaatsanwalt bei dem Oberlandesgericht Dr. Meyer-Abich an Staatsanwaltschaft bei dem Oberlandesgericht z. Hd. Min.Rat Dr. Eichler in Celle, 6 October 1947, S. 31–32.

6. HStAH, Hann. 173a, Nds. 711, Acc. 6/95, Nr. 361, Dr. Möricke, Niedersächsisches Ministerium der Justiz an 229 HQ Mil Gov Land Niedersachsen, 7 November 1947, S. 27–28; Generalstaatsanwalt Dr. Staff bei dem Oberlandesgericht Braunschweig an Generalstaatsanwalt Dr. Möricke, 17 April 1945, S. 8.

7. "Direktive Nr. 19: Grundsätze für die Verwaltung der deutschen Gefängnisse und Zuchthäuser," *Zeitschrift für Strafvollzug* (hereafter *ZfS*) 1 (March 1950): 30–32.

8. Albert Krebs, "Die Durchführung der Kontrollratsdirektive Nr. 19 in den vier Besatzungszonen Deutschlands, insbesondere in der US-Zone (1)," *ZfS* 1 (March 1950): 17–29.

9. "Leitgedanken für eine Reform des Vollzugs der Freiheitsstrafe," *ZfS* 3 (1952): 5–9; "Resolution der Arbeitsgemeinschaft für Reform des Strafvollzugs vom 4.9.1948 und Resolution der Arbeitsgemeinschaft für Reform des Strafvollzugs vom 23.3.1950," *ZfS* 1 (1950): 57–59.

10. Vormbaum, *Einführung*, 223–45; Kai Naumann, *Gefängnis und Gesellschaft: Freiheitsentzug in Deutschland in Wissenschaft und Praxis, 1920–1960* (Münster: LIT, 2006), 230–34.

11. HStAH, Hann. 173a, Nds. 711, Acc. 6/95, Nr. 364, Generalstaatsanwalt an Vorstände [der Strafanstalten] Hannover, Celle, Hameln, Sandbostel, 7 June 1950, S. 87–88.

12. Viola Roggenkamp, "Den 'Fluch' schnell vergessen," *Die Zeit*, 6 January 1989, accessed 8 June 2012, http://www.zeit.de/1989/02/den-fluch-schnell-vergessen/seite-1.

13. Walther Buhl, "Erziehungsvollzug? Eine kritische Betrachtung," *ZfS* 3 (1952): 69–70.

14. Ibid., 77.

15. Ina Heldmann, "Auf die Atmosphäre kommt es an?," *ZfS* 3 (1952): 118–21.

16. Fred Krüttner, "Nochmals: Erziehungsstrafvollzug," *ZfS* 3 (1952–53): 330–34.

17. Goehl, "Der Besserungsgedanke in den Justizvollzugsanstalten," *ZfS* 4 (1954): 59–63.

18. Joseph Strüder, "Erziehungsstrafvollzug?," *ZfS* 3 (1952–53): 244.

19. Franz Böttcher, "Kritische Gedanken zum modernen Erziehungsstrafvollzug," *ZfS* 3 (1952–53): 269.

20. Liebert Müller, "Über den Strukturwandel im Gefängnispersonal und seine Bedeutung für die Persönlichkeit des Gefangenen," *ZfS* 5 (1955): 38.

21. Panse, "Die psychologiche Problematik des Strafvollzugs im Hinblick auf den Besserungsgedanken," *MfKuS* 39 (1956): 5–17.

22. Gödecke, "Criminal Law after National Socialism."

23. Landesarchiv Baden-Württemberg, Hauptstaatsarchiv Stuttgart (hereafter HS-

tAS), EA 4/605, Nr. 10, Franz Geiger, Kath. Anstaltspfarrer beim Landesgefängnis Ludwigsburg an Justizministerium BW, Abt. Strafvollzug. Ludwigsburg, 15 September 1956; W. Heinsius, "Persönlichkeitserforschung und Seelsorge," *ZfS* 4 (1954): 315–20.

24. Baumann, *Dem Verbrechen auf der Spur*, 127.

25. Hans Krüger, "Die Kriminalpsychologische Abteilung der Gefängnisbehörde der Freien und Hansestadt Hamburg," *ZfS* 6 (1956): 247.

26. Ibid., 245.

27. Hans Krüger, "Richter und Täterpsychologie: Fehlerquellen bei der Persönlichkeitsbewertung des Angeklagten," *Deutsche Richterzeitung* 30 (1952): 54–57.

28. Krüger, "Die Kriminalpsychologische Abteilung," 304–12, 364–68; HStAH, Hann. 173a, Nds. 711, Acc. 6/95, Nr. 363, Hildebrandt, "Kurzbericht über die Arbeitsweise der Kriminologischen Untersuchungsstelle bei dem Strafgefängnis und der Untersuchungshaftanstalt Hannover," 29 January 1954, S. 127–29. Tests included the Hamburg-Wechsler test; the Binet-Simon-Kramer test; the Szeno test; the Wartegg-Zeichen and Wartegg-Erzähl tests; the intelligence structure test, a modification of Klemm's Ablegeprobe; and the Rorschach test.

29. Adolf Däumling, "Die Aufgaben des Psychologen im sozialpsychagogischen Strafvollzug," *ZfS* 2 (1951): 7–11; Günther Suttinger, "Über die Tätigkeit des Psychologen im Strafvollzug insbesondere im Jugendvollzug," *ZfS* 1 (1950): 12–17.

30. Mitchell G. Ash, "Wissenschaft und Wissenschaftsaustausch," in *Die USA und Deutschland im Zeitalter des Kalten Krieges, 1945–1990*, vol. 1, ed. Detlef Junker (Stuttgart: Deutsche Verlags-Anstalt, 2001), 634–45.

31. Pieter J. van Strien, "The American 'Colonization' of Northwest European Social Psychology after World War II," *Journal of the History of the Behavioral Sciences* 33 (1997): 349–63. In the United States, unlike in continental Europe, sociology had been abandoning pathological explanations for deviant behavior since the 1930s, while the field of criminology was developed mainly by sociologists and was taught within the liberal arts. See Colin Sumner, *The Sociology of Deviance: An Obituary* (New York: Continuum, 1994), 53–138; Denis Carroll, *The University Teaching of Social Sciences: Criminology* (Paris: UNESCO, 1957).

32. The figure was reported by Ernst Kretschmer in "Was ist Psychotherapie? Ein Streit um ihre formale und faktische Inhaltsbestimmung," *Psyche* 1 (1948): 459.

33. Albert Krebs, "Das Berufsbild des Strafanstaltsfürsorgers," *ZfS* 4 (1954): 51–53.

34. On police programs, see BArch, B 106/15656, Statut über Aufbau, Verwaltung und Aufgabengebiet der Zentral-Polizeischule Hiltrup, ca. 1951.

35. Maria Jankowski, "Zusammentstellung methodischer und organisatorischer Gesichtspunkte bei der Ausbildung vor allem der Aufsichtsbeamten," *ZfS* 5 (1955): 16–26.

36. Thomas Würtenberger, "Défense sociale—Ziele und Wege einer neuen kriminalpolitischen Bewegung," special issue, *MfKuS* (1957): 60–65; Albert Krebs, "Kulturnationen erörtern Strafvollzugsfragen," part 2, "Bericht über den 3. Kriminologenkongreß in London," *ZfS* 5 (1955): 333–50; Albert Krebs, "Entwicklung der Persönlichkeitsforschung im deutschen Gefängniswesen," *ZfS* 4 (1954): 241–52; Josef Schafheutle, "Der erste Kongreß der Vereinten Nationen über Verbrechenverhütung und Behandlung von Straffälligen vom 22. August bis 3. September 1955 in Genf," *ZfS* 5 (1955): 259–64.

37. Up until then, they had been required only in juvenile and preventive detention cases. See Wolfgang Mittermaier, "Neue Entwicklungen im deutschen Strafvollzug," *ZfS* 4 (1954): 33–36.

38. Michael Gallmeier, "Das Klassifizieren in der Strafanstalt als Gemeinschaftsleistung," *ZfS* 4 (1954): 252–60.

39. Johannes Feige, "Über die Mitwirkung des Aufsichts- und Werkdienstes bei der Erfassung der Gefangenenpersönlichkeit," *ZfS* 4 (1954): 261–65.

40. This was also a trend evident in the postwar American human sciences. See James H. Capshew, *Psychologists on the March: Science, Practice, and Professional Identity in America, 1929–1969* (Cambridge: Cambridge University Press, 1999); Ellen Herman, *The Romance of American Psychology: Political Culture in the Age of Experts* (Berkeley: University of California Press, 1996).

41. Th. Grunau, "Die Persönlichkeitsforschung im Schleswig-Holsteinischen Strafvollzug," *ZfS* 4 (1954): 270–76.

42. Tests included the so-called Wechsler test, the Rorschach test, the Wartegg-Zeichen test, the thematic apperception test, Hetzer's Zahlenquadrat-Staffel test, and a variety of aptitude tests for specific trades. See H. B. Greiner, "Persönlichkeitsforschung im Strafvollzug," *ZfS* 3 (1952): 52–59.

43. Sebastian Wannemacher, "Stand der Persönlichkeitsforschung im Strafvollzug des Landesgefängnisses Mannheim," *ZfS* 5 (1955): 31–32.

44. The building of Stammheim Prison during the second half of the 1950s, for instance, was widely represented in the media in just these terms, as a state-of-the-art facility designed to replace existing facilities, most of which had been built in the nineteenth century. See, for instance, BArch, B 141/42082, "Die Strafanstalten des Landes sind mit 8000 Insassen überbelegt," 7 February 1959.

45. Naumann, *Gefängnis und Gesellschaft*, 241–51; Schattke, *Die Geschichte der Progression im Strafvollzug*, 211–21.

46. HStAS, EA 4/605, Nr. 125, "Beiträge zum Vollzug und zur bedingten Entlassung aus der Sicherungsverwahrung," Erfahrungsbericht des Oberrregierungsrat Dr. Rudolph, *Die Justiz*, September 1955, 252.

47. The list of experts was dominated by individuals who had had successful careers during the Third Reich, including Edmund Mezger, Richard Lange, Thomas Würtenberger, Rudolf Sieverts, Wilhelm Gallas, Hellmuth Mayer, and Hellmuth von Weber.

48. The Bundestag members were Hoogen (CDU/CSU), Rehs (SPD), Schneider (FDP), Czermak (BG/BHE [Gesamtdeutscher Block/Bund der Heimatvertriebenen und Entrechteten]), and Merkatz (Deutsche Partei); the legal scholars, Paul Bockelmann, Wilhelm Gallas, Hans-Heinrich Jescheck, Richard Lange, Edmung Mezger, Eberhard Schmidt, and Hans Welzel; the representatives of the Bundesgerichtshof, Baldus and Weichmann. Others included Resch, Dahs, Koffka, Niethammer, Richter, Schäfer, and Skott.

49. Tim Busch, *Die deutsche Strafrechtsreform: Ein Rückblick auf die sechs Reformen des Deutschen Strafrechts (1969–1998)* (Baden-Baden: Nomos, 2005), 39–130; Sozialdemokratische Partei Deutschlands, "Das Programm der Sozialdemokratischen Partei Deutschlands zur Strafrechtsreform," *MfKuS* 36 (1953): 51–52.

50. Overall, historian Marc von Miquel has named nineteen civil servants working in the Federal Ministry of Justice during the 1960s who had close past ties to the Nazi

Party and the Nazi regime. Marc von Miquel, *Ahnden oder amnestieren? Westdeutsche Justiz und Vergangenheitspolitik in den sechziger Jahren* (Göttingen: Wallstein, 2004), 385–86.

51. BArch, B 141/37701, Sauer an Dreher, 30 April 1953, S. 13–14.

52. Ibid., Bohne an Dreher, 4 May 1953, S. 15–16.

53. Ibid., Weber an Dreher, 22 December 1954, S. 61. In March 1933, Weber cowrote a now infamous report that justified retroactive punishment following the Reichstag fire.

54. Ibid., Wahl, 6 May 1955, S. 72–76, quote from S. 73.

55. In November 1954, this subcommission consisted of Baldus, Dahs, Jescheck, Krille, Lange, Mezger, Rösch, Schäfer, Schmidt, Sievets, Skott, Voll, Welzel, and Wiechmann.

56. BArch, B 141/90132, Anlage 2, S. 177–91.

57. BArch, B 141/90132, Große Strafrechtskommission, Niederschrift über die 33. Sitzung am 27. Oktober 1955, S. 91–94.

58. Ibid., S. 100.

59. Ibid., S. 103–4.

60. Ibid., S. 111.

61. Thomas Fuchs, ed., *Strafgesetzbuch für das Deutsche Reich vom 15. Mail 1871: Historisch-synoptische Edition 1871–2011* (Mannheim: Lexetius.com, 2011), 207.

62. BArch, B 141/90133, "Typologie der Gewohnheitsverbrecher oder Rezidivisten," Referat von Prof. Dr. Hellmuth Mayer auf 11. Tagung der Kriminalbiologschen Gesellschaft am 6. Oktober 1961; Erwin Frey, "Frühdiagnostik von Gewohnheitsverbrechern," gehalten am 9. Dezember 1955 vor der Juristischen Studiengesellschaft beim BGH in Karlsruhe.

63. Friedrich Geerds, "Zur kriminologischen Prognose," *MfKuS* 43 (1960): 92–119, quote from 113–14.

64. See sec. 51 of the Reichsstrafgesetzbuch for the years 1934–75.

65. BArch, B 141/82033, Dahs, Strafrechtsausschuß der Deutschen Rechtsanwaltskammern, "Leitsätze zum Thema 'Unzurechnungsfähigkeit und verminderte Zurechnungsfähigkeit,'" 3 July 1956, S. 12.

66. BArch, B 141/82030, Villinger and Ehrhardt, "Stellungnahme der Gesellschaft deutscher Neurologen und Psychiater zu Fragen medizinischen Einschlags," 6 September 1955, S. 110.

67. Mitchell G. Ash, "Émigré Psychologists after 1933: The Cultural Coding of Scientific and Professional Practices," and Edit Kurzweil, "Psychoanalytic Science: From Oedipus to Culture," in *Forced Migration and Scientific Change: Émigré German-Speaking Scientists and Scholars*, ed. Mitchell G. Ash and Alfons Söllner (New York: Cambridge University Press, 1996), 117–38, 139–55.

68. Karen Brecht, "In the Aftermath of Nazi-Germany: Alexander Mitscherlich and Psychoanalysis—Legend and Legacy," and Anson Rabinbach, "Response to Karen Brecht," *American Imago* 52 (1995): 291–312, 313–28.

69. BArch, B 141/82030, A. Mitscherlich, "Stellungnahme der Deutschen Gesellschaft für Psychotherapie und Tiefenpsychologie zu Fragen medizinischen Einschlags," 21 September 1955, S. 126–53.

70. Tobias Freimüller, *Alexander Mitscherlich: Gesellschaftsdiagnose und Psychoanalyse nach Hitler* (Göttingen: Wallstein, 2007), 160–76.

71. BArch, B 141/82030, Sander, "Stellungnahme der Deutschen Gesellschaft für Psychologie zu den Fragen der großen Strafrechtskommission mit psychologischem Einschlag," 24 May 1956, S. 184.

72. BArch, B 141/82033, Große Strafrechtskommission, Niederschrift über die 44. Sitzung am 11. Juli 1956, S. 122, 129.

73. BArch, B 141/82036, Material für die Sitzung der Unterkommission am 15. Januar 1960, S. 74a–b.

74. BArch, B 141/82034, Schneider to Gallas, 12 September 1957, S. 173.

75. BArch, B 141/82036, Ergebnis der schriftlichen Abstimmung zur Stellungnahme der Deutschen Gesellschaft für Psychiatrie und Nervenheilkunde und zum Thema Schuldunfähigkeit und verminderte Schuldfähigkeit," 14 January 1960, S. 105.

76. BArch, B 141/82037, Rosentahl-Pelldram to Schwalm, 8 March 1960, S. 31–32.

77. BArch, B 141/82038, W. Metzger, Vorsitzender, DGfP to Georg Schwalm, Bundesministerium der Justiz (hereafter BMJ), 5 December 1961, S. 34–49.

78. BArch, B 141/82040, Hans Thomae, "Unter Ausschluß der Psychologie," 33–36.

79. BArch, B 141/82041, 12. Sitzung des Sonderausschusses für die Strafrechtsreform, Bonn, 10. März 1966, 243.

80. Zweites Gesetz zur Reform des Strafrechts (2. StrRG) vom 4. Juli 1969, *Bundesgesetzblatt, Teil I*, 56 (1969): 717–42, quote from 720 (§ 20).

81. Busch, *Die deutsche Strafrechtsreform*, 45–50.

82. Franz-Werner Kersting, ed., *Psychiatriereform als Gesellschaftsreform: Die Hypothek des Nationalsozialismus und der Aufbruch der sechziger Jahre* (Paderborn: Ferdinand Schöningh, 2003).

83. Fussinger, "'Therapeutic Community,' Psychiatry's Reformers, and Antipsychiatrists."

84. Bundesministerium der Justiz, *Tagungsberichte der Strafvollzugskommission*, vols. 1–13 (Bonn: Bundesministerium der Justiz, 1967–70), vol. 1 (1967), *Erste Arbeitstagung vom 4. bis 7. Dezember 1967 in Heidelberg*, 145–55.

85. Günther Neulandt, "Zum Problem der sogenannten Resozialisierung," *ZfS* 10 (1961): 325–31.

86. Baumann, *Dem Verbrechen auf der Spur*, 248–68.

87. *Tagungsberichte der Strafvollzugskommission*, vol. 6 (1969), *Sechste Arbeitstagung vom 14. bis 18. April 1969 in Bensheim-Auerbach*, 78–79.

88. Ibid., 6:80–88.

89. Ibid., 6:69.

90. Ibid., 6:70.

91. Ibid., 6:66.

92. *Tagungsberichte der Strafvollzugskommission*, vol. 3 (1968), *Dritte Arbeitstagung vom 8. bis 11. April 1968 in Tübingen*, 44.

93. Ibid., 3:11–13.

94. Ibid., 3:49.

95. Ibid., vol. 4 (1969), *Vierte Arbeitstagung vom 9. bis 13. September 1968 in Kaiserslautern*, 4–34.

96. Ibid., vol. 5 (1969), *Fünfte Arbeitstagung vom 6. bis 10. Januar 1969 in Bremen*, 145–52.

97. Ibid., vol. 8 (1969), *Achte Arbeitstagung vom 13. Bis 17. Oktober 1969 in München*, 164.

98. Ibid., vol. 9 (1970), *Neunte Arbeitstagung vom 24. Bis 28. November 1969 in Hamburg*, 123–25.

99. Ibid., 8:160.

100. Ibid., vol. 11 (1971), *Elfte Arbeitstagung vom 19. bis 23. Oktober 1970 in Münster*, 18

101. *Sonderband zu den Tagungsberichten der Strafvollzugskommission,* vols. 11–13: *Erster Arbeitsentwurf eines Strafvollzugsgesetzes erstellt unter Berücksichtigung der Grundsätze und Empfehlungen der Strafvollzugskommission. Stand—1. Oktober 1970* (Bonn: Bundesministerium der Justiz, 1971), 2. An alternative to point 1 was also submitted, stating, "The prison sentence should contribute to the prisoner leading a future life without any criminal offenses (treatment goal)."

102. Hans Heike Jung, "Ist der Alternativ-Entwurf eine Alternative oder Utopie?," *ZfS* 23 (1974): 50–57.

103. Hans-Dieter Schwind, Ulrich Jany, and Rüdiger Wohlgemuth, "Der Resozialisierungsgedanke gewinnt an Boden," *Zeitschrift für Strafvollzug und Straffälligenhilfe* (hereafter *ZfSuS*) 25 (1976): 103–9; Wolfgang Kampen und Theo Rasehorn, "Die Einstellung der Bevölkerung der Bundesrepublik zum Strafrecht und Strafvollzug," *Zeitschrift für Rechtspolitik* 5 (1972): 21–22.

104. Jürgen Hohmeier, *Aufsicht und Resozialisierung* (Stuttgart: Ferdinand Enke, 1973); Adolf Däumling, "Die psychologische Situation der Aufsichtsbeamten im Justizvollzug des Landes Nordrhein-Westfalen 1969," and Kurt Possehl, "Zum Image des Aufsichtsbediensteten," in *Selbstbild und Fremdbild der Aufsichtsbeamten im Strafvollzug* (Stuttgart: Ferdinand Enke, 1970).

105. K. Pietsch, "Der Psychotherapeut in der Strafanstalt," *ZfS* 7 (1957): 102–16, 143–55.

106. Otto Brink, "Die Kriminalität ist eine Krankheit!," *ZfS* 13 (1964): 150, 155.

107. Bundesministerium der Justiz, *Tagungsberichte der Strafvollzugskommission*, 3: 40.

108. Günter Suttinger, "Persönlichkeit und Strafvollzug," *MfKuS* 43 (1960): 1–19, 76–91.

109. Erhard Brunmayr, "Musikalische Improvisation als Therapie," and Paul Braeuniger, "Versuch zur Selbsterziehung,"*ZfS* 15 (1966): 153–58, 151–53; Johannes Feige, "Neue psychologische Methoden für die Behandlung der Gefangenen," *ZfS* 11 (1962): 316–26; Erich Pakesch, "Der Einfluß des Strafvollzuges auf die Psyche des Häftlings," *MfKuS* 44 (1961): 65–85; Wilhelm Bitter, ed., *Heilen statt Strafen: Ein Tagungsbericht* (Göttingen: Verlag für medizinische Psychologie, 1957).

110. Hellmuth Mayer, "Resozialisierungsbedürftigkeit, -Willigkeit, und -Fähigkeit der Straftäter," *ZfS* 15 (1966): 323–99.

111. Paul H. Bresser, "Ziele und Grenzen der Sozialtherapie—eine Diskussionsbemerkung," *ZfSuS* 24 (1975): 34–37; Heinz E. Wolf, "Beurteilungen der Besserungsmöglichkeiten des Strafvollzugs durch Strafgefangene," *ZfS* 20 (1972): 263–74.

112. Paul Nolte, "Von der Gesellschaftsstruktur zur Seelenverfassung: Die Psychologisierung der Sozialdiagnose in den sechziger Jahren," in *Psychoanalyse und Protest*, ed. Tobias Freimüller, (Götttingen: Wallstein, 2008), 70–94.

113. Gerhard Deimling, "'Resozialisierung' im Spannungsfeld von Strafanstalt und Gesellschaft," *ZfS* 17 (1968): 260.

114. Hermine Rasch-Bauer, "Erziehung und Menschenführung in der Gegenwart," *ZfS* 13 (1964): 255, 257.

115. Bernd Maelicke, "Möglichkeiten und Grenzen der Resozialisierung," *ZfSuS* 24 (1975): 198–203; Walter Rieger, "Die Subkultur im Strafvollzug," *ZfSuS* 24 (1975): 218–21; Volker Menke, "Ausländische Gefangene im Strafvollzug," *ZfS* 22 (1973): 41–43; Steffen Harbordt, *Die Subkultur des Gefängnisses: Eine soziologische Studie zur Resozialisierung*, 2nd ed. (Stuttgart: Enke, 1972).

116. Wolfgang Mittermaier, *Gefängniskunde: Ein Lehrbuch für Studium und Praxis* (Berlin: Franz Vahlen, 1954).

117. Günther Kaiser, Heinz Schöch, Hans-Heinrich Eidt, and Hans-Jürgen Kerner, *Strafvollzug: Eine Einführung in die Grundlagen* (Karlsruhe: C. F. Müller Juristischer Verlag, 1974).

118. Günther Kaiser, *Stand und Entwicklung der kriminologischen Forschung in Deutschland* (Berlin: Walter de Gruyter, 1975).

119. Siegfried Hellmund, "Pastoralpsychologie in der Gefangenenfürsorge," *ZfS* 24 (1975): 101–5; Ellen Stube, "Probleme der Seelsorge im Strafvollzug," *ZfS* 23 (1974): 213–21.

120. HStAS, EA 4/605, Nr. 23, Justizminister, Abt. VI to Ministerialdirektor, 9 October 1973.

121. HStAS, EA 4/605, Nr. 19, Justizministerium to Pädagogische Hochschule Rheinland, Abt. Aachen, Seminar für Psychologie und Soziologie, 22 June 1973.

122. HStAH, Hann. 1973a, Nds. 711, Acc. 6/95, Nr. 58, Müller, Dipl.-Psychologe Hannover, Justizvollzugsanstalt to Generalstaatsanwalt in Celle, 10 January 1972, S. 34; Nds. 711, Acc. 6/95, Nr. 102, Vorstand des Strafgefängnisses und der Untersuchungshaftanstalt Hannover to Generalstaatsanwalt Celle, 4 December 1970, S. 244–57, and Vorstand der Strafanstalt und Sicherungsanstalt Celle an Generalstaatsanwalt Celle, 16 November 1970, S. 239–43.

123. Karl Peters, "Die ethischen Voraussetzungen des Resozialisierung und Erziehungsvollzugs," in *Festschrift für Ernst Heinitz zum 70. Geburtstag*, ed. Hans Lüttger (Berlin: Walter de Gruyter, 1972), 501.

124. Ludwig Mayer, "Reformaufgaben im Justizvollzug und ihre Voraussetzungen," *ZfSuS* 24 (1975): 125–28.

125. "Dumme Gedanken," *Der Spiegel,* 10 November 1975, 111–12.

126. Christie, *Limits to Pain.*

127. Marlene Hilbers and Wolf Lange, "Abkehr von der Behandlungsideologie?," *Kriminologisches Journal* 5 (1973): 52–59.

128. Albin Eser, "Resozialisierung in der Krise?," in *Seminar: Abweichendes Verhalten III*, vol. 2, ed. Klaus Lüderssen and Fritz Sack (Frankfurt: Suhrkamp, 1977), 276–90.

129. Hans-Dieter Schwind, "Einführung in das Tagungsthema," in *10 Jahre Strafvollzugsgesetz: Resozialisierung als alleiniges Vollzugsziel?*, ed. Hans-Dieter Schwind, Gernot Steinhilper, and Alexander Böhm (Heidelberg: Kriminalistik, 1988), 24–25.

130. Günther Kaiser, *Kriminologie: Ein Handbuch* (Heidelberg: C. F. Müller, 1996), 1042.

131. Ulrich Greiner, "Mein ist die Rache," *Die Zeit*, 13 January 1984, 29–31.

132. Helmut Kury and Theodore Ferdinand, "Public Opinion and Punitivity," *International Journal of Law and Psychiatry* 22 (1999): 376.

133. Charlotte Maria Rath, "Die Kritik am Behandlungsvollzug" (JD diss., Georg-August-Universität Göttingen, 1987).

134. Hans-Heinrich Jescheck, "Die Krise der Kriminalpolitik," *ZfdgS* 91 (1979): 1037–64.

135. Günther Kaiser, "Resozialisierung und Zeitgeit," in *Kultur, Kriminalität, Strafrecht*, ed. Rüdiger Herren, Diethelm Keinapfel, and Heinz Müller-Dietz (Berlin: Duncker und Humblot, 1977), 359–72.

136. Michael Power, *The Audit Society: Rituals of Verification* (New York: Oxford University Press, 1997).

137. Heinz Eyrich, "Hat sich das Strafvollzugsgesetz bewährt?," in Schwind, Steinhilper, and Böhm, *10 Jahre Strafvollzugsgesetz*, 29–37.

138. Michael Bock, "Kriminologie und Spezialprävention: Ein skeptischer Lagebericht," *ZfdgS* 102 (1990): 504–33.

139. Gabriele Dolde, "Neuere Forschungsvorhaben zur Sozialtherapie im Strafvollzug der Bundesrepublik Deutschland: Ein Überblick und Ergebnisse," *ZfSuS* 34 (1985): 148–54.

140. Helmut Kury, *Die Behandlung Straffälliger*, vol. 2 (Berlin: Duncker und Humblot, 1987), 336–37.

141. Peter-Alexis Albrecht, "Spezialprävention angesichts neuer Tätergruppen," *ZfdgS* 97 (1985): 839.

142. Stäcker, *Die Franz von Liszt-Schule*, 256–58.

143. Erstes Gesetz zur Verbesserung der Stellung des Verletzten im Strafverfahren vom 18. 12. 1986, *Bundesgesetzblatt, Teil I*, 68 (1986): 2496–2500.

144. Hans-Dieter Schwind, *Kriminologie* (Heidelberg: Kriminalistik, 2009), 387–438.

145. A Federal Constitutional Court decision in 1983 declaring resocialization not the sole purpose of prison provided a further legal justification for reforming therapeutic penology. See "BVerfG, Beschluß vom 28–06–1983—2 BvR 539, 612/80," *Neue Juristische Wochenschrift* 37 (1984): 33.

146. Rüdiger Wulf, "Opferbezogene Vollzugsgestaltung—Grundzüge eines Behandlungsansatzes," *ZfSuS* 34 (1985): 66–77.

147. Klaus Meyer, "Zehn Jahre Strafvollzugsgesetz—das Gesetz im Rückblick," and Günther Kaiser, "Das deutsche Strafvollzug in internationaler vergleichender Sicht," *ZfSuS* 36 (1987): 4–11, 24–31.

148. Eberhard Krott, "Kognitive Therapie—eine Möglichkeit kurzfristiger psychotherapeutischer Intervention im Strafvollzug," *ZfSuS* 36 (1987): 278–81.

149. Rainer Goderbauer, "Soziales Training im Strafvollzug," *ZfSuS* 33 (1984): 13–18.

150. Margit Braun-Heinitz, Walther Schradin, and Ernst-Ulrich Wehle, *Weiterbildung im Strafvollzug*, vol. 1, *Grundlagen des Sozialen Trainings* (Heidelberg: AfeB-Taschenbücher Weiterbildung, 1981), 139–40.

151. Margit Braun-Heinitz, Walther Schradin, and Ernst-Ulrich Wehle, *Weiterbil-*

dung im Strafvollzug, vol. 2, *Praktische Erfahrungen mit dem Sozialen Training* (Heidelberg: AfeB-Taschenbücher Weiterbildung, 1981).

152. Katrin Becker, Judith Marggraf, Ekkehard Nuissl, and Hannelore Sutter, *Leitfaden für das soziale Training: Zwölf Lerneinheiten für Bildungsarbeit im Strafvollzug* (Heidelberg: AfeB-Taschenbücher Weiterbildung, 1988), 6–8, 203–204.

153. This trend had been emerging since the 1960s in the psychological sciences. See Maik Tändler and Uffa Jensen, ed., *Das Selbst zwischen Anpassung und Befreiung: Psychowissen und Politik im 20. Jahrhundert* (Göttingen: Wallstein, 2012).

154. Ezzat A. Fattah, "Victimology: Past, Present, and Future," *Criminologie* 33 (2000): 17–46.

CHAPTER 6

1. "Sittlichkeitsverbrecher," *Neue Württembergische Zeitung*, 28 July 1950, 3.

2. BArch, B 141/4070, Bundesminister der Justiz Dehler to Neue Württembergische Zeitung, 11 August 1950, S. 19–21.

3. Ernst Sturm, "Die Zunahme der Sexualverbrechen," *Zeitschrift für die gesamte kriminalistische Wissenschaft und Praxis* 5 (1951): 32–35.

4. BArch, B 141/4070, Schafheutle to Bundesgeschäftsstelle Verwaltung, Recht-CDU, 20 January 1954, S. 63–65.

5. Stefan Mörchen, *Schwarzer Markt: Kriminalität, Ordnung, und Moral in Bremen 1939–1949* (Frankfurt: Campus, 2011), 453–77.

6. Sybille Steinbacher, *Wie der Sex nach Deutschland kam: Der Kampf um Sittlichkeit und Anstand in der frühen Bundesrepublik* (Munich: Siedler, 2011), 21–85, 347–58.

7. BArch, B 141/4070, BMJ, Statistisches Übersicht über die Häufigkeit der Verurteilungen auf Grund der §§ 171 bis 184a StGB im Bundesgebiet, 15 January 1954, S. 60.

8. Rudolf Sieverts, "The Evolution of Sexual Criminality in the Federal Republic of Germany," in *Sexual Crime Today*, ed. Institute of Criminal Law and Criminology of the University of Leiden (Hague: Martinus Nijhoff, 1960), 51–75.

9. BArch, B 141/4070, E.J. to Bundeskanzler Adenauer, 26 April 1952, S. 34.

10. BArch, B 141/4070, E.J. to Bundesminister der Justiz, 15 May 1952, S. 36.

11. BArch, B 141/4070, Mehrere Familienväter und Gewerkschaftler, 29 October 1952, S. 43.

12. BArch, B 141/4070, BMJ to Vorsitzende des Petitionsausschusses des Deutschen Bundestages, 24 May 1955, S. 78–81.

13. Franz Meixner, "Kriminalität und Sexualität," *Kriminalistik* 5 (1951): 134–37, quotes from 134–35.

14. Gustav Nass, "Unzucht mit Kindern—das Sexualdelikt unserer Zeit, Ursachen und Bekämpfung," *MfKuS* 37 (1954): 69–82.

15. Joachim Gerchow, "Neue Ergebnisse über die Bedeutung soziologischer, psychologischer und psychopathologischer Faktoren bei Inzesttätern der Nachkriegszeit," *MfKuS* 38 (1955): 168–83.

16. Rohlfs, "Wie helfen wir den Sittlichkeitsverbrechern?," *MfKuS* 37 (1954): 113–14.

17. Hans Kühler, "Zur Behandlung der sexuell Straffälligen im Ausland," *MfKuS* 38 (1955): 93–108; F. Krüger-Thiemer, "Zur psychoanalytischen Studie 'Der Sexualverbrecher,'" *Zeitschrift für die gesamte kriminalistische Wissenschaft und Praxis* 5 (1951): 88–91.

18. F. Schleyer, "Studien über das Delikt der gewalttätigen Kindesmißhandlung," *MfKuS* 41 (1958): 65–76.

19. Kerstin Brückweh, *Mordlust: Serienmorde, Gewalt und Emotionen im 20. Jahrhundert* (Frankfurt: Campus, 2006), 221–25; Hommen, *Sittlichkeitsverbrechen*, 74–86.

20. Greg Eghigian, "A Drifting Concept for an Unruly Menace: A History of Psychopathy in Germany," *Isis* 106 (2015): 283–309.

21. Hans W. Gruhle, "Die Unterbringung psychopathischer Verbrecher," *MfKuS* 36 (1953): 6–10, quote from 6.

22. HStAS, EA 4/605, Nr. 118, Justizministerium Baden-Württemberg, Niederschrift über eine Besprechung beim Innenministerium, Abt. Gesundheitswesen vom 25. Januar 1957, 25 January 1957; Inneministerium Baden-Württemberg to Justizministerium, 31 December 1955,

23. HStAH, Hann. 173a, Nds. 711, Acc. 6/95, Nr. 148, Niederschrift über die Arbeitstagung der Strafvollzugsreferenten und Anstaltsvorstände der selbständigen Justizvollzugsanstalten Niedersachsens in Wolfenbüttel am 2.–4. Nov 1954, S. 80.

24. BArch, B 141/82061, Besprechung der Unterabteilung IIa mit Herrn Prof. Dr. Mannheim, 3 August 1955, S. 26; Horst Herrmann, "Die mit Freiheitsentziehung verbundenen Maßnahmen der Sicherung und Besserung," Universität Freiburg 0734 (Heft 6): 83–98, undated [ca. summer 1954], S. 1–16.

25. HStAS, EA 4/605, Nr. 118, Auszugsweise Abschrift aus dem Bericht des Medizinalreferenten Obermedizinalrat Dr. Ernst, Bruchsal vom 15. November 1956. From 1950 until 1958, West German courts annually committed fewer than two hundred individuals to preventive detention, in contrast to Nazi Germany, which committed over one thousand a year from 1939 until 1942. See Jörg Kinzig, *Die Sicherungsverwahrung auf dem Prüfstand* (Freiburg: Max-Planck-Institut für ausländisches und internationales Strafrecht, 1996), 20, 132.

26. HStAS, EA 4/605, Nr. 118, Justizministerium to alle Landesjustizverwaltungen, Gefängnisverwaltung Hamburg, Bundesminister der Justiz, 20 September 1956.

27. HStAS, EA 4/605, Nr. 118, Prof. Dr. Ernst, Obermedizinalrat, Psychiatrisches Landeskrankenhaus Weinsbert to Regierungspräsidium Nordwürttemberg, 18 October 1957.

28. See their statements in BArch, B 141/82061.

29. BArch, B 141/82061, Große Strafrechtskommission, Niederschrift über die 32. Sitzung am 26. Oktober 1955 in Schwangau, S. 31–33.

30. Georg K. Stürup, *Treating the Untreatable: Chronic Criminals at Herstedvester* (Baltimore: Johns Hopkins University Press, 1968).

31. BArch, B 141/82062, Grosse Strafrechtskommission, Niederschrift über die 45. Sitzung am 12. Juli 1956 in Edenkoben.

32. Georg K. Stürup, "The Treatment of Criminal Psychopaths in Herstedvester," *British Journal of Medical Psychology* 25 (1952): 31–38.

33. BArch, B 141/82062, Prof. Dr. Sieverts, 28 March 1956, S. 2.

34. BArch, B 141/82062, Grosse Strafrechtskommission, Niederschrift über die 45. Sitzung am 12. Juli 1956 in Edenkoben.

35. Ibid.

36. BArch, B 141/82062, Grosse Strafrechtskommission, Niederschrift über die 46. Sitzung am 13. Juli 1956 in Edenkoben.

37. Ibid.

38. BArch, B 141/82062, Grosse Strafrechtskommission, Niederschrift über die 47. Sitzung am 14. Juli 1956 in Edenkoben,

39. BArch, B 141/82063, Wilfert, Betreff: Entwurf des Allgemeinen Teiles eines Strafgesetzbuches, 11 March 1959.

40. Kontrollratsgesetz Nr. 11 vom 30. Januar 1946, accessed 29 December 2012, http://www.verfassungen.de/de/de45-49/kr-gesetz11.htm.

41. BArch, B 141/18984, Schwalm, BMJ, Referenten-Vorentwurf für ein Gesetz über freiwillige Unfruchtbarmachungen, 13 August 1963.

42. BArch, Z 21/803, Dr. Pophal und Dr. Lua to Oberstaatsanwalt beim Landgericht, 12 April 1946, S. 3.

43. BArch, Z 21/803, Koch, Präsident des Zentral-Justizamts für die britische Zone an Generalstaatsanwalt Hamburg, 15 October 1946, S. 4.

44. BArch, B 141/3785, Langelüddeke to Bundesministerium der Justiz, 24 July 1951, S. 8.

45. Ernst Klee, *Das Personenlexikon zum Dritten Reich* (Frankfurt: S. Fischer, 2003), 357.

46. BArch, B 141/3785, BMJ internal memo, no day, October 1951, S. 10.

47. BArch, B 141/3785, BMJ to Landesjustizverwaltungen, 9 October 1951, S. 13. Eventually, the consortium awarded Langelüddeke DM 10,000, in the summer of 1955. See BArch, B 141/3787, Dreher internal note, 2 August 1955, S. 114.

48. BArch, B 141/3786, Langelüddeke to Dreher, 11 May 1953, S. 94; B 141/3785, Senator für Justiz, Berlin to BMJ, 13 March 1952, S. 64.

49. BArch, B 141/63331, 123. Sitzung des Sonderausschusses für die Strafrechtsreform, 19 November 1968, 2485.

50. Albrecht Langelüddeke, *Die Entmannung von Sittlichkeitsverbrechern* (Berlin: Walter de Gruyter, 1963), 117.

51. BArch, B 141/18985, Urteil, 4. Senat des Bundesgerichtshofs in der Sitzung vom 13. Dezember 1963.

52. Hermann Plenge, "Die Behandlung erheblich rückfälliger Sexualdelinquenten vornehmlich der Homosexuellen, unter besonderer Berücksichtigung der Kastration," *MfKuS* 44 (1961): 15–41; Dr. Blau, "Ist die frewillige Entmannung homosexueller Sittlichkeitsverbrecher während der Straf- oder Maßregelvollzuges zulässig und angezeigt?," *MfKuS* 43 (1960): 41–43.

53. BArch, B 141/18984, Schwalm, BMJ, Referenten-Vorentwurf für ein Gesetz über freiwillige Unfruchtbarmachungen, 13 August 1963.

54. BArch, B 141/18985, Sturm to Schwalm, 2 March 1964.

55. BArch, B 141/18993, Haddenbrock to Inneministerium Baden-Württemberg, 15 September 1967.

56. Ibid.

57. BArch, B 141/18993, Horstkotte, BMJ to Haddenbrock, 25 October 1967.

58. BArch, B 141/63331, 123. Sitzung des Sonderausschußes für die Strafrechtsreform, 19 November 1968, 2511.

59. BArch, B 141/63331, 124. Sitzung des Sonderausschußes für die Strafrechtsreform, 21 November 1968, 2520.

60. Anthony D. Kauders, "Drives in Dispute: The West German Student Movement, Psychoanalysis, and the Search for a New Emotional Order, 1967–1971," *Central European History* 44 (2011): 711–31.

61. BArch, B 141/63331, 124. Sitzung des Sonderausschußes für die Strafrechtsreform, 21 November 1968, 2522.

62. Gesetz über die freiwillige Kastration und andere Behandlungsmethoden, 15 August 1969, accessed 18 February 2013, http://www.buzer.de/gesetz/6323/index.htm.

63. Plenge, "Die Behandlung," 18.

64. BArch, B 141/18992, Justizamt Hamburg, Besprechung des Arbeitsstabes zur Bekämpfung von Triebverbrechen in der Justizbehörde am 8. Mai 1967, 19 May 1967.

65. BArch, B 141/4070, A.M. to Justizminister Stammberger, 16 August 1962, S. 145.

66. Ibid., 22 September 1962, S. 148.

67. BArch, B 141/63807, L.S. to Heinemann, 7 January 1968.

68. "Immer nur lächeln," *Der Spiegel*, 3 November 1965, 86, 89.

69. "Blutige Ernte," *Der Spiegel*, 10 November 1965, 38–47.

70. BArch, B 141/18989, Horstkotte, 11 November 1965.

71. Ibid., F. Baier (Mitglied des Bundestages) to Dr. R. Jaeger (BMJ), 2 December 1965.

72. Brückweh, *Mordlust*, 303–35.

73. BArch, B 141/63805, Verband zur Verhütung und Wiedergutmachung von Straftaten, undated newsletter [ca. fall 1965].

74. BArch, B 141/18991, "Strafen oder heilen? Forderungen und Möglichkeiten zur Bekämpfung von Sittlichkeitsverbrechen," *Stuttgarter Zeitung*, 25 April 1966, 25.

75. BArch, B 141/63807, Verband zur Verhütung und Wiedergutmachung von Straftaten, "Konzept für das Gespräch mit dem Sonderausschuß für Strafrechtsreform," 17 March 1967.

76. BArch, B 141/63805, Zita Zehner, Vorstizende der Frauenarbeitsgemeinschaft der CSU in Bayern an Bundesminister der Justiz Jaeger, 28 June 1967.

77. BArch, B 141/63806, Hedwig Kömmerling-Fitzler, 1. Vorsitzende des Frauenring-Pirmasens, "Aktion des Frauenring-Pirmasens zur Erreichung eines besseren Schutzes der Kinder vor Triebverbrechern," 11. September 1967–6. Oktober 1967.

78. BArch, B 141/63806, "Unsere Jugend ist kein Freiwild! Schützt unsere Kinder vor Triebverbrechern! Aufruf von Frauenring und Kinderschutzbund," *Pirmasener Zeitung*, 11 September 1967.

79. BArch, B 141/63806, "Fast 700 Unterschriften," *Pirmasener Zeitung*, 13 September 1967.

80. Kerstin Brückweh, "Fantasies of Violence: German Citizens Expressing Their Concepts of Violence and Ideas about Democracy in Letters Referring to the Case of the Serial Killer Jürgen Bartsch (1966–1971)," *Crime, Histoire et Sociétés / Crime, History and Societies* 10 (2006): 53–81.

81. BArch, B 141/18989, Corves, Betr. Fragestunde des Deutschen Bundestages: Fragen der Abg. Lemper und Huys betreffend Triebverbrechen an Kindern, 10 November 1965; BArch, B 141/18994, Bundesminister der Justiz Gustav Heinemann to Präsident des Deutschen Bundestages, 13 November 1967.

82. BArch, B 141/63806, Bundesministerium der Justiz, reply to question of Abg. J. Hoffmann (CDU, Mainz) vom 5. Dezember 1967, undated.

83. BArch, B 141/18988, Schwalm, Bemerkungen zum Referenten-Vorentwurf für ein Gesetz über freiwillige Unfruchtbarmachungen, 17 November 1964.

84. BArch, B 141/18991, Horstkotte, 24 January 1966; Jaeger to Schulhoff, 24 January 1966.

85. BArch, B 141/63807, Corves, 13 December 1967.

86. BArch, B 141/63330, BMJ (Horstkotte), Übersicht über die von den Landesjustizverwaltungen, den Bundesressorts, dem Bundeskriminalamt und den Referaten der Abt. I und IV des BMJ abgegebenen Äußerungen, 5 August 1968.

87. Ibid., Bockelmann to Dreher (BMJ), 12 August 1968.

88. BArch, B 141/18989, Corves (BMJ), Betr. Fragestunde des Deutschen Bundestages, 10 November 1965.

89. BArch, B 141/18991, Werner Krause (Institut für Sexualforschung, Universität Hamburg) to Sturm, 3 November 1966.

90. BArch, B 141/63330, Ursula Laschet to Horstkotte (BMJ), 18 September 1968.

91. BArch, B 41/63331, 123. Sitzung des Sonderausschußes für die Strafrechtsreform, 19 November 1968, 2489–98.

92. Ibid., 2496.

93. Greg Eghigian, "Hypersexual Disorder: An Encounter with Don Juan in the Archives," *Psychiatric Times* 29 (August 2012): 18.

94. BArch, B 41/63331, 123. Sitzung des Sonderausschußes für die Strafrechtsreform, 19 November 1968, 2500.

95. Ibid., 2504.

96. Ibid., 2506.

97. Kastrationsgesetz, accessed 18 February 2013, http://www.buzer.de/gesetz/6323/a87792.htm.

98. Owen Bowcott, "Human Rights Groups Call for End to Surgical Castration of Sex Offenders," *Guardian*, 21 February 2012, accessed 18 February 2013, http://www.guardian.co.uk/law/2012/feb/22/surgical-castration-sex-offenders-cpt-report; Paul Moor, "Ganz gewöhnliche Schlamperei," *Die Zeit*, 28 April 1978, accessed 18 February 2013, http://www.zeit.de/1978/18/ganz-gewoehnliche-schlamperei.

99. Reinhard Wille and Klaus M. Beier, "Castration in Germany," *Sexual Abuse: A Journal of Research and Treatment* 2 (1989): 103–32, figures cited on 111.

100. BArch, B 141/4070, R.R. to Bundesminister Schäffer, 17 January 1959, 103.

101. A number of these letters from the years 1961–62 can be found in BArch, B 141/4070.

102. Ibid., Goßrau (BMJ) to H.K., 16 March 1962, 118–19.

103. BArch, B 141/82064, Herzog (BMJ), internal memo, 19 December 1961, 8; Gesellschaft für Psychiatrie und Nervenheilkunde to BMJ, 18 September 1961, 1; Deutsche Vereinigung für Jugendpsychiatrie to the Vorstand der Deutschen Vereinigung für Jugendgerichte und Jugendgerichtshilfen, 9 September 1961, 2–3.

104. Ibid., Schwalm to *Heidelberger Tageblatt*, 24 May 1963, 39–41.

105. Ibid., Opp, Direktor des Landschaftsverbandes Rheinland to Justizminister NRW, 25 April 1963, 48.

106. Ibid., Associated Press Wire, "Billigen die Gerichte zu oft den Paragraph 51 zu?," 24 April 1964, 54–55.

107. Ibid., Deutscher Bundestag, Sonderausschuß Strafrecht, 42. Sitzung, 11 February 1965, 56–63.

108. For these discussions and exchanges, see ibid., 113–27.

109. "Zweites Gesetz zur Reform des Strafrechts (4. Juli 1969)," *Bundesgesetzblatt, Teil I*, 56 (1969): 728–29.

110. On the history of social psychiatry in the FRG, see Kersting, *Psychiatriereform als Gesellschaftsreform.*

111. BArch, B 141/72673, Strafvollzugskommission, "Grundsätze und Empfehlungen der Strafvollzugskommission zum Thema 'Sozialtherapeutische Anstalt,'" Munich, 15 October 1969, 12–24.

112. Ibid., Niederschrift über die Tagung des Unterausschusses des Strafvollzugsausschusses der Länder vom 1. Bis 3. Dezember 1969 in Mainz, 30 December 1969, 78–111.

113. Ibid.

114. BArch, B 141/72674, Justizministerium Baden-Württemberg, "Niederschrift über die Tagung des Unterausschusses des Strafvollzugsausschusses der Länder vom 24. Bis 26. Februar 1970 in Stuttgart," 20 April 1970, 21–42.

115. Ibid., Dr. Günter Suttinger, Entwurf für eine Sozialtherapeutische Anstalt mit Diagnosezentrum, 9 June 1969, 47–51.

116. Frieder Dünkel, "Sozialtherapie," in *Kleines kriminologisches Wörterbuch*, ed. Günther Kaiser (Heidelberg: C. F. Müller, 1985), 423.

117. "Straf- und Maßregelvollzug," *ZfS* 20 (1972): 359–64.

118. Inge Rieber and Volkmar Sigusch, "Psychosurgery on Sex Offenders and Sexual 'Deviants' in West Germany," *Archives of Sexual Behavior* 8 (1979): 523–27.

119. K. Freund, D. Sedlacek, and K. Knob, "A Simple Transducer for Mechanical Plethysmography of the Male Genital," *Journal of the Experimental Analysis of Behavior* 8 (1965): 169–70.

120. Gerald Streitberg, "Die Behandlung von Sexualstraftätern im Vollzug," *ZfS* 24 (1975): 147–54.

121. Hans-Jürgen Horn, "Die Behandlung der Sexualdelinquenten (unter besonderer Berücksichtigung der somatischen Behandlungsmethoden)," in *Kriminaltherapie heute*, ed. Heinz Müller-Dietz (Berlin: Walter de Gruyter, 1974), 19–34.

122. "Abzüglich gewisser Rechte," *Der Spiegel*, 15 February 1971, 57, 60.

123. Mayer, "Resozialiserungsbedürftigkeit."

124. Wilfried Rasch, "Die Errichtung von Bewahrungsanstalten: Vorplanung und erste Schritte," *MfKuS* 50 (1967): 339–44.

125. Wilfried Rasch, "Organisatorische Sicherung sozialtherapeutischer Orientierung: Das Dürener Modell," in Müller-Dietz, *Kriminaltherapie heute*, 3–15.

126. Marcel Streng,"'Sozialtherapie ist eine Therapie, die sozial macht': Therapeutisierungsprozess im westdeutschen Strafvollzug der langen 70er Jahren," in *Das beratene Selbst: Zur Genealogie der Therapeutisierung in den "langen" Siebzigern*, ed. Sabine Maasen, Jens Elberfeld, Pascal Eitler, and Maik Tändler (Bielefeld: Transcript, 2011), 265–90.

127. W. Rasch and K.-P. Kühl, "Psychologische Kriterien für die Unterbringung in einer sozialtherapeutischen Anstalt," in *Forensische Sozialtherapie: Erfahrungen in Düren*, ed. Wilfried Rasch (Karlsruhe: C. F. Müller Jurististischer Verlag, 1977), 259.

128. Ulrich Eisenberg, "Zum Behandlungskonzept der sozialtherapeutischen Anstalten," *Neue Juristische Wochenschrift* 22 (1969): 1553–58.

129. "Nicht böse," *Der Spiegel*, 11 May 1970, 95, 97

130. Gerhard Mauch and Roland Mauch, *Sozialtherapie und die sozialtherapeutische Anstalt: Erfahrung in der Behandlung Chronisch-Krimineller* (Stuttgart: Ferdinand Enke, 1971).

131. Gerhard Mauch, "Sozialtherapie," in Bundesministerium der Justiz, *Tagungsberichte der Strafvollzugskommission*, 8: 89.

132. Ibid., 91–95.

133. Ibid., 95–100.

134. See, for instance, the case of B.T. (b. 1943) in HStAS, EA 4/602, Nr. 179–222.

135. On the notion of "technologies of hope," see Sarah Franklin, *Embodied Progress: A Cultural Account of Assisted Conception* (London: Routledge, 1997).

136. HStAS, EA 4/602, Nr. 74–130, T.R. to Leiter der sozialtherapeutischen Abteilung Hohenasperg, 30 July 1972.

137. HStAS, EA 4/602, Nr. 1–73, G.B. to Justizministerium Baden-Württemberg, 6 October 1968.

138. Ibid., E.M., Rechtsanwalt to Direktor der Strafanstalt, Landesgefängnis Rotteburg, 4 October 1968.

139. Ibid., R., Anstaltsarzt, Landestrafanstalt Bruchsal to Justizministerium Baden-Württemberg, 5 February 1968.

140. Ibid, EA 4/602, Nr. 114, Gienger to Justizministerium Baden-Württemberg, 30 July 1971; Nr. 103, Justizministerium Baden-Württemberg, internal memo, 24 May 1971.

141. Ibid., EA 4/602, Nr. 228, Schmitt, Justizvollzugsanstalt Ludwigshafen, Sozialtherapeutische Anstalt to Ministerium der Justiz Rheinland-Pfalz, 7 June 1979.

142. Ibid., Vollzugsanstalt Stuttgart, Einweisungskommission, Beschluss vom 11. Februar 1980.

143. Ibid., EA 4/602, Nr. 341, Vollzugsanstalt Stuttgart, Einweisungskommission, Beschluss vom 4. Juli 1980.

144. Ibid., EA 4/602, Nr. 99, Mauch to Vollzugsleiter, 29 May 1970, and Nr. 1–73, Mauch and Ziegler to Vorstand, 21 February 1969.

145. Ibid., EA 4/602, Nr. 249, Liebeler, Sozialtherapeutische Anstalt Ludwigsburg, Sitz Hohenasperg to Justizministerium Baden-Württemberg, 15 August 1978.

146. Ibid, EA 4/602, Nr. 339, Engell, Sozialtherapeutische Anstalt Ludwigsburg, Sitz

Hohenasperg to Leiter der Vollzugsanstalt Bruchsal, 18 July 1980; Nr. 131–78, Einweisungskommission, Vollzugsanstalt Stuttgart to Justizministerium, 20 September 1973.

147. Schwind, Jany, and Wohlgemuth, "Der Resozialisierungsgedanke," 106–7.

148. Dünkel, "Sozialtherapie," in Kaiser, *Kleines Kriminologisches Wörterbuch*, 420–27, figures cited on 423.

149. Bernd Volckart and Rolf Grünebaum, *Maßregelvollzug: Das Recht des Vollzugs der Unterbringung nach §§ 63, 64 StGB in einem psychiatrischen Krankenhaus und in einer Entziehungsanstalt* (Munich: Luchterhand, 2003), 3–4.

150. Rolf Driebold, "Keine Zukunft für die sozialtherapeutische Anstalt? Überlegungen zur Fortentwicklung der Sozialtherapie im Justizvollzug," *ZfS* 32 (1983): 195–200; Rudolf Egg, *Sozialtherapie und Strafvollzug* (Frankfurt: Haag und Herchen, 1979).

151. Dolde, "Neuere Forschungsvorhaben zur Sozialtherapie." One study, for instance, showed that those applying for social therapy were significantly more positively predisposed to the law than those not applying.

152. Rudolf Egg, *Straffälligkeit und Sozialtherapie: Konzepte, Erfahrungen, Entwicklungsmöglichkeiten* (Cologne: Carl Heymann, 1984). See also Karl Peter Rotthaus, "Sozialtherapie: Wie soll es weitergehen?," *ZfS* 35 (1986): 79–80.

153. Rainer Goderbauer and Rudolf Engell, "Aus der Sozialtherapeutischen Anstalt Baden-Württemberg," *ZfS* 37 (1988): 84–87.

154. Edwin H. Sutherland, "The Sexual Psychopath Laws," *Journal of Criminal Law and Criminology* 40 (1950): 543–54.

155. "Gesetz zur Bekämpfung von Sexualdelikten und anderen gefährlichen Straftaten vom 26. January 1998," *Bundesgesetzblatt, Teil 1* (1998): 160–63.

156. Kriminologische Zentralstelle e.V., accessed 8 March 2013, http://www.krimz.de/sozialtherapie.html.

157. Imanuel Baumann, "Sicherungsverwahrung in Baden-Württemberg, 1959 bis 1980" (Freiburg, 2005), http://www.freidok.uni-freiburg.de/volltexte/1582/pdf/SVAnalyse.pdf, accessed 15 April 2015. See also Kinzig, *Sicherungsverwahrung auf dem Prüfstand*, 166.

CONCLUSION

1. C. Stadtland, M. Hollweg, N. Kleindienst, J. Dietl, U. Reich, and N. Nedopil, "Rückfallprognosen bei Sexualstraftäter—Vergelich der prädiktiven Validität von Prognoseinstrumenten," *Der Nervenarzt* 77 (2006): 587–95.

2. While still sanctioned in the GDR until 1987, capital punishment was rarely administered there after the 1950s.

3. Giorgio Agamben, *State of Exception* (Chicago: University of Chicago Press, 2005), and *Homo Sacer: Sovereign Power and Bare Life* (Stanford: Stanford University Press, 1998).

4. This, in part, is one of the reasons why Germany's preventive detention system has been cited for violations by the European Court on Human Rights. See Grischa Merkel, "Case Note—Retrospective Preventive Detention in Germany: A Comment on the ECHR Decision *Haidn v. Germany* of 13 January 2011," *German Law Journal* 12 (2011): 968–77.

5. Simon, *Governing through Crime*; Michaelis Lianos and Mary Douglas, "Dangerization and the End of Deviance," *British Journal of Criminology* 40 (2000): 261–78.

6. Lianos and Douglas, "Dangerization," 267.

7. For example, scholars have noted this development within contemporary medicine. See Jason Adam Wasserman and Brian Philip Hinote, "Chronic Illness and Incalculable Risk: Scientific Uncertainty and Social Transformations in Medicine," *Social Theory and Health* 9 (2011): 41–58; Jeremy A. Greene, *Prescribing by Numbers: Drugs and the Definition of Disease* (Baltimore: Johns Hopkins University Press, 2007); David Armstrong, "The Rise of Surveillance Medicine," *Sociology of Health and Illness* 17 (1995): 393–404.

8. Nikolas Rose, *The Politics of Life Itself: Biomedicine, Power, and Subjectivity in the Twenty-First Century* (Princeton: Princeton University Press, 2007).

9. Kriminologiche Zentralstelle, "Rückfälligkeit von Sexualstraftätern," accessed 9 April 2013, http://www.krimz.de/sexrckfall.html; Jutta Elz, "Zur Rückfälligkeit von Sexualstraftätern in der DDR," in *Sexualstraftaten: Forensische Begutachtung, Diagnostik, und Therapie*, ed. Detlef Schläfke, Frank Häßler, and Jörg Michael Fegert (Stuttgart: Schattauer, 2005), 181–93; Jutta Elz and Almut Fröhlich, *Sexualstraftäter in der DDR: Ergebnisse einer empirischen Untersuchung* (Wiesbaden: Kriminologische Zentralstelle, 2002). Elz found that only 10 percent of those in her East German sample did not reoffend in some way.

10. Wolfgang Heinz, "Rückfall- und Wirkungsforschung—Ergebnisse aus Deutschland," paper presented at Kansai University (Japan), 5 April 2007, accessed 9 April 2013, http://www.uni-konstanz.de/rtf/kis/Heinz_Rueckfall-und_Wirkungsforschung_he308.pdf.

11. Lothar Kolb and Siegfried Klarhöfer, *Zur Erhöhung der erzieherischen Wirksamkeit des Vollzuges der Freiheitsstrafe* (Berlin: Hochschule der Deutschen Volkspolizei, 1988).

12. Garland, *Punishment and Modern Society*, 288.

13. George C. Rosenwald, "Why Operationism Doesn't Go Away: Extrascientific Incentives of Social-Psychological Research," *Philosophy of the Social Sciences* 16 (1986): 303–30, quote from 308.

14. Erving Goffman, *Asylums: Essays on the Social Situation of Mental Patients and Other Inmates* (Garden City: Anchor, 1961), 74.

15. Ibid., 186.

16. Greg Eghigian, "Psychagogy: Psychotherapy's Remarkably Resilient Predecessor," *Psychiatric Times* 29 (November 2012): 12

17. Personal communication with the author.

18. See Wanda J. Olikowski, "Using Technology and Constituting Structures: A Practical Lens for Studying Technology in Organizations," *Organization Science* 11 (2000): 404–28, and "The Duality of Technology: Rethinking the Concept of Technology in Organizations," *Organization Science* 3 (1992): 398–427.

19. Hans-Jörg Albrecht, "Sentencing in Germany: Explaining Long-Term Stability in the Structure of Criminal Sanctions and Sentencing," *Law and Contemporary Problems* 76 (2013): 229.

Selected Bibliography

PRIMARY SOURCES

Archives

Brandenburgisches Landeshauptarchiv
    Rep. 601 Bezirkstag und Rat des Bezirkes Frankfurt
Bundesarchiv (BArch)
    B 106 Bundesministerium des Innern
    B 141 Reichsministerium der Justiz
    B 160 Kriminalbiologische Forschungsstelle des Reichsgesundheitsamtes
    DO 1 Ministerium des Innern
    DP 1 Ministerium der Justiz
    DP 2 Oberstes Gericht
    DP 3 Generalstaatsanwaltschaft
    DQ 1 Ministerium für Gesundheitswesen
    R 3001 Reichsministerium der Justiz
    Z 21 Zentral-Justizamt für die britische Zone
Bundesbeauftragte für Stasiunterlagen (BStU)
    Einzelfallakten
    HA II Hauptabeilung II
    HA VII Hauptabteilung VII
    MfS Arbeitsbereich Neiber 239
Institut für Geschichte der Medizin, Berlin (IGM)
    Charité Forensik, 1950–67
Landesarchiv Baden-Württemberg, Hauptstaatsarchiv Stuttgart (HStAS)
    EA 4 Justizministerium, Abteilung Strafvollzug
Landesarchiv Berlin (LAB)
    A Rep. 003-02 Magistrat Berlin
    A Rep. 369 Gefängnis Plötzensee
Niedersächsisches Hauptstaatsarchiv Hannover (HStAH)
    Hann. 173a Staatsanwaltschaft beim Oberlandesgericht in Celle
    Nds. 711 Staatsanwaltschaft beim Oberlandsgericht Celle
Staatsarchiv Hamburg (StAHH)
    Bestand 213-8 Staatsanwaltschaft Oberlandsgericht-Verwaltung

Bestand 241-1 Justizverwaltung
Bestand 241-1 I Justizverwaltung I
Bestand 242-4 Kriminalbiologische Sammelstelle, 1926–45
Stadtarchiv Frankfurt am Main
Personalakten, Robert Ritter, 18.576

Journals and Periodicals

Allgemeine Zeitschrift für Psychiatrie und ihre Grenzgebiete
Allgemeine Zeitschrift für Psychiatrie und Psychisch-Gerichtliche Medizin
Archives of Sexual Behavior
Archiv für Kriminalpsychologie
Blätter für Gefängniskunde (BfG)
Bundesgesetzblatt
Der Spiegel
Deutsche Justiz
Deutsche Richterzeitung
Die deutsche Sonderschule
Die Zeit
Guardian
Journal of the Experimental Analysis of Behavior
Kriminalistik
Kriminalistik und forensische Wissenschaften
Kriminologisches Journal
Monatsblätter des Deutschen Reichszusammenschlusses für Gerichtshilfe, Gefangenen- und Entlassenenfürsorge der freien Wohlfahrtspflege
Monatsblätter für Gerichtshilfe, Gefangenen- und Entlassenenfürsorge (MfGGE)
Monatsblätter für Straffälligenbetreuung und Ermittlungshilfe
Monatsschrift für Kriminalpsychologie und Strafrechtsreform, 1904–36; *Monatsschrift für Kriminalbiologie und Strafrechtsreform*, 1937–44; *Monatsschrift für Kriminologie und Strafrechtsreform*, 1953– (*MfKuS*)
Neue Juristische Wochenschrift
Neue Justiz
Psychiatrie, Neurologie, und medizinische Psychologie (PNumP)
Zeitschrift für die gesamte kriminalistische Wissenschaft und Praxis
Zeitschrift für die gesamte Strafrechtswissenschaft (ZfdgS)
Zeitschrift für psychische Hygiene
Zeitschrift für Rechtspolitik
Zeitschrift für Strafvollzug, 1950–74 (*ZfS*); *Zeitschrift für Strafvollzug und Straffälligenhilfe*, 1975– (*ZfSuS*)

Published Primary Sources

Akademie der Pädagogischen Wissenschaften der DDR and Akademie der Pädagogischen Wissenschaften der UdSSR, ed. 1972. *Psychologische Probleme der Entwicklung sozialistischer Persönlichkeiten*. Berlin: Volk und Wissen.

Albrecht, Heinz, Lothar Blei, and Erich Weber. 1982. *Handbuch für Betriebsangehörige*. Berlin: Ministerium des Innern.

Albrecht, Peter-Alexis. 1985. "Spezialprävention angesichts neuer Tätergruppen." *ZfdgS* 97: 831–70.

Ayass, Wolfgang, ed. 1998. *"Gemeinschaftsfremde": Quellen zur Verfolgung von "Asozialen" 1933–1945*. Koblenz: Bundesarchiv.

Bader, Karl S. 1949. *Soziologie der deutschen Nachkriegskriminalität*. Tübingen: J. C. B. Mohr.

Bayerischer Landesverband für Wanderdienst, München, ed. 1938. *Der nichtseßhafte Mensch: Ein Beitrag zur Neugestaltung der Raum- und Menschenordnung im Großdeutschen Reich*. Munich: C. H. Beck.

Becker, Katrin, Judith Marggraf, Ekkehard Nuissl, and Hannelore Sutter. 1988. *Leitfaden für das soziale Training: Zwölf Lerneinheiten für Bildungsarbeit im Strafvollzug*. Heidelberg: AfeB-Taschenbücher Weiterbildung.

Betzendahl, Walter. 1933. "Über maskierte Verrücktheit und ihre sozialen Folgen." *Allgemeine Zeitschrift für Psychiatrie und psychisch-gerichtliche Medizin* 100: 141–85.

Bitter, Wilhelm, ed. 1957. *Heilen statt Strafen: Ein Tagungsbericht*. Göttingen: Verlag für medizinische Psychologie.

Blau. 1960. "Ist die frewillige Entmannung homosexueller Sittlichkeitsverbrecher während der Straf- oder Maßregelvollzuges zulässig und angezeigt?" *MfKuS* 43: 41–43.

Bock, Michael. 1990. "Kriminologie und Spezialprävention: Ein skeptischer Lagebericht." *ZfdgS* 102: 504–33.

Böhme, Albrecht. 1935. *Psychotherapie und Kastration: Die Bedeutung der Psychotherapie als Erziehungs- und Ausscheidungsmethode für sexuell Abwegige und Sittlichkeitsverbrecher, dargestellt an Fällen aus der Kriminalpraxis, unter Heranziehung der Graphologie als Hilfswissenschaft*. Munich: J. F. Lehmanns Verlag.

Bormann. 1936. "Ein Beitrag zur Selbshilfe der Gefangenen." *MfGGE* 11: 182–97.

Bormann, W. 1935. "Die Wiedereingliederung des politischen Gefangenen in die Volksgemeinschaft." *MfGGE* 10: 129–30.

Böttcher, Franz. 1939. "Erziehung und praktische Auslesearbeit in der Gefangenenanstalt." *Die deutsche Sonderschule* 6: 567–70.

Braeuniger, Paul. 1966. "Versuch zur Selbsterziehung." *ZfS* 15: 151–53.

Braun-Heinitz, Margit, Walther Schradin, and Ernst-Ulrich Wehle. 1981. *Weiterbildung im Strafvollzug*. Vols. 1–2. Heidelberg: AfeB-Taschenbücher Weiterbildung.

Bresser, Paul H. 1975. "Ziele und Grenzen der Sozialtherapie—eine Diskussionsbemerkung." *ZfSuS* 24: 34–37.

Brink, Otto. 1964. "Die Kriminalität ist eine Krankheit!" *ZfS* 13: 150–70.

Brunmayr, Erhard. 1966. "Musikalische Improvisation als Therapie." *ZfS* 15: 153–58.

Buhl, Walther. 1952. "Erziehungsvollzug? Eine kritische Betrachtung." *ZfS* 3: 69–70.

Bundesministerium der Justiz. 1967–70. *Tagungsberichte der Strafvollzugskommission*. Vols. 1–13. Bonn: Bundesministerium der Justiz.

Bunsmann, Franz. 1938. *Überblick über die Entwicklung der Entmannung sowie Beobachtungen an 30 auf Grund des Gesetzes vom 24.11.1933 entmannten Sittlichkeitsverbrechern*. Würzburg: Richard Mayr.

Burian, Rudolf. 1970. "Über eine durch sexuelle Prägung entstandene Form der Pädophilie." *PNumP* 22: 249–53.

Burmeister, J., H. Dettenborn, and H.-H. Fröhlich. 1975. "Zur Kritik bürgerlicher Sozialtherapie im Strafvollzug." *Kriminalistik und forensische Wissenschaften* 21: 153–89.

Büttner. 1937–38. "Die Zusammenarbeit der NSV mit den Kreisstellen der Sächsischen Straffälligenbetreuung und Ermittlungshilfe." *MfGGE* 13: 44–45.

Carroll, Denis. 1957. *The University Teaching of Social Sciences: Criminology*. Paris: UNESCO.

Creutz, W. 1939. "Psychiatrische Erfahrungen mit §§ 42b und 42c des Gesetzes gegen gefährliche Gewohnheitsverbrecher und über Maßregeln der Sicherung und Besserung vom 24. November 1933." *Allgmemeine Zeitschrift für Psychiatrie und ihre Grenzgebiete* 111: 137–68.

Däumling, Adolf. 1951. "Die Aufgaben des Psychologen im sozialpsychagogischen Strafvollzug." *ZfS* 2: 7–11.

Däumling, Adolf. 1970. "Die psychologische Situation der Aufsichtsbeamten im Justizvollzug des Landes Nordrhein-Westfalen 1969." In *Selbstbild und Fremdbild der Aufsichtsbeamten im Strafvollzug*, 1–42. Stuttgart: Ferdinand Enke.

Deimling, Gerhard. 1968. "'Resozialisierung' im Spannungsfeld von Strafanstalt und Gesellschaft." *ZfS* 17: 251–60.

Dettenborn, Harry, and Hans-H. Fröhlich. 1971. *Psychologische Probleme der Täterpersönlichkeit*. Berlin: VEB Deutscher Verlag der Wissenschaften.

Dolde, Gabriele. 1985. "Neuere Forschungsvorhaben zur Sozialtherapie im Strafvollzug der Bundesrepublik Deutschland: Ein Überblick und Ergebnisse." *ZfSuS* 34: 148–54.

Dra, Konrad. 1939. "Was heißt Besserung im Strafvollzug?" *BfG* 70: 44–48.

Driebold, Rolf. 1983. "Keine Zukunft für die sozialtherapeutische Anstalt? Überlegungen zur Fortentwicklung der Sozialtherapie im Justizvollzug." *ZfS* 32: 195–200.

Dummer, Werner, and Diether Rudolf Burian. 1978. "Eine Behandlungskonzept für sexuelle Deviationen (Methodik und bisherige Ergebnisse)." *PNumP* 39: 599–607.

Dziembowski, W. 1936. "Strafvollzug im nationalsozialistischen Staate und Erziehungsmöglichkeiten an Strafgefangenen durch den Anstaltspädagogen." *BfG* 67: 142–59.

Eberhard, Werner. 1942–43. "Ein Beitrag zur Frage der Beziehungen zwischen Krankheit und Verbrechen." *BfG* 73: 107–14.

Egg, Rudolf. 1979. *Sozialtherapie und Strafvollzug*. Frankfurt: Haag und Herchen, 1979.

Egg, Rudolf. 1984. *Straffälligkeit und Sozialtherapie: Konzepte, Erfahrungen, Entwicklungsmöglichkeiten*. Cologne: Carl Heymann.

Eichler, Hans. 1938. "Die Entlassung aus der Sicherungsverwahrung." *BfG* 69: 265–83.

Eisenberg, Ulrich. 1969. "Zum Behandlungskonzept der sozialtherapeutischen Anstalten." *Neue Juristische Wochenschrift* 22: 1553–58.

Elster, Alexander, and Heinrich Lingemann, eds. 1936. *Handwörterbuch der Kriminologie und der anderen Strafrechtlichen Hilfswissenschaften* Vol. 2. Berlin: Walter de Gruyter.

Erlebach, E., U. Ihlefeld, and K. Zehner. 1971. *Psychologie für Lehrer und Erzieher*. Berlin: Volk und Wissen.

Eser, Albin. 1977. "Resozialisierung in der Krise?" In *Seminar: Abweichendes Verhalten III*, vol. 2, ed. Klaus Lüderssen and Fritz Sack, 276–90. Frankfurt: Suhrkamp.

Exner, Franz. 1936. "Aufgaben der Kriminologie im neuen Reich." *MfKuS* 27: 3–17.

Exner, Franz. 1937. "Bemerkungen zu dem vorstehenden Aufsatz von Dr. H. Trunk über 'Soziale Prognose an Strafgefangenen.'" *MfKuS* 28: 227–30.

Exner, Franz. 1934. "Das System der sichernden und bessernden Maßregeln nach dem Gesetz v. 24. November 1933." *ZfdgS* 53: 629–65.

Exner, Franz. 1935. *Kriminalistischer Bericht über eine Reise nach Amerika*. Berlin: Walter de Gruyter.

Exner, Franz. 1936. "Über Rückfall-Prognosen." *MfKuS* 27: 401–9.

Exner, Franz. 1943. "Wie erkennt man den gefährlichen Gewohnheitsverbrecher?" *Deutsche Justiz* 11 (6 August): 377–79.

Eyrich, Heinz. "Hat sich das Strafvollzugsgesetz bewährt?" In *10 Jahre Strafvollzugsgesetz: Resozialisierung als alleiniges Vollzugsziel?*, ed. Hans-Dieter Schwind, Gernot Steinhilper, and Alexander Böhm, 29–37. Heidelberg: Kriminalistik, 1988.

Fink. 1935. "Der zukünftige Strafvollzug." *MfKuS* 26: 537–40.

Fehlow, Paul. 1975. "Der weibliche Sexualstraftäter." *PNumP* 27: 612–18.

Fehlow, Paul. 1989. "Pädophil-voyeuristisches Verhalten." *PNumP* 41: 109–11.

Fehlow, Paul. 1980. "Zur Persönlichkeit des Notzuchtstraftäters." *PNumP* 32: 164–69.

Feige, Johannes. 1962. "Neue psychologische Methoden für die Behandlung der Gefangenen." *ZfS* 11: 316–26.

Feige, Johannes. 1954. "Über die Mitwirkung des Aufsichts- und Werkdienstes bei der Erfassung der Gefangenenpersönlichkeit." *ZfS* 4: 261–65.

Feix, Gerhard. 1961. *Die Bekämpfung von Sexualverbrechen an Kindern*. Berlin: Verlag des Ministeriums des Innern.

Fikentscher, E., H. Hinderer, K. Liebner, and H. Rennert. 1978. "Sexualstraftaten an Kindern und Jugendlichen unter Berücksichtigung latenter Kriminalität." *Kriminalistik und forensische Wissenschaften* 33: 67–82.

Finke. 1935. "Anlage und Umwelt als kriminalpädagogisches Problem." *MfGGE* 10: 67–69.

Freisler, Roland. 1938. "Ein Querschnitt durch die Fragen der Sicherungsverwahrung." In *Dringende Fragen der Sicherungsverwahrung, Gemeinschaftsarbeit aus der Praxis für die Praxis*, ed. Roland Freisler et al., 7–14. Berlin: R. von Decker's Verlag.

Freisler, Roland. 1941. "Gedanken über das Gesetz zur Änderung des Reichsstrafgesetzbuches." *Deutsche Justiz, Rechtspflege und Rechtspolitik* 103 (26 September): 929–38.

Freisler, Roland. 1942. "Wiedereingliederung—Abschlußteil des Strafrechts." *Monatsblätter für Straffälligenbetreuung und Ermittlungshilfe* 17: 6–10.

Freund, K., D. Sedlacek, and K. Knob. 1965. "A Simple Transducer for Mechanical Plethysmography of the Male Genital." *Journal of the Experimental Analysis of Behavior* 8: 169–70.

Fröhlich, Hans-H. 1980. "Die Sexualkriminalität im Blickwinkel menschlicher Sexualität und sexueller Normen." *Kriminalistik und forensische Wissenschaften* 41: 43–54.

Fröhlich, Hans-H. 1982. "Zur Konzeption und Methodik der Behandlung funktioneller Sexualstörungen—Erfahrungen und Probleme." *PNumP* 34: 554–62.

Fuchs, Thomas, ed. 2011. *Strafgesetzbuch für das Deutsche Reich vom 15. Mail 1871: Historisch-synoptische Edition 1871–2011*. Mannheim: Lexetius.com.

Gallmeier, Michael 1954. "Das Klassifizieren in der Strafanstalt als Gemeinschaftsleistung." *ZfS* 4: 252–60.

Geerds, Friedrich. 1960. "Zur kriminologischen Prognose." *MfKuS* 43: 92–119.

Gentz, Werner. 1925. "Der moderne Strafvollzug." *ZfdgS* 6: 132–33.

Gentz, Werner. 1948. "Reform des Stravollzuges." In *Beiträge zur Demokratisierung der Justiz*, ed. Max Fechner, 231–57. Berlin: Dietz.

Gentz, Werner. 1948. "Straffälligen-, Gefangenen-, und Entlassenenfürsorge." *Neue Justiz* 2: 72.

Gerchow, Joachim. 1957. *Die ärztlich-forensische Beurteilung von Kindesmörderinnen*. Halle: Carl Marhold.

Gerchow, Joachim. 1955. "Neue Ergebnisse über die Bedeutung soziologischer, psychologischer und psychopathologischer Faktoren bei Inzesttätern der Nachkriegszeit." *MfKuS* 38: 168–83.

Gerecke, Werner. 1937–38. "Eindrücke vom Strafvollzug im Staate New York." *BfG* 68: 379–83.

Gerecke, Werner. 1939. "Zur Frage der Rückfallprognose." *MfKuS* 29: 35–38.

Gertig, B., and R. Schädlich. 1955. *Lehrbuch für Kriminalisten: Die allgemeinen Verfahren und Arbeitsmethoden der Kriminalistik*. Berlin: Verlag für Fachliteratur der Volkspolizei.

Glueck, Sheldon, and Eleanor Glueck. 1930. *500 Criminal Careers*. New York: Knopf.

Goderbauer, Rainer. 1984. "Soziales Training im Strafvollzug." *ZfSuS* 33: 13–18.

Goderbauer, Rainer, and Rudolf Engell. 1988. "Aus der Sozialtherapeutischen Anstalt Baden- Württemberg." *ZfS* 37: 84–87.

Goehl. 1954. "Der Besserungsgedanke in den Justizvollzugsanstalten." *ZfS* 4: 59–63.

Gold, C., and R. Gold. 1980. "Zur Problematik der befristeten ärztlichen Einweisung durch Anordnung bei Alkoholismus: Ein kritischer Beitrag zur Anwendung des Gesetzes über die Einweisung in stationäre Einrichtunge für psychisch Kranke vom 11. Juni 1968." MD diss., Akademie für Ärztliche Fortbildung der DDR.

Greger, J., and E. Popella. 1968. "Zur forensisch-psychiatrischen Beurteilung motivisch unklarer Diebstähle." *PNumP* 20: 302–12.

Gregor, Adalbert, and Albert Zink. 1942. "Soziale Eingliederung und Prognose aus dem Jugendgefängnis Entlassener." *BfG* 72: 241–91.

Greiner, H. B. 1952. "Persönlichkeitsforschung im Strafvollzug." *ZfS* 3: 52–59.

Gruhle, Hans W. 1953. "Die Unterbringung psychopathischer Verbrecher." *MfKuS* 36: 6- 10.

Grunau, Th. 1954. "Die Persönlichkeitsforschung im Schleswig-Holsteinischen Strafvollzug." *ZfS* 4: 270–76.

Gummersbach, H. 1934. "Die Erziehung zur Lebenstauglichkeit als Strafvollzugsziel der Reformen." *Monatsblätter des Deutschen Reichszusammenschlusses für Gerichtshilfe, Gefangenen- und Entlassenenfürsorge der freien Wohlfahrtspflege* 9 (January–February): 11–17.

Gummersbach, H. 1934. "Die Neugestaltung des italienischen Strafvollzugs im Vergleich mit den deutschen Reformen." *MfKuS* 25: 369–82.

Hacker, E. 1935. "Beiträge zum Problem der rückfälligen und unverbesserlichen Verbrecher." *MfKuS* 26: 247–53.

Harbordt, Steffen. 1972. *Die Subkultur des Gefängnisses: Eine soziologische Studie zur Resozialisierung*. 2nd ed. Stuttgart: Enke.

Harno, Albert J., Andrew A. Bruce, Ernest W. Burgess, and John Landesco. 1928. *The Workings of the Indeterminate-Sentence Law and the Parole System in Illinois*. Chicago: State of Illinois.

Hegemann. 1941. "Zu der Frage nach Überlegung bei einer Anklage auf Mord." *Allgemeine Zeitschrift für Psychiatrie und ihre Grenzgebiete* 118: 380–91.

Heim, Michael, and Joachim Morgner. 1985. "Der pädophile Straftäter." *PNumP* 37: 107–12.

Heinsius, W. 1954. "Persönlichkeitserforschung und Seelsorge." *ZfS* 4: 315–20.

Heldmann, Ina. 1952. "Auf die Atmosphäre kommt es an?" *ZfS* 3: 118–21.

Hellmund, Siegfried. 1975. "Pastoralpsychologie in der Gefangenenfürsorge." *ZfS* 24: 101–5.

Hess, Albert Günter. 1934. *Die Kinderschändung: Unter besonderer Berücksichtigung der Tatsituation*. Leipzig: Ernst Wiegandt.

Hesse, Peter, et al., ed. 1974–78. *Sexuologie: Geschlecht, Mensch, Gesellschaft*. 3 vols. Leipzig: Hirzel.

Heydt, Arthur von der. 1952. *Querulatorische Entwicklungen*. Halle: Marhold.

Heyme,Torsten, and Felix Schumann. 1991. *"Ich kam mir vor wie'n Tier"—Knast in der DDR*. Berlin: BasisDruck.

Hiebsch, Hans, and Reiner Werner. 1968. "Aufgaben der forensischen Psychologie." *Neue Justiz* 22: 713–15.

Hilbers, Marlene, and Wolf Lange. 1973. "Abkehr von der Behandlungsideologie?" *Kriminologisches Journal* 5: 52–59.

Hilgenfeldt. 1942. "Kriegsaufgaben der Straffälligenbetreuung." *Monatsblätter für Straffälligenbetreuung und Ermittlungshilfe* 17: 1–5.

Hoeniger, Walther. 1947. "Bewährungseinsatz statt Strafvollzug." *Neue Justiz* 1: 178–80.

Hoeniger, Walther. 1948. "Über das richtige Strafmaß und verwandte Probleme." In *Beiträge zur Demokratisierung der Justiz*, ed. Max Fechner, 211–28, Berlin: Dietz.

Hohmeier, Jürgen. 1973. *Aufsicht und Resozialisierung*. Stuttgart: Ferdinand Enke.

Hürten, Ferdinand. 1937. "Die ersten Hundert auf Grund des Gesetzes vom 24. November 1933 in der westfälischen Prov.-Heilanstalt Eickelborn untergebrachten geistig abnormen Rechtsbrecher." *Allgemeine Zeitschrift für Psychiatrie und Psychisch-Gerichtliche Medizin* 106: 255–338.

International Society for Criminology. 1960. *4th International Criminological Congress*. Hague: CIC.

Jähnig, Heide-Ulrike, and Eckard Littmann, eds. 1985. *Kriminalpsychologie und Kriminalpsychopathologie*. Jena: Gustav Fischer.

Jankowski, Maria. 1955. "Zusammentstellung methodischer und organisatorischer Gesichtspunkte bei der Ausbildung vor allem der Aufsichtsbeamten." *ZfS* 5: 16–26.

Jarosch, K. 1960. "Zur Psychopathologie einzelner Deliktformen." *PNumP* 12: 266–73.

Jensch, Nikolaus. 1944. *Untersuchungen an entmannten Sittlichkeitsverbrechern*. Leipzig: Georg Thieme.

Jensen, A. R. 1958. "The Maudsley Personality Inventory." *Acta Psychologica* 14: 314–25.

Jescheck, Hans-Heinrich. 1979. "Die Krise der Kriminalpolitik." *ZfdgS* 91: 1037–64.

Jung, Hans Heike. 1974. "Ist der Alternativ-Entwurf eine Alternative oder Utopie?" *ZfS* 23: 50–57.

Kaiser, Günther. 1987. "Das deutsche Strafvollzug in internationaler vergleichender Sicht." *ZfSuS* 36: 24–31.

Kaiser, Günther, ed. 1985. *Kleines kriminologisches Wörterbuch*. Heidelberg: C. F. Müller.

Kaiser, Günther. 1977. "Resozialisierung und Zeitgeit." In *Kultur, Kriminalität, Strafrecht*, ed. Rüdiger Herren, Diethelm Keinapfel, and Heinz Müller-Dietz, 359–72. Berlin: Duncker und Humblot.

Kaiser, Günther. 1975. *Stand und Entwicklung der kriminologischen Forschung in Deutschland*. Berlin: Walter de Gruyter.

Kaiser, Günther, Heinz Schöch, Hans-Heinrich Eidt, and Hans-Jürgen Kerner. 1974. *Strafvollzug: Eine Einführung in die Grundlagen*. Karlsruhe: C. F. Müller Juristischer Verlag.

Kampen, Wolfgang, und Theo Rasehorn. 1972. "Die Einstellung der Bevölkerung der Bundesrepublik zum Strafrecht und Strafvollzug." *Zeitschrift für Rechtspolitik* 5: 21–22.

Kampmann, Erik. 1934. "Das Gefängniswesen in Dänemark nach dem neuen Strafgesetz von 1930." *BfG* 65: 95–118.

Kapp, Franz. 1935. "Kriminal-psychotherapeutische Einzelfälle." Part 1, "Ein Neurotiker mit Mordphantasien," and part 2, "Ein Neurotiker mit vielseitigen (polytropen) verbrecherischen Neigungen." *Allgemeine Zeitschrift für Psychiatrie und psychischgerichtliche Medizin* 103: 1–25.

Kapp, Franz. 1937. "Über die Beobachtungsabteilungen bei den Gefangenenanstalten der Justizverwaltung." *Zeitschrift für psychische Hygiene* 10: 3–15.

Kern, Herbert. 1958. *Die Erziehung im Strafvollzug*. Berlin: VEB Deutscher Zentralverlag.

Kersten, Günther. 1939. "Besonderheiten in der Betreuung weiblicher Strafgefangener." *Monatsblätter für Straffälligenbetreuung und Ermittlungshilfe*. 14 (January): 49–56.

Kertész, Imre. 1970. "Zu einigen Problemen der kriminalpsychologischen Methodologie." *Kriminalistik und forensische Wissenschaften* 1: 63–68.

Keyserlingk, H. v. 1951. "Psychopathische Persönlichkeiten, ihre Kriminalität und ihre Stellung vor dem Gesetz." *PNumP* 3: 180–90, 207–22.

Koch, Rudolf. 1940. *Über Sittlichkeitsverbrecher*. Leipzig: Ernst Wiegandt.

Kolb, Lothar. 1979. *Mitwirkung Strafgefangener im Erziehungsprozeß*. Berlin: Ministerium des Innern.

Kolb, Lothar, and Siegfried Klarhöfer. 1988. *Zur Erhöhung der erzieherischen Wirksamkeit des Vollzuges der Freiheitsstrafe*. Berlin: Hochschule der Deutschen Volkspolizei.

Kothe, A. 1933. "Der Wert der Persönlichkeit im Strafvollzuge." *MfKuS* 24: 602–9.

Kothe, A. 1935. "Zum künftigen Strafvollzug." *MfKuS* 26: 127–35.

Kozarska-Dworska, Jadwig. 1972. "Die Rehabilitation von Psychopathen im Strafvollzug." *Kriminalistik und forensische Wissenschaften* 8: 57–71.

Krebs, Albert. 1954. "Das Berufsbild des Strafanstaltsfürsorgers." *ZfS* 4: 51–53.

Krebs, Albert. 1950. "Die Durchführung der Kontrollratsdirektive Nr. 19 in den vier Besatzungszonen Deutschlands, insbesondere in der US-Zone (1)." *ZfS* 1: 17–29.

Krebs, Albert. 1954. "Entwicklung der Persönlichkeitsforschung im deutschen Gefängniswesen." *ZfS* 4: 241–52.

Krebs, Albert. 1955. "Kulturnationen erörtern Strafvollzugsfragen." Part 2, "Bericht über den 3. Kriminologenkongreß in London." *ZfS* 5: 333–50.

Krempler, Herbert. 1939. *Die Sittlichkeitsdelikte im Bezirk des Landgerichts Eisenach in den Jahren 1905–1936*. Jena: Frommann.

Kretschmar. 1942. "Die Sächsische Straffälligenbetreuung." *Monatsblätter für Straffälligenbetreuung und Ermittlungshilfe* 17: 60–62.

Krott, Eberhard. 1987. "Kognitive Therapie—eine Möglichkeit kurzfristiger psychotherapeutischer Intervention im Strafvollzug." *ZfSuS* 36: 278–81.

Krüger, Fritz. 1940. "Die Aufgaben der Gefangenenfürsorge im Kriege." *Monatsblätter für Straffälligenbetreuung und Ermittlungshilfe* 16: 4–6.

Krüger, Hans. 1956. "Die Kriminalpsychologische Abteilung der Gefängnisbehörde der Freien und Hansestadt Hamburg." *ZfS* 6: 243–56, 299–312, 366–77.

Krüger, Hans. 1952. "Richter und Täterpsychologie: Fehlerquellen bei der Persönlichkeitsbewertung des Angeklagten." *Deutsche Richterzeitung* 30: 54–57.

Krüger-Thiemer, F. 1951. "Zur psychoanalytischen Studie 'Der Sexualverbrecher.'" *Zeitschrift für die gesamte kriminalistische Wissenschaft und Praxis* 5: 88–91.

Krutoff, Anne. 1951. "Ein sozialhygienischer Beitrag zum Strafvollzugsproblem." MD diss., Humboldt University of Berlin.

Krüttner, Fred. 1952–53. "Nochmals: Erziehungsstrafvollzug." *ZfS* 3: 330–34.

Kühler, Hans. 1955. "Zur Behandlung der sexuell Straffälligen im Ausland." *MfKuS* 38: 93–108.

Kühn, Ernst. 1942. "Kriminalpsychiatrische Untersuchungen an geistig abnormen politischen Rechtsbrechern." *Allgemine Zeitschrift für Psychiatrie und ihre Grenzgebiete* 120: 158–85.

Kury, Helmut. 1987. *Die Behandlung Straffälliger*. Vol. 2. Berlin: Duncker und Humblot.

Langelüddeke, Albrecht. 1963. *Die Entmannung von Sittlichkeitsverbrechern*. Berlin: Walter de Gruyter.

Langelüddeke, Albrecht. 1943. "Resozialisierung durch Entmannung: Bemerkungen zu der gleichnamigen Arbeit von W. Meywerk." *MfKuS* 34: 148–53.

Lemke, Eva. 1936. "Hausbesuch und Familienforschung, eine wichtige Vorarbeit zweckmäßiger Gefangenen- und Entlassenenfürsorge." *MfGGE* 11: 164–69.

Leonhard, Karl. 1957. *Aufteilung der endogenen Psychosen*. Berlin: Akademie-Verlag.

Leonhard, Karl. 1948. *Grundlagen der Psychiatrie*. Stuttgart: Ferdinand Enke.

Leonhard, Karl. 1963. *Individualtherapie der Neurosen*. Jena: Gustav Fischer.

Leonhard, Karl. 1964. *Instinkte und Urinstinkte in der menschlichen Sexualität*. Stuttgart: Ferdinand Enke.

Leonhard, Karl. 1968. "Was ist eine Sexualstörung?" *PNumP* 20: 1–3.

Leonhard, Karl, and Sieglinde von Trostorff. 1964. *Prognostische Diagnose der endogenen Psychosen*. Jena: Gustav Fischer.

Lewark. 1935. "Resozialisierungsmaßnahmen." *MfGGE* 10: 139–41.

Liebner, K. 1969. "Das EEG bei Psychopathen." *PNumP* 21: 373–76.

Linden, Herbert. 1939. "Bekämpfung der Sittlichkeitsverbrechen mit ärztlichen Mitteln." *Allgemeine Zeitschrift für Psychiatrie und ihre Grenzgebiete* 112: 405–23.

Liszt, Franz von. 1883. "Der Zweckgedanke im Strafrecht." *ZfdgS* 3: 1–47.

Lotz, Ludwig. 1939. *Der gefährliche Gewohnheitsverbrecher*. Leipzig: Ernst Wiegandt.

Lüttger, Hans, ed. 1972. *Festschrift für Ernst Heinitz zum 70. Geburtstag*. Berlin: Walter de Gruyter.

Maelicke, Bernd. 1975. "Möglichkeiten und Grenzen der Resozialisierung." *ZfSuS* 24: 198–203.

Mallow, Siegfried. 1933. *Beitrag zur Kastration von Sexualverbrechern*. Leipzig: August Hoffmann.

Martinson, Robert. 1974. "What Works? Questions and Answers about Prison Reform." *Public Interest* 35: 22–54.

Mauch, Gerhard, and Roland Mauch. 1971. *Sozialtherapie und die sozialtherapeutische Anstalt: Erfahrung in der Behandlung Chronisch-Krimineller*. Stuttgart: Ferdinand Enke.

Maurach, Reinhart. 1933. "Der neue Strafvollzug in Sowjetrußland." *MfKuS* 24: 705-19.

Mayer, Hellmuth. 1966. "Resozialisierungsbedürftigkeit, -Willigkeit, und -Fähigkeit der Straftäter." *ZfS* 15: 323–99.

Mayer, Ludwig. 1975. "Reformaufgaben im Justizvollzug und ihre Voraussetzungen." *ZfSuS* 24: 125–28.

Mayr, Hans. 1937. "Die Entlassung aus der Sicherungsverwahrung: Bisherige süddeutsche Erfahrungen." *MfKuS* 28: 84–86.

Mehner, Heinrich, Gerhard Meier, and Hermann Bodenburg. 1972. *Die Erziehung der Strafgefangenen zu Ordnung und Disziplin: Anerkennungen, Disziplinar- und Sicherungsmaßnahmen*. Berlin: Ministerium des Innern.

Meixner, Franz. 1951. "Kriminalität und Sexualität." *Kriminalistik* 5: 134–37.

Menke, Volker. 1973. "Ausländische Gefangene im Strafvollzug." *ZfS* 22: 41–43.

Meyer, Alfred, Franz Irro, and Rudi Rödszus. 1974. "Informatischer Bericht über die Tätigkeit von Expertengruppen zur Bekämpfung der Rückfallfrkiminalität und Erziehung kriminell Gefährdeter und die Möglichkeiten der Psychiater, dabei wirksam mitzuhelfen." *PNumP* 26: 98–103.

Meyer, Klaus. 1987. "Zehn Jahre Strafvollzugsgesetz—das Gesetz im Rückblick." *ZfSuS* 36: 4–11.

Meywerk, Wilhelm. 1938. "Beitrag zur Bestimmung der sozialen Prognose an Rückfallsverbrechern." *MfKuS* 29: 422–44.

Meywerk, Wilhelm. 1943. "Resozialisierung durch Entmannung." *MfKuS* 34: 1–61.

Mezger, Edmund. 1932. "Arbeitsmethode und Bedeutung der kriminalbiologischen Untersuchungsstellen für Strafrechtspflege." *MfKuS* 23: 415–16.

Mezger, Edmund. 1923. "Die Behandlung der gefährlichen Gewohnheitsverbrecher." *MfKuS* 14: 135–75.

Ministerium des Innern [Alfred Meyer, Otto Adam, and Lothar Bohmüller]. 1970. *Die Wiedereingliederung Strafentlassener in das gesellschaftliche Leben und die Erziehung kriminell gefährdeter Bürger*. Berlin: Ministerium des Innern.

[Ministry of Interior of the USSR, ed.]. 1970–73. *Beiträge zur Strafvollzugspsychologie*. Vols. 1–4. Berlin: Ministerium des Innern.

[Ministry of Interior of the USSR]. 1970. *Lehrbuch der Strafvollzugspädagogik*. Berlin: Ministerium des Innern.

Mittermaier, Wolfgang. 1954. *Gefängniskunde: Ein Lehrbuch für Studium und Praxis*. Berlin: Franz Vahlen.

Mittermaier, Wolfgang. 1954. "Neue Entwicklungen im deutschen Strafvollzug." *ZfS* 4: 33–36.

Möller, Heinz. 1939. *Die Entwicklung und Lebensverhältnisse von 135 Gewohnheitsverbrechern*. Leipzig: Ernst Wiegandt, 1939.

Morgner, Joachim. 1977. "Exhibitionistische sexuelle Fehlentwicklungen." *Kriminalistik und forensische Wissenschaften* 30: 105–8.

Müller, Karl. 1971. "Über das Suchtproblem bei sexuellen Deviationen." *PNumP* 23: 267–73.

Müller-Dietz, Heinz, ed. 1974. *Kriminaltherapie heute*. Berlin: Walter de Gruyter.

Narr, Wilhelm. 1936. "Der Erziehungsgedanke und seine Verwirklichung im Strafvollzug." *Die deutsche Sonderschule* 2: 933–35.

Nass, Gustav, 1954. "Unzucht mit Kindern—das Sexualdelikt unserer Zeit, Ursachen und Bekämpfung." *MfKuS* 37: 69–82.

Neulandt, Günther. 1961. "Zum Problem der sogenannten Resozialisierung." *ZfS* 10: 325–31.

Neureiter, Ferdinand von. 1940. *Kriminalbiologie*. Berlin: Carl Heymann, 1940.

Pakesch, Erich. 1961. "Der Einfluß des Strafvollzuges auf die Psyche des Häftlings." *MfKuS* 44: 65–85.

Panse. 1956. "Die psychologiche Problematik des Strafvollzugs im Hinblick auf den Besserungsgedanken." *MfKuS* 39: 5–17.

Pietsch, K. 1957. "Der Psychotherapeut in der Strafanstalt." *ZfS* 7: 102–16, 143–55.

Piroshkov, W. F. 1972. "Der Gegenstand, die Aufgaben und die Methoden der sowjetischen Strafvollzugspsychologie." In *Beiträge zur Strafvollzugspsychologie*, [ed. Ministry of Interior of the USSR], 3:13–59. Berlin: Ministerium des Innern.

Plenge, Hermann. 1961. "Die Behandlung erheblich rückfälliger Sexualdelinquenten vornehmlich der Homosexuellen, unter besonderer Berücksichtigung der Kastration." *MfKuS* 44: 15–41.

Possehl, Kurt. 1970. "Zum Image des Aufsichtsbediensteten." In *Selbstbild und Fremdbild der Aufsichtsbeamten im Strafvollzug*, 43–111. Stuttgart: Ferdinand Enke.

Quentin, Leopold, and Rudolf Sieverts. 1937. "Die Behandlung der jungen Rechtsbrecher im Alter von 17 bis 23 Jahren in England unter besonderer Berücksichtigung des Borstal-Systems." *BfG* 68: 165–239.

Rasch, Wilfried. 1967. "Die Errichtung von Bewahrungsanstalten: Vorplanung und erste Schritte." *MfKuS* 50: 339–44.

Rasch, Wilfried, ed. 1977. *Forensische Sozialtherapie: Erfahrungen in Düren*. Karlsruhe: C. F. Müller Jurististischer Verlag.

Rath, Charlotte Maria. 1987. "Die Kritik am Behandlungsvollzug." JD diss., Georg-August-Universität Göttingen.

Ratinow, A. R. 1970. *Forensische Psychologie für Untersuchungsführer*. Berlin: Ministerium des Innern.

Rattenhuber, Franz. 1939. *Der gefährliche Sittlichkeitsverbrecher*. Bottrop: Wilhelm Postberg.

Rennert, Helmut. 1954. "Psychiatrische Betrachtungen zum Inzest und seiner Verbreitung." *PNumP* 6: 80–87.

Rieber, Inge, and Volkmar Sigusch. 1979. "Psychosurgery on Sex Offenders and Sexual 'Deviants' in West Germany." *Archives of Sexual Behavior* 8: 523–27.

Rieger, Walter. 1975. "Die Subkultur im Strafvollzug." *ZfSuS* 24: 218–21.

Reuter, Fritz. 1936. *Aufartung durch Ausmerzung*. Berlin: Reimar Hobbing.

Ritter, Robert. 1942. "Die Artung jugendlicher Rechtsbrecher." *Deutsches Jugendrecht* 4: 33–60.

Rodewald. 1937. "Entmannung und Entmannungsuntersuchungen: Text und Erläuterung der AV des Reichsjustizministers vom 10. Okt 1936." *MfKuS* 28: 3–11.

Rohden, Friedrich von. 1933. "Gibt es unverbesserliche Verbrecher?" *MfKuS* 24: 74–92.

Rohlfs. 1954. "Wie helfen wir den Sittlichkeitsverbrechern?" *MfKuS* 37: 113–14.

Röhner, K.-H. 1982. "Bedeutung und Rolle einer ungenügenden Sexualerziehung für die Begehung gewaltsamer Sexualstraftaten durch Jugendliche." *Kriminalistik und forensische Wissenschaften* 45: 101–6.

Rösler, Hans-Dieter, Hans-Dieter Schmidt, and Hans Szewczyk, eds. 1970. *Persönlichkeitsdiagnostik: Probleme und Ergebnisse persönlichkeitsdiagnostischer Forschungen in der klinischen Psychologie der DDR*. Berlin: Deutsche Verlag der Wissenschaften.

Rossner, Mahnolf. 1979. "Zur Frage der operativen Kastration von Sexualdelinquenten—Aktuelle Literaturübersicht und der Ansatz einer Meinungsbildung." *PNumP* 31: 321–29.

Rupperath. 1937. "Individuelle Behandlung der Gefangenen." *MfGGE* 12: 115–20.

Saupe, Volker, and Brigitte Wende. 1985. "Gruppengesprächstherapie mit ausgewählten forensisch-psychiatrischen Patienten (Dissoziale Fehlentwicklung)." *PNumP* 37: 300–304.

Schaffstein, Friedrich. 1936. "Die Bedeutung des Erziehungsgedankens im neuen deutschen Strafvollzug." *ZfdgS* 55: 275–90.

Schaffstein, Friedrich. 1939. "Vorbeugungshaft, Verwahrung, und Bewahrung." *ZfdgS* 58: 307–13.

Schafheutle, Josef. 1955. "Der erste Kongreß der Vereinten Nationen über Verbrechenverhütung und Behandlung von Straffälligen vom 22. August bis 3. September 1955 in Genf." *ZfS* 5: 259–64.

Schafheutle, Josef, and Fritz Hauptvogel. 1936. "Sicherungsverwahrung." In *Handwörterbuch der Kriminologie und der anderen Strafrechtlichen Hilfswissenschaften*, vol. 2, ed. Alexander Elster and Heinrich Lingemann, 597–610. Berlin: Walter de Gruyter.

Schiedt, Robert. 1936. *Ein Beitrag zum Problem der Rückfallsprognose*. Munich: Münchener Zeitungs-Verlag.

Schiefer. 1938. "Der Verwahrungsvollzug in der Sicherungsanstalt Waldheim." *BfG* 68: 448–65.

Schläger. 1944. "Abartige Geisteszustände und die Rechtsprechung." *Allgemeine Zeitschrift für Psychiatrie und ihre Grenzgebiete* 123: 112–21.

Schleyer, F. 1958. "Studien über das Delikt der gewalttätigen Kindesmißhandlung." *MfKuS* 41: 65–76.

Schmidt, E. 1937. "Sinn und Zweck des Strafvollzugs." *BfG* 68: 42–52.

Schmidt, Hans-Dieter. 1970. *Allgemeine Entwicklungspsychologie*. Berlin: Deutscher Verlag der Wissenschaften.

Schmieschek, Hansgeorg. 1977. "Verhaltenstherapie bei sexuellen Deviationen." *PNumP* 29: 725–31.

Schmitz, Käte. 1938. "Soziale Stellung—äußere Faktoren in ihrer Bedeutung für die Beurteilung der rechtsbrecherischen Frau." *Monatsblätter für Straffälligenbetreuung und Ermittlungshilfe* 13: 129–32.

Schnabl, Siegfried. 1972. *Intimverhalten, Sexualstörungen, Persönlichkeit.* Berlin: Deutscher Verlag der Wissenschaften.

Schneickert, Hans. 1942. "Die Schwierigkeit der Charakterbestimmung." *Archiv für Kriminalpsychologie* 111: 86–91.

Schneider, Kurt. 1935. *Pathopsychologie der Gefühle und Triebe: Ein Grundriss.* Leipzig: Georg Thieme.

Schnell, Karl. 1935. *Anlage und Umwelt bei 500 Rückfallsverbrechern: Ein Beitrag zum Problem des Gewohnheitsverbrechertums erarbeitet an einem Material der Bayerischen Kriminalbiologischen Sammelstelle.* Leipzig: Ernst Wiegandt.

Scholz, Hedwig. 1953. *Sie sollen wieder vollwertige Menschen werden: Über den demokratischen Strafvollzug in der Deutschen Demokratischen Republik.* Berlin: Verlag Kultur und Fortschritt.

Schottky, Johannes. 1941. "Psychiatrische und kriminalbiologische Fragen bei der Unterbringung in einer Heil- und Pflegeanstalt nach § 42b and c des Strafgesetzbuches." *Allgmemeine Zeitschrift für Psychiatrie und ihre Grenzgebiete* 117: 287–355.

Schulz, H., and G. Mainusch. 1969. "Beitrag der klinischen Elektroencephalographie zur forensischen Begutachtung." *PNumP* 21: 266–75.

Schwaab, Fritz. 1939. *Die soziale Prognose bei rückfälligen Vermögensverbrechern.* Leipzig: Ernst Wiegandt.

Schwarz, Hanns, ed. 1961. *Das milieubeschädigtes Kind.* Jena: Gustav Fischer.

Schwarz, Hanns, ed. 1971. *Kriminalität der Frau—Alterskriminalität—Psychiatrische Begutachtungsfrage im Zivilrecht.* Jena: Gustav Fischer.

Schwind, Hans-Dieter, Ulrich Jany, and Rüdiger Wohlgemuth. 1976. "Der Resozialisierungsgedanke gewinnt an Boden." *ZfSuS* 25: 103–9.

Schwind, Hans-Dieter, Gernot Steinhilper, and Alexander Böhm, ed. 1988. In *10 Jahre Strafvollzugsgesetz: Resozialisierung als alleiniges Vollzugsziel?* Heidelberg: Kriminalistik.

Seifart, Wolfgang. 1968. "Zur Rolle der Information und Dokumentation bei der prognostischen Tätigkeit der Rechtspflegeorgane." *Neue Justiz* 22: 13–14.

Siebenbrodt, Joachim, ed. 1969. *Bericht über den 2. Kongreß der Gesellschaft für Psychologie in der DDR.* Berlin: Deutscher Verlag der Wissenschaften.

Sieber. 1940. "Die Ehre als Schnittpunkt in der Tendenz des Strafvollzuges, der Straffälligenbetreuung und Strafanstaltsseelsorge." *BfG* 71: 53–60.

Sieverts, Rudolf. 1960. "The Evolution of Sexual Criminality in the Federal Republic of Germany." In *Sexual Crime Today*, ed. Institute of Criminal Law and Criminology of the University of Leiden, 51–75. Hague: Martinus Nijhoff.

Silbereisen, Sigmund. 1940. *Die spätere Straffälligkeit jugendlicher Rechtsbrecher: Eine Nachuntersuchung über die im Jahre 1928 in München verurteilten Jugendlichen.* Leipzig: Ernst Wiegandt.

Sozialdemokratische Partei Deutschlands. 1953. "Das Programm der Sozialdemokratischen Partei Deutschlands zur Strafrechtsreform." *MfKuS* 36: 51–52.

Staatsrat der Deutschen Demokratischen Republik. 1963. *Rechtpflegeerlaß—bedeutsame Weiterentwicklung unserer sozialistischen Demokratie*. Berlin: Staatsverlag der Deutschen Demokratischen Republik.

Statistisches Bundesamt. *Statistisches Jahrbuch für die Bundesrepublik Deutschland, 1962–1991*. Stuttgart: W. Kohlhammer, 1962–91.

Steigertahl, Georg. 1937. "Die Zusammenhänge zwischen Zwangsfürsorge und Maßregeln der Sicherung und Besserung in Hamburg." *MfKuS* 28: 128–40.

Steinwallner, Bruno. 1934. "Faschistischer Strafvollzug: Die italienische Strafvollzugsverordnung von 1931." *BfG* 65: 191–200.

Stettner. 1934. "Die Erziehung im deutschen Strafwesen, von der Strafentlassenenfürsorge aus gesehen." *Monatsblätter des Deutschen Reichszusammenschlusses für Gerichtshilfe, Gefangenen- und Entlassenenfürsorge der freien Wohlfahrtspflege* 9 (January–February): 40–64.

Stiller, Gerhard, ed. 1964. *Kriminalitätsursachen und ihre Überwindung*. Berlin: Staatsverlag der Deutschen Demokratischen Republik.

Stiller, Gerhard. 1965. "Theoretische und methodologische Grundlagen der kriminologischen Forschungen in der Deutschen Demokratischen Republik." Habilitationsschrift, Wiss. Scientific Council of the Institute for State and Legal Science Research of the "Walter Ulbricht" German Academy for State and Legal Science, Potsdam-Babelsberg.

Stiller, Gerhard. 1968. "Zur Rolle der Prognose in der bürgerlichen Kriminologie." *Neue Justiz* 22: 599–601.

Strauss, Ewald Heinz, and Jürgen Mehl. 1977. "Zu einigen neueren Problemen und Ergebnissen der Verhaltenstherapie." *PNumP* 29: 705–11.

Streitberg, Gerald. 1975. "Die Behandlung von Sexualstraftätern im Vollzug." *ZfS* 24: 147–54.

Striehn, Otto. 1938. *Kastration nach § 14 II des Gesetzes zur Verhütung erbkranken Nachwuchses und nach § 42 k des Reichsstrafgesetzbuches unter Berücksichtigung der an der Kreis-Heil- und Pflegeanstalt zu Frankenthal vorhandenen Fälle*. Bleicherode: Carl Nieft.

Strüder. 1933. "Gedanken über die Erziehbarkeit der Zuchthausgefangenen." *MfKuS* 24: 519–25.

Stube, Ellen. 1974. "Probleme der Seelsorge im Strafvollzug." *ZfS* 23: 213–21.

Sturm, Ernst. 1951. "Die Zunahme der Sexualverbrechen." *Zeitschrift für die gesamte kriminalistische Wissenschaft und Praxis* 5: 32–35.

Stürup, Georg K. 1968. *Treating the Untreatable: Chronic Criminals at Herstedvester*. Baltimore: Johns Hopkins University Press.

Stürup, Georg K. 1952. "The Treatment of Criminal Psychopaths in Herstedvester." *British Journal of Medical Psychology* 25: 31–38.

Suttinger, Günther. 1960. "Persönlichkeit und Strafvollzug." *MfKuS* 43: 1–19, 76–91.

Suttinger, Günther. 1950. "Über die Tätigkeit des Psychologen im Strafvollzug insbesondere im Jugendvollzug." *ZfS* 1: 12–17.

Szewczyk, Hans. 1978. "Die Bedeutung sexueller Erlebnisse für die Persönlichkeits- und Sexualentwicklung von Kindern und Jugendlichen." In *Sexualität: Fakten, Normen, gesellschaftliche Verwantwortung*, ed. Hans Szewczyk and Horst Burghardt, 192–202. Berlin: Verlag Volk und Gesundheit.

Szewczyk, Hans, ed. 1966. *Die Begutachtung und Behandlung erwachsener und jugendlicher Täter: Bericht über das III. Internationale Symposion "Über aktuelle Fragen der Gerichtspsychiatrie," 21. bis 23. 9. 1964, Charité zu Berlin*. Jena: Gustav Fischer.

Szewczyk, Hans, ed. 1964. *Die Gerichtspsychiatrie in der neuen Rechtspflege: Bericht über das Symposion "Über aktuelle Fragen der Gerichtspsychiatrie," 8. und 9. März 1963, Charite zu Berlin*. Jena: Gustav Fischer.

Szewczyk, Hans. 1969. "Die 'seelische Notlage' als Motiv für Tötungsdelikte." *PNumP* 21: 262–65.

Szewczyk, Hans, ed. 1972. *Kriminalität und Persönlichkeit: Psychiatrisch-psychologische strafrechtliche Aspekte*. Jena: Gustav Fischer.

Szkibik, Heinz. 1969. *Sozialistischer Strafvollzug: Erziehung durch Arbeit*. Berlin: Staatsverlag der Deutschen Demokratischen Republik.

Thierack. 1936. "Der Strafvollzug im Dienste der Volksgemeinschaft." *MfGGE* 11: 209–15.

Trunk, Hans. 1937. "Soziale Prognose an Strafgefangenen." *MfKuS* 28: 209–27.

Trunk, Hans. 1936. "Unterbringung in Heil- und Pflegeanstalten als Sicherheitsmaßnahme." *Zeitschrift für psychische Hygiene* 9: 120–26.

Viernstein, Theodor. 1922. "Die Einführung eines Stufensystems in den bayrischen Strafanstalten." *Zeitschrift für Medizinalbeamte* 35: 538–53.

Vietze, G. 1976. "Indikationen, Kontraindikationen, und rechtliche Problematik bei der Antiandrogen-Behandlung." *PNumP* 28: 684–89.

Vogelsang, Heinz. 1935. "Organisatorischer Aufbau und Zielsetzung der neuen deutschen Straffälligenfürsorge." *MfGGE* 10: 152–57.

Voigtländer, Else. 1937. "Über den Strafvollzug an Frauen." *BfG* 68: 268–78.

Vorstand der Gesellschaft für Psychologie in der DDR, ed. 1965. *Psychologie als gesellschaftliche Prodkuktivkraft: Bericht über den 1. Kongreß der Gesellschaft für Psychologie in der DDR vom 21.–23. Mai 1964 in Dresden*. Berlin: Deutscher Verlag der Wissenschaften.

Wagner, Gerhard. 1974. "Zur Motivation der Brandstiftung." *PNumP* 26: 155–64.

Wannemacher, Sebastian. 1955. "Stand der Persönlichkeitsforschung im Strafvollzug des Landesgefängnisses Mannheim." *ZfS* 5: 31–32.

Weber, Franz. 1938. "Erfahrungen in der Sicherungsanstalt." *BfG* 68: 429–48.

Weissenrieder, Otto. 1935. Review of *Kriminalistischer Bericht über eine Reise nach Amerika*, by Franz Exner. *BfG* 66: 183–86.

Weissenrieder, Otto. 1935. "Selbsterziehung eines 'Unverbesserlichen.'" *BfG* 66: 391–97.

Weissenrieder, Otto. 1933. "Vorwort." *BfG* 64: 113–17.

Weissheit, Gertraude. 1986. "Erfahrungen der Bezirksnervenklinik Brandenburg mit der Einweisung von Patienten nach § 6 des Gesetzes über die Einweisung in stationäre Einrichtungen für psychisch Kranke vom 11. 6. 1968." MD diss., Akademie für Ärztliche Fortbildung der DDR.

Werner, Paul. 1944. "Die Einweisung in die polizeilicher Jugendschutzlager." *Deutsches Jugendrecht* 4: 95–106.

Wessel, Gerhard. 1939. *Das Delikt der Kinderschändung im Landgerichtsbezirk Bonn*. Düsseldorf: Dissertations-Verlag G. H. Nolte.

Wilhelm, Josef Georg, ed. 1946. *Einführung in die praktische Kriminalistik*. Stuttgart: W. Kohlhammer.

Wolf, Heinz E. 1972. "Beurteilungen der Besserungsmöglichkeiten des Strafvollzugs durch Strafgefangene." *ZfS* 20: 263–74.

Wolf, Helmut. 1941. *Beitrag zur Frage der Kastration unter Berücksichtigung von Fällen der Heil- und Pflegeanstalt Göttingen*. Göttingen: Martin Sass.

Wulf, Rüdiger . 1985. "Opferbezogene Vollzugsgestaltung—Grundzüge eines Behandlungsansatzes." *ZfSuS* 34: 66–77.

Würtenberger, Thomas. 1957. "Défense sociale—Ziele und Wege einer neuen kriminalpolitischen Bewegung." Special issue, *MfKuS,* 60–65.

Xingas, Georg. 1937. *Die Kastration als Sicherungsmaßnahme gegen Sittlichkeitsverbrecher*. Berlin: R. Pfau.

Zeugner, Franz. 1935. "Zur Kritik der Erziehungsmethoden im Strafvollzug." *MfKuS* 26: 267–70.

SECONDARY SOURCES

Agamben, Giorgio. 1998. *Homo Sacer: Sovereign Power and Bare Life*. Stanford: Stanford University Press.

Agamben, Giorgio. 2005. *State of Exception*. Chicago: University of Chicago Press.

Albrecht, Hans-Jörg. 2013. "Sentencing in Germany: Explaining Long-Term Stability in the Structure of Criminal Sanctions and Sentencing." *Law and Contemporary Problems* 76: 211–36.

Alexopoulos, Golfo. 2005. "Amnesty 1945." *Slavic Review* 64: 274–306.

Allen, Francis A. 1981. *The Decline of the Rehabilitative Ideal*. New Haven: Yale University Press.

Altner, Peter, and Günter Kröber, eds. 1986. *KPD und Wissenschaftsentwicklung, 1919-1945*. Berlin: Dietz.

Ammerer, Gerhard, and Alfred Stefan Weiss. 2003. "Zucht- und Arbeitshäuser in Österreich um 1800—Recht, Konzepte, und Alltag." In *Gefängnis und Gesellschaft: Zur (Vor-)Geschichte der strafenden Einsperrung*, ed. Gerhard Ammerer, Falk Bretschneider, and Alfred Stefan Weiß, 149–76. Leipzig: Leipziger Universitätsverlag.

Ansorg, Leonore. 2005. *Politische Häftlinge imn Strafvollzug der DDR: Die Strafvollzugsanstalt Brandenburg*. Berlin: Metropol.

Armstrong, David. 1995. "The Rise of Surveillance Medicine." *Sociology of Health and Illness* 17: 393–404.

Arnauld, Andreas von. 2006. *Rechtssicherheit: Perspektive Annäherungen an eine idée directrice des Rechts*. Tübingen: Mohr Siebeck.

Ash, Mitchell G. 1996. "Émigré Psychologists after 1933: The Cultural Coding of Scientific and Professional Practices." In *Forced Migration and Scientific Change: Émigré German-Speaking Scientists and Scholars*, ed. Mitchell G. Ash and Alfons Söllner, 117–38. New York: Cambridge University Press.

Ash, Mitchell G. 1999. "Kurt Gottschaldt and Psychological Research in Nazi and Socialist Germany." In *Science under Socialism*, ed. Kristie Macrakis and Dieter Hoffmann, 286–301, Cambridge, MA: Harvard University Press.

Ash, Mitchell G. 1995. "Verordnete Umbrüche—Konstruierte Kontinuitäten: Zur Entnazifizierung von Wissenschaftlern und Wissenschaften nach 1945." *Zeitschrift für Geschichtswissenschaft* 43: 903–23.

Ash, Mitchell G. 1997. "Wissenschaft, Politik, und Modernität in der DDR: Ansätze zu einer Neubetrachtung." In *Wissenschaft und Politik: Genetik und Humangenetik in der DDR (1949–1989)*, ed. Karin Weismann, Peter Kröner, and Richard Toellner, 1–25. Münster: LIT.

Ash, Mitchell G. 2001. "Wissenschaft und Wissenschaftsaustausch." In *Die USA und Deutschland im Zeitalter des Kalten Krieges, 1945–1990*, vol. 1, ed. Detlef Junker, 634–45. Stuttgart: Deutsche Verlags-Anstalt.

Baganz, Carina. 2005. *Erziehung zur "Volksgemeinschaft": Die frühen Konzentrationslager in Sachsen 1933–1934/37*. Berlin: Metropol.

Baird, Jay W. 1992. *To Die for Germany: Heroes in the Nazi Pantheon*. Bloomington: Indiana University Press.

Barnes, Steven A. 2011. *Death and Redemption: The Gulag and the Shaping of Soviet Society*. Princeton: Princeton University Press.

Baumann, Immanuel. 2006. *Dem Verbrechern auf der Spur: Eine Geschichte der Kriminologie und Kriminalpolitik in Deutschland 1880 bis 1980*. Göttingen: Wallstein.

Beachy, Robert. 2010. "The German Invention of Homosexuality." *Journal of Modern History* 82: 801–38.

Becker, Peter, and Richard F. Wetzell. 2006. *Criminals and Their Scientists: The History of Criminology in International Perspective*. New York: Cambridge University Press.

Behnke, Klaus, and Jürgen Fuchs, eds. 1995. *Zersetzung der Seele: Psychologie und Psychiatrie im Dienste der Stasi*. Hamburg: Rotbuch.

Berkowitz, Michael. 2007. *The Crime of My Very Existence: Nazism and the Myth of Jewish Criminality*. Berkeley: University of California Press.

Bierwisch, Manfred. 1990. "Wissenschaft im realen Sozialismus." *Kursbuch* 101: 112–23.

Bochnik, H. J. 2004. "Erinnerung an Professor Dr. med. Karl Leonhard." *Hessisches Ärzteblatt* 3:158–59.

Borchert, Jens. 2002. *Erziehung im DDR-Vollzug: Theoretische und gesetzliche Grundlagen sowie die Durchführung in der Strafvollzugseinrichtung Torgau*. Herbolzheim: Centaurus.

Bouvier, Beatrix. 2002. *Die DDR—ein Sozialstaat? Sozialpolitik in der Ära Honecker*. Bonn: Dietz.

Bowker, Geoffrey C., and Susan Leigh Star. 2000. *Sorting Things Out: Classification and Its Consequences*. Cambridge, MA: MIT Press.

Bratke, Gerrit. 1999. *Die Kriminologie in der Deutschen Demokratischen Republik und ihre Anwendung im Bereich der Jugenddelinquenz: Eine zeitgeschichtlich- kriminologische Untersuchung*. Münster: LIT.

Brecht, Karen. 1995. "In the Aftermath of Nazi-Germany: Alexander Mitscherlich and Psychoanalysis—Legend and Legacy." *American Imago* 52: 291–312.

Bretschneider, Falk. 2008. *Gefangene Gesellschaft: Eine Geschichte der Einsperrung in Sachsen im 18. und 19. Jahrhundert*. Konstanz: UVK.

Brückweh, Kerstin. 2006. "Fantasies of Violence: German Citizens Expressing Their Concepts of Violence and Ideas about Democracy in Letters Referring to the Case of the Serial Killer Jürgen Bartsch (1966–1971)." *Crime, Histoire et Sociétés / Crime, History and Societies* 10: 53–81.

Brückweh, Kerstin. 2006. *Mordlust: Serienmorde, Gewalt und Emotionen im 20. Jahrhundert*. Frankfurt: Campus.

Burgmair, Wolfgang, Matthias M. Weber, and Nikolaus Wachsmann. 1999. "'Die soziale Prognose wird damit sehr trübe . . .'—Theodor Viernstein und die Kriminalbiologische Sammelstelle in Bayern." In *Polizeireport München, 1799– 1999*, ed. Michael Farin, 250–87. Munich: Belleville.

Burleigh, Michael, and Wolfgang Wippermann. 1991. *The Racial State: Germany, 1933–1945*. New York: Cambridge University Press.

Busch, Tim. 2005. *Die deutsche Strafrechtsreform: Ein Rückblick auf die sechs Reformen des Deutschen Strafrechts (1969–1998)*. Baden-Baden: Nomos.

Busse, Stefan. 1998. "'Von der Sowjetwissenschaft lernen': Pawlowismus und Psychologie." *Psychologie und Geschichte* 8: 150–73.

Capshew, James H. 1999. *Psychologists on the March: Science, Practice, and Professional Identity in America, 1929–1969*. Cambridge: Cambridge University Press.

Castoriadis, Cornelius. 1987. *The Imaginary Institution of Society*. Cambridge, MA: MIT Press.

Christie, Nils. 1982. *Limits to Pain*. Oxford: Martin Robertson.

Cole, Simon A. 2000. "From the Sexual Psychopath Statute to 'Megan's Law': Psychiatric Knowledge in the Diagnosis, Treatment, and Adjudication of Sex Criminals in New Jersey, 1949–1999." *Journal of the History of Medicine and Allied Sciences* 55: 292–314.

Cowen, Michael. 2008. *Cult of the Will: Nervousness and German Modernity*. University Park: Pennsylvania State University Press.

Dahle, Klaus-Peter. 1995. *Zur Versorgung forensisch-psychiatrischer Patienten in den neuen Bundesländern: Bestandaufnahme und Empfehlungen*. Baden-Baden: Nomos.

Diemer, Susanne. 1994. *Patriarchalismus in der DDR: Strukturelle, kulturelle, und subjektive Dimensionen der Geschlechterpolarisierung*. Opladen: Leske und Budrich.

Downes, David. 2001. "The *Macho* Penal Economy: Mass Incarceration in the United States—a European Perspective." *Punishment and Society* 3: 1–80.

Dressen, Wolfgang. 1982. *Die pädagogische Maschine: Zur Geschichte des industrialisierten Bewußtseins in Preußen/Deutschland*. Frankfurt: Ullstein.

Drost, M.-P. 1988. "Sartre's Concept of a Person as a Project." *Dialogos* 23: 97–108.

Dumont, Kitty. 1999. *Die Sozialpsychologie der DDR: Eine wissenschaftshistorische Untersuchung*. Frankfurt: Lang.

Dunbabin, Jean. 2002. *Captivity and Imprisonment in Medieval Europe, 1000–1300*. Basingstoke: Palgrave Macmillan.

Eghigian, Greg. 2003. "Der Kalte Krieg im Kopf: Ein Fall von Schizophrenie und die Geschichte des Selbst in der sowjetischen Besatzungszone." *Historische Anthropologie* 11: 101–22.

Eghigian, Greg. 2015. "A Drifting Concept for an Unruly Menace: A History of Psychopathy in Germany." *Isis* 106 (June): 283–309.

Eghigian, Greg. 2012. "Hypersexual Disorder: An Encounter with Don Juan in the Archives." *Psychiatric Times* 29 (August): 18.

Eghigian, Greg. 2012. "Psychagogy: Psychotherapy's Remarkably Resilient Predecessor." *Psychiatric Times* 29 (November): 12.

Eghigian, Greg. 2002. "Was There a Communist Psychiatry? Politics and East German Psychiatric Care, 1945–1989." *Harvard Review of Psychiatry* 10: 364–68.

Eghigian, Greg, Andreas Killen, and Christine Leuenberger, eds. 2007. *The Self as Project: Politics and the Human Sciences*. Osiris 22. Chicago: University of Chicago Press.

Elz, Jutta. 2005. "Zur Rückfälligkeit von Sexualstraftätern in der DDR." In *Sexualstraftaten: Forensische Begutachtung, Diagnostik, und Therapie*, ed. Detlef Schläfke, Frank Häßler, and Jörg Michael Fegert, 181–93, Stuttgart: Schattauer.

Elz, Jutta, and Almut Fröhlich. 2002. *Sexualstraftäter in der DDR: Ergebnisse einer empirischen Untersuchung*. Wiesbaden: Kriminologische Zentralstelle.

Emmerich, Norbert. 1989. "Die forensische Psychiatrie 1933–1945: Das Schicksal der wegen einer Straftat eingewiesenen Kranken." In *Totgeschwiegen 1933–1945*, ed. Arbeitsgruppe zur Erforschung der Geschichte der Karl-Bonhoeffer- Nervenklinik, 105–23. Berlin: Edition Hentrich.

Engstrom, Eric J. 2009. "Die Psychologie als Argument für die Abschaffung des Strafmasses." In *Psychologie als Argument in der juristischen Literatur des Kaiserreichs*, ed. Mathias Schmoeckel, 43–55. Baden-Baden: Nomos.

Ernst, Anna-Sabine. 1997. *"Die beste Prophylaxis ist der Sozialismus": Ärzte und medizinische Hochschullehrer in der SBZ/DDR, 1945–1961*. Münster: Waxmann.

Ernst, Anna-Sabine. 1993. "Vom 'Du' zum 'Sie': Die Rezeption der bürgerlichen Anstandsregeln in der DDR der 1950er Jahre." *Mitteilungen aus der kulturwissenschaftlichen Forschung* 16, no. 33: 190–209.

Eser, Albin. 2001. "Zur Entwicklung von Maßregeln der Besserung und Sicherung als zweite Spur im Strafrecht." In *Grundfragen staatlichen Strafens*, ed. Guido Britz, 213–36. Munich: C. H. Beck.

Essig, Karen. 2000. *Die Entwicklung des Strafvollzuges in den neuen Bundesländer*. Mönchengladbach: Forum Verlag Godesberg.

Evans, Jennifer V. 2010. "Decriminalization, Seduction, and 'Unnatural Desire' in East Germany." *Feminist Studies* 36: 553–77.

Fattah, Ezzat A. 2000. "Victimology: Past, Present, and Future." *Criminologie* 33 (2000): 17–46.

Fenemore, Mark. 2009. "The Recent Historiography of Sexuality in Twentieth-Century Germany." *Historical Journal* 52: 763–79.

Fenemore, Mark. 2007. *Sex, Thugs, and Rock 'n' Roll: Teenage Rebels in Cold-War East Germany*. New York: Berghahn.

Fings, Karola. 2010. "The Public Face of the Camps." In *Concentration Camps in Nazi Germany: The New Histories*, ed. Jane Caplan and Nikolaus Wachsmann, 108–26. London: Routledge.

Fischer, Dirk, ed. 2006. *Transformation des Rechts in Ost und West*. Berlin: Berliner Wissenschafts-Verlag.

Foucault, Michel. 2003. *Abnormal: Lectures at the Collège de France, 1974–1975*. New York: Picador.

Foucault, Michel. 1995. *Discipline and Punish: The Birth of the Prison*. New York: Vintage.

Foucault, Michel. 1990. *The History of Sexuality: An Introduction*. Vol. 1. New York: Vintage.

Franklin, Sarah. 1997. *Embodied Progress: A Cultural Account of Assisted Conception*. London: Routledge.

Freimüller, Tobias. 2007. *Alexander Mitscherlich: Gesellschaftsdiagnose und Psychoanalyse nach Hitler*. Göttingen: Wallstein.

Fricke, Karl Wilhelm, ed. 1999. *Humaner Strafvollzug und politischer Mißbrauch*. Dresden: Sächsischer Staatsministerium der Justiz.

Fuchs, Jürgen. 1993. "'Zelleninformatoren': Über die 'Inoffiziellen Mitarbeiter' des MfS im Strafvollzug." In *Verriegelte Zeiten: Vom Schweigen über die Gefängnisse in der DDR*, ed. Rolf Hanusch, 24–27. Tutzing: Evangelische Akademie.

Fussinger, Catherine. 2011. "'Therapeutic Community,' Psychiatry's Reformers, and Antipsychiatrists: Reconsidering Changes in the Field of Psychiatry." *History of Psychiatry* 22: 146–63.

Galassi, Silviana. 2004. *Kriminologie im deutschen Kaiserreich: Geschichte einer gebrochenen Verwissenschaftlichung*. Stuttgart: Franz Steiner.

Garland, David. 2001. *The Culture of Control: Crime and Social Order in Contemporary Society*. Chicago: University of Chicago Press.

Garland, David. 2010. *Peculiar Institution: America's Death Penalty in an Age of Abolition*. Cambridge, MA: Belknap Press of Harvard University Press.

Garland, David. 1990. *Punishment and Modern Society: A Study in Social Theory*. Chicago: University of Chicago Press.

Gellately, Robert, and Nathan Stoltzfuss, ed. 2001. *Social Outsiders in Nazi Germany*. Princeton: Princeton University Press.

Geltner, G. 2008. *The Medieval Prison: A Social History*. Princeton: Princeton University Press, 2008.

Getty, J. Arch, Gábor T. Rittersporn, and Viktor N. Zemskov. 1993. "Victims of the Soviet Penal System in the Pre-War Years: A First Approach on the Basis of Archival Evidence." *American Historical Review* 98: 1017–49.

Gesellschaft für christlich-jüdische Zusammenarbeit Göttingen e.V. und dem evangelisch-lutherischen Pfarramt Moringen, ed. 1983. *KZ Moringen: Männerlager, Frauenlager, Jugendschutzlager*. Göttingen: Steidl.

Gieseke, Jens. 2001. *Mielke-Konzern: Die Geschichte der Stasi, 1945–1990*. Stuttgart: Deutsche Verlags-Anstalt.

Gödecke, Petra. 2014. "Criminal Law after National Socialism: The Renaissance of Natural Law at the Beginning of Penal Reform in West Germany." In *Crime and Criminal Justice in Modern Germany*, ed. Richard F. Wetzell, 270–301. Oxford: Berghahn.

Goeschel, Christian, and Nikolaus Wachsmann. 2010. "Before Auschwitz: The Formation of the Nazi Concentration Camps, 1933–9." *Journal of Contemporary History* 45: 515–34.

Goffman, Erving. 1961. *Asylums: Essays on the Social Situation of Mental Patients and Other Inmates*. Garden City: Anchor.

Goffman, Erving. 1986. *Stigma: Notes on the Management of a Spoiled Identity*. New York: Simon and Schuster.

Goldstein, A. P. 1973. *Structured Learning Therapy: Toward a Psychotherapy for the Poor*. New York: Academic.

Goltermann, Svenja. 2009. *Die Gesellschaft der Überlebenden: Deutsche Kriegsheimkehrer und ihre Gewalterfahrungen im Zweiten Weltkrieg*. Munich: Deutsche Verlags-Anstalt.

Götte, Petra. 2003. *Jugendstrafvollzug im "Dritten Reich": Diskutiert und realisiert—erlebt und erinnert*. Bad Heilbrunn: Julius Klinkhardt.

Gottschalk, Marie. 2006. *The Prison and the Gallows: The Politics of Mass Incarceration in America*. Cambridge: Cambridge University Press.

Greene, Jeremy A. 2007. *Prescribing by Numbers: Drugs and the Definition of Disease*. Baltimore: Johns Hopkins University Press.

Greiner, Bettina. 2010. *Verdrängter Terror: Geschichte und Wahrnehmung sowjetischer Speziallager in Deutschland*. Hamburg: Hamburger Edition.

Greve, Ylva. 2004. *Verbrechen und Krankheit: Die Entdeckung der "Criminalpsychologie" im 19. Jahrhundert*. Cologne: Böhlau.

Gruchmann, Lothar. 1988. *Justiz im Dritten Reich 1933–1940: Anpassung und Unterwerfung in der Ära Gürtner*. Munich: Oldenbourg).

Gusfield, Joseph R. 1980. *The Culture of Public Problems: Drinking-Driving and the Symbolic Order*. Chicago: University of Chicago Press.

Habermas, Rebekka, and Gerd Schwerhoff, eds. 2009. *Verbrechen im Blick: Perspektiven der neuzeitlichen Kriminalitätsgeschichte*. Frankfurt: Campus.

Harcourt, Bernard E. 2003. "From the Ne'er-Do-Well to the Criminal History Category: The Refinement of the Actuarial Model in Criminal Law." *Law and Contemporary Problems* 66: 99–150.

Hartl, Benedikt. 2000. *Das nationalsozialistische Willensstrafrecht*. Berlin: Weissensee.

Hellbeck, Jochen. 2006. *Revolution in My Mind: Writing a Diary under Stalin*. Cambridge, MA: Harvard University Press.

Henze, Martina. 2007. "Netzwerk, Kongressbewegung, Stiftung: Zur Wissenschaftsgeschichte der internationalen Gefängniskunde 1827 bis 1951." In *Verbrecher im Visier der Experten: Kriminalpolitik zwischen Wissenschaft und Praxis im 19. und frühen 20. Jahrhundert*, ed. Desiree Schauz and Sabine Freitag, 55–77. Stuttgart: Franz Steiner.

Henze, Martina. 2003. *Strafvollzugsreformen im 19. Jahrhundert: Gefängniskundlicher Diskurs und staatliche Praxis in Bayern und Hessen-Darmstadt*. Darmstadt: Hessische Historische Kommission und Historische Kommission für Hessen.

Herman, Ellen. 1996. *The Romance of American Psychology: Political Culture in the Age of Experts*. Berkeley: University of California Press.

Herzog, Dagmar. 2005. *Sex after Fascism: Memory and Morality in Twentieth-Century Germany*. Princeton: Princeton University Press.

Herzog, Dagmar. 2011. *Sexuality in Europe: A Twentieth-Century History*. Cambridge: Cambridge University Press.

Hohmann, Joachim S. 1991. *Robert Ritter und die Erben der Kriminalbiologie: "Zigeunerforschung" im Nationalsozialismus und in Westdeutschland im Zeichen des Rassismus*. Frankfurt: Lang.

Hohmann, Joachim S., ed. 1991. *Sexuologie in der DDR*. Berlin: Dietz.

Hommen, Tanja. 1999. *Sittlichkeitsverbrechen: Sexuelle Gewalt im Kaiserreich*. Frankfurt: Campus.

Ivanov, Konstantin. 2002. "Science after Stalin: Forging a New Image of Soviet Science." *Science in Context* 15: 317–38.

Janus, Eric S. 2000. "Sexual Predator Commitment Laws: Lessons for Law and the Behavioral Sciences." *Behavioral Sciences and the Law* 18: 5–21.

Jarausch, Konrad H., ed. 1999. *Dictatorship as Experience: Towards a Socio-Cultural History of the GDR*. New York: Berghahn.

Jenkins, Philip. 1998. *Moral Panic: Changing Concepts of the Child Molester in Modern America*. New Haven: Yale University Press.

Jureit, Ulrike, 1995. *Erziehen, Strafen, Vernichten: Jugendkriminaliät und Jugendstrafrecht im Nationalsozialismus*. Münster: Waxmann.

Kailer, Thomas. 2011. *Vermessung des Verbrechers: Die kriminalbiologische Untersuchung in Bayern, 1923–1945*. Bielefeld: Transcript.

Kaiser, Günther. 1996. *Kriminologie: Ein Handbuch*. Heidelberg: C. F. Müller.

Kauders, Anthony D. 2011. "Drives in Dispute: The West German Student Movement, Psychoanalysis, and the Search for a New Emotional Order, 1967–1971." *Central European History* 44: 711–31.

Kebbedies, Frank. 2000. *Außer Kontrolle: Jugendkriminalität in der NS-Zeit und der frühen Nachkriegszeit*. Essen: Klartext.

Kerchner, Brigitte. 2000. "Kinderlügen? Zur Kulturgeschichte des sexuellen Mißbrauchs." In *Mißhandlung, Vernachlässigung und sexuelle Gewalt in Erziehungsverhältnissen*, ed. Urte Finger-Trescher and Heinz Krebs, 15–41. Giessen: Psychosozial.

Kerchner, Brigitte. 2003. "'Sexualdiktatur': Macht und Gewalt in Gerichtsverfahren der Weimarer Republik." In *Unzucht—Notzucht—Vergewaltigung: Definitionen und Deutungen sexueller Gewalt von der Aufklärung bis heute*, ed. Christine Künzel, 137–63. Frankfurt: Campus.

Kerchner, Brigitte. 1998. "'Unbescholtene Bürger' und 'gefährliche Mädchen' um die Jahrhundertwende." *Historische Anthropologie* 6: 1–32.

Kersting, Franz-Werner, ed. 2003. *Psychiatriereform als Gesellschaftsreform: Die Hypothek des Nationalsozialismus und der Aufbruch der sechziger Jahre*. Paderborn: Ferdinand Schöningh.

Kesper-Biermann, Sylvia. 2009. *Einheit und Recht: Strafgesetzgebung und Kriminalrechtsexperten in Deutschland vom Beginn des 19. Jahrhunderts bis zum Reichsstrafgesetzbuch von 1871*. Frankfurt: Vittorio Klostermann.

Kesper-Biermann, Sylvia, and Petra Overath, eds. 2007. *Die Internationalisierung von Strafrechtswissenschaft und Kriminalpolitik (1870–1930): Deutschland im Vergleich*. Berlin: Berliner Wissenschafts-Verlag.

Kharkhordin, Oleg. 1999. *The Collective and the Individual in Russia: A Study of Practices*. Berkeley: University of California Press.

Kinzig, Jörg. 1996. *Die Sicherungsverwahrung auf dem Prüfstand*. Freiburg: Max-Planck-Institut für ausländisches und internationales Strafrecht.

Klee, Ernst. 2003. *Das Personenlexikon zum Dritten Reich*. Frankfurt: S. Fischer.

Knabe, Hubertus. 1997. "'Weiche' Formen der Verfolgung in der DDR: Zum Wandel der repressiven Strategien in der Ära Honecker." *Deutschland Archiv* 30: 709- 19.

Kopstein, Jeffrey. 1994. "Ulbricht Embattled: The Quest for Socialist Modernity in the Light of New Sources." *Europe-Asia Studies* 46: 597–615.

Korzilius, Sven. 2005. *"Asoziale" und "Parasiten" im Recht der SBZ/DDR*. Cologne: Böhlau.

Kossakowski, Adolf. 1994. "Die pädagogische Psychologie der DDR im Spannungsfeld zwischen kindorientierter Forschung und bildungspolitischen Forderungen." In *Pädagogik in der DDR*, ed. Ernst Cloer and Rolf Wernstedt, 205–18. Weinheim: Deutscher Studien.

Kott, Sandrine. 2001. "Die Unerreichbaren der sozialistischen Gesellschaft: Die Arbeiterjugend in der DDR (1970–1989)." In *Der Schein der Stabilität: DDR- Betriebsalltag in der Ära Honecker*, ed. Renate Hürtgen and Thomas Reichel, 229–48. Berlin: Metropol.

Kozulin, Alex. 1986. "The Concept of Activity in Soviet Psychology." *American Psychologist* 41: 264–74.

Kury, Helmut, and Theodore Ferdinand. 1999. "Public Opinion and Punitivity." *International Journal of Law and Psychiatry* 22: 373–92.

Kurzweil, Edit. 1996. "Psychoanalytic Science: From Oedipus to Culture." In *Forced Migration and Scientific Change: Émigré German-Speaking Scientists and Scholars*, ed. Mitchell G. Ash and Alfons Söllner, 139–55. New York: Cambridge University Press.

Laatz, Horst. 1990. *Klassenstruktur und soziales Verhalten: Zur Entstehung der empirischen Sozialstrukturforschung in der DDR*. Cologne: Wissenschaft und Politik.

Laitko, Hubert. 1997. "Wissenschaftspolitik." In *Die SED: Geschichte—Organisation—Politik; Ein Handbuch*, ed. Andreas Herbst, Gerd-Rüdiger Stephan, and Jürgen Winkler, 405–20. Berlin: Dietz.

Landesjugendamt Brandenburg, ed. 1996. *"Wir hatten noch gar nicht angefangen zu leben": Materialien zur Ausstellung über die Jugendkonzentrationslager Moringen und Uckermark*. Bernau: Landesjugendamt.

LaPierre, Brian. 2012. *Hooligans in Khrushchev's Russia: Defining, Policing, and Producing Deviance during the Thaw*. Madison: University of Wisconsin.

Lappi-Seppälä, Tapio. 2012. "Penal Policies in the Nordic Countries 1960–2010." Supplement, *Journal of Scandinavian Studies in Criminology and Crime Prevention* 13: 85–111.

Lassleben, Wolfgang. 2008. "Zur Rehabilitierung von Verurteilungen nach § 249 StGB/DDR." *Horch und Guck* 60: 42–45.

Lemke, Thomas. 2011. *Biopolitics: An Advanced Introduction*. New York: New York University Press.

Leonhard, Hans-Walter. N.d. "Psyche und Psychosen: Zum wissenschaftlichen Werk von Karl Leonhard." Accessed 3 March 2011. http://www.menschenkunde.net/artikel/kl-werk.htm.

Leukel, Sandra. 2014. "Reforming Women's Prisons in Imperial Germany." In *Crime and Criminal Justice in Modern Germany*, ed. Richard F. Wetzell, 86–111. New York: Berghahn.

Liang, Oliver. "The Biology of Morality: Criminal Biology in Bavaria, 1924–1933." In *Criminals and Their Scientists: The History of Criminology in International Perspective*, ed. Peter Becker and Richard F. Wetzell, 425–46. New York: Cambridge University Press.

Lianos, Michaelis, and Mary Douglas. 2000. "Dangerization and the End of Deviance." *British Journal of Criminology* 40: 261–78.

Lindenberger, Thomas. 2008. "'Asociality' and Modernity: The GDR as a Welfare Dictatorship." In *Socialist Modern*, ed. Katherine Pence and Paul Betts, 211–33. Ann Arbor: University of Michigan Press.

Loetz, Francisca. 2009. "Sexualisierte Gewalt in Europa 1520–1850: Historisierung von 'Vergewaltigung' und Missbrauch.'" *Geschichte und Gesellschaft* 35: 561–602.

Lombardo, Giovanni Pietro, and Renato Foschi. 2001. "The Concept of Personality in 19th-Century French and 20th-Century American Psychology." *History of Psychology* 6: 123–42.

Ludz, Peter Christian. 1964. "Soziologie und empirische Sozialforschung in der DDR." In "Studien und Materialien zur Soziologie der DDR," ed. Peter Christian Ludz, special issue, *Kölner Zeitschrift für Soziologie und Sozialpsychologie* 8: 327–418.

Maasen, Sabine. 1998. *Genealogie der Unmoral: Zur Therapeutisierung sexueller Selbste*. Frankfurt: Suhrkamp.

Malycha Andreas. 2002. "Frost nach dem Tauwetter: Wissenschaft und Politik in der DDR in den fünfziger Jahren." *Deutschland Archiv* 35: 237–52.

Mansnerus, Laura. 2006. "Time Served: Zoning Laws That Bar Pedophiles Raise Concerns." *New York Times*, 27 November. Accessed 20 March 2013. http://www.nytimes.com/2006/11/27/nyregion/27sex.html.

Markovits, Inga. 2010. *Justice in Lüritz: Experiencing Socialist Law in East Germany*. Princeton: Princeton University Press.

McConville, Sean. 1981. *A History of English Prison Administration*. Vol. 1, *1750–1877*. London: Routledge and Kegan Paul.

McLellan, Josie. 2011. *Love in the Time of Communism: Intimacy and Sexuality in the GDR*. Cambridge: Cambridge University Press.

Mehner, Heinrich. 1992. "Aspekte zur Entwicklung des Straf- und Untersuchungshaftvollzugs in der ehemaligen sowjetischen Besatzungszone Deutschland (SBZ) sowie in den Anfangsjahren der DDR." *Zeitschrift für Strafvollzug und Straffälligenhilfe* 41: 91–98.

Merkel, Grischa. 2011. "Case Note—Retrospective Preventive Detention in Germany: A Comment on the ECHR Decision Haidn v. Germany of 13 January 2011." *German Law Journal* 12: 968–77.

Merkel, Ina.1999. *Utopie und Bedürfnis: Die Geschichte der Konsumkultur in der DDR*. Cologne: Böhlau.

Meyer, Hansgünter. 1990. "Wissenschaftspolitik, Intelligenzpolitik: Das Personal für Wissenschaft, Forschung, und Technik in der DDR." In *Intelligenz, Wissenschaft, und Forschung in der DDR*, ed. Hansgünter Meyer, 1–51. Berlin: Walter de Gruyter.

Miquel, Marc von. 2004. *Ahnden oder amnestieren? Westdeutsche Justiz und Vergangenheitspolitik in den sechziger Jahre*. Göttingen: Wallstein.

Mörchen, Stefan. 2011. *Schwarzer Markt: Kriminalität, Ordnung, und Moral in Bremen 1939–1949*. Frankfurt: Campus.

Morré, Jörg. 2010. "Vom Niedergang des Erziehungsgedankens im Strafvollzug der DDR." In *Hinter Gittern: Zur Geschichte der Inhaftierung zwischen Bestrafung, Besserung und politischem Ausschluss vom 18. Jahrhundert bis zur Gegenwart*, ed. Silke Klewin, Herbert Reinke, and Gerhard Sälter, 241–54. Leipzig: Leipziger Universitätsverlag.

Morris, Norval, and David J. Rothman, eds. 1995. *The Oxford History of the Prison*. New York: Oxford University Press.

Mosse, George, 1996. *The Image of Man: The Creation of Modern Masculinity*. New York: Oxford University Press.

Mothes, Jörn, Gundula Fienbork, Rudi Pahnke, Renate Ellmenreich, and Michael Stognienko, ed. 1996. *Beschädigte Seelen: DDR-Jugend und Staatssicherheit*. Bremen: Edition Temmen.

Müller, Christian. 1997. *Das Gewohnheitsverbrechergesetz vom 24. November 1933: Kriminalpolitik als Rassenpolitik*. Baden-Baden: Nomos.

Müller, Christian. 2004. *Verbrechensbekämpfung im Anstaltsstaat: Psychiatrie, Kriminologie und Strafrechtsreform in Deutschland, 1871–1933*. Göttingen: Vandenhoeck und Ruprecht.

Naumann, Kai. 2006. *Gefängnis und Gesellschaft: Freiheitsentzug in Deutschland in Wissenschaft und Praxis, 1920–1960*. Münster: LIT.

Neugebauer, Manuela. 1997. *Der Weg in das Jugendschutzlager Moringen*. Mönchengladbach: Forum.

Niemann, Heinz. 1995. *Hinterm Zaun: Politische Kultur und Meinungsforschung in der DDR; Die geheimen Berichte an das Politbüro der SED*. Berlin: Edition Ost.

Nolte, Paul. 2008. "Von der Gesellschaftsstruktur zur Seelenverfassung: Die Psychologisierung der Sozialdiagnose in den sechziger Jahren." In *Psychoanalyse und Protest*, ed. Tobias Freimüller, 70–94. Götttingen: Wallstein.

Nutz, Thomas. 2001. *Strafanstalt als Besserungsmaschine: Reformdiskurs und Gefängniswissenschaft, 1775–1848*. Munich: Oldenbourg, 2001.

Obertreis, Gesine. 1986. *Familienpolitik in der DDR 1945–1980*. Opladen: Leske und Budrich.

Oleschinski, Brigitte. 1993. "'Nur für den Dientgebrach?' Das Tabu Strafvollzug in der DDR." In *Verriegelte Zeiten: Vom Schweigen über die Gefängnisse in der DDR*, ed. Rolf Hanusch, 7–13. Tutzing: Evangelische Akademie Tutzing.

Olikowski, Wanda J. 1992. "The Duality of Technology: Rethinking the Concept of Technology in Organizations." *Organization Science* 3: 398–427.

Olikowski, Wanda J. 2000. "Using Technology and Constituting Structures: A Practical Lens for Studying Technology in Organizations." *Organization Science* 11: 404–28.

Orlob, Stefan. 2001. "War der deutsche forensische Psychiater Hans Szewczyk der erste moderne Profiler?" *Archiv für Kriminologie* 207: 65–72.

Peukert, Detlev. 1986. *Grenzen der Sozialdisziplierung: Aufstieg und Krise der deutschen Jugendfürsorge von 1878 bis 1932*. Cologne: Bund-Verlag.

Pfeiffer, Christian. 2005. "Weniger Verbrecher, mehr Panikmache." *Die Zeit*, 2 June, 9.

Pine, Lisa. 1995. "Hashude: The Imprisonment of 'Asocial' Families in the Third Reich." *German History* 13: 182–97.

Pingel-Schliemann, Sandra. 2003. *Zersetzen: Strategie einer Diktatur*. Berlin: Robert-Havemann-Gesellschaft.

Pitscheider, Sabine. 2010. "'Biz zur Besserung': Die Praxis von Einweisung, Anhaltung, und Entlassung im Provinzialzwangsarbeitshaus Schwaz/Innsbruck 1825 bis 1860." In *Orte der Verwahrung: Die innere Organisation von Gefängnissen, Hospitälern, und Klostern seit dem Spätmittelalter*, ed. Gerhard Ammerer, Arthur Brunhart, Martin Scheutz, and Alfred Stefan Weisse, 131–48. Leipzig: Leipziger Universitätsverlag.

Poiger, Uta G. 2000. *Jazz, Rock, and Rebels: Cold War Politics and American Culture in a Divided Germany*. Berkeley: University of California Press.

Power, Michael. 1997. *The Audit Society: Rituals of Verification*. New York: Oxford University Press.

Pratt, John, 2002. *Punishment and Civilization: Penal Tolerance and Intolerance in Modern Society*. London: Sage.

Rabinbach, Anson. 1995. "Response to Karen Brecht." *American Imago* 52: 313–28.

Raphael, Lutz. 1996. "Die Verwissenschaftlichung des Sozialen als methodische und konzeptionelle Herausforderung für eine Sozialgeschichte des 20. Jahrhunderts." *Geschichte und Gesellschaft* 22: 165–93.

Raschka, Johannes. 2000. *Justizpolitik im SED-Staat: Anpassung und Wandel des Strafrechts während der Amtszeit Honeckers*. Cologne: Böhlau.

Ritscher, Bodo. 1993. "Die Abteilung Spezlager: Anmerkungen zur Struktur und zum Funktionsbereich einer NKWD/MWD-Behörde in Deutschland." In *Das Torgau-Tabu*, ed. Norbert Haase and Brigitte Oleschinski, 135–45. Leipzig: Forum.

Rodden, John. 2002. *Repainting the Little Red School House: A History of Eastern German Education, 1945–1995*. New York: Oxford University Press.

Rode, Christian. 1996. *Kriminologie in der DDR*. Freiburg: Edition Iuscrim.

Rodmell, Sue. 1981. "Men, Women, and Sexuality: A Feminist Critique of the Sociology of Deviance." *Women's Studies International Quarterly* 4: 145–55.

Roesler, Jörg. 1990. "Die Wirtschaftsreform der DDR in den sechziger Jahren: Einstieg, Entwicklungsprobleme, und Abbruch." *Zeitschrift für Geschichtswissenschaft* 38: 979–1003.

Roodenburg, Herman, and Pieter Spierenburg, eds. 2004. *Social Control in Europe, 1500–1800*. Columbus: Ohio State University Press.

Rose, Nikolas. 2007. *The Politics of Life Itself: Biomedicine, Power, and Subjectivity in the Twenty-First Century*. Princeton: Princeton University Press.

Rosenblum, Warren. 2008. *Beyond the Prison Gates: Punishment and Welfare in Germany, 1850–1933*. Chapel Hill: University of North Carolina Press.

Rosenwald, George C. 1986. "Why Operationism Doesn't Go Away: Extrascientific Incentives of Social-Psychological Research." *Philosophy of the Social Sciences* 16: 303–30.

Ross, Corey. 2000. *Constructing Socialism at the Grass-Roots: The Transformation of East Germany, 1945–1965*. New York: St. Martin's.

Roth, Thomas. 2010. *"Verbrechensbekämpfung" und soziale Ausgrenzung im nationalsozialistischen Köln*. Cologne: Emons.

Rothmaler, Christiane. 1999. "Von 'haltlosen Psychopathinnen' und 'konstitutionellen Sittlichkeitsverbrechern': Die Kriminalbiologische Untersuchungs- und Sammelstelle der Hamburgischen Gefangenenanstalten 1926 bis 1945." In *Wissenschaftlicher Rassismus: Analysen einer Kontinuität in den Human- und Naturwissenschaften*, ed. Heidrun Kaupen-Haas and Christian Saller, 257–303. Frankfurt: Campus.

Rüping, Hinrich, ed. 1994. *Von der Aufklärung bis zur doppelten Staatsgründung*. Vol. 2 of *Studien- und Quellenbuch zur Geschichte der deutschen Strafrechtspflege*, ed. Wolfgang Sellert and Hinrich Rüping. Darmstadt: Scientia Verlag Aalen, 1994.

Sander, Günther. 1979. *Abweichendes Verhalten in der DDR: Kriminalitätstheorien in einer sozialistischen Gesellschaft*. Frankfurt: Campus.

Schädler, Sarah. 2009. *"Justizkrise" und "Justizreform" im Nationalsozialismus: Das Reichsjustizministerium unter Reichsjustizminister Thierack (1942–1945)*. Tübingen: Mohr Siebeck.

Schattke, Herbert. 1979. *Die Geschichte der Progression im Strafvollzug und der damit zusammenhängenden Vollzugsziele in Deutschland*. Frankfurt: Lang.

Schauz, Desiree. 2008. *Strafen als moralische Besserung: Eine Geschichte der Straffälligenfürsorge, 1777–1933*. Munich: Oldenbourg.

Schauz, Desiree, and Sabine Freitag. 2007. *Verbrecher im Visier der Experten: Kriminalpolitik zwischen Wissenschaft und Praxis im 19. und frühen 20. Jahrhundert*. Stuttgart: Franz Steiner.

Schenk, Christina. 2001. *Bestrebungen zur einheitlichen Regelung des Strafvollzugs in Deutschland von 1870 bis 1923*. Frankfurt: Lang.

Scherpe, Klaus R. 1982. "Erzwungener Alltag: Wahrgenommene und gedachte Wirklichkeit in der Reportageliteratur der Nachkriegszeit." In *Nachkriegsliteratur in Westdeutschland 1945–1949*, vol. 1, *Schreibweisen, Gattungen, Institutionen*, ed. Jost Hermand, Helmut Peitsch, and Klaus R. Scherpe, 35–102. Berlin: Argument.

Schivelbusch, Wolfgang. 1998. *In a Cold Crater: Cultural and Intellectual Life in Berlin, 1945–1948*. Berkeley: University of California Press.

Scholz, Sabine. 1996. "Die Einweisung und Unterbringung gerichtspyschiatrischen Patienten in der DDR am Beispiel der Bezirksnervenklinik Brandenburg." MD diss., Medizinische Fakultät der Humboldt-Universität Berlin.

Schörken, Rolf. 1995. *Jugend 1945: Politisches Denken und Lebensgeschichte*. Frankfurt: Fischer.

Schröder, Wilhelm Heinz, and Jürgen Wilke. 1997. *Politische Gefangene in der DDR—eine quantitative Analyse*. Wissenschaftliche Expertise für die Enquete-Kommission des Deutschen Bundestages "Überwindung der Folgen der SED-Diktatur im Prozeß der deutschen Einheit." Cologne: Zentralarchiv für Empirische Sozialforschung.

Schröder, Wilhelm Heinz, and Jürgen Wilke. 1998. "Politische Strafgefangene in der DDR: Versuch einer statistischen Beschreibung." *Historical Social Research* 23: 3–78.

Simon, Jonathan. 2007. *Governing through Crime: How the War on Crime Transformed American Democracy and Created a Culture of Fear*. New York: Oxford University Press.

Simon, Jürgen. 2001. *Kriminalbiologie und Zwangssterilisation: Eugenischer Rassismus, 1920–1945*. Münster: Waxmann.

Skyba, Peter. 2000. *Vom Hoffnungsträger zum Sicherheitsrisiko: Jugend in der DDR und Jugendpolitik der SED 1949–1961*. Cologne: Böhlau, 2000.

Snacken, S., K. Beyens, and H. Tubex. 1995. "Changing Prison Populations in Western Countries: Fate or Policy?" *European Journal of Crime, Criminal Law, and Criminal Justice* 3: 18–53.

Spierenburg, Pieter. 2007. *The Prison Experience: Disciplinary Institutions and Their Inmates in Early Modern Europe*. Amsterdam: Amsterdam Academic Archive.

Spierenburg, Pieter. 2004. "Punishment, Power, and History: Foucault and Elias." *Social Science History* 28: 607–36.

Spierenburg, Pieter. 2004. "Social Control and History: An Introduction." In *Social Control in Europe*, vol. 1, *1500–1800*, ed. Herman Roodenburg and Pieter Spierenburg, 1–22. Columbus: Ohio State University Press.

Stäcker, Therese. 2012. *Die Franz von Liszt-Schule und ihre Auswirkungen auf die deutsche Strafrechtsentwicklung*. Baden-Baden: Nomos.

Stadtland, C., M. Hollweg, N. Kleindienst, J. Dietl, U. Reich, and N. Nedopil. 2006. "Rückfallprognosen bei Sexualstraftäter—Vergelich der prädiktiven Validität von Prognoseinstrumenten." *Der Nervenarzt* 77: 587–95.

Stahlmann, Martin, and Jürgen Schiedeck. 1991. *"Erziehung zur Gemeinschaft—Auslese durch Gemeinschaft": Zur Zurichtung des Menschen im Nationalsozialismus*. Bielefeld: Karin Böllert/KT-Verlag.

Steinbacher, Sybille. 2011. *Wie der Sex nach Deutschland kam: Der Kampf um Sittlichkeit und Anstand in der frühen Bundesrepublik*. Munich: Siedler.

Steinböck, Herbert R. 2009. "New Developments in Preventive Detention in Germany." *Current Opinion in Psychiatry* 22: 488–91.

Stoff, Heiko. 2003. "Degenerierte Nervenkörper und regenerierte Hormonkörper: Eine kurze Geschichte der Verbesserung des Menschen zu Beginn des 20. Jahrhunderts." *Historische Anthropologie* 11: 224–39.

Stoff, Heiko. 2004. *Ewige Jugend: Konzepte der Verjüngung vom späten 19. Jahrhundert bis ins Dritte Reich*. Cologne: Böhlau.

Stokes, Raymond G. 2000. *Constructing Socialism: Technology and Change in East Germany, 1945–1990*. Baltimore: Johns Hopkins University Press.

Stolpmann, Gerhard. 2010. "Psychiatrische Maßregelbehandlung." *Aus Politik und Zeitgeschichte* 60: 28–33.

Strauss, Claudia. 2006. "The Imaginary." *Anthropological Theory* 6: 322–44.

Streng, Marcel. 2011. "'Sozialtherapie ist eine Therapie, die sozial macht': Therapeutisierungsprozess im westdeutschen Strafvollzug der langen 70er Jahren." In *Das beratene Selbst: Zur Genealogie der Therapeutisierung in den "langen" Siebzigern*, ed. Sabine Maasen, Jens Elberfeld, Pascal Eitler, and Maik Tändler, 265–90. Bielefeld: Transcript.

Strien, Pieter J. van. 1997. "The American 'Colonization' of Northwest European Social Psychology after World War II." *Journal of the History of the Behavioral Sciences* 33: 349–63.

Sumner, Colin. 1994. *The Sociology of Deviance: An Obituary*. New York: Continuum.

Süss, Sonja. 1999. *Politisch mißbraucht? Psychiatrie und Staatssicherheit in der DDR*. Berlin: Ch. Links.

Sutherland, Edward. 1950. "The Diffusion of Sexual Psychopath Laws." *American Journal of Sociology* 56: 142–48.

Sutherland, Edward. 1950. "The Sexual Psychopath Laws." *Journal of Criminal Law and Criminology* 40: 543–54.

Szöllösi-Janze, Margrit. 2004. "Wissensgesellschaft in Deutschland: Überlegungen zur Neubestimmung der deutschen Zeitgeschichte über Verwissenschaftlichungsprozesse." *Geschichte und Gesellschaft* 30: 277–313.

Tändler, Maik, and Uffa Jensen, ed. 2012. *Das Selbst zwischen Anpassung und Befreiung: Psychowissen und Politik im 20. Jahrhundert*. Göttingen: Wallstein.

Taylor, Charles. 2002. "Modern Social Imaginaries." *Public Culture* 14: 91–124.

Thulfaut, Geril. 2000. *Kriminalpolitik und Strafrechtslehre bei Edmund Mezger (1883–1962)*. Baden-Baden: Nomos, 2000.

Vicedo, Marga. 2013. *The Nature and Nurture of Love: From Imprinting to Attachment in Cold War America*. Chicago: University of Chicago Press.

Vigarello, Georges. 2001. *A History of Rape: Sexual Violence in France from the 16th to the 20th Century*. Cambridge: Polity.

Vogel, Jakob. 2004. "Von der Wissenschafts- zur Wissensgeschichte: Für eine Historisierung der 'Wissensgesellschaft.'" *Geschichte und Gesellschaft* 30: 639–60.

Vogel, Joachim. 2004. *Einflüsse des Nationalsozialismus auf das Strafrecht*. Berlin: Berliner Wissenschafts-Verlag.

Volckart, Bernd, and Rolf Grünebaum. 2003. *Maßregelvollzug: Das Recht des Vollzugs der Unterbringung nach §§ 63, 64 StGB in einem psychiatrischen Krankenhaus und in einer Entziehungsanstalt*. Munich: Luchterhand.

Vormbaum, Thomas. 2011. *Einführung in die moderne Strafrechtsgeschichte*. Heidelberg: Springer.

Wachsmann, Nikolaus. 2002. "Between Reform and Repression: Imprisonment in Weimar Germay." *Historical Journal* 45: 416–17.

Wachsmann, Nikolaus. 2001. "From Indefinite Confinement to Extermination: 'Habitual Criminals' in the Third Reich." In *Social Outsiders in Nazi Germany*, ed. Robert Gellately and Nathan Stoltzfuss, 165–91. Princeton: Princeton University Press.

Wachsmann, Nikolaus. 2004. *Hitler's Prisons*. New Haven: Yale University Press.

Wachsmann, Nikolaus. 2008. "The Policy of Exclusion: Repression in the Nazi State, 1933–1939." In *Nazi Germany*, ed. Jane Caplan, 122–45. Oxford: Oxford University Press.

Wagner, Patrick, 1996. *Volksgemeinschaft ohne Verbrecher: Konzeptionen und Praxis der Kriminalpolizei in der Zeit der Weimarer Republik und des Nationalsozialismus*. Hamburg: Christians.

Wagner, Walter. 2011. *Der Volksgerichtshof im nationalsozialistischen Staat*. Munich: Oldenbourg.

Walmsley, Roy. 2003. "Global Incarceration and Prison Trends." *Forum on Crime and Society* 3: 65–78.

Wanitschke, Matthias. 2001. *Methoden und Menschenbild des Ministeriums für Staatssicherheit der DDR*. Cologne: Böhlau.

Ward, Tony, and Shadd Maruna. 2007. *Rehabilitation*. London: Routledge.

Wasserman, Jason Adam, and Brian Philip Hinote. 2011. "Chronic Illness and Incalculable Risk: Scientific Uncertainty and Social Transformations in Medicine." *Social Theory and Health* 9: 41–58.

Weber, Petra. 2000. *Justiz und Diktatur: Justizverwaltung und politische Strafjustiz in Thüringen 1945–1961*. Munich: Oldenbourg.

Wentker, Hermann. 2001. *Justiz in der SBZ/DDR 1945–1953: Transformation und Rolle ihrer zentralen Institutionen*. Munich: Oldenbourg.

Werlinder, Henry, 1978. *Psychopathy: A History of the Concepts; Analysis of the Origin and Development of a Family of Concepts in Psychopathology*. Stockholm: Almqvist och Wiksell International.

Wetzell, Richard F. 2006. "Criminology in Weimar and Nazi Germany." In *Criminals and Their Scientists: The History of Criminology in International Perspective*, ed. Peter Becker and Richard F. Wetzell, 401–23. New York: Cambridge University Press.

Wetzell, Richard F. 2004. "From Retributive Justice to Social Defense: Penal Reform in Fin-de- Siécle Germany." In *Germany at the Fin-de-Siécle: Culture, Politics, and Ideas*, ed. Suzanne Marchard and David Lindenfeld, 59–77. Baton Rouge: Louisiana State University.

Wetzell, Richard F. 2000. *Inventing the Criminal: A History of German Criminology, 1880–1945*. Chapel Hill: University of North Carolina Press.

Whitman, James Q. 2003. *Harsh Justice: Criminal Punishment and the Widening Divide between America and Europe*. Oxford: Oxford University Press.

Whooley, Owen. 2010. "Diagnostic Ambivalence: Psychiatric Workarounds and the Diagnostic and Statistical Manual of Mental Disorders." *Sociology of Health and Illness* 32: 452–69.

Wierling, Dorothee. 1994. "Die Jugend als innerer Feind: Konflikte in der Erziehungsdiktatur der sechziger Jahre." In *Sozialgeschichte der DDR*, ed. Hartmut Kaelble, Jürgen Kocka, and Hartmut Zwahr, 404–25. Stuttgart: Klett-Cotta.

Wierling, Dorothee. 1999. "Das weiblich-proletarische Tüchtigkeitsideal der DDR." In *Arbeiter in der SBZ-DDR*, ed. Peter Hübner and Klaus Tenfelde, 831–48. Essen: Klartext.

Wierling, Dorothee. 2000. "Über die Liebe zum Staat—der Fall der DDR." *Historische Anthropologie* 8: 236–63.

Wille, Reinhard, and Klaus M. Beier. 1989. "Castration in Germany." *Sexual Abuse: A Journal of Research and Treatment* 2: 103–32.

Williams, Robert A., Jr. 2012. *Savage Anxieties: The Invention of Western Civilization*. New York: Palgrave Macmillan.

Willing, Matthias, 2003. *Das Bewahrungsgesetz (1918–1967): Eine rechtshistorische Studie zur Geschichte der deutschen Fürsorge*. Tübingen: Mohr Siebeck.

Winter, David G., and Nicole B. Barenbaum. 1999. "History of Modern Personality Theory and Research." In *Handbook of Personality: Theory and Research*, ed. Lawrence A. Pervin and Oliver P. John, 3–27. New York: Guilford.

Wunschik, Tobias. 1997. "Der Strafvollzug als Aufgabe der Deutschen Volkspolizei in den fünfziger Jahren." *Archiv für Polizeigeschichte* 8: 74–91.

Zarusky, Jürge. 2006. "Von der Sondergerichtsbarkeit zum Endphasenterror: Loyalitätserzwingung und Rache am Widerstand im Zusammenbruch des NS- Regimes." In *Terror nach Innen: Verbrechen am Ende des Zweiten Weltkrieges*, ed. Cord Arendes, Edgar Wolfrum, and Jörg Zedler, 103–21, Göttingen: Wallstein.

Zimmermann, Verena. 2004. *"Den neuen Menschen schaffen": Die Umerziehung von schwererziehbaren und straffälligen Jugendlichen in der DDR (1945–1990)*. Cologne: Böhlau.

Index